STRENGTH OF A WOMAN

The Phyllis Hyman Story

JASON A. MICHAEL
IN COOPERATION WITH GLENDA GRACIA AND THE ESTATE OF PHYLLIS HYMAN

STRENGTH OF A WOMAN: The Phyllis Hyman Story © 2007 by Jason A. Michael. All rights reserved. Printed in the United States of America. No part of this book may be used or reproduced in any manner whatsoever without written permission except in the case of brief quotations embodied in critical articles and reviews. For information address JAM Books, LLC, 75 Chestnut St., River Rouge, MI 48218.

"PHYLLIS HYMAN" is a Registered Trademark (U.S.P.T.O. Reg. No. 3,108,778) of The Estate of Phyllis Hyman (Glenda Gracia, Executrix) and is used with the permission of the Estate.

This work contains references to certain letters, documents and photographs the copyrights for which are owned by The Estate of Phyllis Hyman (Glenda Gracia, Executrix) and which are used with the permission of the Estate.

THIRD EDITION

ISBN 0-9794890-0-8

New Acknowledgements

It's been just over a decade since I first released this book. After being told by dozens of publishing houses that there was no market for a book about Phyllis, I was forced to self-publish. The book went on to become an Essence magazine bestseller. Despite this initial success I was unable to keep the book in print and eventually after a second printing the book disappeared.

But even with no books to sell, I always continued to promote Phyllis Hyman. I love talking about her and helping folks to understand her better. Whether I'm speaking to a book group or giving an interview on the radio or even one on one with the folks who contact me through social media, keeping Phyllis's legacy alive is and will always be my lifelong mission.

I said in the acknowledgments section of the first edition that I credited Phyllis with bringing so many wonderful people to me while writing the book. Phyllis has the most amazing fans and she has continued to bring incredible people into my life like Jeffrey Graham, Darryl Pressley, Craig Wiggins, Michael Coleman, Mikeisha Best, Rudy Chapman, Leo Brown, Quentin Harrison, Douglas Says, Jerry Aultmon and David Aaron Moore.

I'd like to thank everyone who promotes Phyllis in some way and continues to help keep her legacy alive. I appreciate everyone who interviewed me for their newspaper or blog or radio program. Thanks to Troy J. Rose for creating the Simply Phyllis Hyman Facebook page. A big shout out to Kendrell Bowman and Anthony Wayne, producers of An Evening with Phyllis Hyman, for bringing Phyllis's story to the stage. Thanks also to Sass and Teri S. from DIVAS DC Productions for their efforts on Phyllis's behalf. Appreciation goes to my attorney Alicia Skillman.

Thanks to dear friends Rev. Dr. Selma Massey and Lady Vonne' for always keeping ahold of me spiritually. My admiration goes to Jey'nce Poindexter Mizrahi for being such a powerful example of someone who walks in her faith. A big shout out goes to my Imagine This Productions partners Robert Tate, Marcus Pratt and Damon "Magic" Percy.

Words cannot express the gratitude I have for Joshua H. Jenkins, another friend I met through the book who is now the webmaster of www.phyllishymanstory.com and the book's Facebook page (www.facebook.com/phyllishymanstory). Josh, you are my hero and I thank you immensely for helping to get the book back out there. I couldn't have done it alone. Thank God he sent me you.

And if you're reading this and you've been waiting to own the book for some time, my sincere apologies for keeping you waiting. I hope after you've finished it you'll feel it was worth the wait.

Peace and Love,

JAM

September 2018

Introduction

Phyllis's story is a tale of woe: extreme sadness and regret still hang in the air. At the end of her life, Phyllis' spirit was threadbare. Her bold sense of humor blurred by bitterness, her strong convictions weakened by self-doubt. Her suffering had been incessant and unfathomably deep.

As one of seven children raised by parents who were challenged by mental illness, alcoholism and an inability to cope with the stressors a large, struggling family presented, she suffered. As an unusually tall teenager and woman, beauty could not compensate her enough for the suffering caused by being different. As an artist who could not express her art in an authentic way, she suffered. As a black woman living in a culture that is hostile toward black women, she suffered. And, as a victim of mental and emotional illness, she suffered.

In the face of all this suffering, Phyllis fought everyday to function and forge a successful career and life path for herself. The result: an incredible body of work bequeathed to the world. A tribute to her great artistry, she offered her voice to us, without holding back one ounce of passion – whether the song deserved the gift of life she gave it or not. Phyllis also offered her humanity. She could cry for you and could care more about you than you did for yourself.

This book puts Phyllis's business in the street: revealing her as a frightened and angry womanchild – and, as a victim, survivor and warrior battling life and herself. For some, this book will become a tool for self-examination and introspection. The process required for healing mental and emotional illness… and, trauma.

A death caused by mental illness is so hard to understand. With heart disease or cancer, you wonder: what will give out or metastasize? Well, for the mentally ill, it's their obligatory sadness that runs rampant and their will that gives out – their will to live and be strong. For them, the expectation of adversity is so ingrained in their emotional fabric that the mere suggestion of joy offers too much of a challenge for their dried up soul.

Of all the illnesses from which one can suffer, mental illness is among the cruelest and most irreverent. It creates a vicious cycle of embarrassment, guilt and shame for its victim and their loved ones. Everyone involved spends their life seeking forgiveness from themselves and others that often never comes. Our society does not support meaningful dialogue about mental illness the way it does for other pathologies that manifest in the physical. As a consequence, millions remain undiagnosed and continue to suffer through "bad days," as the people in their lives try to cheer them on or leave them to fend for themselves because it's too hard to engage with them.

If Phyllis had cancer – she may have been better off. She may have received more support, compassion and understanding. She may have been nurtured into a survivor until she healed or made a transition with dignity.

An HIV victim has support from family and society. A diabetes victim has support from family and society.

Not the victim of mental illness. Why do you suppose? There are brilliant professionals available to help when given the opportunity. Indeed, opportunity is the operative word. The shame and guilt about mental illness keeps victims and their loved ones closeted, hurting alone till the bitter end. The regretful afterthought always haunting those who are left behind: "we should a…"

We must raise our awareness about mental illness to create more consciousness as a society for the sake of the humanity of those who suffer. They need our love, support and compassion just like the next person suffering from an illness.

At the end of her turbulent and battered 45 years, Phyllis had become indifferent – robbed of her enthusiasm for life and the sweet spot that music and performance once held for her. Across many traditions, people pray for deliverance from attachment and aversion – but not to the point of becoming indifferent. Indifference forbids joy, hope, meaning and love. A sad way, indeed, to walk in this world.

Ironically, Phyllis was referred to as the Goddess of Love. Within her world, as Goddess, she could create and destroy, be benevolent and wrathful. However, at the end of the day, Phyllis did not want to be objectified or worshipped. She wanted passion, sweet passion: yes. But, she longed for the experience of true love:

accepting, forgiving, unconditional. Don't get me wrong. Phyllis was offered love all the time. Yet, it was the cruelty of her illness that never allowed her to accept the experience of true love. The discord in the love song heard by Phyllis was inaudible to those who came willing to share all they had with her. When it was not enough, they simply left.

By the age of 13, I had become enamored with James Baldwin. What a gifted American writer! His wisdom framed life for me in ways that made my coming of age magical. For example, he touched me indelibly with this observation: "the moment we refuse to hold one another, the moment we break faith with one another, the sea engulfs us and the light goes out."

Each day, we must find the light in those we love and hold them. Phyllis' light went out. Perhaps, it didn't have to…

Glenda
31 May, 2007

Author's Note

Wherever possible, it has been my goal to let Phyllis tell her own story, and I'm happy to have been able to include many rare and insightful quotes of hers here. At times, these quotes may appear inconsistent, but that does not in any way imply insincerity. Phyllis was diagnosed with bipolar disorder in her thirties, though she was likely affected by the onset of manic depression much earlier than that.

Bipolar disorder is a cyclical condition characterized by extreme and uncontrollable swings in mood. These swings go from extreme highs and/or irritability to intense hopelessness and despair and back again, sometimes with periods of normal mood in between. Phyllis's comments, which portrayed at times both great optimism and great hopelessness, were colored by where she was on this spectrum when she made them. So even if Phyllis appears to contradict herself within these pages, it is simply no more than a graphic illustration of the dramatic shifts in mood she struggled with.

If, like Phyllis, you believe that you or someone you know may be suffering from bipolar disorder, please visit the National Institute of Mental Health online at www.nimh.nih.gov/ for more information and consult with a mental health specialist in your area.

To Phyllis, for bravely battling her demons as long as she managed to so that she could share with the world her incredible gift and leave us, her fans and friends, with such a rich legacy of love and music.

And to her siblings, Ann, Jeannie, Sakinah, Mark, Anita and Michael, who continue to wake up every day and fight the good fight.

*"The truly creative mind in any field is no more than this:
A human creature born abnormally, inhumanly sensitive.
To him...
a touch is a blow,
a sound is a noise,
a misfortune is a tragedy,
a joy is an ecstasy,
a friend is a lover,
a lover is a god,
and failure is death."*
Pearl S. Buck, Nobel laureate

"Phyllis is such a mystery, even to me."
Phyllis Hyman

Prologue

Life is about choices, and I choose to go.

Leonard Feather, renowned jazz critic and author of the *Encyclopedia of Jazz*, was backstage at the Phoenix Theatre in New York on June 25, 1959. Billie Holiday, for whom he had produced several shows and a successful European tour some years earlier, was scheduled to perform. But as she passed him backstage, Feather could not conceal his shock at her ragged appearance. She looked painfully tired and well beyond her 44 years. "What's the matter, Leonard?" Holiday asked as she walked by. "Seen a ghost or something?"

Just minutes later, the show was over. Holiday managed to make it through her opening number, the telling "Ain't Nobody's Business If I Do," but she was unable to finish a second song and instead stumbled off stage and promptly collapsed. The following week, Holiday was found unconscious on the floor of her Upper West Side apartment and rushed to nearby Knickerbocker Hospital. Holiday had been abusing her body for years made extra long by the perils of the road and the burden of being a black cabaret singer in the era of segregation. From alcohol and marijuana she graduated to opium and later heroin. Now, the toll had to be paid.

Yet even as she lay in the hospital, her body riddled with cirrhosis of the liver, Holiday could not abandon her excesses. Somehow, she was able to procure heroin even then and was soon enough fingerprinted, photographed while lying flat on her back and weighing a mere 80 pounds, and, say some sources, actually handcuffed to her bed by members of the New York Police Department. Worse yet, they confiscated her portable record player taking away her single source of solace.

When her estranged husband, Louis McKay, flew in from California, he found Holiday in a pitiful shape, her battle-weary body unable to fight both withdrawal and heart disease at the same time. "Daddy," she told him, "I didn't know they could be this cruel to nobody." Days later, deflated and defeated, the woman known to the world as Lady Day was dead.

This was the sort of ending that Phyllis Hyman knew was in store for her, and that she wanted at all costs to avoid. By June of 1995 – 36 years after Holiday's passing – Phyllis, who had once been christened by *Black American* magazine "the next Billie Holiday," knew that she, too, had fallen victim to her own excesses, and that like Lady Day she was killing herself slowly. Twice she had made month-long treks to high-priced rehabilitation facilities, and twice she failed to maintain sobriety. Like Billie, she was now finding it virtually impossible to finish her shows, to find any joy in the one place she was once guaranteed to find it. She had difficulty remembering the words to her songs, and in between them she was reduced intermittently to crying jags and fits of outrage. Hers was a pain the size of the ocean, an anger as hot as the sun.

And like Billie, Phyllis was now getting double takes left and right. Gone were the last vestiges of her once regal beauty and her statuesque supermodel physique. Like alcohol, cocaine and pills, food was nothing but another of her addictions, one more substance with which she had a disastrously unhealthy love affair. Pushing up on 300 pounds, she was bloated and bordering on obese, her crystalline features now contorted and transfigured.

Finally the food, the booze and the drugs all began to taste the same: bitter. Bitterness was the pill she could not swallow, it stayed lodged painfully in her throat. But while her self-awareness and sense of reality may have fluctuated in years past, Phyllis had moments of clarity; and on one point she was certain – the end was near. Phyllis confessed this to her longtime friend Tina Stephens. "She told me she loved to eat and she loved to do drugs so she was going kill herself … she knew she was going to die," Tina recalled. "She didn't want to stop getting high, and the doctor told her if she didn't stop, she'd die."

So Phyllis, who once aptly stated that if the toilet had to be flushed she might as well flush it herself, decided to orchestrate her own departure. She didn't want to wither away like Billie, or binge herself to death unexpectedly like Dinah Washington, who accidentally overdosed on a lethal combination of alcohol and diet pills. Phyllis had long been an advocate of suicide and had twice before attempted it. This time though, she vowed there would be no mistakes.

Phyllis spent days on the preparations. Birthdays had always been important to her. She usually oversaw the planning of an annual party and even handed out very specific wish lists to her staff members. This year's celebration would be one of a kind, though, and her wish list was short. Phyllis wanted peace.

She phoned friends and asked them to come out to her concert at the famed Apollo Theatre, scheduled for Friday, June 30, 1995. To the masses, Phyllis simply said it would be her last date for a while and that she planned on going away. To intimates, she was more specific. Phyllis called Danny Poole, an old boyfriend from her days on Broadway in *Sophisticated Ladies*, on Thursday, June 29. Bluntly, she told him she planned to take an overdose of sleeping pills on July 6, her 46th birthday.

"She started off by saying that she was just existing, and she was unhappy," Poole remembered. "She'd had some good days but not enough in her life. She was depressed and she was tired of having to worry about other people and getting jobs. I knew in the first five minutes that she was serious about doing it. She seemed convinced that it was something she wanted to do."

Danny, who was speaking to Phyllis from his office in Denver, where he was working as a real estate broker, said Phyllis seemed content with her decision to end her life. "She was jovial, she laughed, she made fun of life." And she made it clear that this time her suicide attempt would not fail. "The last time, I didn't know what I was doing. This time I do," she said, telling Poole that her best bet was to use a gun, but since she didn't have one pills would have to do. "I'm not going out of the window because it would hurt all the way down," she said with a laugh, dismissing the option of a 33-story plunge. "I'm just going to take some pills and go to sleep.

"I'm unhappy. The only bright light is to die so I won't have to worry about a job and other people. I have no personal life and no energy."

Billie Holiday had made the same argument backstage at the Phoenix Theatre. In her dressing room, she confessed to clarinetist Tony Scott that she hadn't eaten in three weeks. "I don't want to live," she said, as the tears began to stream down her sallow face. "I'm all alone, I ain't got nobody."

The loneliness of the female jazz singer has long been a special kind of beast. For Phyllis, this was complicated by her manic depression. She had known several loves throughout her years, but she had never been able to master self-love, and without it, she proved incapable of sustaining a lasting relationship. Phyllis liked to say that men were intimidated by her, and no doubt many were. But there were a select group of other men who were exasperated by her mood swings.

She teetered between two personas: that of an obnoxious, boisterous and aggressively singularly-minded woman hell bent on pleasing herself at all costs, and that of a fragile little girl with a delicate ego, unable to comprehend why others were upset by her actions. "She would go into this childlike behavior and show playfulness," said Portia Hunt, Ph.D., Phyllis's psychologist for several years. "She would lose herself in it, and then come back with rage."

That is, after all, what manic-depressive illness is and what it does. A disorder of the brain also known as being bipolar, it causes unusual and severe shifts in a person's mood, energy, and ability to function. In her book *An Unquiet Mind*, Dr. Kay Redfield Jamison, an expert on manic-depressive illness and someone who has suffered from it for decades herself, speaks about the down side of the disorder.

"Depression is awful beyond words or sounds or images," she writes. "It bleeds relationships through suspicion, lack of confidence and self-respect, the inability to enjoy life, to walk or talk or think normally, the exhaustion, the night terrors, the day terrors. There is nothing good to be said for it except that it gives you the experience of how it must be to be old and sick, to be dying; to be slow of mind; to be lacking in grace, polish and coordination; to be ugly; to have no belief in the possibilities of life, the pleasures of sex, the exquisiteness of music, or the ability to make yourself and others laugh."

This was the dismal abyss Phyllis was wandering through when she spoke to Danny Poole. "All I want to do is go," she told him. He tried to persuade Phyllis to reconsider, telling her she was too young to die. Her response was to hang up the phone. He dialed her back immediately, and she answered and quickly reiterated the ground rules.

"I told you, Danny, if you try to talk me out of it, I'm going to hang up on you," she stated firmly. So Danny just listened. "I'm trying to be nice and say goodbye to everyone and everyone is trying to talk me out of it ... I'm not going to debate you over my life ... you can't help ... life is about choices and I choose to go."

Typical of Phyllis, she spoke with Danny until her doorman called to tell her that her lunch had arrived. Then, she rushed him off the phone and, once finished with her lunch, continued about the business of making her final preparations.

The show the next day, Friday, June 30, was supposed to have been Phyllis's final hurrah. But something happened to convince her to hasten her exit. She had made several goodbye calls, and sent cryptic and vague messages to many others. Perhaps she feared an intervention was in the works, or possibly she was just truly too tired to get up on stage and give one more performance. Whatever the reason, Phyllis chose not to play the Apollo one last time. Phyllis told her personal assistants, Lennice Molina and Leo Lord, that she planned to sun for a bit on the roof of her building before sound-check and sent them out on errands.

But Phyllis never made it to the roof. Instead, once her assistants had left the apartment, and knowing her time was short, Phyllis walked into the bedroom of her tiny midtown Manhattan apartment, locked the door behind her, sat down on the edge of her king-sized bed, and swallowed handfuls of her favorite sleeping pills, Tuinal®. Afterward, she put on a sleeping mask to block out the blinding sunshine pouring in from the windows, and lay down. For years, serenity had eluded Phyllis. Now she made one final attempt to find it. Hers was a mind that worked overtime, packed full of loud and robust thoughts. But as the darkness began to envelop her, her restless mind was quieted at last.

Of Billie Holiday, Feather once said, "Her voice was the voice of living intensity, of soul in the true sense of that greatly abused word. As a human being, she was sweet, sour, kind, mean, generous, profane, lovable and impossible, and nobody who knew her expects to see anyone quite like her ever again."

It was likewise a fitting eulogy for Phyllis Hyman.

Chapter 1

*I never experienced being a girl.
I was always a woman.*

Ismael X paid thirty-five dollars to Solomon Hyman for the right to use his name to buy land in his native North Carolina. The son of slaves, Ismael, a humble farmer, worked hard to build a better life than the one he had known for his children. Ishmael's grandchildren were the first generation to head north in search of that better life. Samuel, Edward and Philip all settled in Philadelphia.

Philip served in the Army during World War II and was stationed in North Africa. After returning to Philly, he began working in his brother Samuel's barbershop at Haverford Avenue and 52nd Street. He met Louise Lively, a waitress, at a local nightclub. Their courtship was short. Philip proposed when Louise announced she was pregnant. Louise was 26 when she gave birth to a daughter, Phyllis Linda, on July 6, 1949. Philip just days shy of 29. Soon he had abandoned the barbershop for a job on the railroad; and the couple moved with their infant to Pittsburgh, where they settled into the public housing of the St. Clair Village area of town. A second daughter, Ann, was born 21 months after the first, and a third, Jeannie, was born 13 months after that.

By this time, Louise was suffering from chronic depression, and she found herself unable to cope. Jeannie was sent to live with family friends, Bill and Esther Quales. When Jeannie finally returned to the fold, at about age six, she was keenly aware that something was amiss in the Hyman household. There was a new sister in the house, Kym, and yet another child, a boy, had been stillborn. "I was a little kid and I remember thinking, 'What's she still doing having babies?'" recalled Jeannie. "Now back then, kids didn't know stuff like they do now. But I remember thinking, 'If she couldn't take care of me, why is she still having children?'

"When you have a severely impaired primary caregiver, lots of little things just don't get taken care of," Jeannie continued. "When I came back into the household, to me, it was utter chaos. It was nasty. It was dirty. The kids were unkempt. There was no order. I couldn't believe people lived like this."

Quarters were cramped in the Hyman household. Philip and Louise lived with their four children in a three-bedroom row house. As Louise spun further and further into the depths of her depression, Philip did little around the house to bring order to the chaos. Working on the railroad, he was often gone a lot when Phyllis was young. Later, back problems caused him to retire on a medical disability and he did barbering part-time. "He had health problems and then he had his drinking problem," said Jeannie. "And often, the two were intermixed."

Two years after Kym came along, Louise gave Philip his first son, Mark. And a year after that, she delivered twins, Michael and Anita, bringing the total to seven. Finally, they moved up the street to a four-bedroom unit, but seven kids sharing three bedrooms was still a pretty tight fit.

"There's a difference between a parent who's just lazy and does not want to do anything and a parent who cannot," said Jeannie. "If my mother had been in a wheelchair and had been paralyzed, everybody would have understood. But because they didn't, I always perceived us as being seen as those dirty little yellow kids in the neighborhood. Plus, not knowing that my mother was mentally ill, not knowing what the issues were, I just saw my parents as trifling, an opinion that I think Phyllis shared.

"When my kids and I were poor, I could take my pennies and put them in layaway for things that I wanted them to have," Jeannie continued. "Or I could go to the secondhand store and get some good buys. My mother didn't have the capacity to do that. We didn't get our hair combed unless I did it. We didn't get baths regularly. It just was a nasty mess."

With Louise overwhelmed and at times out of commission, and Philip incapacitated in his own right, Jeannie stepped up and became a surrogate caregiver for her siblings. Phyllis, meanwhile, had free reign to lord a certain power over her brothers and sisters.

"She liked to bully us," said Ann. "She had to be in charge." Jeannie concurred. "She was a terrible bully," she said. "We were her little peons."

Phyllis intimidated her younger siblings into doing her bidding, unwittingly adding to the burden on the rest of the older children in the house, who scrambled to fill the gap created by their mother's mental illness.

"Jeanie was our caretaker," said Kym. "She was the one who combed our hair, got us ready for school, made sure we ate, even made sure we had dessert."

It was a great deal of work, but Jeannie did it gladly. "That was my role," she said. "I think because I didn't live there for several years, when I came back my attitude was 'We've got to get this together.' I was really little. I was under 10 taking the three little ones to the baby clinic for their shots and stuff. But I loved that. I think because I didn't live at home for those years, I felt like I didn't really have a place there, that there must have been something defective with me that I was given away and no one else was. So I found a place for myself, and I liked that place. It made me feel a part of the solution."

In later years, when she reflected on her childhood, Phyllis rarely touched on the dysfunction of the Hyman family home. She made it clear, however, that her family's poverty was an impetus to her quest for fame. "We were a below-middle income family," Phyllis said. "We were rich in human areas. We didn't have material things, but then I didn't miss them either. My parents, I felt, were not obligated to give me things. Money can't buy a moral attitude."

From a very young age, Phyllis was perplexed by the notion that a woman could want no more than to raise children and take care of her family. As a child, not fully comprehending the extent of her mother's illness, Phyllis faulted her mother for not doing more, for appearing to want so little. Following her father's lead, Phyllis even began to take her mother for granted, to verbally abuse her. "I didn't respect my mother's opinion. I thought, 'What has she done? Had seven children?' I never had to carry a key when I was growing up because she was always home. I always thought I didn't want to be like that. That woman didn't ask for enough. There was a whole world out there."

Phyllis knew she wanted to explore that world. She considered her family's poverty a curse. "When I was real little, I used to have daydreams about being very wealthy, very famous and very loved," she said. Phyllis began taking after her father, who didn't provide much aide with the young children in the house. Phyllis's mother did not ask Phyllis for help, and she didn't offer any. Philip, according to Phyllis, was a shadow around the house. The family patriarch ate and slept there, but was not, exactly, an involved parent. "He never said much," Phyllis remembered.

The lack of visible affection between her parents left a lasting impression on Phyllis. It helped her to form a negative opinion of marriage and family that stayed with her for most of her life. "I didn't like being part of a large family, not just because there was a lack of money, toys and things like that, but because I didn't witness a lot of caring or passion between my mother and father. With the intense pressure of trying to feed and raise seven of us properly, I guess there just wasn't enough energy left for that." If Phyllis was aware that it was more than just seven children draining her mother's energy, that it was also her intense depression, she kept that knowledge, as well as her sadness and shame surrounding it, out of interviews.

For her part, if Louise had any awareness of what was happening to her, as depression held her firmly in its clutches, she had little to hold on to in the way of faith. Raised Catholic, she no longer attended church. Philip was the son of a fundamentalist Baptist minister, but he no longer regularly attended services either. The Hyman children were, however, often invited to church by neighbors and permitted by their parents to go. "We were not encouraged or discouraged," said Jeannie. "We were given an opportunity to go."

When she attended services with her siblings, Phyllis had her own issues with God and religion. "Can you really imagine me as a little girl, in a ruffle dress, being quiet for any length of time? I think not." Church was far too constraining for young Phyllis. "You had to keep your legs crossed. You couldn't eat. I couldn't wait till church was over so we could get in the basement and eat that good old church food. I was slightly afraid because the preacher would be shoutin'. I thought, well, who the hell is he mad at today? He'd be screaming at you, 'And the Lord sayeth.' I wanted to say, 'And I ain't deaf. I hear real doggone good.'"

There was at least one perk, though. "You know the collection box in the church? It had change in it. So I thought it was mine. That's what I got for an allowance. I was always trying to go for it. Of course, I got slapped on the back of the head a lot. It's very flat back there." Outside of church, Phyllis had few spiritual thoughts. "I can remember my mom teaching me a prayer, 'Now I lay me down to sleep; I pray the Lord the soul to keep; If I should die before I wake; I pray the Lord my soul to take.' Does that sound like a nightmare to you? I didn't want to go to sleep – *ever*. I was petrified. God's coming."

Pittsburgh in the 1960s was still somewhat segregated. St. Clair Village was one of the poorest neighborhoods on the north side of the river. It was the projects, and the only projects in the area. "It was a nice neighborhood and real communal," Phyllis said. "If I misbehaved in some way, the neighbor down the street was permitted to give me a licking. So I couldn't get away with much. I was a pretty good kid. I played hooky just one time and, wouldn't you know it, I got caught."

There was no high school in St. Clair Village. The all-black high schools were located on the south side of the Allegheny River. But Phyllis chose to attend Carrick High School, just above the all-white Mt. Oliver section of town. Though their parents might have, the other black kids in the school did not look down on their classmates from St. Clair Village. Just the opposite, they idolized and emulated them. The kids from St. Clair Village were cooler, hipper. They dressed with a certain flare and listened to the newest music. Kids from the integrated sections of town, like Beltzhoover, would sneak into St. Clair Village and hang out at the community center in search of some fun and puppy love.

Phyllis was well liked in the predominantly white high school. She was a member of the student council, the human relations club, intramurals and, of course, the chorus. At Carrick, music teacher David Tamburri took a special interest in Phyllis. A jazz pianist by trade, Tamburri had only started teaching to be able to provide a steady income for his family. When Phyllis joined the chorus at Carrick, Tamburri "recognized immediately that Phyllis had something besides just a normal kind of voice," recalled his widow, Trudy Tamburri.

"I always knew I could sing, but I didn't always want to do it professionally," Phyllis once said. "In fact, the first time I sang at a talent show, it must have been in junior high, I remember my legs shaking and my voice quaking."

The problem for Phyllis was not the singing. That came effortlessly. She could do it with her eyes closed and probably did in those early days. Phyllis didn't like being watched, for she couldn't comprehend what made her watchable or why anyone would care. She was never asked to sing by her parents, or encouraged by them to perform for visiting friends, as parents are sometimes want to do. So Phyllis sang for herself, for her own enjoyment, and when others started catching on, it confused her. "As long as I thought no one was paying any attention to me, I could relax and sing," she said. "But as soon as people stopped talking and started to listen, I froze."

Music was not readily available in the Hyman household. "We had a little cheap radio that was played," said Jeannie. "I don't remember music ever being a big thing, except when Phyllis would sing. My father and mother would have parties and I remember music from that, Nat King Cole and Dinah Washington, but I don't remember music being a big part of our home."

Radio was Phyllis's link to a whole new world. "We didn't have a record player in the house, but I always managed to listen to music somewhere," she said. "When I first heard Nancy Wilson sing, it was the greatest sound I'd ever heard. I knew from that moment on, scared or not, that's what I had to do."

Jeannie may have thought her oldest sister a terrible bully, but she also knew from an early age that she was a terrific talent. "Even though I didn't like her as a child, it was so astounding to me that she sounded like an adult. We were kids. She couldn't have been more than 10, 12 years old and she sounded like an adult singing with another adult. I knew at a very early age that she had a really special voice."

On occasion, Phyllis would recruit Jeannie and Ann to be her backup singers. "She would bring us in if she needed us," said Jeannie. "She would make us learn songs. We wouldn't want to do it, but we didn't have a choice. She made us do it anyway, and we did it and we did it well. I mean, she would train us and whip us in shape."

"I remember when we were little kids and Motown was what was happening," said Ann. "I told my sister, I said, 'Phyllis, we'll just get on the Greyhound bus and go to Detroit and just walk up to [Berry Gordy's] doorstep and as soon as he comes out, just start singing. Cause brothaman's gonna hire you.' I knew it. I believed it. I said, 'All we gotta do is get on his sidewalk and you start singing.' She had a beautiful voice."

By the time that Phyllis, Jeannie and Ann were entering their teen years, their mother was beginning to make some headway with her illness. As a result, Phyllis's four youngest siblings recall their formative years – and their mother – differently than the oldest children. "She wasn't cold, she wasn't mean, but she was just blank," said Jeannie. "My mother never touched me growing up. She didn't hug me. She didn't spank me. Now not hugging me, that was not inconsistent with the '50s, but never spanking me – never touching me – that's kind of hard for a parent to do."

On the opposite end of the spectrum, Kym, who has converted to the Muslim faith and now goes by Sakinah, recalls her mother as "extremely loving and caring despite her depression. A lot of it was that the four younger ones kind of forced her to be like that. We were a little bit more affectionate and closer to her and more needy, I guess. Also, by the time that I was coming up my mother started to get some help for her illness. It was the only help that was available, Valium and amphetamines. But by the time I was coming up, she had some more coping skills with her illness. So we had a different kind of childhood."

For Anita, the baby, childhood was a half and half experience. "I got some distance and I got some love," she said. "I got both of that. My mom did the best that she could."

Whatever their birth order, it's safe to say that all the Hyman children felt some resentment toward one or both of their parents, and Phyllis was likely no exception. "I think she both resented and did not understand why they kept having children that they couldn't take care of," said Jeannie. Meanwhile, Sakinah remembers that Phyllis used to pretend she was her parents' only child. "I think Phyllis felt like we were like cousins, and actually when she was little she used to tell people that, that we were her cousins. She had her little fantasy world that she really didn't belong."

Phyllis continued to sing in the citywide talent contests that took place in various schools of the Pittsburgh district. Donna Hubbard was a student at Knoxville Junior High when she heard Phyllis, who was auditioning for a talent show that was to be held at that school, for the first time. "Phyllis never needed a microphone," Hubbard recalled. "Her voice would resonate through the hallways in the school. She could carry anything off. She sang 'Somewhere Over The Rainbow' as an audition piece, from *The Wizard of Oz*. Everybody else was doing The Supremes or Mary Wells or Martha Reeves. But Phyllis chose 'Somewhere Over The Rainbow' and stopped traffic. We couldn't believe that this girl had pulled this off. But she had that kind of voice."

Phyllis was a standout not only for her voice and her unusual repertoire, but for the fact that she sang solos as well. It was the era of the boy groups and girl groups, and most of the kids sang in groups of three or four that tried to imitate The Supremes or The Temptations. Phyllis sang in talent shows at all the local schools, and more often than not, she won. "Phyllis just blew the city out," said Hubbard. "Any talent show that she was in, forget it, you weren't going to win. Forget it if Phyllis was going to be in it. That's the type of reputation she got."

Soon enough, all the kids around town knew Phyllis, if not by name, than as "the big girl," as she was often called. She was popular for her talent, but already nearly six feet tall, she was not at all popular as a possible romantic interest for the boys in her school. "Nobody called me, not very much," she said of her high school years. "I was as big as the guys or bigger. They'd tease me – I wasn't dainty like the other girls. Guys never followed me around. I never experienced being a girl, I was always a woman."

If a part of Phyllis felt shunned by the lack of attention, another part of her was relieved. Boys and love led to marriage and kids, a road Phyllis had no desire to go down. "I was one of seven kids and I knew I didn't want to be a mother of seven children. It was all I ever saw. I wanted to be a working woman, an independent woman, and not have to depend on a man."

Phyllis took the energy her classmates were expending on the opposite sex and put it into her singing. "I can't pinpoint it, but I always seemed to have more of an ambition than those around me," she said. In addition to talent shows and music class, Phyllis sang with the prestigious Pittsburgh All-City Choir. She suffered from stage fright, and singing as part of the choir was easier than doing solos. "At least if people looked, they were looking at all of us," she said.

Though Phyllis may have felt awkward, her sisters recall her as popular. She was attractive, talented and stylish. "She took her babysitting money, her lunch money, to make sure that she had the jazziest earrings, the newest color in lipstick, fingernail polish," said Jeannie. "That was the way she was. The entertainment business did not create that. Phyllis Hyman was the star in our neighborhood. I don't know how our two brothers felt, but as her sisters, we were her court. When she went out on a date, we all had a role to play. I'm Miss Get Her Something to Drink, iced tea, hot tea, help her zip up her dress. We never complained. That's just what we did. 'She's going out on a date. We must be there to assist her.'"

Phyllis's brother Michael saw this, too. "She was always a person who commanded attention, even as a sibling," he said. "She had everybody waiting on her. My sister had the same type of dominating way about her as my father. I'd have to say even at that point, as she was getting older, you couldn't tell her anything. You could never correct Phyllis."

If Phyllis had nice things, they were hers and hers alone. She worked for them, she earned them and she didn't see the need to share her clothes or jazzy jewelry with her sisters. Phyllis's room was a fun play spot for her younger siblings, but only when she was out of the house. Once, twins Anita and Michael had a little too much fun in Phyllis's room playing with matches and accidentally set her clothes on fire. "My mother was so afraid that she was going to do something," said Michael. "She actually hid us from her. It's something that I will never forget. At one point, she had us in the closet. Phyllis kept saying, 'Where are they? I want to talk to them,' and my mother would not let her."

Phyllis cherished her personal space, which was often hard to come by in the packed Hyman house. She guarded herself.

Sleeping on the edge of the bed, she also kept whichever sibling may have been sharing the bed with her on the edge of the other side. And if you happened to cross that line into her territory, there was hell to pay. "When you slept with her, you did not want to touch her," remembered Jeannie. "You did not want to hog up the blankets; and you did *not* want to take her pillow by mistake."

As Phyllis matured in the tumultuous '60s, she was proud to be black. Being a woman, though, that was another matter. "I found being black to be pleasurable because everybody else around me was black, but everyone else around me was not a lady," she said. "I found being a woman to be really difficult to deal with because you suffered so much. I consider women in this whole society the 'niggers of the world.' Women are really the lowest on the totem pole all over the world.

"It was frightening when I realized it was going to be like this the rest of my life; that I was never going to be able to get away from it. I could never be anything else. I just kept seeing that I couldn't make any headway in the things that I wanted to do. I was a girl. I couldn't do certain things. Girls were expected to act a certain way and to perform a certain way in front of guys, and I didn't know how to do that."

Phyllis's first real boyfriend was Richard Wall. The two met at a picnic in South Park in the summer of 1967. Phyllis had just graduated from high school and Richard, whom everyone called Richie, had just returned from a tour of duty in Vietnam. "I noticed Phyllis right off," said Richie. "She was hard to miss. She was extremely attractive. She seemed to me to be a part of but apart from everybody else in her neighborhood." As the two got to know each other and began to grow serious, Richie considered it quite a coup that he'd claimed Phyllis as his girl. "She always carried herself in a very proud, special way. I thought I was really doing something to have gotten together with her."

After high school, Phyllis joined a group called The Sounds of Ebony. A trio, The Sounds of Ebony sang what Phyllis referred to as "message songs," and even shared a bill with The Last Poets during a Black Week celebration at Pitt University. Phyllis's old music teacher David Tamburri, meanwhile, had left Carrick and taken a position with the Robert Morris Business College. The school was attempting to expand its focus from business into a fully accredited state university. As part of the accreditation process, the school needed to start a music department, and they brought Tamburri onboard to head it. Tamburri accepted the post with Phyllis in mind, and soon had used his influence to ensure that Phyllis became the recipient of the school's first ever music scholarship.

Around this time, a major shakeup occurred in the Hyman household. Phyllis's father left her mother and moved in with another woman. "My mother was crushed," Sakinah recalled. But Philip didn't go far. He moved in with his girlfriend, Willa, in Beltzhoover. The kids disliked her at first, but watching their father with this new woman was also an eye opener.

"She put him in check," said Jeannie. "She was his equal, and he was in no way with her the way he was with our mother. So that really let me know that one, my parents should have never been together. They probably wouldn't have been had my mother not gotten pregnant. Two, that because my mother was not able to stand up to him, he just ran over her. See, he needed a woman who could hold up her end and stand up to him, and my mother wasn't able to do that."

Philip wasn't always awful to Louise, though. "She just completely loved him, and even though he was a jerk sometimes he wasn't always a jerk," said Sakinah. "My father loved my mother. It's just that their relationship was her depression and his alcoholism."

Not long after her father left the house, Phyllis moved out, too. Her first home away from home was a small apartment on the south side at Tenth Street and East Carson. "It was a hallway apartment," said Jeannie. "It was so narrow that you could almost extend your arms and touch both sides." Sometimes, Anita would go over and help Phyllis clean house. "I just remember how eccentric she was, how she just stood out and how her girlfriends just really idolized her. If she had something on, everybody wanted to emulate her. She just definitely stood out."

At home, Louise's mother helped her pick up the slack. Some of Phyllis's siblings, though, think that it was their grandmother who predisposed their mother to being abused. "Oh yes, my father picked up right where her mother left off," said Jeannie. Anita's recollections were similar. "To me, what I saw was a love and hate relationship," she said. "It was love and hate." And brother Mark recalled that with his father out of the house, it was his grandmother who ruled the roost. "My grandmother was a disciplinarian. She didn't take no mess. She was loving and kind and affectionate, but if you got on her nerves she'd get on your case."

Initially, Phyllis wasn't sure she wanted to attend college. She was interested in becoming an AmeriCorps VISTA volunteer. "My father told me VISTA would always be there, but this scholarship wouldn't. So I took it. But I didn't finish college. I wasn't really prepared for it."

Phyllis did try for a time to get with the program. She respected Tamburri and she wanted to make him proud. Tamburri started a chorus at Robert Morris and took the 30 or so students in it all over the city and suburbs to perform. He showcased Phyllis and let her sing songs like "Satin Doll" and "Here's That Rainy Day." With his jazz background, Tamburri understood the importance of contemporary standards. He wasn't grooming Phyllis merely to be the best possible chorus member – he truly believed that she could have a successful career as a vocalist.

In his spare time, Tamburri began working with her privately. He would pick Phyllis up on Sunday mornings and drive her to his home in the suburb of Gibstonia, some 20 miles away. There he would spend hours training Phyllis and teaching her new songs. Then, in the evening, Tamburri's wife would drive Phyllis back to the city.

Phyllis's father wasn't particularly fond of the notion that his daughter might pursue a career in the arts, and he grew suspicious of the Tamburri family's influence. "He did call me a couple times and it was almost sort of like, 'Well, what are you going to do with my daughter?'" recalled Trudy Tamburri with a laugh. "It was amusing to me. I mean, he didn't say, 'I'm happy that you have such an interest in her and she's doing so well.' Nothing like that.

"Actually, when she went to Robert Morris College, my husband was always getting her out of the frying pan. She'd miss classes and everything. He wanted her to stay in school so not only would she have a showcase, but she would have something to fall back on just in case a career in show business didn't work out."

Tamburri still had connections in the music business, and a host of friends that played in several well-known jazz clubs around Pittsburgh. With his wife's blessing, Tamburri began to prepare Phyllis to sing solo in these clubs. The Tamburris convinced their family dentist to cap Phyllis's front teeth for free, and Trudy went about fashioning Phyllis some proper stage wear. "I bought this pink brocaded satin," said Trudy Tamburri. "I made her some palazzo pants with real wide legs at the bottom – because Phyllis was so tall she could wear anything – and a halter top."

Tamburri took Phyllis to places like the Crawford Grill and the Lowendi Club, where his friends in the band would let him and his young protégé sit in. "People just went crazy over her," said Trudy Tamburri.

"At first, when I started to do little clubs, I was okay as long as you weren't looking at me," Phyllis said of this period. "I used to think people were out of their minds for paying good money to come and hear me sing."

But if Phyllis was blind to her incredible talent, the Tamburris certainly were not, and in later years she reflected upon their influence in the early stages of her career. "People pushed me and advised me to go into entertainment," she said. "I mean, they *pushed* me. I kept saying, 'You're crazy. There are too many great people out there. I'll never make it.'"

After a year at Robert Morris, Phyllis dropped out. She took a break from singing and briefly worked as a file clerk for General Electric and as a secretary for Westinghouse before settling into a position with Neighborhood Legal Services. "I thought business would be my future," she said. "I was never the greatest secretary, but I was always a concerned secretary." Perhaps the result of living in a crowded house, where bathroom access wasn't always guaranteed, Phyllis developed a tardiness problem that stayed with her for the rest of her life. "I lived six blocks away and I was late every day."

Phyllis and Richie continued to see each other. The two would take in a concert – acts such as The Temptations or a talented new artist named Roberta Flack – or simply stay in and talk. "We had a relationship and a friendship, I think," said Richie, who said

Phyllis's budding talent already astounded him. "Occasionally, we would be talking and just in conversation she'd sing. She had a really amazing voice. One time she just imitated my voice and she got it perfectly. It was like listening to myself on a tape recorder. She had a tremendous talent. She could do almost anything with her voice."

Phyllis was excited by the possibilities of where her voice could take her. But Richie was able to detect a certain sadness hiding beneath Phyllis's warm personality. The drinking age was 18, and Phyllis indulged regularly. It was also not unusual to find marijuana in the house. "She smoked weed but she also liked to take pills. Phyllis was an escapist. She liked to get away from things. I think, in retrospect, that she was just depressed. I think she could have had everything and she would have had the same problem. I think she was just a depressed person, that she was genetically predisposed to it."

From time to time, Phyllis would find a way to sing a little bit here and there. Her first major break came when she was asked to sing at a charity benefit. "The timing was right," Phyllis said. "Dick Morgan heard me and asked me to join his group, which had just lost its lead singer." Phyllis accepted the offer, which required her to quit her job and put her relationship with Richie on hold, without hesitation.

Morgan, a Washington-based pianist, was working with a booking agent in New York who helped him plan an impressive tour. New Directions, Morgan's quartet, traveled to cities like Las Vegas, Chicago, Cleveland, Miami, and even Nassau, Bahamas and Puerto Rico. Each engagement lasted a week to two weeks, and New Directions was booked into some of the best lounges in the country.

Phyllis knew by now that she was not meant to be a secretary and had no problem giving up that work. Initially, though, she had a hard time adjusting to life on the road, far from friends and family. The road is not easy, and making it more difficult still was the fact that she was the only woman accompanying an all-male quartet composed of essentially four strangers. For a time, she didn't think she was going to make it. From her hotel room in Vegas' flashy Flamingo Hotel, where the group was playing,

Phyllis felt homesickness overwhelm her. "I remember calling and telling my dad I wanted to come home," she said, "and at age 20 no less."

Her father encouraged her to stick it out, and after the first few dates, life on the road became a little easier. Morgan took her under his wing and tried to help her become a better live performer. "It was my first gig and I had to learn how to dress, apply makeup and work with choreography," recalled Phyllis. "Since I wasn't into any of that jazz, it was like a crash course." The group would rehearse in the afternoons and Phyllis was grateful for the knowledge that Morgan shared. She soaked it all up, and eagerly asked questions. "I used to say, 'Dick, teach me how to stand.' And he'd say, 'Forget it, Phyllis. That's how we found you. Stand like that.'"

What Morgan did teach Phyllis was stage manners, microphone technique and "how to blend in with the group without being out of sorts visually," he recalled. "Her talent was so effortless, it took no effort on her part to do what she needed to do to create those vocal and visual effects. She was a natural talent, so it was just a matter of fine-tuning."

In addition to vocal talent, Morgan found that Phyllis had a natural charm and a bold, outgoing personality that he quickly put to work for him. "I would let her make all the announcements about the tunes and songs and the intermissions. She would insert her own little brand of humor, which would fit sometimes and sometimes it didn't. I let her do it because I felt like her honesty and sincerity was going to come out."

To be sure, the tour was a turning point for Phyllis. It was the first time she considered that a career in music was a real option for her. "In six months I got this incredible view of what this business is about," she reflected. "For me at the time, in my first job, it was just fascinating; hard work, but fascinating. I had never done this before. I had never put makeup on, or done anything to my hair, or concentrated on the image of an entertainer. I learned a lot. I found that it wasn't really a fantasy world. It was just work. I rehearsed all day long. I hated it because all I wanted to do was get up and sing. But you had to prepare. I didn't know that."

After about six months on the road, the dates dried up. Morgan's booking agent had left the firm he worked for, and the band took a hiatus. Phyllis returned to Pittsburgh, open to considering that her voice could be a viable vocation, but uncertain she really wanted to pursue a career as a vocalist. "I came back to Pittsburgh to kind of get the cobwebs out of my head," she said. "I really wasn't sure if I wanted to do it."

Phyllis knew by now that she was talented. But deep inside she wondered if she was talented enough – good enough – to really make it. "One of the reasons I never got in the business until very late was Nancy Wilson. I thought, if you can't be that good don't bother. She got my act together. I just believed in order to be in line with her you had to try to be as good. I didn't want to just wade through it." Unsure if she could ever be Nancy Wilson good, Phyllis took a break.

"I don't remember consciously seeking this business but friends say I always wanted it," said Phyllis. "I was probably telling them something I wasn't telling myself." While she weighed her options, Phyllis, now in her early 20s, took a job as a live-in babysitter of sorts. "A friend of mine with a big house was having a kid and her husband was working two jobs, and he wanted me to keep her company. So I got free room and board and the work was real simple: sleeping and talking."

But after about eight months on the job, Phyllis grew restless. "One day I said to myself, 'This will never do!'" There was only one way out of the job for Phyllis, and out of the city, which was her ultimate goal. Phyllis auditioned for and quickly got a job with another band. All The People was Phyllis's "ticket out of Pittsburgh," she said proudly. The band was "a loud R&B horn band and it used to drive me crazy. I don't like loud music, but they got me to Miami."

Chapter 2

Florida was very strange ... but that's where I learned to be an entertainer.

Things moved fast for Phyllis in Miami. In no time, she was securing dates for herself as a solo vocalist and would often sit in with several local bands. Tee To Green quickly became one of Phyllis's regular spots to perform. While the club was not nearly as upscale as its name might imply, it did attract a high caliber of talent to its tiny stage. Along with Phyllis, other regular performers of the time included Gwen Dickey, who by 1976 would be topping the pop charts as lead singer for the group Rose Royce, with the hit "Car Wash," and Margaret Reynolds, who went on to become a founding member of Fire, the trio known for the elaborately lush backing vocals they added to the sound of Miami superstars KC & The Sunshine Band. But in early 1972, when Phyllis arrived on the scene, they were all still a bunch of underpaid unknowns.

Phyllis became friends with a drummer and percussionist named Chico Lopez. But Chico didn't play in Phyllis's band. He had a regular – and better paying – gig with Joe Donato. A brass man who played a variety of instruments, Donato was a white man fronting an all black band. Donato and his group primarily played trendy private clubs in toney Coconut Grove. At Chico's insistence, Joe accompanied him to Tee To Green one night to hear Phyllis sing. "I really wasn't interested but I would go along with Chico because he's very, very convincing," remembered Donato. "We went to hear her and, of course, she was fantastic."

Donato had just signed a contract to play at Coconut Grove's newest nightspot, Sausalito. The club was very chic and often attracted visiting celebrities such as Sonny and Cher and Bob Dylan. With Donato, there was not a lot of time for rehearsals, which Phyllis really didn't require anyway. When it came to her portion of the show the band just made sure to play songs she was familiar with. "Everything was just off the cuff," Donato said. "She'd come on stage, take her shoes off, and that was it. She'd just open it up and go for it."

Phyllis sang standards with Donato's band, songs such as "Here's That Rainy Day," which she had learned from David Tamburri. She would also, on occasion, sing a few contemporary numbers like Marvin Gaye's "What's Going On," which was a favorite of hers at the time.

"Then she would do this other thing," said Donato. "She liked to be in the background, using her voice as a horn or another instrument. It was a beautiful sound. It added so much because of the tone and musicality in whatever she did." Phyllis called Donato "Professor Jazz," and his influence led her to experiment with jazz and Caribbean-driven beats, two ingredients that would remain a part of her music throughout the length of her career.

Phyllis quickly attracted attention around town. In 1973, choreographer turned director Bob Fosse was in Miami shooting a biopic of controversial comedian Lenny Bruce. Starring Dustin Hoffman, the film was appropriately titled *Lenny* and Fosse tapped Phyllis for a cameo. Fosse "was a sweetheart, very kind and patient," Phyllis recalled. "He asked me if I could laugh. I said, 'If something's funny, believe me, I *can* laugh.'" Before he had finished shooting the scene, Fosse, himself, had to get down on hands and knees and hold Phyllis's feet. "I was knocking over stuff," Phyllis explained. "When I laugh, my arms go flying and everything else goes which way. I am not a quiet laugher."

Phyllis was not exclusive to Donato's band. She did the occasional solo date, and she also sang with a few other groups, such as the Hondo Beat. An all-purpose outfit that played jazz, R&B and Caribbean tunes, the Hondo Beat regularly played weeklong stints on assorted cruise ships within the Norwegian Caribbean line. Phyllis was in her cabin aboard the MS Skyward when she heard a spectacularly sexy voice just outside her door and decided to investigate. "I was getting ready for work so I peeked out to see who he was. I said, 'Wow!' It was truly love for me at first sight," Phyllis said of her first glimpse of Larry Alexander.

Larry fit Phyllis's physical taste to a tee. He was taller than she was – and at 6 feet ½ inches, that was saying something – with deep eyes and an even deeper Jamaican-accented voice. Like Phyllis, he was a vocalist working on the ship, and the pair struck up a quick friendship. "It's funny, but as a child coming up I would always have this dream about this man in my life, but he never had a face," Phyllis said. "As strange as it may seem, when I met Larry the dream disappeared. I never had it again. We were talking marriage in a couple of months."

Phyllis was also talking about another change in her life. Joe Donato's contract with Sausalito was for one year. When it ran out in early 1974, he decided to take the band on tour. Phyllis, meanwhile, decided to form a band of her own. She called on bassist Mark Egan and drummer Billy Bowker from the Hondo Beat to help her out. Egan and Bowker had both studied at the University of Miami's School of Music. Another of their classmates, guitarist Hiram Bullock, signed on, and Howie Schneider rounded out the group on keyboards. Egan, though, favored fellow classmate and keyboardist Clifford Carter, who was currently on tour with the Four Tops, and set out to persuade him to join the group.

"I remember he called me from the road and asked if I wanted to play with the Tops," recalled Egan. To Carter's surprise, Egan immediately declined the offer. "I said, 'No, I want to play with Phyllis.' He said, 'Whoah! Must be something happening there if you're really not willing to go on the road with the Four Tops.' And there was. It was a great band with Billy and Hiram. So Clifford left the Tops and decided to come with Phyllis."

Thus, Phyllis Hyman and the P/H Factor were born. Their sound, as Egan described it, was eclectic. "It was a real melting pot. We played everything including funk, Latin music, Brazilian music, straight ahead jazz. Phyllis just fit into it all. If left to her own devices, I think Phyllis would have had us doing cover tunes of rhythm and blues. But she had a bunch of progressive heads in the band and we pulled her in other directions. Then she pulled us in hers, and it was a great thing."

For her part, Phyllis enjoyed diversifying her show. "Once I realized I was capable of interpreting all different kinds of music, I decided, 'Why not?' I became kind of the 'in thing' in Florida because there weren't many other singers at the time who could do all different types of material, who could do Latin, who could do 'Satin Doll,' who could do The Isley Brothers and then go into a Cole Porter tune. It was in Miami where I really perfected my singing style and stage presence."

"She just morphed into whatever it was and she just would be really strong and do it in a different way," said Egan. "She didn't sing the be-bop kind of jazz, she didn't have that background. So she did it in her own way, which was the unique thing about that band."

Phyllis and the P/H Factor quickly developed a reputation – and a regular following – and were soon enough gigging six nights a week. One of the band's regular spots to play was the Checkmate Lounge in South Miami, which was owned by entertainment attorney Leonard Levinstein. Lenny, as his friends called him, took an interest in Phyllis and arranged an audition with Steve Alaimo of Alston Records.

Alston was the precursor to TK Records, the empire responsible for the advent of disco and such acts as KC and the Sunshine Band, George McCrae, Latimore and Timmy Thomas. It was at the time, however, still a fledgling empire and Phyllis, who went to the audition with Larry, was not impressed. "Levinstein said, 'She's great,' so I went down to hear her and I said, 'Yes, she is really great,'" recalled Alaimo. "So we came in and cut a couple things with her." Alaimo was interested in Phyllis, but ultimately no deal was signed. "Levinstein wanted to manage her. But she didn't want that. I don't think she thought we were big enough. She wanted to sign with a major. She was very, very headstrong. She thought she was going to be a star, and she ended up being one."

The trip wasn't a total loss, though. While at the Tone Building in Hialeah, Alston's headquarters, Phyllis met the label's first lady. Betty Wright had burst onto the soul music scene in a big way with 1971's million-selling record "Clean Up Woman." Wright was immediately taken with Phyllis's bubbly personality and the two hit it off. "I remember thinking, 'That's the tallest lady I've ever seen,'" Wright said. "She had a scarf on her head like a gypsy and she had shining eyes. She said, 'I always wanted to meet you,' and she was so friendly to me that I instantly fell in love with her. She just didn't meet no stranger."

Though she was still a relative newcomer – especially as a bandleader – the P/H Factor boys were duly impressed by Phyllis. "I learned my work ethic from her," recalled guitarist Hiram Bullock. "She showed me that no matter how many people were in the room, you should still give it your all. It was the same show for two or 2,000. Phyllis taught me a lot, man. She was the first person who referred to the gig as work. I was sort of coming at it from this hippy rocker stance, 'We're gonna go play;' and she'd say, 'No, we're gonna go work.'"

According to Bullock, Phyllis was a musical genius. "I don't think many people realize just what a creative artist Phyllis was. She was a creative genius on the order of Miles Davis. At the Checkmate, she did vocal improvisations that could hold their own with anyone. Phyllis was more creative than even she realized."

Phyllis and crew would always secure a regular gig as the house band someplace, and then do additional gigs on the side. Members of the band made on average $200 "for five nights a week, sometimes five sets a night," Bullock said. "You'd start with the dinner set, playing 'Satin Doll' and jazz, then you'd work your way into boogie down. It basically was one of the contributing factors to me having versatility as a performer. We played everything, every type of music."

Larry was on the scene, when he wasn't singing on the cruise ship circuit. But his role with the band was unofficial. Often, he was simply Phyllis's chauffeur. "In the beginning I tried to handle all the business aspects myself," Phyllis said. "The most I would let him do was drive me around to different gigs." More often that not, though, it was Mark or Hiram who drove Phyllis. "She was quite comfortable watching soaps all day and making some smothered pork chops," said Bullock. "I'd pick her up with her hair in curlers and drive her to the gig, and she'd hit the stage and it was like, bam!"

"Florida was very strange," Phyllis said of her time as a bandleader in Miami. "Music wasn't very exciting during the period I was there. People were into drinking and picking up the girl or the guy across the table. But that's where I really learned how to be an entertainer. I would joke around and do all kinds of crazy things from the stage."

"She was always wild," said Mark Egan. "You never knew what she was going to say. I remember we used to do this tune called 'The Creator Has A Master Plan,' and she would, basically, rap. We would be vamping in the background and she'd start to speak. I used to say, 'Whoah! Phyllis, come back,' because she would start talking about religion and she just went a little far."

Phyllis's "Creator" monologues revealed a philosophical and spiritually aware side of Phyllis that she didn't often offer a glimpse into when not on stage. The following is a transcript of one of them.

"When you're a kid and over and over again the creator is called by so many different names, the Lord, God, Jesus, the messiah, Allah, sometimes even 'the man.' That confuses you when you're a child. It has to, because you don't know. But as you grow up and you begin to give very heavy consideration to just who or what the creator is and what relationship that being has with you, then you begin to ask some very serious questions. One, is the creator a man or a woman? Is the creator black or white? Asian? Indian? Exactly what is the scope? Being practical, being sensible, looking at it from all angles, I had to arrive at the feeling, at the thought, at wanting to believe that the creator is not a man, is not a woman, is not black nor white Asian or otherwise, but a mass of very positive, loving energy that each of us has to cup from daily. We cannot survive without that energy. We need it to live. We use it everyday whether you go to church or not, whether you want to believe or not that energy comes from it, from that, from everything."

After several months at the Checkmate, Phyllis and the band moved to Cahoots in the Fort Lauderdale Ramada Inn. While she was there, Phyllis decided to host her younger brothers for a summer visit. She invited Mark, 16, and Michael, two months shy of 15, to Miami. The two boys had lots of fun in the Sunshine State. Mark had just failed Algebra and English and was required to attend summer school if he wanted to enter his junior year in the fall. Phyllis arranged for him to take classes in Miami. Phyllis cooked for her brothers, saw that Mark got to school, and on the weekends, she let them accompany her to her gigs.

"She'd perform and I'd get a plate of food, some lobster or some shrimp or some steak," recalled Mark. "We'd sit and dance and have a good time."

Michael, too, was impressed with Cahoots, which sat right on the water and afforded him his first ever view of the ocean. "That was my first taste of watching her work as a singer and watching her as a leader of a band. It was amazing watching her interact with an audience and how they responded to her. You could tell that there were big things ahead of her."

Phyllis enjoyed looking after her brothers and even took them to Disney World over the Independence Day holiday weekend. "I remember Phyllis as a happy, bubbly, life-of-the-party person," said Mark. "Phyllis was a real charmer, too. She could charm her way out of any situation in the world."

It wasn't always charm, though, that she used on her live-in boyfriend Larry Alexander. Sometimes, it was brute force. Mark recalled that the balance of power in Phyllis's relationship with Larry leaned heavily in her favor. "Larry was real kind to my sister," Mark said. "He was real gentle with her and I liked him for that. But they would argue, and he always had some drama. She would laugh at him. She would beat him up. She would dog him out. I didn't like that."

While still at Cahoots, Phyllis met Sid Mauer, who along with Freddy Frank owned a label called Roadshow Records. Distributed at the time by Scepter, Roadshow had made a name for itself a year earlier with the number one single "Do It ('Till You're Satisfied)" by B. T. Express.[1] They were instantly taken with Phyllis and interested in adding her to the Roadshow roster of artists. After an entertaining evening at the club, Sid and Freddy spent the next few days talking with Phyllis and Larry. "It took us a little bit of time but we finally signed her to one of our labels," recalled Sid.

---

[1] Roadshow would soon switch to United Artists for distribution and go on to score additional hits by such groups as Brass Construction and Enchantment.

That label was Desert Moon Records, a new start-up. Shortly thereafter, Larry, who had finally begun making a little headway in his efforts to assert some influence over Phyllis's career, approached producer George Kerr. George had scored a million-selling record ("Hypnotized") on Linda Jones in 1967. Larry put him in contact with Phyllis's new label bosses and, once satisfied with his credentials, they gave him the go ahead to take Phyllis into the studio. George, of course, wanted to see the goods. So he, like Sid and Freddy had just weeks before, flew to Florida to see Phyllis. By then she had moved on to the Love Lounge inside Miami Beach's historic Eden Roc hotel. "Seeing her that one time is all it took," George said. "I took her to dinner and she told me she felt she had what it takes to be a big star. Three weeks later, I flew her to New York."

It was actually in West Orange, New Jersey, that Phyllis went into the studio with George. She traveled there with Larry, but without the band, and laid down the vocals for "Leavin' The Good Life Behind" to a prerecorded track. "Leavin'" was an upbeat disco number written by gospel artist Alvin Darling. A year shy of the 12-inch craze, "Leavin'," which was mixed by popular engineer Tom Moulton, was released as a two-sided 45 single, with a nearly three minute radio edit on one side and an extended mix on the other that finished at just over five minutes. Sid and Freddy arranged with their friend Larry Uttal to have the record released on his Private Stock label while they worked on setting up distribution for Desert Moon. Serviced to radio in July of 1975, the song went to number nine on Billboard's disco singles chart. But it didn't manage to crack either the pop or black singles chart.

Sid and Freddy had faith in Phyllis and asked George to fly to Miami to record some additional tracks. They arranged for studio time in Miami's famous Criteria Studios, a favorite with such acts as Eric Clapton, The Eagles and Crosby, Stills & Nash. During this period, the studio was often booked for months at a time by the Bee Gees. But Phyllis somehow got squeezed in. At Criteria, the whole band played on a couple of Larry's original compositions, including "And That Would Be," "Baby (I'm Gonna Love You)" and "Do Me," on which Hiram shared writer's credit and contributed an amazing guitar solo. Recording went smoothly.

"I was amazed at how fast she learned the tunes and got herself into the songs," said Kerr. "She was a one-take artist. She took very, very good direction," including how to start a song gently and gradually work up to a fevered pitch. "She used to start a song off at a climax, so there was no place to go. I told her, 'Smooth it out, stay with the melody and then do your thing.'"

Despite Kerr's praise, neither Phyllis nor the rest of the band was too pleased with the results of the sessions. "I always thought that she had much more talent than got across in those records," said Mark Egan, who played bass on the sessions. "I thought they over produced her. They got her out there, but I knew her potential. She was a monster, monster vocalist."

If Phyllis was, as Hiram Bullock saw her, a creative genius, she was still to many just a girl singer. Developing her artistry was not nearly as important a concern to Desert Moon/Roadshow as making a quick buck was. Larry likely loved Phyllis deeply, but for his part was trying to forge a path of his own. So his actions were dictated not only by what he thought was best for Phyllis's career, but what he felt was best for his, too. The result was precedent setting in Phyllis's career. She was singing what other people wanted her to, and it would be some time before she found a voice of her own.

Sid and Freddy, along with George, thought the simplest way to break Phyllis as a new artist was to follow the current trend. "We recorded a couple of sides with her that she wasn't too crazy about," explained Maurer. "This was the disco era. Everything on the charts was disco, from Kool & the Gang to KC and the Sunshine Band, and she was more into jazz, top of the line R&B, etcetera."

From the Love Lounge, Phyllis and the band moved on to Scamps, a club in Coconut Grove not far from where Phyllis had played with Joe Donato. But the band was not destined to enjoy a lengthy partnership with the club. Phyllis attracted a lot of attention, and in this case from the club's owner. According to Hiram Bullock, the owner made a sexual advance toward Phyllis, who turned him down cold. "The next night, we got to the gig and our equipment was off the stage," said Bullock. "They hired another band." But the P/H Factor still had a gig. Two "high rollers," as Bullock recalled them, had offered to book the band for a week in Belize. Now the P/H Factor was free to take them up on the offer.

Belize, British Honduras is nestled between Mexico and Guatemala on the Caribbean coast. There, Phyllis found a beautiful mix of tropical forests, mountains, mysterious Maya temples, and a host of diving and fishing experiences. Belize is also home to enormous poverty. The shows, which more often that not took place in tiny outdoor pavilions, were not well attended. At one show, somewhere in the Belizean jungle, Phyllis started singing at dusk. Just as she began, a colony of bats swarmed the bandstand. Phyllis, fighting back a fit of laughter, had to duck down for several minutes.

The trip to Belize affected Phyllis and forced her to take her career more seriously than she ever had before. "The poverty was frightening," she said. "Somehow it got me thinking I was going to have to come to New York and try to make it." Bullock recalls it wasn't just the poverty that convinced Phyllis, but the issue at Scamps as well. "When we got back, Phyllis was like, 'This whole scene sucks. Let's go to New York.'"

The band arrived in the Big Apple on December 21, 1975. Miraculously, they managed to secure a gig the first day, a two-week engagement at a club called Rust Brown's. Larry's brother, jazz pianist Monty Alexander, lived nearby and Larry and Phyllis stayed with him during the job. The rest of the band, meanwhile, stayed in the basement of Clifford Carter's parents' house in Westchester, a half an hour away.

Phyllis opened at Rust Brown's and was an instant hit. "People came because we weren't doing the usual New York club scene," explained Mark Egan. Phyllis's rendition of "Everything Must Change" was second to none. Her take on the Quincy Jones produced-Minnie Ripperton number "If I Ever Lose This Heaven" was also unique, and she had carefully crafted Leon Russell's "Song For You" into a medley with "You Are So Beautiful To Me." Other popular hits that regularly found themselves included in the act were "Reasons" by Earth, Wind and Fire, "Rock The Boat" by the Hues Corporation, Maria Muldaur's "Midnight At The Oasis" and "I Can See Clearly Now" by Johnny Nash.

Phyllis was still doing her share of straight ahead jazz. But she could just as easily switch gears and add vocals to a disco instrumental such as "Express," a big hit that had launched the career of her Roadshow label mates B.T. Express, or "Discotizer," an original written by Hiram and Larry that B.T. Express had actually recorded on their follow-up album. The band's diverse repertoire immediately attracted the attention of the New York crowd, where bands at the time usually focused on a specific genre. "Not many people were doing it all," said Egan. "A lot of folks were attracted to it because it was different."

It was so different – and so good – that at the end of the run the management of Rust Brown's asked the band to stay on. Phyllis and the gang had two days to return to Miami, pack up or put out all their belongings, let go of their apartments and return to New York. Amazingly, they made it back in time, where their new fans were waiting.

"One night George Benson would be there, then Stevie Wonder would come by, he lived around the corner," said Mark Egan, remembering those heady days at Rust Brown's. "Then George Harrison would be in town. A lot of people were checking us out."

For Phyllis, it was all a bit overwhelming. "It was frightening and puzzling," she said. "I couldn't figure out why all those people came to hear me." As always, Phyllis appeared to be the last one to realize just how incredibly talented she really was.

Chapter 3

> *People tell me, 'You're going to be a star in two or three years.'*

One of the many celebrities to find their way into the club was Norman Connors. A multitalented drummer and composer from Philadelphia, Connors had studied music at Philly's Temple University and the famous Juilliard School of Music. Soon after, he secured a touring gig with Pharoah Sanders that led to a deal with Cobblestone Records, a subsidiary of Buddah, in 1972. Connors had put out a total of five albums. But it was only on his most recent, 1975's *Saturday Night Special*, that he'd really begun to find his niche – as well as his first taste of commercial success.

Connors was known for finding and featuring new talent on his releases. On *Saturday Night Special*, he teamed two very gifted vocalists together, Michael Henderson and Jean Carn. Henderson was a child prodigy, playing bass with groups such as the Fantastic Four, the Detroit Emeralds and Billy Preston by the time he was 13. He spent seven years in the band of jazz legend Miles Davis before joining up with Connors, who allowed him to showcase his vocal skills for the first time. Jean Carn, meanwhile, made her Connors debut on his 1974 release, *Slewfoot*. Known as a jazz diva, Carn had already released four albums with her husband, Doug, on the Ovation label. After both the marriage and musical partnership dissolved, she sang with Duke Ellington before recording for Connors.

"Valentine Love" was a tune that Henderson had composed. A syrupy-sweet duet, Henderson alternated between his rich tenor voice and full, soaring falsetto while trading lush lines with Jean. It was a good match, and the song was a certified hit on the R&B charts, going to number 10. Connors shrewdly planned to re-team Henderson with Carn on his new album, hoping to rekindle the

But Carn had just signed a solo contract with Philadelphia International Records, and the powers at PIR – none other than industry veterans Kenny Gamble and Leon Huff – were not interested in loaning out Carn outside of the label.

One look at – and listen to – Phyllis, and Connors knew he had solved the problem. He wasted no time in approaching her after she finished her first set.

"I walked up and said, 'Phyllis, I'm Norman Connors and I'd like to take you into the studio,'" he recalled.

But Phyllis wasn't one to be easily impressed.

"She said, 'Yeah, everybody says that.'"

"No, no. I've got the perfect song for you, 'Betcha By Golly Wow,'" Connors continued.

The name rang no bells for Phyllis.

"She said, 'What kind of song is that?'"

Unbeknownst to Phyllis, who had never owned a record player, it was the kind of song that hits were made of. "Betcha" had gone to number two R&B, number three pop for the Stylistics in 1972. Written by Thom Bell and Linda Creed – two writers who would contribute significantly to Phyllis's recording career in the years to come – "Betcha" was already a Philly soul classic.

Phyllis was also as unfamiliar with Connors as she was with the song he was proposing for her to record. "I hadn't really heard of him up to that point," she recalled. "But it was a chance to make a record and I said, 'Sure.' I had made a record before," she said, referring to the "Leavin' The Good Life Behind" single, "but that really doesn't count. It was pretty obscure. Even I don't have a copy of it."

Norman wanted to get Phyllis in the studio right away, but there was one hurdle to jump first. Phyllis was a signed artist and he had to get permission from her label bosses at Roadshow. Sid and Freddy weren't too keen on the idea, but they allowed Phyllis to record not just one, but three songs with Connors. In addition to "Betcha," Norman asked Phyllis to sing on "Just Imagine," which had been written by arranger Onaje Allen Gumbs, and "We Both Need Each Other," the newest Henderson-penned duet on which Connors had originally planned to re-team him with Carn.

With the proper permissions in place, Connors took Phyllis into Electric Lady Studios, the recording studio originally built by Jimi

Hendrix in 1970. Phyllis recorded "We Both" first, and immediately impressed those gathered in the studio, including producer Skip Drinkwater. "Skip and the others were not familiar with Phyllis at all," said Gumbs, who was another local talent Phyllis had impressed with her sets at Rust Brown's. "So every time she answered Michael Henderson, she blew him, and everybody else in the studio, away.

When Drinkwater went out of town, Gumbs was left with the responsibility of recording Phyllis's vocals for "Betcha," which didn't go all together well. Phyllis was running late for her show at Rust Brown's and growing more impatient as the seconds passed. Gumbs and company didn't want to keep the crowd at Rust Brown's waiting, but they did think Phyllis had a better take in her. "I told him I had to leave to go to work and that I'd come back to finish," Phyllis recalled. But Onaje convinced her to sing the song just one more time before leaving. "He calmed me and I said, 'OK,' and we did it, and that was the take that made the album."

Phyllis may have thought that, but actually the vocal Gumbs finally used was not any one particular take. Rather it was a composite of several of them, which when meshed together offered listeners, said Gumbs, the "crème de la crème of her vocal interpretation." During this session, Gumbs saw firsthand how Phyllis's manager/boyfriend really felt about her. Listening to Phyllis lay down the vocals for "Betcha," Larry lost it. "The man was reduced to tears," said Gumbs. "He was so overwhelmed. She was a goddess to him, not just the woman he shared his bed with. He worshipped Phyllis."

Connors may not have been reduced to tears, but he, too, was moved by Phyllis's gift. Phyllis was "very talented," he said, "doing things in one or two takes. She was very easy to work with. Very sensitive to a point. But she would look at me and try to listen to whatever I had to say."

Phyllis was likewise appreciative of Norman. "He was so wonderful to me. We had a certain kind of chemistry between us that just worked. He brought out notes in me that I didn't know were there."

Phyllis, by early 1976, was building a throng of fans across New York. From Rust Brown's, Phyllis moved a few blocks away to Mikell's, where she became the house band, playing Sunday through Thursday nights. Located on the corner of 97th Street and Columbus Avenue, and owned by husband and wife Pat and Mike Mikell, Mikell's was very in at the time. The pub was frequented by a clientele that included its share of celebrities. Among them, Cat Stevens and Stevie Wonder could often be spotted sipping a Planter's Punch, the house specialty, which consisted of 150-proof rum and fresh fruit juice.

Soon enough, just as Norman Connors had approached Phyllis, the rest of the band began getting offers. One by one, they defected. Hiram got a gig with saxophonist David Sanborn; Mark Egan and Cliff Carter accepted an offer to go on the road with the Pointer Sisters, and Billy Bowker tired of New York and decided to return to Florida.

"That was a turning point and very difficult decision for me to make," said Egan. "But we saw that Phyllis was doing stuff with Roadshow, that they were sort of producing the records for her. So we thought it would be a good opportunity to move onto other things.

"I've never in all my experience before or since played with anyone with such a dynamic personality as Phyllis," Egan continued. "I've never met anyone who was the entertainer she was."

In need of a new band, Larry turned to Onaje Allen Gumbs and asked him to put one together. Taking on the role of musical director, Onaje played keyboards and brought in Alex Blake on bass and Brian Brake on drums. It had only been three months since Phyllis arrived in New York, and already she was something of a local legend. She and Larry were still staying in his brother Monty's apartment. There, one day in late March, Phyllis entertained a reporter from the *Associated Press*. The reporter, Dolores Barclay, wrote a piece she titled "Phyllis Hyman – Remember That Name," that ran in papers across the country. Phyllis was still playing at Mikell's, and had no immediate plans to tour, but it put the rest of the nation on notice to get ready.

"Her voice filled the small Westside nightclub, piercing the air with a dramatic shrill and then falling to an incredibly husky whisper as she sang the Quincy Jones song 'Everything Must Change,'" began the introduction to the piece. "Her name is Phyllis

Hyman. She's a 26-year-old Pittsburgh, Pa. native who was virtually unknown in New York until her first club appearances in December. Since then, she has attracted as avid and loyal a following among patrons of Manhattan's Westside nightclubs as some of the nation's top recording stars."

For her part, Phyllis was frank. "My gimmick, if artists are to have one, is to be me. I don't make up speeches for the stage, and I'm not into theatrics when I sing because I want people to enjoy my singing." Between puffs on a Marlboro, Phyllis waxed philosophical about her future. "I don't know what it is I'm supposed to be looking for. People tell me, 'You're going to be a star in two or three years.' Well, I'm already a star. I have a job and a husband who has helped mold my career. What I have now is enough to sustain myself. What else comes will be added on. My career, since I first started, is at the right speed. I'm not rushing."[2]

The new band was still eclectic, but its repertoire was not quite as diverse as the P/H Factor. A few of Phyllis's straight ahead jazz tunes were kept, like Pharoah Sanders' "The Creator Has A Master Plan." But she added several new cover tunes, most of which had originally been performed by male vocalists. A fan of Bill Withers, Phyllis incorporated a couple songs from his recent *Making Music* album, including "I Wish You Well" and "She's Never Lonely," which she changed to "I'm Never Lonely." Phyllis also sang Stevie Wonder's "Superstition" and the Bobby Hebb classic "Sunny."

Between songs, Phyllis would keep the pace moving with her hilarious patter. Then there was the whistle, already her trademark. When she would decide to whistle a verse instead of sing it, "it's like the heavens would open up," said Gumbs. "If you had any imaginings of what world peace would be like, you felt it at the point she started whistling. There were no problems. Everything was fine. Everything could be overcome. And when you watched her, it seemed to be one of the few times she was at peace with herself.

---

[2] While Phyllis often referred to Larry as her husband, the two were not actually married at this time.

"Her head would sway back and forth. These notes would come out with this incredible vibrato and she was transfixed. She was in a trance. It was almost cathartic for her. That was her special time, and we had a chance to witness it."

Offstage, however, Gumbs had a chance to witness another side to Phyllis. "Her communication with her husband was not always the most pleasing to witness. There was tension. I felt, in a way, she wore the pants in the relationship. Pretty much whatever she wanted, he would have to do. He'd give in.

"It was a volatile relationship," Gumbs continued. "I'd pass by their place and walk into the middle of stuff. I'd always stay out of it. There were never any blows, but they definitely raised the decibel a lot. The decibel level was pretty intense."

By now, Phyllis was the talk of the town and making the society pages with great regularity. The combination of her comeliness and commanding stage presence had made fans out of the likes of Ashford & Simpson, George Benson, Lenny White and Dee Dee Bridgewater. Sometimes the celebrities became more than just fans, and Phyllis grew especially close to Roberta Flack. For her part, Flack was so impressed by Phyllis that she called upon the president of her record label, Atlantic's Ahmet Ertegun, to come out and see Phyllis for himself.

Phyllis and the Onaje-led band played at Mikell's for a few months, until the release of Connors' *You Are My Starship* album. Connors asked Phyllis to join him on his summer tour. Trying to duplicate the success of "Valentine Love," Norman chose "We Both Need Each Other" as the album's first single, a song that ironically, while it was featured on his album, he had not even played on. Adding to the irony was the fact that Michael Henderson was not initially on the tour, leaving Norman to actually sing the song with Phyllis. The song peaked at number 23 R&B, number 101 pop. Phyllis, of course, also sang "Betcha," a song that many felt should have been the album's first single but was actually still six months shy of being released.

Hoping to capitalize on the momentum of "We Both Need Each Other," Freddy Frank and Sid Maurer of Roadshow decided to release a second single on Phyllis. "Baby (I'm Gonna Love You)" came out just as the Norman Connors-produced track was climbing the charts. Culled from the recording sessions with

George Kerr, "Baby" was one of Larry's tunes. Released directly on Frank and Maurer's own Desert Moon label, "Baby" spent a mere six weeks on the charts and peaked at number 76 R&B.

After "We Both," Norman chose the album's title cut, another song written by and featuring the lead vocals of Michael Henderson, to be the album's second single. Phyllis received good marks for her part on the tour, and a healthy share of notices. Still, it wasn't the same as doing her own show, and during an August stopover in San Francisco she spoke about fronting her own band. "It's an interesting and challenging position for a woman. I like running the show anyway. But I'm not just a singer. I am involved in all facets of the business, singing, recording and promotions. Just singing isn't enough for me."

Even if she wasn't just a singer, it was hard to deny she was a singer first and foremost. "I enjoy performing. I really come alive when I'm out there. When you learn your audience, you better know how to approach them. It's an art, and I am an artist."

For the moment though, she was a guest artist on the Connors tour, and she gave him generous praise in any press coverage she received. "It's great working with Norman. I feel very fortunate that he put me on the album. It gave me a major recording on the market. I've learned a lot from working with him. He's patient and a very quiet person."

Not too quiet. It was while on this tour that Norman began speaking to Phyllis and Larry about signing to the label he called his creative home. Buddah Records began as an offspring of Kama Sutra Records in 1967. Initially the label was known for releasing "bubblegum music," light, airy songs absent of any social commentary and heavy on meaningless fun. The sound was cultivated by Buddah's number two guy, Neil Bogart. But it was owner Art Kass who would usher in an era of greater sophistication for the label in 1973 when he signed R&B super group Gladys Knight & the Pips. Knight and company came to the label bitter over being relegated to Motown's B list – overshadowed by acts like the Temptations, Marvin Gaye and the burgeoning solo career of Diana Ross – and instantly found themselves big fish in the small pond of Buddah.

Kass allowed the group – for the first time in their career – to have a strong say in the production of their music and the decision paid off nicely for him. Gladys and the Pips scored immediately with a string of hits that included the number one singles "Best Thing That Ever Happened To Me," "I Feel A Song (In My Heart)" and "I've Got To Use My Imagination." By 1976, Gladys was still doing relatively well, though no longer visiting the top ten, and the label was seeing very little action from the other artists on its roster.

Kass switched Norman Connors, who recorded for Buddah's jazz subsidiary, Cobblestone Records, over to Buddah direct. Connors then became the in-house musical director for Buddah and also acted as a sort of talent scout for the label as many of the acts he worked with on his own records won Buddah contracts.

"We decided to go with Buddah because we liked what we saw in terms of the promotion the company was doing with Norman," Phyllis explained. "So they bought my contract from Desert Moon and when we came off the road we started working on the album."

According to Maurer, there was no buyout involved. "We just let her go," he said. "All we could do was accede to her wishes, which came through her husband, Larry. I said, 'C'mon Freddy. If she wants to do this, we'll catch her later.'"

Though Phyllis may not have realized it, Buddah was already a sinking ship by the time she came onboard in 1977. That year would mark the last time Gladys Knight would make it to the R&B top ten while on the label, and it was a sign of things to come. Outside of Norman and his recruits, Melba Moore was about the only other thing making any R&B noise on the label. But after two years on Buddah, she'd only managed to crack the lower half of the R&B top 20 twice. In short, Buddah was releasing more greatest hits packages than new music.

Phyllis began work on her debut album in September, recording four songs co-produced by Larry and Sandy Torano at Record Plant in New York City. Larry called on Onaje to arrange these songs and play keyboards. In fact, one of them, "Deliver The Love," was a tune that Onaje had helped write. Hiram came back to play guitar on two of the tracks, and Phyllis, Larry and Sandy added backing vocals where necessary. One of these songs, "Children of the World," was a tune Phyllis had been singing live for the past year or so. It featured a young guitarist by the name of Reggie Lucas.

Buddah's Lewis Merenstein, the album's executive producer, encouraged Phyllis to use three different producers on the project, thus adding versatility to Phyllis's debut and showing her in several different lights. Production duties on the rest of the album were split between Jerry Peters and John Davis. Larry contributed a song to the album called "Beautiful Man of Mine." "It's how he thinks of himself in relation to me, and I go along with that," Phyllis explained. "The cat's been a wonderful inspiration to me, and singin' it's my way of thanking him for putting up with me these past four years."

All told, the album took six months to record and cost about $60,000 – or six times its original budget. "Buddah's been very fair in that they've never dictated policy," said Phyllis. "They've always said, 'We think you know what you're doing. So use your own judgment on the album.'" The creative control afforded to Phyllis – the same approach the label used to lure Gladys Knight some years earlier – may have ultimately hurt her cause more than it helped. In Gladys and the Pips' case, *All Music* called that control "a factor that they were mature and sophisticated enough to exploit to the fullest." But Phyllis and Larry were not the recording veterans that Gladys and company were by the time they came to Buddah from the school of Motown.

This control, whether she was experienced enough to handle it or not, was likely a leading factor in Phyllis choosing to sign with Buddah. Several other labels had expressed interest, including Warner Bros. and Atlantic, in signing her. Acting as her manager, though, Larry obviously found the Buddah deal the most attractive as it afforded him the opportunity to write and produce a portion of Phyllis's album. Phyllis may have seen this as a good thing. But neither Larry nor either of the additional two up-and-coming producers Buddah brought on board had enough name recognition to add any real prestige to the project; and Buddah certainly was without the resources to launch a proper marketing campaign.

The buzz about Phyllis only intensified as she returned to Mikell's for a special holiday engagement. "New York City was her oyster," said Barbara Shelley, a publicist Phyllis befriended shortly after signing with Buddah. "Everyone wanted to meet her because she was tall and gorgeous and talented. There wasn't anybody who wasn't talking about her. She made such an impression. When you would introduce her to someone she'd be down-home and friendly and warm. Andy Warhol loved to run into her. I could take her anyplace, and I did."

Buddah finally released "Betcha By Golly Wow" as a single on January 15, 1977. The third single from the *You Are My Starship* album, the ship was low on steam at this point, having been out nearly a year. Still, "Betcha" spent nine weeks on the charts and made it to number 29 R&B, number 102 pop.

Just as Connors was celebrating his first gold album, Phyllis was preparing for the release of her debut set. "It really turned out to be extensions of what Larry and I had been planning for four years and I learned a great deal from the whole experience," Phyllis said. "Everybody had the freedom they needed to be creative. I wanted the album to project what I want to say to the public, and I think it does just that."

Sadly, if the album said anything at all it affirmed the old adage "a little power is a dangerous thing." In allowing Phyllis, via Larry, to control the concept and production of the album, Buddah unintentionally perpetuated the same mistake made by Roadshow. In their attempt to ensure that her product was contemporary and commercial, they sacrificed a great deal of the eclecticism that Phyllis's live show had become known for.

Stereo Review summed up the unfortunate mistake in their November issue:

Her producers have wrought a miracle in reverse by managing to make her sound like just about everybody else. In an obvious attempt to 'popularize' her sound in order to sell her to a broader pop-soul audience, her enormous talent has been shaved down to fit sound-alike songs with banal lyrics and repetitious arrangements.

Though she stooped to the occasion, Ms. Hyman did not completely camouflage her artistry. There are moments here when her exceptional vocal control and interpretive skill come through, particularly in the introspective 'Was Yesterday Such A Long Time Ago,' which she sings with such fluidity and rare sensitivity as to evoke shivers.

Chosen as the album's important first single was the Thom Bell penned "Loving You, Losing You," which began eking its way up the charts in early April. Eventually, it reached number 32 R&B, number 103 pop. On the bright side, the song reached the top 40, yet it hadn't made it as far as either of the Norman Connors collaborations. Buddah released a second single from the album, "No One Can Love You More," written by Skip Scarborough, in July. "No One" was just the silky, smooth type of ballad that Phyllis could wrap herself in so easily. But despite the perfect fit between singer and song, "No One" made it no further than number 58 R&B. Meanwhile, the album these songs were culled from had stalled out at number 49 R&B, number 107 pop.

Phyllis toured throughout the summer of 1977 to promote the album, opening for a cross-section of acts from jazz luminary Ramsey Lewis to the disco dancing family group the Sylvers. She also opened several shows for Teddy Pendergrass. On average, Phyllis earned between $1,250 and $2,000 for these shows, which were booked for her by Gemini Artists Management out of New York. One highlight of the summer tour was playing Newark's Symphony Hall in July. Roberta Flack brought along Mick Jagger to hear Phyllis. News of the surprise backstage visit spread across the country when Anita Summer mentioned it in her column, which was syndicated to 330 papers nationally, and a photo of the trio was circulated to all the trades.

Barbara Shelley expertly handled the press for Phyllis and waged a massive media campaign. She even went the extra mile by making sure that Phyllis was seen at all the "in" parties around New York. At these soirees, it was customary for cocaine to be served, and Phyllis often indulged. Everyone in the scene did it. It was a perk of gaining access to the VIP room, a sign you had arrived, and a way of keeping your energy level up while you danced the night away.

Shelley took every ounce of good press Phyllis received, mashed it all together and made a gigantic media snowball she used to bust down any door that refused to open. Working every angle, she got Phyllis a pre-show interview with a booker from *The Tonight Show* in hopes that it would lead to a spot for Phyllis on Carson's couch. On a free day from the road, Shelley took Phyllis out to lunch with Rona Barrett's personal assistant, assuring some future column inches for the new star.

Still, despite all of Shelley's efforts, the fact that the album and its two singles hadn't fared well commercially made the determined publicist's job that much more difficult. "I don't know why my records haven't gone further up the charts," Phyllis said. "It's not that easy for me in the recording industry because everything is based on, 'Do you have a hit?' If you don't have anything on the charts, nobody wants to talk to you. That can be very disheartening. It could make you feel less about yourself. But I don't intend to let it do that to me, because it's just a job. It's a J-O-B, and I have other things in my life that are much more important."

This was bold talk, but also blatantly untrue and the beginning of a pattern for Phyllis: She told it as she wished it were – but not like it really was. The truth was that there was little besides her career happening in Phyllis's life. Even her relationship with Larry was consumed by it as he continued to act as her manager. Everything Phyllis did was done to better her professional image. She was traveling, performing to solid reviews from coast to coast and earning a national reputation. She had a record out, and even if it wasn't a smash it was one she was proud of. No doubt about it, her career was taking off.

During this time, Phyllis and Larry were rarely apart. "It's beautiful being married to your manager 'cause you don't have to hunt him down when you want to talk business," Phyllis said. "He's always right there." More often than not, Larry accompanied her on the road and to her performances. Phyllis appreciated his diligence and was pleased with the results. "Since Larry's taken over as manager, I've recorded with Norman Connors, Jon Lucien and the Fatback Band. I've done a commercial with Burger King, and I had the chance to perform at the Amsterdam Lente Festival with artists like George Benson and Charlie Rich. Plus, he got me a beautiful contract with Buddah."

When he wasn't working on Phyllis's career, Larry focused on his own. In addition to his songwriting for B.T. Express, Brass Construction and other acts signed to the Roadshow label, Larry and Sandy Torano, with whom he co-produced much of Phyllis's first album, had formed the band Tornader. The group's debut album, *Hit It Again*, was released in 1977 on the Polydor label. Much of it was written or co-written by Larry. But the single "(Back Up) Hit It Again" only made it to number 52 on the black singles chart. Phyllis claimed to be as supportive of Larry as he was of her and said their individual egos never got in the way. "There is no such thing as competition between two good people. That's a myth, an inside jealousy. That's not really necessary. We don't have that. I won't let our careers get in the way of our personal lives. It doesn't have to be that way."

Larry was once again employed as her producer in early 1978 as Phyllis began working on her second album for Buddah. Larry had decided to tackle producing the entire album this time, and he enlisted the help of Skip Scarborough, who served as his co-producer. Scarborough was riding high off of the success of his recent production for Con Funk Shun. Simply titled "Ffun," the song spent two weeks at number one at the first of the year. Scarborough was also a gifted writer, having penned such hits at L.T.D.'s "Love Ballad" and "Don't Ask My Neighbors" by the Emotions. Phyllis had recorded Skip's song "No One Can Love You More" on her debut album, and it was one of the highlights. Surprisingly, and disappointingly, Scarborough only brought one of his own compositions to Phyllis's sophomore project, the song "Livin' Inside Your Love."

For the first time in her career, Phyllis was exercising her own writing chops. She wrote a tune – her first song ever – in tribute to Black Panther Angela Davis. The song was simply called "Gonna Make Changes." "I remember when Angela was put in jail," Phyllis said. "Black and white people alike rallied to that lady's defense. It was so beautiful to see. I never met Angela, but I knew she was well educated and that she was doing things to help other people. Her release affirmed that there's power in the masses. If we stick together, we can make changes. Angela proved it. So many people – especially *our* people – are quietly being shafted and railroaded into a penal system into which they disappear."

Never one to be afraid of speaking out, Phyllis had done so with great finesse through her song. A powerful and moving ballad, "Changes" alluded to Phyllis's compassion for those who were struggling and seeking to bring about positive social change.

It also revealed a writing skill that once finely honed could have secured her a spot among the greats of the era. But as she openly admitted, writing was not something that came easily to her.

"Writing is something that's not natural for me," she said. "Being a stage performer is natural to me; being a singer is natural to me. Ideas come to me at different times, but most of them I lose. If I were a serious writer, I'd jot everything down or I'd tape everything. But I figure I'm not gonna get any ideas. So when I really get a hot one it's gone in two seconds."

Sing A Song, as the album came to be called, far outshined Phyllis's debut effort. Scarborough's experienced hand factored largely in this. He helped Larry guide her from the contemporary ("Livin") to the beautiful ballads that were already becoming her trademark, such as "Changes," "The Answer Is You," and "Here's That Rainy Day," the classic Phyllis had first learned from her music teacher David Tamburri. On this version, Phyllis was accompanied by Larry's brother Monty on the piano. Phyllis was at her best on these sorts of numbers. The spare accompaniment kept the focus firmly on her voice.

But quality was not the issue. Money was. Buddah was no longer able to stay financially afloat, and the label was close to folding. Soon after the release of *Sing A Song*, Buddah, still owned by Art Kass, inked a distribution deal with a new record label called Arista.

Arista was run by one Clive Davis, already something of an icon in the recording industry. When Davis looked at what Buddah could bring to his new label, he was particularly interested in Gladys Knight. But Kass was not in a position to throw Knight into the bargain. Her contract was up for renewal and she wanted out. Phyllis was the logical consolation prize. She was still under contract to Buddah and Arista could absorb her without issue.

Suddenly, Phyllis found herself an Arista recording artist, without any say-so in the matter whatsoever. This was a fact that did not sit well with her. And when Phyllis was unhappy, she was not one to keep quiet about it for long.

Chapter 4

*I don't think anyone has captured the true
essence of what I'm about in the studio yet.*

By 1978, Clive Davis was somewhat of a controversial figure. A Harvard-educated attorney, Davis was 28 when he joined the Columbia Records legal staff in 1960. Seven years later he was president of the company. The flagship label of the CBS Records Group, Columbia was the leading label in the industry by the late 1950s. But during his rapid rise to the top, Davis noticed that the label's Broadway and mainstream pop sales – the genres that had only a decade before been responsible for Columbia's prominence – were beginning to wane. So throughout his six years at the helm of Columbia, Clive spent much of his time changing the company's course and steering it into more contemporary waters.

He had an epiphany of sorts at the Monterey Pop Festival in 1967. "It was clear that a social revolution was occurring, clear that a musical revolution was occurring," Davis said. Shortly afterward, back in his office in New York, Clive became convinced that rock was the wave of the future and began signing a long list of future superstars that included Carlos Santana, Billy Joel, Bruce Springsteen and a rowdy redhead named Janis Joplin, whom Clive had first seen at Monterey.

But while rock may have been Clive's biggest contribution to Columbia, it wasn't his only one. Clive realized that Columbia was clueless when it came to rhythm and blues. Indeed, Aretha Franklin was signed to the label the same year Clive came on board and left it – virtually hitless – just before he took over the presidency. Clive knew as he watched Aretha move on to instant success at Atlantic that there was money to be made in rhythm and blues as the genre continued to cross over to white audiences. It was quite a stroke of luck then when Philadelphia-based producers

Kenny Gamble and Leon Huff approached him about a distribution deal for their fledgling Philadelphia International Records label in 1971.

The deal quickly proved beneficial to both parties as Gamble and Huff's stable of stellar talent, acts such as the O'Jays, Harold Melvin & the Blue Notes and Billy Paul, took to the top of the charts within a year. In fact, four out of Columbia's nine gold singles for 1972 were on the PIR label. By the following year, however, the party was over for Clive at Columbia.

Actually, it was the party – or more precisely the bar mitzvah – that ended his association with the label. On February 6, 1973, Clive was one of eight men indicted in a massive payola sting. CBS fired him on May 29, the same day they served him with a lawsuit that accused him of embezzling nearly $100,000 from the company over the past six years. Most of the funds were traced through a series of falsified receipts, including $18,000 billed as a party for the label's newest act, Liza Minnelli, that never happened and was actually spent on an October 1972 bar mitzvah for Clive's son.

In May 1976, the government dropped all but one charge against Clive, and he pleaded guilty to a single count of tax evasion stemming from $8,800 worth of personal vacation expenses that had been charged to CBS. The following year was spent settling the civil case CBS had brought against him and writing his memoir, *Clive: Inside the Record Business*.

Inside the record business was exactly where he wanted to be once more and, soon enough, he was. Barely a year after settling the civil suit with CBS, Clive accepted an offer to head up the records division of the CBS-owned Columbia Pictures, Bell Records. Clive quickly changed the label's name to Arista and that was just the beginning. He let go of virtually all the artists on Bell's roster save one: a young piano-playing balladeer named Barry Manilow.

Despite how Phyllis found her way into this mix, there were many reasons why she and Arista had the potential to be a good match. For starters, Clive had been given $10 million to start the label, which was approximately the amount Buddah president Art Kass was said to be in the hole. And though Kass had earned a reputation through the years as a compassionate executive, he had neither the power nor the influence that Clive wielded by this time.

If anything, Clive was more determined to prove himself in the wake of the payola scandal. Like a prize racehorse out the gate, he wasted no time in establishing his new label and making it an industry frontrunner. Indeed, the first record Arista released, "Mandy" by Barry Manilow, became not only Arista's first number one, but also its first gold record. The following year Mandy was nominated for a Grammy, by which time the album it was culled from had already achieved platinum status.

Despite all this, and not to mention the generous $50,000 advance she received for signing with the label, Phyllis was not at all happy to be an Arista artist. "From the moment the deal was signed she was pissed," recalled publicist Barbara Shelley, who made the transition from Buddah to Arista with Phyllis. "She was pissed that no one thought to make a deal with Phyllis Hyman. But, if anything, Clive could have made the deal and not taken her as part of it. He took her because he appreciated her talent. He was enamored with her. He really saw the talent that was there."

That was not enough for Phyllis though. The money and perks meant little to her compared to the things the deal did not include. For starters, Phyllis liked small spaces. Growing up in a crowded apartment with six other siblings provided little breathing room for Phyllis. She grew accustomed to that, comfortable with that, if not always happy about it. When Phyllis moved out on her own, it was into a hallway apartment barely larger than an oversized closet. Currently, she and Larry were still sharing a one-bedroom apartment with Larry's brother Monty. Arista was too big for Phyllis. Even Clive Davis, himself, or his ego at least, was too large. It was not a place where Phyllis felt she could thrive.

That Buddah was a small independent, albeit with mounting debts and no real budget for promotion, meant that her role at the label – her role in the creation of her own music – was larger. She was the proverbial big fish in a little pond at Buddah. At Arista, however, she would be just a minnow. Moving to Arista represented losing control to Phyllis. There was a great need in Phyllis to remain in control of all things at all times – it was the only way she felt safe – and there was no way Clive Davis was going to leave Phyllis and Larry to their own devices as Art Kass had.

Phyllis would never admit her discontent to the press though, at least not at this point in her career. She still had the power to control her public image, and her comments on the label switch dripped with nonchalance. "I just outgrew my surroundings and wanted to expand on myself," she said, making it sound as if the decision to leave Buddah had been her own.

Despite her misgivings, Arista wasted no time in focusing some much-needed attention on Phyllis's career. Clive decided to pull the *Sing A Song* album and retool it, adding, most noticeably, a track to be produced by none other than his number one artist, Barry Manilow. It was decisions like this one that bothered Phyllis though. She was happy with *Sing A Song*, and she found the fact that Clive felt it was missing something insulting. He made the call to cut three of album's songs, "Sweet Music," "Love Is Free" and the album's title track.

The Manilow session took place in New York in August 1978, a full eight months after the Alexander/Scarborough-produced portion of the album had been recorded in San Francisco. Ron Dante, who co-produced the session with Manilow, was quite pleased with Phyllis's performance. Larry, on the other hand, who happened to be in the studio with Phyllis, proved to be quite an annoyance to the veteran producers.

He "kind of hovered over her," said Dante. "He watched our every move, trying to get some tips on making good records, I think." Phyllis, though, "was very charming and a piece of cake to direct. She wanted to sing the song a little bigger than Barry and I wanted her to, but she went along with us and sang a beautiful vocal that day."

Phyllis went along with Manilow's urgings if for no other reason than the way he phrased them. "He actually asked if I minded him making suggestions about the way he might like me to sing a particular phrase or word. He approached me a whole different way from the way everyone else has."

That Clive would pair Barry up with Phyllis said much about his appreciation of both Phyllis's talent and potential. But when Phyllis found she had received the offer by default, and that the song Clive had helped select for the Manilow production was not initially intended for her, she was disillusioned. "Originally, we believed Gladys Knight would cut 'Somewhere in My Lifetime,'" Davis revealed in an interview with *Soul* magazine, shortly after the album's release, for a story they were doing on Manilow.

Clive had been forced to let go of his dream of uniting Knight and Manilow when Gladys, whose contract with Buddah was at an end, turned down Clive's offer to sign with Arista and opted instead to sign with his former label, Columbia. While the opportunity was still a good one for Phyllis, she understandably did not enjoy being anyone's second choice, and she was angry with Clive for publicly announcing that she had been.

The album's three final songs, produced by newcomer T. Life, who had recently hit it big with Evelyn "Champagne" King's "Shame," were recorded a few weeks later. These tracks took Phyllis back in an old direction – to disco, which was by now at its frenzied peak. Sadly, the three tracks T. Life contributed to Phyllis's album, "Kiss You All Over," which the group Exile had taken to the number one spot on the pop charts just months earlier, "So Strange" and "Lookin' For a Lovin,'" originally recorded by Ann Peebles, were not standouts. Phyllis's perfect diction, reminiscent of Dinah Washington's, was evident even on these frenetically paced tracks. But as disco goes, the songs – both their lyrics and arrangements – were pedestrian.

Still, Phyllis claimed to be happy with the album overall. "To me, the album represents a progression," she said. "It shows growth, although I will say that I don't think anyone has captured the true essence of what I'm about in the studio yet. Maybe it's because I don't think I've worked with anyone who's allowed me to have all the time I need to work on my vocal performance. Not that I'm unhappy with what's there. It's just that I feel with more time I could do so much more."

Though she was no great fan of working in the studio, Phyllis, perhaps in an effort to regain some semblance of control over her recording career, pledged to become more involved in the process for her future efforts. "Yes, I intend to get into more songwriting and that should help my involvement even more. I feel we're getting closer to capturing all the things I know I can do in the studio. It's just a matter or time."

Time was something Phyllis had precious little of at this point. In addition to recording and touring, and being escorted to all the right places to be seen by Barbara Shelley, Phyllis was also doing endorsements. With Shelley's help, Phyllis was named the ambassador for Revlon's Polished Amber line of cosmetics and traveled frequently to promote it. Phyllis was always up for anything that meant increased exposure, and she was eager to branch out and see what other mediums she could conquer.

In the midst of all this, Phyllis miraculously found time to escape from New York just after the album's final recording sessions and returned to Florida, where she and Larry, the man she had referred to as her husband for the past few years, were finally married in a small ceremony in Coral Gables on September 18th. The two married in Florida to accommodate Larry's mother, who lived there. No one in Phyllis's family, however, attended. They weren't invited – undoubtedly, because they all believed Phyllis and Larry had married some years earlier.

"I thought they were married when we met him," said Phyllis's sister Jeannie, recalling the couple's trip to Pittsburgh a year earlier. "As a matter of fact, my mom let them sleep in the same room. So, that wouldn't have been happening if we didn't believe they were married." Hiram Bullock, from Phyllis's group the P/H Factor, said the couple had even pretended to be married as far back as Miami. "When they weren't married, they said they were, and when they actually were married, they said they weren't," he recalled. "They were a very odd couple."

Little changed in Phyllis and Larry's relationship after they were, in fact, legally married, least of all her name. "There was no question that I would not take Larry's name," Phyllis said. "I'm a Hyman. Phyllis Hyman-Alexander. I was a Hyman before I met him and I'll be a Hyman forever. To me, it would be ludicrous to give up my name."

Back in New York, Phyllis began promoting her heavily revamped and long awaited sophomore release, now called *Somewhere In My Lifetime*. *Somewhere* was officially released in January of 1979 to mixed reviews. The disco craze was in full swing. It was the year of *Saturday Night Fever*. Acts like the BeeGees and KC and the Sunshine Band were all the rage.

In fact, when "Somewhere in My Lifetime" made its debut on the R&B top 40 in December, the number one spot on the chart was solidly locked down by "Le Freak," the latest hit from the Nile Rodgers-fronted group Chic. "Le Freak" remained at number one for five solid weeks. It would be another four months before a ballad would once again top the chart, when "Reunited" by Peaches & Herb made it to number one. America was without a doubt in dancing mode at this time. So, in hindsight, it's quite impressive that a traditional ballad like "Somewhere" made it as far as it did on the R&B chart at that time.

If "Somewhere" was not the smash that Arista was hoping it would be, Phyllis wasn't surprised. "I thought the record was incredible, but I didn't think it would be a big seller, which it wasn't," she said. "It happened to be a big turntable success and a great performance song. When I do it in concert to large black audiences, they go crazy. They just go absolutely nuts."

Even if it wasn't a big seller, Phyllis still expressed interest in working with Manilow again. "He's so busy and everyone is seeking him out for productions," she said. "I only hope we can get together again." Despite Phyllis's wish, Clive would ultimately only allow the match this one shot, preferring instead to pair his star artist up with acts he thought would have a better chance of charting well in the pop arena.

In all likelihood, the R&B charts were not the primary concern of the promotion team at Arista. Clive Davis knew better than anyone that the key to superstardom lie in crossover success. Clive thought "Somewhere" would have mass appeal, and had the country not been in the midst of disco fever, he might have been proven right. Producers Barry Manilow and Ron Dante tried diligently to constrain Phyllis's performance and keep her from carrying its emotional level over the top. Though they were smart enough not to tell Phyllis as much at the time, what they were actually doing was trying to limit the soulfulness of the song so as not to alienate potential pop fans. Still, pop radio wasn't buying.

"Phyllis had already begun building an R&B base and they didn't respond well to that song, and she was an unknown quantity at pop radio," explained David Nathan, then a reporter for Britain's *Blues & Soul* magazine and today affectionately referred to as the British Ambassador of Soul. "I think the assumption that because the song was produced by Barry Manilow it was going to get an automatic response at pop radio was the problem."

Though the single fizzled out just short of the R&B top ten, the album it came from sold well and would go on to peak at number 12 R&B/ number 70 pop in the spring of 1979. A second single, "Kiss You All Over" backed with "So Strange," was issued as a 12-inch to the clubs, but managed to make its way no further than a meager number 75 on the Club Play Singles chart.

Phyllis hit the road to promote the album in February. She teamed up with Capitol artist Peabo Bryson for an extensive and tightly scheduled two-month, 30-city outing. It was her first major tour, and her opening portion of the show received positive, and sometimes peculiar, reviews. Once again illustrating the effortlessness of Phyllis's talent, she managed to outshine Peabo with reviews of her performance that were oftentimes quite mixed. Consider this one, from the nation's paper of record, *The New York Times*:

The roof that Miss Hyman raised with her bravura performance fell in when she surrendered the stage to Mr. Bryson's crashing boredom. Miss Hyman had almost everything going against her. Her sound system, band, arrangements and material ran the gamut from bad to worse. But by the end of her set, her gorgeous voice had blown away every obstacle. Her command of dynamics is what makes Miss Hyman a remarkable singer. One moment she is tenderly burnishing a deep, golden note, the next she is belting out a chorus with a brassy blare.

This sort of review was the norm for Phyllis on this tour. The problem here was that Phyllis was a critically acclaimed cabaret singer, most comfortable – by her own admission – performing in small clubs. So her act did not always translate well to larger venues, and her efforts to commercialize her show often removed some of the depth from it. It was 1979 after all, and Phyllis was performing a disco-heavy set. She opened with a bit of "As You Are," a Norman Connors-produced track from Pharoah Sanders' latest album that Phyllis had contributed vocals to. The rest of the set was comprised of seven of the ten tracks from *Somewhere In My Lifetime*, including all the dance numbers, plus "Betcha By

Golly Wow" and a spirited version of "Close The Door," a song that Teddy Pendergrass had recently taken to number one on the R&B chart, was thrown in for good measure.

Not completely comfortable with either the material or the venues, Phyllis did not always come out on top in the reviews the tour generated. The *Chicago Sun-Times* said, "Bryson's glow outshines even 'the next Billie Holiday.'" Meanwhile, the *Los Angeles Times* said of the tour's three-night stop at The Roxy, which brought out the likes of Norman Connors and Natalie Cole, that Phyllis "is a wealth of un-mined charisma. She flashed it at times and it was overwhelming. Most of the time, however, she only projected uneasiness."

Reviews aside, the Phyllis-Peabo shows sold out across the country. It was a hectic time for Phyllis. Not only was the tour tightly scheduled, but Arista arranged for her to do in-store visits to promote the album in most cities, as well as radio interviews wherever possible. In Seattle, for example, Phyllis had only minutes between her live interview with radio station KYAC and her scheduled appearance at the Wide World of Music record store. Phyllis did the best she could to keep up the pace, including asking her fans to help out.

"If someone would please bring me a Burger King fish sandwich with tartar sauce and lots of pickles and an order of fries," she asked on-air as she started the interview. "I just want to see if someone's gonna bring it. And a small Coca Cola. I'll give you the money back."

Phyllis spoke about the future and her career goals. "I'd like to expand on what I'm doing now, which includes the cosmetic industry. I'd love to do some fashion layouts and work more with fashion. I'd like to keep up with making better records. My first record was great. The second record is great. I seem to be setting up a certain amount of consistency in recording. I really want to do that because I've been accepted by the general public and I feel that they are due good music from me. Once they've accepted me, I have no right to ever slack up."

Disk jockey Greg Collins couldn't conceal his pleasure at chatting up Phyllis. "I cannot tell you how much I have enjoyed sitting here with you," he said. "I know how tough your schedule is, and I know you'd love to be having your cheeseburger, right? Or was it the hamburger?"

"I tell you, if I don't do this there is no cheeseburger," Phyllis said. "And no, it's a fish sandwich, Burger King preferably, lots of tartar sauce, heavy on the pickle, French fries, small Coca Cola, lots of ice. Thank you very much."

While in Seattle, Phyllis took time out to meet with Thom Bell. One of the originators of the 'Philly Sound,' Bell had played a role in Phyllis's recording career virtually from the beginning, having co-written "Betcha By Golly Wow" with his frequent lyrical collaborator Linda Creed. His latest effort was producing the soundtrack for an upcoming film called *The Fish That Saved Pittsburgh*.

Phyllis was a natural to work on the soundtrack. She was, of course, a native of Pittsburgh, and Bell had been pleased by her renditions of his songs "Betcha" and "I Don't Want To Lose You." Indeed, lots of folks had been taking notice of not only Phyllis's own recordings, but also of her guest and album appearances on the recordings of other artists of various genres. "Normally, I tend to work harder for other people," Phyllis said. "If someone takes the time out to hire me for a job that they could have hired a number of other people to do, I always put my best foot forward, and so far it's worked for me."

Bell found this attitude refreshing. "You didn't have to take all day changing lyrics around and trying your darnedest to make her do something," he said. "She was what she was, but she could give you different sounds, different attitudes. She could give you anything you wanted."

The Fish That Saved Pittsburgh was a comedy about the NBA's Pittsburgh franchise. When most of the team walks out, horrified by a horrendous losing streak, the team's faithful owner takes a tip from the ball boy and holds an open tryout. The catch is, he can only hire ball players born under the astrological sign of Pisces – so says the team's astrologer and all-around good luck charm, Miss Mona Mondieu. The film starred legendary basketball players Julius "Dr. J" Erving and Meadowlark Lemon alongside actors Margaret Avery, Jonathan Winters, Flip Wilson and Stockard Channing, who played the aforementioned Mona.

Released in the fall of 1979, the film bombed. But the soundtrack, which featured an interesting assortment of artists that included the likes of trumpeter Doc Severinsen, the Spinners, the Four Tops and the first lady of country music, Loretta Lynn, was hailed as a critical smash. Phyllis's contribution to the soundtrack was "Magic Mona," an ode to the Mighty Pisces' astrologer. With lines like, "Mystic lady of the Zodiac, come and set us on the winning track" and "Tell us how we should be functioning, tell us of the star's conjunctioning," the song was downright silly, which is what made it work.

Phyllis also recorded a second more serious song while in Seattle. "Believe In You (And Life Will Too)," which featured lyrics by Linda Creed, was an inspirational, anthem-like number, which Phyllis sang with passionate conviction. Bell submitted it, but room couldn't be found for the song in the film, and so it was left off the soundtrack.

Chapter 5

What kind of woman would Billie Holiday have been if she had a couple of kids?

Arista wanted to get Phyllis back into the studio quickly, and the only question was with whom. She had expressed an interest in working again with Barry Manilow, which might have offered her a second chance at conquering the pop charts. But Clive pooh-poohed that idea. He had recently acquired a new artist to add to his growing stable at Arista, the legendary Dionne Warwick. An industry veteran known for her string of Burt Bacharach-produced hits on Scepter Records, her fortunes at Warner, her last label, had been few.

Clive thought he could revive her career and quickly teamed her up with Manilow. Unlike Phyllis, though, who only got one song, Warwick got an entire Manilow produced album. Warwick fared far better than Phyllis in her musical marriage with Manilow. The album, simply titled *Dionne*, was considered her comeback and quickly went platinum. In addition, the single "I'll Never Love This Way Again" soared to number 5 pop/number 18 R&B/number 5 adult contemporary and went gold, while "Déjà Vu" went to number 15 pop/number 25 R&B/number 1 adult contemporary. [3]

With Manilow not an option, Phyllis's first choice was Quincy Jones. But Clive vetoed the idea as well. Most likely because he feared such a collaboration would take Phyllis back to her jazz roots, which he thought she needed to abandon in order to achieve across-the-board commercial success. It was another incorrect

---

[3] The following year, Warwick went on to win a Grammy for Best Pop Vocal Performance Female for "I'll Never Love This Way Again" and a second one for Best R&B Vocal Performance Female for "Déjà Vu."

calculation on Clive's part, and another indication of how he and Phyllis disagreed about the course her career should take.

At about this time, Clive brought Larkin Arnold on board to head the label's black music division. A powerful black attorney and A&R man from the West Coast, Arnold had recently had great success bringing Capitol Records' black music division to life. Arnold brought with him to Arista Andre Perry, an up and coming A&R man from Warner Records. Perry assumed the responsibilities of product manager to most of Arista's black acts, including Phyllis, Angela Bofill, Tom Browne, GQ, Ray Parker, Jr. & Raydio and, of course, Dionne Warwick who, because of her stature in the industry, was a top priority.

Initially, at least, Phyllis was considered a priority of sorts, too. "I think Clive wanted to go with someone that had more R&B potential than Dionne had," said Perry. "Dionne, obviously, was a pop diva, and Phyllis became a high priority because he saw the potential she had."

Perry saw the potential, too. It was he, in fact, who suggested the production team of Lucas/Mtume as possible producers for Phyllis. And once Clive blessed the idea, Arnold made the call. Reggie Lucas and James Mtume had met in the early 70s when they, like former Phyllis collaborator Michael Henderson, were members of Miles Davis' band. The two had their first taste of chart success as songwriters the year before when Roberta Flack and Donny Hathaway took one of their compositions, "The Closer I Get To You," to the number one spot on the R&B chart (number 2 pop).

Most recently, Lucas and Mtume had helped Stephanie Mills transition her success from the Broadway stage, where'd she starred as Dorothy in *The Wiz* for the past four years, to the record charts. Producing her debut album for the 20th Century label, they scored big with the single "Whatcha Gonna Do With My Lovin'." It peaked at number 8 R&B/ number 22 pop, giving Mills her first taste of pop success and proving that Lucas and Mtume were quite capable of producing crossover hits.

Phyllis had known Lucas and Mtume since her earliest days in New York, when the duo would often take in her club gigs around town. So she was agreeable to working with them when Arnold approached her with the idea. Once in the studio, however, the match appeared to be made in a place far south of Heaven. Phyllis was a live performer and liked to have a crowd in the studio to sing to. But her new producers weren't having it. "We didn't want an entourage in the studio with her, and after the very first session I took her aside and told her that," Mtume recalled. Phyllis acquiesced and never brought another soul back to the studio, not even Larry.

It was one of the first indicators for Phyllis, who stated after the release of her last album that she wanted to become more involved in the recording process, that she wouldn't be able to exert much influence here. Phyllis was trying, to the best of her ability, to keep Clive happy and stay in his good graces. She'd released two albums – three if you counted the limited release of *Sing A Song* – and still had no substantial hits to show for it. Lucas and Mtume had proved they could make a hit, a number one hit, and Phyllis knew she needed them. But Phyllis didn't like having to rely on anyone. Losing control caused her to become fearful. And that fear, more often that not, took the form of anger when Phyllis tried to express herself.

One of the biggest conflicts took place while recording what would become the album's title track and its first single, "You Know How To Love Me." Journalist David Nathan, who had passed by the session at Mtume's invitation, recalled the fury of Phyllis's short fuse in his book *The Soulful Divas*.

The relatively long, seven-minute-plus song called for Phyllis to sing and hold a note that extended over several bars. As was their usual practice as producers, James and Reggie kept insisting that Phyllis repeat the note until they were satisfied. After about four or five takes on the exact same musical passage, Phyllis was getting mad.

"I'm not singing this fucking thing anymore," she yelled through the recording booth.

James tried to appease her: "C'mon, Phyllis, I know you got one more great one in there...."

"Fuck, man, I can't sing this shit anymore," she responded.

James pushed: "I promise, this will be the last one," and probably out of rage and frustration, Phyllis sang the hell out of the phrase."

"Look, motherfucker, it's OK, but just as well you got that one on tape because I'm through."

Lucas and Mtume had written four songs, including the title track, especially for the project, and brought two more to the table that had been written by collaborators of theirs. Phyllis found two songs for the project on her own, "This Feeling Must Be Love" and "Complete Me," and also contributed "Give A Little More," a song she had co-written with Larry and old her pianist, Howie Schneider.

In August, Phyllis appeared on the cover of *Sepia* magazine donning a rhinestone-studded veil attached to a pillbox hat, and bearing the words "Phyllis Hyman: Breathing New Life into the Frazzled Word, 'Star.'" In the feature story, Phyllis spoke about her precarious position on the cusp of stardom. "To be honest, I don't even know what superstardom is," she said. "I don't know what that phrase really means. Is it the kind of person on a level with Judy Garland or what? I don't think there are any more superstars."

Phyllis was frank about being viewed as a commodity by industry bigwigs such as Clive Davis, though she was wise enough not to mention him by name – at least, not yet. "When I got into this business, I just thought it was more different than what it is. I thought there was more sensitivity and creativity. I cried a lot and was very hurt that I would be looked upon as product more than as a creative individual. But now, I realize that I am merely looked at as a business entity."

Even without a monster hit under her belt, the spotlight was still on Phyllis as she prepared to release her second Arista album. Mtume recalled that Clive claimed to be a "little disappointed" by the album he and his partner turned in to him. Nevertheless, *You Know How To Love Me* did well for Phyllis. The single once again leveled out at number 12 R&B – the exact same spot "Somewhere" had stopped – and made it to number 101 pop, not nearly the result Clive was hoping for. The album sold better than *Somewhere*, though, reaching number 10 R&B/number 50 pop.

In the November issue of the gentlemen's magazine *Players*, Phyllis beat out Lena Horne and Diana Ross to be named the world's most exciting black woman. There, Phyllis gave a glowing review of Lucas and Mtume's methods in the studio and failed to mention any of the friction that existed between them while recording. "We worked it out and went into the studio and laughed the whole session," she claimed, trying to save face both for her and producers. "We just laughed every day. We worked until six every night. No drugs, no liquor – everything was right on the money and totally professional, which is right up my alley. I want to just get in there and do it. It's work for me. It's a fun gig and a loose gig, but it's still work. It costs somebody a lot of cash. I'm looking forward to working with them on my upcoming album."

Arista was looking forward to that, too. But the same could not be said of Lucas and Mtume. It was easy enough to overlook her antics in the studio – Phyllis certainly wasn't the only temperamental artist in the business – but they had been turned off by an earlier interview Phyllis gave to a jazz critic, wherein she candidly reflected on her disappointments with *You Know How To Love Me* during the first week of its release. "She fell right into the trap and talked about how she felt the album was very formulaic," said Mtume. "She said she wanted to use her own musicians but that wasn't how we worked as producers. The bottom line was she was saying she didn't think it was a good album. Remember, this is the week the album comes out! After I read the interview, I called Reggie and we agreed we didn't need to do another album with Phyllis. After it started taking off, Arista offered us a ton of money to do another record, but that's the reason we didn't do a follow up with her."

If Phyllis didn't think that *You Know How To Love Me* was the best it could be, she wasn't the only one with qualms about the album. Reviews were once again mixed across the board, with some unnecessarily vicious in their attack of the project. Calling the album "a waste," a critic at *Stereo Review* summed up *You Know How To Love Me* like this:

Alas, poor Phyllis Hyman. Every time it seems she's beginning to move in a direction that could develop her considerable potential as a singer and stylist, she's drawn back into such mediocrity that my only response is a moan of profound disappointment. ... Someone, somewhere, should be able to come up with the proper songs, arrangements, and settings to highlight what has always promised to be a major talent, instead of again subjecting us to songs that all sound amazingly like each other and also just about everything else Hyman has recorded. Phyllis Hyman could be a class act and should be treated as such, but no one seems to know how – or care.

The review was perhaps unduly harsh. Yet the point was valid. The album did have its moments, but not enough of them. "You Know How To Love Me" was a classic dance performance. But still, the audiences who'd watched the supper-club chanteuse weave her magic at such intimate settings as Mikell's and Rust Brown's knew she could do so much more. How to capture that magic and spin it onto vinyl was the problem. How did you give Phyllis commercial appeal without giving the impression that she'd sold out?

No one seemed to know. And Phyllis was by no means alone in the battle. Jean Carn, for instance, released three albums between 1977 and 1979 on the Philadelphia International label. Each produced major critical acclaim and zero top ten hits. Angela Bofill, another artist often compared to Phyllis, was in the midst of the same struggle. Recording on the Arista-distributed GRP label, the jazz-flavored vocalist was also having a hard time conquering the mainstream. Artists such as these were really misplaced in the era they found themselves recording in. Jazz would not get them hits and disco did them no justice. So where, exactly, did they belong?

"They've got to get a new name for what I think I am, for what Jean Carn is, for what Dee Dee Bridgewater is," Phyllis complained to a reporter. "It's a new era, with new vocalizing. I don't know what to call it, and nobody seems to have come up with a name for it yet."

David Nathan explained the constraints of the industry that had confounded Phyllis since the start of her career. "I think it was a marketing nightmare for the record label," he said. "I think they really did not know what to do with her. I mean, the most obvious thing to do was to take her music to R&B radio. Back at that time, there was really no smooth jazz format. There was no quiet storm.

All there really was was R&B radio, and jazz radio was its own other world. But the two genres didn't really meet.

"The only place they could take her was R&B radio and that was it," Nathan continued. "I think she got caught in not being just one type of artist. Then, of course, when Buddah got absorbed into Arista, then she became under the dominion of Clive Davis, whose primary interest was selling as many records as possible. So his consistent interest was how do we cross you over? How do we get you from R&B to pop? Not, how do we get you from R&B to jazz. There was no jazz department at Arista. So if you were a black music artist you either were R&B or pop. So I think she was right in that there was really no way to categorize her. But it presented a dilemma because there was no structure to be able to handle someone who did what she did, which was this kind of amalgam of jazz, R&B and pop. It was a uniqueness that there was no setup for."

While she may have been confusing to radio and record executives, Phyllis was growing more comfortable with herself. "I am beginning to discover who Phyllis Hyman is vocally," she said. "I have a lot of styles mixed up in me, which is good since it broadens my appeal. But I would like to find the center, vocally. I want to be distinctive from other singers."

As Phyllis searched for her vocal center, her album continued to sell briskly. Arista issued a second single, "Under Your Spell," in March. It spent 11 weeks on the charts, just grazing the top 40 at number 37, and by April the album, despite its flaws, had sold nearly 400,000 copies. While that number easily made *You Know How To Love Me* Phyllis's biggest-selling album to date, it was still short of the current industry marker for a hit album: gold status, representing 500,000 in sales.

To Andre Perry, that goal was still attainable. Sitting in an Arista sales meeting, Perry took the opportunity to make his case when the subject turned to Phyllis. "I said, 'We've got to get another 100,000 albums and force it out there. Get another single out and go ahead and force it gold,'" Perry recalled. "Then we'd really be able to establish her as an artist and break her wide open."

But Clive was not interested in Perry's argument, or in putting out another single from *You Know How To Love Me*.

"Andre," he said, looking up from his notes. "When is the new Angie Bofill album going to be ready?"

Perry was confused and tried to keep the focus on Phyllis.

"Clive, I'm talking about Phyllis's album on the verge of being gold," he said, as others in the room suddenly grew silent.

Clive asked again, "When is Larry Rosen shipping the Angie Bofill album?"

The discussion was dropped, and Perry realized that "at that point, he had written Phyllis off."

Why was Clive already tired of this talented vocalist whom he had signed to his label only a little over a year ago? For starters, he felt Phyllis was difficult and she didn't roll over if she had an opinion or preference. Clive's ego – according to Andre – was "bigger than the United States *and* Europe." He had already built countless careers and had introduced many newcomers to stardom. He wasn't accustomed to being challenged or questioned.

Phyllis, likewise, was not used to having her input ignored. "I remember once we ran into each other very shortly after she'd had a meeting with Clive, and she was just fuming," recalled David Nathan. "She was like, 'He doesn't understand what I'm trying to do.'

"They didn't get along and Phyllis was not a passive person," Nathan continued. "When she didn't agree with something she would say 'no' or 'I don't agree.' And Clive's whole thing is how can we sell the most number of records? How can we get you into the most number of homes? How can we get the record on pop radio? How can we turn you into a mainstream artist? I think that probably some of his strategy didn't go well with her."

Nathan theorized that Phyllis feared her black base was being sacrificed in Clive's efforts to cross her over, and she put her foot down. "I think she was very conscious of the support of black audiences from the beginning, from the very beginning, and, essentially, it was black audiences throughout her entire career that kept her going. She wasn't willing to forsake them. I also think it was personal. It wasn't just about the audiences, but it was a certain kind of pride.

"I think that because she wasn't a straight-ahead R&B artist that you could just easily turn into a pop diva, that you could easily crossover, there was this conflict." Summing up the strain between

Clive and Phyllis, Nathan said simply, "It wasn't a good relationship. They just didn't work together well."

Phyllis was self-aware enough to realize that she was not always easy to deal with. "I'm an explosive person, and I sometimes get irritated over the slightest things," she told *Black Stars*. "I do try to be even-tempered, but when something goes wrong, I can blow the situation way out of proportion and overreact."

All artists are sensitive, but Phyllis was especially so. When Clive tried to change Phyllis's style in the name of marketability, she took it as a personal criticism. She felt that Clive did not see her, and she was hurt that he didn't feel she was good enough just as she was. Phyllis felt attacked and, as a result, her insecurities flared up and she began attacking herself from the inside.

"I think that up to this point I may not have put forth all the effort to make it happen totally because I maybe had a fear of getting too big, and that's maybe made me a little laidback," Phyllis told Nathan for an April 1980 interview with *Blues & Soul*. Unwittingly, she had let the cat out of the bag. Her fear of success, combined with the insecurity that had festered within her since she was the awkward and lanky girl none of the boys talked to in junior high, caused her to feel she didn't deserve it.

Phyllis's father had walked out on her. Her mother had been incapable of showing her love, either through affection or discipline, and now the industry, hell bent on categorizing her and unable to accept her simply for what she had to offer, was making her feel less than, too. This is what prompted her to lash out at those, such as James Mtume and Clive Davis, who were trying to make success happen for her.

A great point of contention between Phyllis and the label was her current manager: husband Larry Alexander, supplemented by Charles Ward, an attorney from San Francisco. "I think there were a couple of managers that Clive felt strongly about, that would have been better managers for Phyllis," said Perry. "I agreed with him. But that was her manager. So far be it from me to tell her, 'Fire your manager,' who also happened to be her husband at the time."

Phyllis had no intention of letting Larry go. In fact, appointing him to the job had been a well thought out and calculated decision. "What I didn't want was some big, fat, cigar-smoking, fast-talkin', rich cat who already had everything come in and take over another potential moneymaker. So I asked myself, 'How do we keep this thing in the family?' I sincerely believe that black people have to start handling themselves in this business. That's the only way you can have any self-esteem and feeling of self-worth."

Be that as it may, Clive's respect level for Larry as a manager was at the bottom of the barrel. "There was always this ongoing battle between them," Perry continued. "Larry Alexander, her husband, and Charles were always fighting with Clive. There was always something going on. There was never any peace in the valley, so to speak.

"While all this is going on, I was trying to push the record through the pipeline and get publicity, get it overseas, do *Top of the Pops*, you name it. But there was always this battle I was fighting. So it became really clear when Clive said to me, 'When's Angie Bofill's album shipping?' At that point, he was finished with Phyllis.

"He decided at that point that he wasn't going to make her career what it could have been," Perry continued. "Can I prove that? No. But let's face it. I worked inside. So I know how things go and don't go."

In Angela Bofill, Clive found a far more cooperative would-be star. Starting with Bofill's third album, she would be signed directly to Arista. And her management would be none other than Vincent Romeo, Clive's close friend. Romeo was Clive's first choice to take over the direction of Phyllis's career, but she wouldn't hear of it.

"Phyllis needed direction and leadership," said Perry. "She couldn't do it on her own. Everybody loved her. Radio loved her. Promoters loved her. TV loved her. People all over Europe loved her. Labels wanted her. But she never had direction, the leadership. The folks that were around her did not guide her properly, and a lot of bad decisions were made."

Bad decisions or not, they were Phyllis's decisions, and she relished in the decision-making power having her husband as a manager afforded her. "You have to accept us anyway," Phyllis said of her professional partnership with her spouse in an interview with *Essence*. The comment was directed to no one in particular, but it's not hard to imagine that she was speaking directly to Clive. "We are married! We have a certain amount of strength in our own home if not within the industry."

Phyllis was careful always to present a unified front in the press. She was so desperate for control, or at least the illusion it, that she continuously talked up Larry even as their relationship was disintegrating. Behind the scenes though, things with the couple were falling apart. "There always was stuff going on," said one close friend of Phyllis's who asked to remain anonymous. "I don't think either of them was ever faithful to the other, and I think it was just a cuckoo marriage."

To be sure, Larry and Phyllis each saw something in the other they needed. Larry needed to protect Phyllis and Phyllis needed protecting. Though she talked big game, the fact is that Phyllis was still in many ways the wounded little girl from junior high. She needed the attention now that she did not get then, and Larry offered it to her. The problem was that the little girl inside of Phyllis too often popped out, through petulance and pettiness. Larry was gentle and mild mannered, much like her distant mother, who Phyllis saw as weak. Like her father had before her, Phyllis exploited that weakness in her mate, bullying and berating him.

It was also from watching her father that Phyllis had learned a little about escapism. As her father had before her, Phyllis had long looked to alcohol to distract her. She had added pills and marijuana to the mix before leaving Pittsburgh. Now, in New York, she and Larry had begun experimenting with cocaine.

While high, the couple's marital issues seemed to drift away on a cloud of smoke. But by the next morning, the issues were glaring and undeniable: Larry was not assertive enough to make her feel safe. That's why she continued to test him, hoping he'd rise to the occasion and begin acting more like her father had, a man that she, herself, had emulated for years.

Soon, the relationship was fraying around the edges and rumors began circulating that Phyllis and Larry were separating. But in a February 1979 profile in the *N.Y. Amsterdam News*, Phyllis attempted to put them to rest. "Larry and I have a very special relationship and have no intentions of splitting up," she said. "We're very happy together."

Phyllis was understandably loyal to her husband in the press. But Clive demanded loyalty, too, and Phyllis wasn't willing to give it. Headstrong, she was blinded to the potential benefits of playing the game Clive's way. Instead, Phyllis fumed. She felt betrayed and victimized by the man with the power to make her a star and his apparent decision to withhold it. And it was not just Clive she blamed. Phyllis's anger spilled over onto Angela Bofill as well.

"There was a resentment toward her because her career was pretty much on hold when Clive decided Angie Bofill was going to become the priority and Phyllis was going to be put on the back burner," said Perry. "That's why she was annoyed. She saw that. Ray Charles could see it. I sat and saw it. I lived it. I was the one that was told point blank: 'The priority is Angie.'"

In a sit down chat with poet Nikki Giovanni for *Eagle & Swan* magazine, Phyllis continued to sing Larry's praises. "He's the brains behind our company, though I'm the president and chief controller of my career. He's a very sensitive man. He's sensitive to me. He's not afraid to show his emotions – to be a whole person. I've told Larry he's it! If this doesn't work, I'm giving up on relationships."

In the *Eagle & Swan* interview, Phyllis also spoke openly about her resistance to start a family. "Sometimes I think about having children," Phyllis said. "I'm still young so I don't have to make any snap decisions. But I think about it. What kind of woman would Billie Holiday have been if she had a couple of kids? One, maybe two children that I could show the world to – that might be nice … sometime. Larry and I haven't rejected the idea. It just hasn't come up."

The Billie Holiday reference was provocative. It showed that Phyllis, subconsciously, saw herself as headed down the same path of destruction the late singer had traveled. But her comments on the topic were just the latest in a series of little white lies she told to the press. She and Larry had, in fact, spoken of children, which Larry wanted. In an interview with *Black Stars*, Phyllis fessed up.

"Larry and I have thought about having children, but I've been concerned about my figure, and the thought of having a gigantic stomach doesn't appeal to me right now," she said. "Besides, my work schedule is so hectic. I wouldn't be able to devote enough time to a baby, and I want to be able to offer the necessary time and energy to raise a well adjusted child."

The issue of children was a critical one in Phyllis and Larry's troubled marriage. Larry knew what Phyllis chose not to openly reveal: despite the fact that she got along with them famously, she did not want children of her own, now or ever. Motherhood represented sacrifice to Phyllis, endless sacrifice, and she was self-actualized enough to realize that sacrifice was not her strong suit.

But even if Phyllis didn't feel she was mother material, she was at times undeniably maternal. She always looked out for friends and staff – indeed, anyone in need – and she worried about projecting a positive image for her young fans. "I'm really concerned about the young girls, about being a role model to them. There are certain things I just won't do because I didn't like that kind of thing when I was young. I wanted to have somebody I could look at and say, 'Wow, I want to be like that. I can do that.'"

By 1980, Arista's black music roster was falling into place with acts like GQ and Ray Parker, Jr. & Raydio scoring big on both the R&B and pop charts. But a great deal of the label's attention was focused on a couple of legendary divas Clive had recently lured to the label. Clive had always regretted that Columbia had not been able to break Aretha Franklin. She languished on the label for six years while they tried to mold her into a jazz singer without commercial success – perhaps the reason he was unwilling to watch Phyllis go in the same direction.

As soon as her contract expired, Aretha signed to Atlantic, where Jerry Wexler let loose the gritty and soulful side of the singer. She went on to score a remarkable 17 number one R&B singles for the label, 14 of them going gold. Now Clive had a second chance to show what he could do with Aretha as she signed to Arista that year. Dionne Warwick, by comparison, had always done better on the pop charts than she had in the R&B world. This tradition continued at Arista when she signed to the label in 1979.

With all this action, it's easy to see how Phyllis could have gotten lost in the shuffle. But Clive wasn't finished with Phyllis just yet, for if he hated dealing with novice managers and uncooperative talent, he hated failure even more. In fact, one might say he detested it. Phyllis still had a contract with the label, and therefore, Clive still wanted to prove himself by making her a star. After all, if the great Clive Davis couldn't make a star out of someone both so naturally talented and beautiful, what did it say about his and his label's hit-making powers?

With James Mtume and Reggie Lucas out of the picture, the search was on for new producers for Phyllis. Larkin Arnold knew Chuck Jackson from his Capitol days, where Jackson had helped launch the career of a young Natalie Cole with songs he co-produced with Cole's husband at the time, Marvin Yancy. Among the classics that musical union produced are "Inseparable," "This Will Be (An Everlasting Love)," "Our Love," "I've Got Love On My Mind" and "I'm Catchin' Hell." The irony here is that Jackson co-wrote each of these songs with Yancy. Yet the Phyllis project contained none of his own tunes.

Arista decided to once again split the recording duties on the album and re-teamed Phyllis with Norman Connors for the second half of the album. Connors was recording for Arista direct these days, and according to the critics he had captured a side of Phyllis on those first singles that no one had been able to find since. Connors was working out of the West Coast by this time, so Phyllis, who preferred to record in New York, reluctantly flew to Los Angeles to work on the album. Connors had been working with a feisty freelance production coordinator and hesitantly offered her the job of helping out on this project.

"He said, 'I don't know if you can handle her, she's pretty tough,'" recalled Tina Stephens, who vividly remembers the first time she met Phyllis in the Kendrun Recorders studio in Burbank.

"Are you that new production person?" Phyllis asked her. "I need you to go to the store for me."

Tina was unmoved. "I'm a production coordinator," she explained. "I arrange the session musicians and schedule the sessions and keep things running smoothly. Someone who goes to the store for you is called a gopher, which I am not."

"I never had any problems with her after that," said Stephens. "Of course, I did end up going to the store for her and running errands from time to time, but only because I wanted to."

Phyllis appreciated Stephens' directness, a quality Phyllis, herself, embodied. Soon enough, the two were close pals and Stephens found herself doing more than just running to the store for Phyllis. "Phyllis had begun freebasing cocaine" said Stephens. "I felt very protective of her. I was always the one to hide her stuff because I didn't want the world to know what a major problem she had developed."

While Tina attempted to hide the problem from everybody else, she saw very clearly what it was doing to Phyllis. "When she was freebasing, she didn't care about how well her records were doing, or having a number one," Stephens said. "She didn't care about getting that best take in the studio. She only cared about getting out of it and getting high."

Phyllis looked to cocaine, something she told friends that Larry had introduced her to, to take her mind off her troubles. After three albums, her career had still not taken off. Worse yet, her marriage was in trouble. Phyllis had found herself pregnant in the summer of 1980 and, despite Larry's urgings that she keep the baby, had an abortion that July.

"They made a decision in their life which I guess they thought was a career decision, when they really should have made a family decision," said Phyllis' old friend Betty Wright, whom she met up with in October when both singers were recording albums in Los Angeles. "Phyllis was a very serious woman, Larry's a very serious man, and when you're that driven you sometimes feel like, 'Well, I don't have the time to do this right now 'cause I've got to go sing.' You should make those decisions based on love of God and family before this business. When you make a decision to have a family, or you make a decision not to have a family, you still have to remember at the end of the day this career stuff, you know, that ain't 24/7."

Chapter 6

I wanted a break from the record industry and the whole concert business was in something of a slump anyway.

For four days in July of 1980, Phyllis returned for a special engagement to Mikell's in New York, where she was once the house band. In the audience was pianist Lloyd Mayers, who had taken on the responsibilities of music director for a Duke Ellington review that was being launched and hoped to head to Broadway. "He came all four nights to hear me sing," Phyllis said. "And when I was about to close, he told me he wanted me to do Ellington's music."

Now that Mayers knew whom he wanted, it was the producers of the show that Phyllis needed to convince. The play had already created a buzz about town, and Phyllis was facing some stiff competition. Marilyn McCoo and Leslie Uggams both auditioned for the part. McCoo had no real theatrical experience at the time. But after several years with the hit group The Fifth Dimension, as well as her recent smash duet with husband Billy Davis, Jr., "You Don't Have To Be A Star (To Be In My Show)," she had bigger name recognition. Uggams, meanwhile, had the stage chops, having won a Tony in 1968 for her role in *Hallelujah, Baby!*

Auditioning was quite an ordeal for Phyllis. In fact, she was so nervous the night before that she overindulged and was unable to keep her appointment. Hung-over, she called on her percussionist and partying pal Mayra Casales to save the day. "I called and acted like I was her secretary," Casales remembered. "I told them that the taxi she was in had been involved in an accident." The producers, likely swayed by the recommendation from Mayers, agreed to reschedule her.

When she finally stood before them, Phyllis was a wreck. "I went to the audition and I was petrified, because auditions and me don't get along very well," Phyllis recounted. "I don't like these charts, working with strange musicians." Phyllis hated charts because she couldn't read them and, as such, it made her feel less than a true musician. Phyllis's insecurity around this issue drew from the same source as her anger and control issues. It was her fear that fed them all.

Phyllis went back to her roots and sang one of the first songs she'd ever learned from Mr. Tamburri, "Satin Doll." "I said, 'stick to the basics' and I sang that, and the girls gave themselves away. They fell in love with my voice and they said, 'Oh, sing another one. Sing another one.' I knew I had the job. I just had this feeling."

Phyllis's feeling was right on the money, and the part, quite effortlessly, was hers. In his 2003 autobiography, *Transcending Boundaries: My Dancing Life*, director Donald McKayle remembered Phyllis as "one of the delicious discoveries of the audition process. She walked into the room slightly over animated from nerves and blew us away with the power and stylishness of her voice. She had a sound that was unique and was equally at home with pulsing jazz tunes, scat singing, or a searing ballad. She was a large and attractive woman and would look wonderful in highly theatrical costumes. There was no point in waiting to tell her of a decision that was unanimous and instantaneous.

'We'd love to have you in our show.'

'You mean I've got the job? For real?'

"As we nodded and babbled effusively, Phyllis burst into a delightful series of whoops and squeals."

That Phyllis secured the role so easily was ironic considering she had an admitted distaste for Broadway. "I never liked the theatre," she said. "It's like being in your bedroom. I get really relaxed because it's dark and I fall asleep."

Whether she'd been interested in Broadway or not, she was now in the throes of it. Rehearsals, which started in October 1980, were challenging for Phyllis, right from the beginning. To allow Phyllis to finish recording her new album in Los Angeles, the show's producers had agreed that she could report for rehearsals a day late. This was a fact that didn't sit well with everyone else in the cast, many of whom had never heard of Phyllis Hyman.

"*Sophisticated Ladies* was an integrated show," explained Ken Hanson, one of the production's three stage managers. "All the producers were white. A lot of the white people connected with the show had no clue who Phyllis was. But then when she opened her mouth, she sounded like, you know, just honey. Her voice was so beautiful that everyone was in awe of her from the second she opened her mouth. So those white people who didn't know who she was, they understood why she was there."

If Broadway promised greater exposure for Phyllis, it also meant a pay cut. To compensate, for much of the time she was rehearsing in New York, she was also doing local appearances and shows whenever possible. "My first recollection of her is that she was in a sweat suit, because she had a personal trainer," recalled Mercedes Ellington, the Duke's granddaughter and a featured performer in the show, as well as its assistant choreographer. "She wanted to get into condition to do all of this movement, and also for doing eight shows a week.

"I remember her leaning over the piano going over one of the songs and talking to Lloyd and my father [Mercer Ellington, the conductor of the Ellington Orchestra]," Ellington continued. "Sometimes they complained about Phyllis being late, and they tried to make sure that she had enough time to reschedule. A lot of the time she was doubling during the rehearsal process. She had club dates and things like that."

Phyllis, a theatrical amateur, suddenly found herself sharing a stage with seasoned veterans. "It was sheer fright and sheer hell," Phyllis said of her first rehearsals. "No one ever told me what 'stage left' and 'stage right' meant, because they were too busy with their own problems and I was too scared to ask."

"She was very insecure because she was one of the few people in the show who had no real theatrical experience," said Ty Stephens, one of the dancers in the show and a longtime fan. "So there was a lot we had to school her on."

Then there was the subject of discipline, which was never one of Phyllis's strong points. She was unaccustomed to the grueling hours and rapid changes in staging and arrangements. "Everyone realized that she had to get used to it," said Ken Hanson. "But when they heard her sing, they allowed for anything because they realized that she was as spectacular as anyone in the show. She brought something that no one else did. No one had a voice as rich as hers."

"When I first started rehearsing, I said, 'Jeeesus Christ,' this is most grueling, time-consuming, intense work I've done in my life," Phyllis moaned. "I've never done nothing like this before. Your whole existence is involved with theatre. You don't get a chance to do anything else. Forget shopping, husbands, wives, and friends; forget that. It's a whole new way of life in theatre, the strict rules and discipline one must be under."

What Phyllis didn't mention but definitely should have was the difficulties of maintaining a successful recording career. Phyllis's next album, tentatively titled *Sunshine In My Life*, was scheduled to be released in February – the same month *Sophisticated Ladies* was to open on Broadway. Arista had the resources to do their part of the promotion, but how much would Phyllis be able to contribute while performing eight shows, six days a week? It didn't matter. Phyllis had already made up her mind. Regardless of any impact it might have on her recording career, she was doing the show.

"I wanted a break from the record industry and the whole concert business was in something of a slump anyway," she told *Blues & Soul*. "I had just undergone a nationwide tour and, truthfully, it hadn't resulted in any real record sales. These days, that's the main reason for being on the road, as far as your career is concerned, because there really isn't money to be made from concerts."

If Phyllis had fibbed in the past, now she was telling a bold faced lie. The main reason most artists toured *was*, in fact, to make money, and most artists did. Most recording artists, and historically most black recording artists in particular, made more money from touring than they did from recording royalties. This was especially true for an artist like Phyllis, who didn't write much of her material or own its publishing rights. Phyllis had already attracted a faithful audience around the country by this point, and it's hard to believe that her tightly-scheduled tour with Peabo Bryson in the spring of 1979, her last major tour, had not made money.

If it didn't make as much as she had hoped, part of the problem may have been the amount of money she spent while on it; or how

Larry, acting on her behalf, managed it. "They would stay at first class hotels and order up champagne," said Sid Maurer, Phyllis's former label head at Roadshow and current New York neighbor. "She wasn't that kind of star yet." And she would never be if she didn't learn to put concentrated attention on her recording career. It was for this reason that Clive did not want Phyllis to do *Sophisticated Ladies*.

"I think Clive saw it as something more of a diversion, something that was not going to primarily benefit her music career," said Milton Allen, Phyllis's new product manager at Arista. "I think Clive also saw it as delving into the jazz idiom, which creatively for her would be a step backwards, because that's where she evolved from with the whole Norman Connors thing. I don't think he looked at it as a plus to her career."

If Phyllis was unwilling to give her recording career her full attention, it was debatable whether she'd do any better with her fledgling stage career. Phyllis didn't care very much for rehearsals, and the combination of her carefree style and her burgeoning drug habit made for some pretty difficult *Sophisticated Ladies* rehearsals. "The producers bent over backwards for her," said Tina Stephens. "They made concessions for her that they wouldn't have made for anybody else because she could really sing those Ellington songs. I mean, look at it, she was the only one of the cast that couldn't dance."

Phyllis was in awe of the dancers, and mystified by the amount of time they spent rehearsing the same number. "We would all do a step over and over and over and over again," recalled Terri Klausner, a principal cast member. "She would be like, 'I don't know how you people can keep doing it. It looks fine to me. Why do you keep doing it over and over again?' Whereas, we were so used to, particularly in the dance world, doing it again until you felt you had perfected it."

It was a very different scene from the recording arena, where Phyllis was known to lay down her vocal tracks in very few takes. And even then, it wasn't necessary to get a completely perfect take. The producer and engineer had the ability to splice together bits from different takes to create one perfect one. "She probably got very good at going, 'Boom! This is what I'm doing. This is how I'm doing it. And can I go home and take a nap now?' That was it," said Klausner. "So the rules of the theatre took a little bit of adapting for her, I'm sure."

Rounding out the cast of *Sophisticated Ladies* were Gregory Hines, a renowned stage actor and tap dancer, and Judith Jamison, a longtime principle with the Alvin Ailey American Dance Theatre, in the other lead role. In featured roles were Klausner, Ellington, P.J. Benjamin, Priscilla Baskerville, Hinton Battle and Gregg Burge. Directing the show was the man who conceived and choreographed it, Donald McKayle. A dancer who worked early in his career with the distinguished companies of Sophie Maslow, Martha Graham and Merce Cunningham, McKayle went on to both star and direct on Broadway before segueing into choreographing for television.

A perfectionist, McKayle envisioned *Sophisticated Ladies* as an extravagant theatrical experience and set out to make it just that. It was reported that he had gone through 500 of Ellington's works and initially chose 50 examples that highlighted the styles of ballet, sacred, popular and classic jazz pieces. That number would continue to be whittled down as rehearsals progressed. The show featured sixteen performers, a twenty-piece band, gobs of glittery costumes and heaps of huge neon lights, backdrops, foredrops and moving platforms. All together, *Sophisticated Ladies* was shaping up to be a massive production with a nifty price tag of $3 million.

But when in December *Sophisticated Ladies* opened at the Forrest Theater in Philadelphia, it was anything but ready. The show was just not coming together, and Phyllis was hard-pressed to keep up with all the changes going on around her. "I was totally wigged out," she said. "Rehearsals were long and arduous. One day a certain song would be in and the next day it was out."

Amid this chaos, not unusual for launching a new show but intensified by the sheer magnitude of such a large production, there was no one to breast feed Phyllis, no one to nurture her. She was going to have to fend for herself. Phyllis did her best, but like the rest of the cast, her performances in Philadelphia, the show's first out-of-town tryout, were less than stellar. One night she was so tense that when she strolled out on stage to begin the song "In a Sentimental Mood," which starts with those very words, she somehow substituted them for "in my solitude," a line that's not even in the song.

"The cast was cracking up, rolling on the floor in hysterics, wondering now what is she going to do?" Phyllis recalled. "Instead of just going on with the song, I went back and sang the first line. I was too freaked out to think how to cover it up."

Phyllis's blooper was by no means the only one in the show. *Sophisticated Ladies* arrived in Washington, D.C., for its second and last out-of-town tryout, in shambles. Scheduled to open at the Kennedy Center Opera House on January 11, the sets were so unmanageable that removing them from the Forrest Theater and installing them in the Opera House caused the show's Washington opening to be delayed by two days. Phyllis used the down time to do some press. Her product manager at Arista, Milton Allen, had introduced her to a former college friend of his from Howard University, Sheila Eldridge, who had recently started up her own PR firm. Phyllis, feeling that Barbara Shelley was too entwined with Clive and all that was bad about the Arista machine, signed Eldridge on to be her personal publicist.

"Because she was not really happy with the way the record thing was going, she wanted to maximize her appeal," said Eldridge. "She saw *Sophisticated Ladies* as a way to really diversify. She always wanted that crossover." As with any new employee, when Eldridge came onboard Phyllis began to test her. It was her way of seeing how far she could go. Moreover, it helped her figure out how far the employee would go for her. This was how Phyllis ascertained if it was safe to extend her trust. Phyllis knew she could be difficult – extremely difficult – so better to know upfront if someone was going to cut and run than to find out in a time of need.

"Whenever you called she was always asleep," said Sheila. "So you had to wake her up; and when she didn't want to be bothered, she didn't want to be bothered." Sheila had never had such a client. "I was scared of her. She was bullying me around." Attorney Charles Ward, now functioning as Phyllis's manager, understood well how she operated, and stepped in to help Sheila. He explained to her that it was just a test, and then he hipped the new publicist to the answer.

"Charles said to me, 'As long as she does not respect you, you'll never get her to do anything, and if you can't get her to do what she needs to do, she's going to fire you.' I got on a plane two days later and headed to New York. We literally went at it, and after that, it was different. She realized, 'Oh, OK, I can't run her.'"

When *Sophisticated Ladies* finally opened in Washington on Tuesday, January 13, 1981, it was still plagued by many of the problems it had in Philly. The show was still too long, and the narration that Gregory Hines was to insert between the endless musical numbers was dull.

"Donald McKayle has contributed some brash and lovely choreography that sits nicely with the music, but time and again the dances start out small and snappy only to end up big and cluttered," wrote a reviewer from *The Washington Post*. "And the bigger the number, the more the choreography edges away from the spirit of Edward Kennedy Ellington to the spirit of Broadway bland. Simplicity is what *Sophisticated Ladies* needs more of across the board."

But things were anything but simple on the set of *Sophisticated Ladies* while it was in Washington. Tensions ran high, particularly between director Donald McKayle and Gregory Hines, with whom a feud had long been in the works. "This was no longer the young man I had worked with from Hines, Hines and Dad, nor the eager, versatile and willing actor who had played in *The Last Minstrel Show*," wrote McKayle in his autobiography. "This was a new and ambitious performer who had a definite agenda in mind: becoming a superstar with this vehicle, whatever it might take."

The battle between director and star came to a head Wednesday morning, when it was announced that Hines had resigned from the show, and that his understudy, Gregg Burge, would assume the role beginning with that day's matinee performance. In truth, Hines had not resigned, but rather been fired by McKayle, who had finally reached the end of his rope. When the rest of the cast learned of this development, things began to unravel. "When Gregory got fired, I went into hysterics," Phyllis said. Mercedes Ellington concurred. "She freaked, and so did Terri Klausner. The two of them cried so much that they had to cancel the matinee. They cried their voices out."

If Phyllis and Terri wanted Gregory back, they weren't the only ones. "We rallied behind Greg because for one, the show was built around him, and he's brilliant and you really can't replace him," said dancer Ty Stephens. "It would have probably killed the show to bring it in with someone other than Greg. On top of that, we were Greg's friends. We had a great time with him."

By Thursday, Hines was back and McKayle was gone, having obviously been voted the lesser of the two talents by the show's producers, who contacted the likes of Alvin Ailey, Arthur Mitchell, Jerome Robbins and Geoffrey Holder in search of a new director. Ultimately, Michael Smuin, director of the San Francisco Ballet, was brought in to take over directorial duties and polish up the choreography.

In the wake of McKayle's departure costumes were redone and songs were dropped. Others were rearranged and a new opening – Gregg Burge and Hinton Battle doing "I've Got To Be A Rug Cutter" – was inserted. Much of the narration, including Hines' oration about Ellington's search for "the perfect note," was trimmed down extensively and the focus once more returned to the music. Day by day, the show was tightening up, or as the *Post* pointed out, "Miraculously, *Sophisticated Ladies* began to find itself."

"We had gone through so many phases and changes that we never thought it would ever run in New York," said Klausner. "We came in to the city and we were exhausted. We had gone through emotional changes like crazy."

Phyllis, by this point, was openly admitting that she and Larry, who was back in Florida, were separated. "I couldn't believe that after caring about someone for so long that I could just wake up one morning and not feel anything for him. We never took our relationship seriously enough. We just thought that it would always be flowers. But you know, flowers die if you don't water them suckers."

To some, Phyllis was more candid about children and the role her disinterest in having them had played in the disintegration of her marriage. "Marriage didn't get in my way, but I would never have had children," she said. "You can't take care of children and do this. I wouldn't subject a child to that, nor myself. At this point in my life, I'm into me. I have no interest in having babies. I can't understand me and a little kid at the same time. I really want to get to know myself first and understand me, so that when I do bring a child into the world, the child gets full attention. There are a lot of tormented children out there, brought into the world through parents who had no business having kids."

It took a certain courage for Phyllis to make these powerful statements, and it's clear she was reflecting on her own childhood as she did so. But the issue of having children was not the only one that permeated her marriage to Larry. "They had a good thing going, but I think Phyllis just started to grow out of it," said Mayra Casales," who had started as percussionist for Phyllis during the Peabo Bryson tour. "She needed more than what Larry could do, and I think that's what kind of tore them apart. I think she needed somebody who had greater connections."

While Larry was managing Phyllis, he was also trying to launch his own career as a musician and songwriter. In short, he had too many irons in the fire and not the know how to juggle them properly. "He was one of those cats that tried to do everything but really wasn't great at any of it," Casales continued. "He was kind of under his brother's thing. Monty was already a great, accomplished musician. But Larry didn't really take the time to study. He was just kind of riding on it, from what I could see. He had really great ideas but, again, not the connections to make them happen.

"He didn't have that for Phyllis. She was growing fast and rapid, and as she was getting bigger and bigger, he was getting smaller and smaller." As Larry's power and ability shrank in Phyllis's eyes, her attraction waned. "They lost interest in each other as lovers, I think. They weren't loyal or faithful to each other. That's a given."

Though Phyllis said in interviews that her career was not the center of her world, this was a skeptical claim. Even her marriage was built around it, with Larry's role as her manager superceding his role as her mate. Now, suddenly single, there was little time to be lonely. Phyllis was doing what she could to promote her recording career outside of the show. On February 23, Phyllis dashed out of a rehearsal to Madison Square Garden to sing the National Anthem at the Tommy Hearns/Juan Benitez fight before rushing back to the theatre. It was an exhausting period for Phyllis, but adrenaline and ambition kept her going as the show began to come together.

Opening night at the Lunt-Fontanne Theatre, on March 1, 1981, was a star-studded event attended by such celebrities as Phyllis's friends Nicholas Ashford and Valerie Simpson and dancing legends Alvin Ailey and Geoffrey Holder, two dance greats who had declined to replace Donald McKayle as the show's director. Against all odds, *Sophisticated Ladies* was an instant smash hit.

"The Duke would have been pleased, I think. I loved it madly," raved Douglas Watt of the *New York Daily News*. "It's just super entertainment," said Liz Smith, in her entertainment column for the same paper. "Never will you see such great-looking talent and energy. Every artist deserves a Tony Award nomination." And it wasn't just the *Daily News* that was impressed. Frank Rich of *The New York Times* said, "There's a lavishness in the show's production and in its performing talent. It just won't quit until it has won over the audience with its dynamic showmanship."

Phyllis was one of the show's standouts, and she generated a great deal of praise in the press. *The New York Times* critic Walter Kerr said Phyllis was "hitherto unknown to me but, I note, recently a most popular recording star. I am now prepared to believe she is a most popular anything she chooses to be." Meanwhile, Christine Arnold, writing for the *Philadelphia News*, wrote this piece of prose about Phyllis:

They never met, and Duke Ellington wrote Sophisticated Lady *in 1933, a couple of decades before she was even an unsophisticated baby. But watch her stride regally, coolly onto the stage of Broadway's Lunt-Fontanne Theatre. Listen to a voice that combines cream and honey, playfulness and the unendurable tears of unrequited love. Let her statuesque beauty, augmented by glittering costumes that are the stuff of fantasy, cast its inevitable spell.*

Do that – and you can, since the splashy revue-style Sophisticated Ladies *has been one of the few musicals with box-office muscle during this New York theater season – and you may become convinced that when he composed it, the Duke was writing under the power of premonition. That he knew that someday Phyllis Hyman would come along to embody that song.*

As the incredible reviews continued to pour in, Phyllis was in shock. "It's freaks me out that my first Broadway show is a big hit," she said. "It's a whole new experience and I'm quite enthralled."

At the Lunt-Fontanne, Phyllis shared her dressing room with Mercedes Ellington and a couple members of the chorus. "She insisted she did not want to be alone," Ellington recalled. "They gave her the star dressing room and she said it was too big for her. So three members of the chorus moved in. That's what she wanted."

In those intimate quarters, Ellington got the opportunity to know Phyllis better than most. "She had a very unique and recognizable sound, and she had a feeling for the musicals of the period. Phyllis was a great musician. Although at first I think she was a bit intimidated by my father and the music, she understood where the music was coming from, absolutely, on a level that very few singers would.

"I think she was one of these complete singers. She didn't rely on gimmicks. She was really, really a great musician, and I don't think anybody really understood that. She never had a witness to her life in that sense, somebody who could really understand where she was coming from. I think it was very important to her to find that person. I mean, my grandfather found it in Billy Strayhorn, and some of us find it in various types of partners whether it be personal or professional. But I think Phyllis's mind was so far out there that there were very few people who could really keep up with her and her needs, her desires, where she wanted to go musically. And I think it frustrated her to no end."

Just weeks after the show opened, RCA acquired the rights to produce the original cast album. This didn't sit well with Phyllis. She was hurt, though likely not surprised, that Clive didn't buy the rights for Arista and instead opted to purchase the rights to the soundtrack to *Woman Of The Year*, the Lauren Bacall-led show playing down the street at The Palace. With RCA in charge, the two-record set was produced by Thomas Z. Shepard with musical direction provided by Mercer Ellington. Less than half the show's numbers actually made it onto the set, of which Phyllis sang four, including "It Don't Mean A Thing (If It Ain't Got That Swing)," "Take The A Train," "In A Sentimental Mood" and "I Got It Bad (and That Ain't Good)"/"Mood Indigo." The latter was a medley of two songs that had been in the show from its first incarnation. Phyllis sang "I Got It Bad," while Terri Klauser tackled "Mood Indigo." The two songs were interspersed, forcing Phyllis and Terri to play off of each other.

"You do a Broadway recording pretty much within the first or second week that you've opened, so they can market that product along with, hopefully, the success of the show," explained Klausner. "It's usually done very quickly. It's done in one day. It's an intense day and everyone's usually totally exhausted. But once you put it down for posterity's sake, to adjust things or change things is just unheard of. You really want to have the recording reflect the show that people are seeing."

This was perhaps the most foreign of all Broadway's traditions to Phyllis, who had great trouble with repetition and preferred to interpret the lyrics a little differently each evening.

"How can you sing the same song the same way every night?" Phyllis would ask her duet partner.

"And I would look at her and go, 'How can you come up with more riffs and more scatting every night?'" said Klausner. "I was just fascinated at how she would do it."

But Klauser was initially a bit put off by it, too. "At first, we were kind of pulling on each other because I wanted to have the consistency of that performance. I also wanted to know what she was doing and where she was going. For the first month, she would really kind of go off a lot. She got notes from the stage managers, saying, 'Phyllis, don't take that too long. Terri's standing on the stage ready to come in.'"

In time, the two eventually began to understand each other enough to work together well. "We always worked at complimenting each other," said Klausner. "I became more flexible, knowing she was going to go off. I embraced it because she couldn't help it. That was her talent and her passion. She also, I think, began to embrace my consistency and understood it as support. So it was good."

As expected, Phyllis outshined the rest of the cast on vinyl, a fact that was confirmed by the music critic for the *Los Angeles Times*. "The singer who emerges with flying tone-colors is Phyllis Hyman," said Leonard Feather, Billie Holiday's old friend. "Her singing and scatting on 'Take the A Train' evoke memories of Betty Roche, who sang it for years in the Duke's band; her 'I Got It Bad' and 'In A Sentimental Mood' are delivered with a jazz-edged timbre that brings new and affecting life to them."

When the Tony nominations were announced just weeks after the show opened, *Sophisticated Ladies* came out a big winner. The show received a total of eight nominations, including musical of the year, Michael Smuin for director, Gregory Hines for leading actor, Hinton Battle for featured actor, costume design, lighting design and choreography. The eighth nomination went to none other than Broadway newcomer Phyllis Hyman for featured actress – the only female in the show to receive a Tony nod.

Ultimately, Phyllis walked away empty handed from the awards ceremony. She watched with great disappointment as Beatrice Arthur, or Maude, as Phyllis – ever the television buff – called her, presented the award to Marilyn Cooper for *Woman of the Year*. Of the eight awards the show was nominated for, it only won two. Hinton Battle took home the award for featured male performer and Willa Kim won for costume design. However, Phyllis did, some time later, win the Theatre World Award for most promising new talent, an honor that put her in the company of such previous prestigious winners as Jane Fonda, Robert Redford and Paul Newman.

"It made a nervous wreck out of me," Phyllis said of receiving the award on *Today's Black Woman*, a new BET talk show hosted by singer Freda Payne. "I had never received any award. I mean, nothing to really speak of. When I got the call, I didn't even know what they were talking about." Phyllis hadn't even heard of the Theatre World Awards, but when she found out other nominees included Elizabeth Taylor and Maureen Stapleton, she was impressed.

Gregory Hines was on hand to present the award to Phyllis, and his comments to the crowd put her at ease. Phyllis, he said, was "one of the most amazing performers I've ever seen, the only girl I know who can eat chicken during intermission, sleep for 15 minutes and go sing her butt off.'"

"At that point I just lost it," Phyllis said. "It was just hysterical. It meant a lot to me."

Even without any Tony Awards for its top players, *Sophisticated Ladies* continued to be the talk of the town. Photos ran in the trades almost weekly depicting members of the cast with whichever visiting dignitaries came their way. Phyllis and friends entertained an odd assortment of famous folks backstage that included everyone from funk star Rick James to Tony and Oscar winner Liza Minnelli, whose husband at the time, Mark Gero, Phyllis thought was "so damn attractive." Nancy Reagan, who was in New York to shop on her way to the royal wedding of Prince Charles and Lady Di in England, even passed by with her son Ron and his wife Daria. "I loved it," said the first lady after the performance.

Several months into the run, Phyllis wasn't as enthralled as she once had been. The show was wearing her out. "I am enjoying it, sure. But it's been a lot of work – six days a week, eight shows. It's been driving me crazy, and it's made me more nervous than I used to be. I can't imagine ever doing this again. There's too much technique involved and not enough entertaining."

Chapter 7

*I often times don't see myself the
way other people see me.*

"You know, recently people have been asking me whether I'm still a recording artist," Phyllis, seated in her dressing room at the Lunt-Fontanne, confessed to an eager reporter. "This album should more than answer that question. It has been a while coming, but I'm back and this one is really me. The diversity of the tunes really reflects my personality and taste in music, and the sound indicates my growth vocally."

Yes, if Clive Davis hadn't wanted Phyllis to take the part in *Sophisticated Ladies* he couldn't deny that the show's success – and in particular Phyllis's Tony nomination – didn't exactly hurt as Arista readied the new album for a July release. The press, who had always loved Phyllis, now absolutely adored her. Called *Can't We Fall In Love Again* to play up her reunion in the studio with Michael Henderson, Clive had given the order to change the album's name from *Sunshine In My Life* against Phyllis's wishes. Regardless, the buzz around Arista was that the album was guaranteed gold in the wake of Phyllis's new Broadway fame.

Arista planned a special debut party for the album to correspond with the Billboard convention that was taking place in New York City. A promotional party was scheduled at a trendy new club, which of course had to be scheduled in the afternoon to avoid conflicting with *Sophisticated Ladies*. This was problematic from the start, as Phyllis was in the habit of partying after the show into the wee hours of the morning with members of the cast, and sleeping the daytime hours away.

For this special event, Arista had flown in Michael Henderson and had a full band ready to play the party. "Phyllis didn't show up for rehearsals," recalled Milton Allen. "Of course, one of my jobs was to make sure Phyllis was there. So it's getting kind of close. Show time was a couple hours away. No one's heard from Phyllis, and all of a sudden I'm becoming alarmed."

Milton was prepared for this possibility, though, and had an emergency plan in place. Phyllis's new apartment at the Carnegie Mews on West Fifty-Sixth Street was only a few blocks away. So he called one of Phyllis's assistants, whom he knew had a key, and made plans to meet him in the lobby of Phyllis's building. "He let us into the apartment and she was just out of it." Milton recalled that Phyllis claimed to have taken Nyquil, though it was probably the result of something a little heavier taken the night before which now caused her to be almost catatonic. "We couldn't get her up. Eventually, she had to be put in the shower under cold water. We got her dressed. We got her fixed up. Meanwhile, I'm biting my nails, thinking, 'This is it. This is the end of my career. It's all over.'"

Downstairs in the car, Phyllis was still totally groggy and unable to focus. "I can't get anything out of her," Milton continued. "She looks great, her hair, makeup. But she's still incoherent. We get to the club. The show has started. The band is playing. We walk to the stage door. I open it and I say, 'Phyllis, this is it. We're here. It's time to go on.'

"All of a sudden, she just snaps out of it. She goes up there and she does a great show. She's talking, and she's flirting and cooing. She does the show, walks off the stage, gets back in the car and falls out again. I mean, she was still out of it. Just gone."

This was not the only time that Milton had had to go the extra mile do get Phyllis to do what she was supposed to. "That was one of the things that fueled the negative side of the fire, her unreliability," he said. "There were plenty of times that we couldn't get her up to go to things. I found myself constantly covering for her." The situation was already made difficult enough with Phyllis's limited availability to promote the album while doing the stage show. "We tried to work, as best we could, around her schedule. There were a lot of things that we could not do that we normally would have. The degree to which that helped or hurt is debatable. But nothing surpasses having an artist make in-person contacts with your radio stations and retail stores, and especially with Phyllis's personality. So we did miss some marketing opportunities there."

Still, the project initially got off to a good start. Both the album and the single were issued in July and quickly began climbing the charts. "It's moving up the charts so fast it's scaring me," gushed Phyllis to *Sepia* magazine. "I'm having the biggest fun with this record because I worked so hard on it, harder than any other I've ever done. We've changed and reworked things to make this the best album possible."

In an effort to be amiable, Phyllis took the opportunity to thank her boss for his role in the album's success. "Clive Davis was so helpful to me," she said. "I want to give credit where credit's due. He was very instrumental in making this recording what it is. He stepped in, and we had some disagreements about it, but as hard as it is to admit, he was right and I was wrong. Once I got past a very emotional point, we were able to improve on the original product. I'm really proud and happy with the way it's come out."

It cannot be disputed that Clive did put some effort into *Can't We Fall In Love Again*. "Clive invested a lot of personal time on this album, in terms of song selection and that sort of thing," said Milton Allen. "This was his attempt to elevate her to another level. It did have a pretty big recording budget and a fairly big marketing budget as well. Once the record came out, we worked it very, very hard. 'Can't We Fall In Love Again' did well on R&B radio, but the overall album did not do as well on what we now call urban radio as we would have liked. Maybe it was because the market was looking for something more like an Mtume/Lucas album, as opposed to a new, more polished sound. So it was not commercially successful."

Phyllis cross-promoted the show and album throughout the summer, appearing on such shows as *Mike Douglas*. But despite the exposure, the album eventually stalled out at number 11 R&B, number 57 pop, digits below the peak of *You Know How To Love Me*, her last album.

Still, it was not a bad showing, and the single climbed to number 9 R&B, making it Phyllis's first top ten single. Reviews for *Can't We Fall In Love Again* were generally positive. *Stereo Review* classified the album as a "recording of special merit" and stated that, "producers Norman Connors and Chuck Jackson have provided a variety of settings that show off Hyman's talent and are diverse enough to maintain the listener's attention."

Phyllis was happy with the album, but she also already had designs on her next recording project. "The one person I would really love to work with is Quincy Jones. That would be a magical experience and I'd do anything for that to happen one day. The only thing is that I wouldn't want to do just one album with him. I'd want to work with him forever."

Phyllis worked hard to promote the album as best she could around her busy theatre schedule. She took time off from the show and flew to Miami to record a television special for WTVJ-Channel 4 that debuted in August. Titled *Phyllis Hyman – A Sophisticated Lady*, the special was essentially a 50-minute music video. Joining Phyllis on the special was guest star Bobby Caldwell, another former Miami resident, who'd scored a smash hit in 1979 with "What You Won't Do For Love."

The taping marked the first time that Phyllis and Bobby had met. "I was a bit taken back because she was a tall gal," Caldwell recalled. "I'm not short. I'm 5'10", but she's well over six feet. She came to the taping with pumps, and I took her aside and I said, 'I'm feeling kind of dwarfed standing next to you. Can somebody give me a box or can you do it in flats?'" Phyllis hadn't brought any flats, and performed in her pumps when the two sang "Come To Me," during which Bobby was seating playing keyboards. But when he stood to sing the second song with her, Phyllis took her shoes off and sang barefoot to help Bobby feel more comfortable.

Phyllis only had a few days off from the show, so rehearsals for the special were limited, and Phyllis and Bobby did their duets in a single take. But Phyllis handled the task like a pro. "Phyllis is a natural," said the special's producer, Greg Simpson. "Television is her medium. It's making love to that lens. You've got to relate to that lens as another person and be one on one with it. You've got to see it as a pair of eyes. If it's a love song, you've got to play to that lens like you're singing to your lover. She's got it. She's got it inside."

In September 1981, Phyllis made her second appearance on *Soul Train*, just as Arista was preparing to release the album's second single, "Tonight You and Me," which disappointingly spent a brief ten weeks on the charts, peaking at number 22 R&B. Still, it had been a remarkable year for Phyllis. She'd debuted on Broadway – receiving a Tony nomination and a Theatre World Award in the process – and had her first top ten hit with "Can't We Fall In Love Again." Yet for all she had gained, her first *Jet* cover story, which hit the stands October 1st, focused on what she didn't have. Looking sexy and sultry in a low-cut, sleeveless black and gold gown, the headline ran "Phyllis Hyman Wants Love To Match Records, Stage Success."

"I'm not ashamed to talk about it because I think that maybe people don't discuss it enough and they're suffering inside," Phyllis said of loneliness in the story. "I really want people to know that what they think and read about entertainers' lives being so glamorous – hell, no! That is far from the truth, and especially for female performers. Men seem to be in awe of you and feel you can't be approached."

Phyllis had always been candid, but she came into the spotlight with a man on her arm. Now separated, though not yet divorced, the *Jet* story for the first time saw Phyllis portrayed as lonely and desperate for love – an image that would only intensify as the years passed and find itself a recurring theme in both her interviews and song lyrics alike.

"I don't really want to say need because to me – an aggressive, liberated woman – need sounds too pathetic," Phyllis said confidently, before dropping the mask completely. "But maybe I'm wrong. Maybe need and want sometimes go together. Maybe I do need and want a man."

Product manager Milton Allen explained the story's sad turn like this: "We had to come up with some kind of angle for the story. *Jet* was resisting putting her on the cover. They didn't feel that Phyllis had the star power. So in addition to buying advertising and doing everything like that, we also had to create a story angle that was, from a publicist's standpoint, somewhat controversial. So that was a publicist's concoction. But that was a milestone."

Phyllis's publicist, Sheila Eldridge, concurred. "At that time, much more than now, *Jet* had to have that headline that would engage people, and I think the feeling was that Phyllis was not a household name. I think that was a way to get her in, and Phyllis in her interviews was talking about wanting a man. So we just kind of played into that."

While the story's angle may have been a "publicist's concoction," it unwittingly created a theme for Phyllis's interviews that would stay with her till the end. Phyllis had learned to advertise her loneliness and her pain, which was not conditional on whether she was seeing someone or how much free time she had on her hands. For in truth, doing eight shows six days a week left Phyllis with little time for a social life. Yet, still, she managed to squeeze one in, which largely consisted of late night parties, often including the usage of cocaine, with members of the cast of *Sophisticated Ladies*. She was accompanied to these by a variety of men, including for a time model Danny Poole. But even with a man on her arm, in the middle of a crowded room, Phyllis could still be lonely – and often she was.

Phyllis's cast mates knew of her loneliness even before the *Jet* cover story appeared on newsstands. They, like Milton Allen, had seen how her substance abuse and irresponsibility was jeopardizing her career. "She was an addictive personality," said Terri Klausner. "You worried for her, and you wondered, 'Is she going to show up on time today? Is she going to make it to the show?' There were times when she would fall asleep during the show. We'd hear her come running down the stairs because she missed a cue or something, and it was like, 'Oh God, Phyllis!'"

If everyone saw Phyllis's stumbles, no one was more acutely aware of them than stage manager Ken Hanson. He tried, whenever possible, to cover for her. But she didn't make the job easy. "She would miss performances. She'd be late for work a lot and she lived right around the corner from the theatre." The Wednesday and Saturday matinees were most challenging for Phyllis. "She would go home after a show and some of the people connected with the show would be there and she'd be up doing drugs all night. She would not even fall asleep until 6 o'clock in the morning, and the shows start at 2 o'clock in the afternoon."

On those days that Phyllis couldn't get out of her bed, her understudy, Anita Moore, would go on in her place. Moore had joined the Duke Ellington Orchestra in 1972, two years before Duke's death, and remained a member of the group as *Sophisticated Ladies* opened. But the crowd was coming to see

Phyllis. "We didn't want to disappoint the audience. We would wait till the last possible moment to make Anita go on. It got so bad that I would call Phyllis. I would wake her up and she would answer the phone like, 'Oh, shit. It's 1:15.' She didn't even know. It was like she was in a daze or something."

Often, once out of her apartment building, Phyllis was unable to catch a cab quickly enough and would just take off running. "I can remember going to the corner and keeping an eye out for her," said Hanson. "I would scream to them, 'She's coming, she's coming,' and they would wait, which is unheard of. If you're not there 30 minutes ahead of time, you're legally not supposed to go on."

Hanson vividly recalls one of Phyllis's most outrageous stunts, which happened approximately 18 months into the show's run. Phyllis had a long break between numbers in the show. After singing 'A-Train,' in the middle of act one, she didn't come back until 'Sentimental Mood,' which was at the start of act two. On this particular day, Phyllis went upstairs to her dressing room and dozed off. As act two started, following the intermission, the orchestra kicked it off with their opening number. Then it was Phyllis's turn.

But Phyllis was missing in action. "They were playing the intro, the band had finished their big number, and Phyllis was not there. They were vamping and vamping. I can remember getting on the microphone and screaming at the top of my lungs, 'Phyllis, Phyllis,' and we didn't know where she was. The audience is waiting. The piano is just playing. Thirty seconds have gone by, nearly a minute." The stage managers made the decision to go on without her, and caught Judith Jamison coming out of her dressing room in time to be shoved on stage to start her number, which normally followed Phyllis's.

By this time, someone had woken Phyllis. She ran down the stairs from her dressing room and rushed to the side of the stage, where she found Judith well into her number. Shrugging her shoulders, Phyllis turned around and headed back upstairs to change for her next song.

"It was against equity rules," Hanson continued. "She was chastised for it. But everyone knew Phyllis, and they knew why she had missed the number. She wasn't going to be fired for it. She was there that night and she did the whole show. There was nothing wrong with her voice. She was just drugged out from the night before and had fallen asleep in the middle of the performance."

"A lot of the time Phyllis's actions had to do with her depression," offered Ty Stephens. "The times you could tell that she was on her game, she was in a relationship. When she wasn't, she was out it. Her life was kind of based on whether she was in love or not."

Terri Klausner saw this, too. "She didn't pick men very well in her life," she said. "Many of the men that I could see her fall for – she just wanted security so much, I think, something stable, and someone to take care of her and tend to her and treat her like a queen. Maybe at the beginning they would, but nothing ever seemed to stay long with her."

Despite Phyllis's erratic behavior, she was still generally popular with the rest of the cast. The dancers, in particular, grew especially close to Phyllis as she opened up her dressing to them. "We hung out in her room," said Ty Stephens. "That was kind of like the central location to chill and hang out. I think she really needed to have people around her to help her feel comfortable."

Phyllis would ask the dancers and other cast members to accompany her to concerts around town. "Phyllis had a lot of public appearances during that time, and most of them were singing her material in clubs," said Ty. "Her disco tracks were very popular. So there was a group of us from the show that went everywhere she went in New York City. We would go after the show. We would hang out all night long, and she would be looking at us for the lyrics that she couldn't remember because we all knew her lyrics better than she did. We were real fans of Phyllis Hyman."

Even those she disappointed still fell prey to her charm and reluctantly joined her at her post-show concerts. "It's not that she would command that you join her," explained Terri. "But there was something about her. She was very charismatic. No matter what she did during the day, for some reason, even if you got annoyed with her, if she turned to you and said, 'You're coming tonight, aren't you? You'll be there with me?' There was something about her that made it almost impossible to say no to her."

Her issues aside, there was a part of Phyllis that was sweet and sincere, almost childlike. "She was very gracious at the stage door," recalled Ken Hanson. "She would sign all the autographs. I can remember people rushing her that were trying to go to dinner. She'd say, 'Oh, no, no. I'm signing every autograph. These are record sales.'"

Indeed, if Phyllis's unpredictability earned her a reputation, so, too, did her generosity. "There was this blind man on the street that was right on the way on her walk," Hanson continued. "She used to give this man money every day when she would go by, and he knew exactly who she was. She'd go over, and as crazy as Phyllis was she was very much like that. She'd be in no makeup, running down the street in big sunglasses. She would stop and say, 'Hi, how you doin'? This is Phyllis.' And he knew who it was. She would give him money and then she'd come on in."

When Phyllis made the decision to call it quits with Larry she lost a husband and a manager. Charles Ward, Phyllis's attorney, had attempted to fill the gap long distance from San Francisco. But by early 1982, Phyllis decided she needed someone more hands on. The label had just released a third single from *Can't We Fall In Love Again*, "You Sure Look Good To Me," but it spent a mere three weeks on the charts, climbing no further than number 76. Her distrust for Arista, and more precisely, Clive Davis, was in full bloom, and she wanted someone local, someone savvy. Phyllis approached her old friend Sid Maurer, the man who had first signed her to his label and then graciously released her to Buddah, and asked him to take over the reigns of her career.

"She said, 'Could you handle me for a while?'" Maurer, who had managed acts such as Donovan in the '60s, recalled. "I said, 'C'mon, Phyllis, you're a pain in the ass, you know that.' But eventually I caved in. She was a handful, and I did the best I could do."

A standard signing photo – Phyllis, in a zebra-print jacket sitting at a desk with a contract on it while Sid, wearing dark sunglasses, stood looking over her shoulder – showed up in all the industry trades, including *Billboard*, in March of 1982. "Phyllis and I go a long way back, all the way back to her days in Florida," Maurer was quoted as saying in the press release that Sheila Eldridge circulated to the media. "I've often counseled her on various decisions. Now she had reached such a plateau in her career that we feel it is time to make it official."

Maurer went on to say that he and Phyllis were "forming an alliance," and that together they would take her career to new heights. "I will be building a network of companies for Phyllis, which will include producing some acts that she has her eyes on, as well as the production of some television shows." Maurer also mentioned that Phyllis's concert appearances would now be booked by the Norby Walters Agency, and that the Light Company in Los Angeles had been contracted to handle television and motion picture bookings.

At the helm of Phyllis's career, Sid found her business affairs and operations at Command Performances, her publishing and production company, in shambles. Larry "mishandled her terribly," said Sid. "He dipped into Arista's tour support fund. He didn't know what he was doing. It was just a matter of mismanagement and not putting the money in the right place. She could have made it, but he was getting in the way of all kinds of stuff. He was making dumb decisions. When you get tour support money it's not a free gift. It's recoupable."

The powers that be at Arista were initially quite pleased with this change in management – something they had been advocating for years. "It helped the working relationship," said Milton Allen. "Sid could communicate better with us than Charles could. Charles was more of an outsider, an agitator. And Sid was your consummate insider. He was charming, affable. He was well known. He was a New Yorker, that sort of thing."

One of the first things Sid did was negotiate for Phyllis to appear on the latest album by jazz pianist McCoy Tyner. An industry veteran, and up to this point pretty much a jazz purist, Tyner had recorded more than thirty albums over the past two decades. He had recently switched from his longtime label, Milestone, to mainstream Columbia and was trying for a more contemporary sound.

Tyner had written three lyrical ballads for Phyllis to sing on the album, including "Love Surrounds Us Everywhere," "In Search of

My Heart" and "I'll Be Around," the latter being co-written and arranged by Stanley Clarke. Phyllis recorded the tracks with Tyner at the Power Station in New York and later arranged to join Tyner onstage for several dates, including the Berkeley Jazz Festival in California in May and at the Kennedy Center in Washington, D.C. in June.

For the most part, Phyllis's career was on autopilot as long as she remained in *Sophisticated Ladies*, which was growing old to her by 1982. "The show wasn't doing for her what she had intended, giving her the visibility in the areas that she had hoped for, and Arista was pitting her up against Angela Bofill and people like that," explained Mercedes Ellington. "The industry does such strange things with people. Treating people as commodities never works."

The longer she stayed with the show, the more lax she became backstage. The cast and crew never ceased to be amazed by her antics, and none amazed them more than the chicken leg incident. There was usually over 45 minutes from the time she finished "Take The 'A' Train" in the first act until the start of "In A Sentimental Mood" in the second. Oftentimes, during matinee days especially, Phyllis would use this time to eat and ordered in.

Most vocalists generally prefer not to eat before singing. But Phyllis was, of course, not the average singer. She could choke down a cheeseburger one minute and scat jazz the next. This particular day, she had a taste for chicken, and she was still eating it when she came down from her dressing room on her way to sing "In A Sentimental Mood." Resplendent in a satin peignoir with enormous ostrich feathers at the wrists, stage manager Ken Hanson had a fit when he spotted her.

"It's against union rules for anyone to be eating in their costumes," he said. "I mean, you're not supposed to be backstage in your costume chowing down on fried chicken. Grease gets on your costume and you're not at a restaurant. You're at work. But of course, Phyllis doesn't care anything about things like that."

Phyllis, followed closely by her dresser, Judy Giles, dismissed Hanson's chastisement and headed toward the stage, drumstick still in hand. As the music for her number began, she took a last bite, chewed and swallowed it, licked her teeth and handed the half-eaten drumstick – and the napkin she was holding it by – to Giles before entering stage right. Phyllis sang "In A Sentimental Mood" as effortlessly as usual, finished the song to her standard hearty round of applause, and exited stage left, the opposite side of the stage. "And when she got off on the other side, Judy was over there with her chicken leg," recalled Hanson, who watched incredulously as Phyllis finished eating while Giles went about switching Phyllis's wig for her next number.

Publicist Sheila Eldridge explained that even if Phyllis's interest in the show was waning, she wasn't about to give it up. She had, in fact, chosen to renew her contract more than once. "It was grueling, but she loved it," Eldridge said. "Phyllis liked that stage. It was stardom. The whole role, the feel, everything. She'd never had that before. So it was a love/hate kind of relationship."

In June, two distinct events happened in Phyllis's career that clearly illustrated her internal struggles and the dueling personalities inside her. The first occurred on June 14, when Phyllis was honored at the Fifth Annual New York Women's Jazz Festival. She appeared on the cover of the conference booklet, *Catalyst*, alongside jazz veterans and fellow honorees Shirley Horn, Dakota Staton, Sarah Vaughan and others.

But in her next cover story, folks would see a different side of Phyllis. No stranger to men's magazines, Phyllis had, in fact, appeared on the cover of *Players* no less than three times. But folks in the industry were still surprised when Phyllis, who only a year prior had declared that she hoped her image projected a "morally righteous aspect," agreed to pose nude for *Oui*. Phyllis appeared in a seven-page spread in the magazine with photos by Oscar Abolafia and a question and answer-style interview by Peter Wolff.

The interview actually took place in a bar not far from the Lunt-Fontanne called Downey's on Broadway, where, over Irish coffees, Phyllis got to look at the proofs from her photo shoot. With her hair pinned up and her face heavily painted, Phyllis was featured in various stages of undress baring her breasts and backside. Phyllis frolicked for the camera in a bubble bath, admired herself in a full-length mirror, squirmed around on satin sheets, sat knock-kneed in a wicker peacock chair and posed with a children's teddy bear strategically placed between her long legs.

During the interview, Phyllis spoke about her take on adult magazines and her reasons for doing the shoot, which she confessed "required a bit of libational lubrication to get through." Sheila Eldridge, who was mortified when she learned that Phyllis had bared it all, thought that all the alcohol nearly constituted coercion. "The understanding was that she was *not* going to do nude," Eldridge said. "I think they started drinking and everybody just got kind of loose. I got a call the next day and I said, 'Oh, no!'"

The *Oui* piece would do Phyllis's career no favors. "Bad move," said Sid Maurer. "But I've got to take the rap because, one way or another, when you're managing somebody, you take the rap for good and bad. I tried to talk her out of it, especially when I saw the shots. It didn't help her. It hurt her."

By this time, Phyllis had done jingles for many popular brand names. "They want all-American, they get all-American," she said of her endorsements and jingle work in the *Oui* interview. "I do it all because I feel it all. I'm a bunch of complex personalities." Perhaps too complex for some of the companies she worked for. Phyllis had been spokesperson for Clairol's Born Beautiful line of hair colors for just over a year. Indeed, Phyllis, who had already recorded two separate radio spots for the company, was scheduled to go on a four-day promotional tour July 11-14 to sing at Clairol's divisional sales meetings across the country.

She had commissioned the creation of a special scrim bearing the words "Sophisticated Ladies" – and paid $1,200 for it out of her own pocket – to be hung on the stage behind her when she sang. The scrim was finished, her vacation time from the show already approved, and her staff – road manager Greg Simpson, pianist Patti Clements, valet Carlos Suarez and hairstylist Danny Wintrode – were all set to make the trip when Clairol abruptly called it off on June 17. Just as her friend Jayne Kennedy had after she posed nude for *Playboy*, Phyllis was about to feel the repercussions of her latest career move.

"We had a deal with Clairol and once that magazine came out, Clairol just squashed the contract," said Sid. Through her agent at the William Morris Agency, Phyllis accused Clairol of anticipatory breach of contract for canceling the performances, for which she was scheduled to earn $5,000 per show plus expenses. But word came back from Clairol, through a memo from the Foote, Cone & Belding advertising agency, that it was Phyllis who was in breach.

Phyllis had violated the contract's morality clause. And it was not just that she posed nude for the magazine. Adding insult to injury for Clairol was the fact that she mentioned the company in the interview that ran with the spread. The problem only intensified when *Oui* sent an image from the shoot to *Jet* magazine without Phyllis's consent. *Jet* ran a photo from the shoot along with quotes pulled from the *Oui* interview in their July 5th issue. Fearing the loss of additional endorsement deals, Phyllis, via Sid, requested a written guarantee from *Oui* that no additional images would be sent out without her expressed consent.

But the Clairol contract wasn't all that was squashed as a result of the spread. Maurer nearly lost his marriage after Phyllis mentioned in the article that he had been dancing with another man when she first met him in Miami back in 1975. "She outed him and almost cost him his marriage," said Phyllis's friend Tina Stephens. "After that, Clive washed his hands of her. That's when he went looking for Whitney Houston."

"That was a PR disaster," agreed Milton Allen. "It was certainly a bad move and that was one of those curve balls that Phyllis would just throw at you."

In the midst of the *Oui* scandal, Phyllis flew to London to perform in *The Sacred Music of Duke Ellington*, a televised special featuring Ellington's gospel works that would later be released on videocassette by MGM Home Video. The only member of the *Sophisticated Ladies* cast invited to be a part of the special, Phyllis, dressed in a white, fur-trimmed Tony Chase gown, sang two songs, "Tell Me It's The Truth" and an Ellington-arranged version of "The Lord's Prayer." Other performers on the show, which was recorded at London's historic St. Paul's Cathedral, where Prince Charles and Lady Di had been married two years earlier, included Tony Bennett and Douglas Fairbanks, Jr., who narrated the special.

Phyllis took some more time off from *Sophisticated Ladies* as summer 1982 wound to a close. Sheila Eldridge had gotten Phyllis booked back on the *Tonight Show with Johnny Carson* based on the continued success of the show. Getting there, though, turned out to be quite a task. "They wouldn't let her off," said Eldridge. "She had to leave the morning of the taping because they would not let her off. I remember fighting with the producer saying, 'Look, this is a great opportunity for both the play and Phyllis.' But Phyllis had missed a lot of shows."

Phyllis's flight to Los Angeles was delayed and, once she finally landed, her driver was also running behind schedule to meet her. "That was one of the most horrifying experiences of my life," Eldridge said. "I had worked hard to get her on the *Tonight Show*. But by the time the car picked her up and got her to the studio, it was too late for rehearsal and they were getting ready to start taping. It was a big opportunity and she was devastated."

Tina Stephens, who met up with Phyllis in L.A., did not recall it that way. "The Johnny Carson show was a big thing, but for Phyllis it was, 'No big deal. Let's go to Hamburger Hamlet.' You never knew what would faze her. Like that, you would expect her to just blow the roof off the car and be impossible, and she's like, 'Hey, shit happens. What I can I say? We didn't make it.' Then there'd be another incident, when somebody would take the last piece of gum in her pack, and she would rant and rave for two or three hours. You just never knew what was going to set her off."

Devastated or not, Phyllis needn't have worried with Eldridge on the job. "I made a promise to her that I'd have her booked back on that show within two weeks, and within the next two weeks she was on the show."[4]

After the Carson taping, it was on to Detroit, where she played the Montreaux Kool Jazz Festival. Later in the month, Phyllis made her debut on Merv Griffin's show. And on October 2, she took yet another night off from the show to open for Lou Rawls at Carnegie Hall. But by now, it was obvious that Phyllis was burning the candle at both ends..

One thing *Sophisticated Ladies* had offered Phyllis was the chance to party and party hard, and Sid soon learned that Phyllis had picked up some nasty habits. "She got involved in some bad

---

[4] To be exact, the initial appearance was scheduled for August 11, 1982 and the rescheduled date was September 2.

stuff," said Sid. "Cocaine. She could not break the drug habit. We'd go on the road for the weekend. We had a bus, and we'd do two or three cities over the weekend. On the way back, as we were dropping her off at five or six in the morning, she'd say to me, 'I need a $1,000.'"

Sid would beg Phyllis not to take the money – not to take the drugs – but Phyllis always remained insistent.

"She'd get insulting and tell me, 'It's my money.'"

"You know what, baby?" Sid would answer. "It is your money. You're right. Take it."

The more Phyllis indulged, the riskier her behavior became. "I remember being on the way to the Dorothy Chandler Pavilion in Los Angeles, and she was freebasing in the back of the limo," recalled Tina Stephens. "I thought, this driver is going to call the police on us. Then, later, she did it in the dressing room with an off duty police officer stationed outside her door."

When Phyllis was freebasing, the only thing that mattered to her was her high. She would use till her stash was exhausted. Then, come morning, she was useless.

"She was incredibly self destructive," Tina said. "She had demons that could not be controlled."

Chapter 8

*I never sang in church, you know.
But I bet you what, when you
black you can fake it.*

In December of 1983, Phyllis again took time off from *Sophisticated Ladies* to go gig. This time, she played three nights at the historic Uptown Theatre in Philadelphia. Between doing eight shows a week and using substantial amounts of cocaine, Phyllis was worn out and there was no hiding it. In his review of her performance, Joseph P. Blake of the *Philadelphia Daily News* said that Phyllis was "more than qualified to send chills up and down your back with her jazzy, deep voice. But she didn't."

Not everyone, of course, shared Blake's opinion and at least one member of the audience was impressed. Glenda Gracia had graduated from Temple University law school and landed a job in the business affairs division of CBS network television right out of school. The granddaughter of famed evangelist Bishop C.M. Grace, better known as "Sweet Daddy Grace," it's arguable that Glenda's gift for oration was inherited. After leaving CBS, Gracia had served as the founding executive director of the Philadelphia-based Black Music Association for three years. Recently, she had headed out on her own to start G. Gracia & Associates, a consulting firm specializing in personal management for entertainment artists.

Glenda had first encountered Phyllis in 1976 having caught her show at Mikell's. "I'd gone there with Roberta Flack, who was telling everybody about this terrific new singer," Gracia recalled. "Well, Roberta wasn't one to exaggerate. First of all, Phyllis came out on the bandstand just drop-dead gorgeous. She had a quality of poise and assurance that was incredible for somebody so young and appearing in front of what sometimes got to be a bit of a rowdy, certainly a really demanding audience. But she silenced the place. You could hear the proverbial pin fall as it hit the floor. She was beautiful, in command, and simply overwhelming with this truly brilliant voice. People were in awe."

Glenda was no less taken with Phyllis in 1982 than she had been six years earlier. In fact, Glenda was so impressed that she asked to meet with Phyllis later in the month in New York. Glenda came highly recommended, and pleased with the fact that she was both black and female, Phyllis quickly agreed to a meeting. "What I felt I already knew about her when we met is that she gave an enormous amount of focus to imaging and style," said Glenda. "But after we met, the thing I quickly learned and loved about her was her candor. Sharing that as a personality trait, I know how often people find honesty difficult to manage. When I find that quality in another person I just love it because it means there won't be any punches pulled."

Phyllis rang in 1983 in a big way, appearing on the CBS New Year's Eve special *Happy New Year America*. Just days later, on January 2, the curtain came down on *Sophisticated Ladies* for the last time when the producers decided to abruptly close the show.

"I'm disappointed and I'll always wonder why it happened like that," Phyllis told *Jet* magazine. "I'm really going to miss the show. For two years, eight shows a week it was my life. The cast members worked and played together. I don't understand the logic behind the closing. The box office was increasing."

Suddenly, Phyllis found herself with a lot of free time on her hands. That was good news to Arista, because it meant that Phyllis would actually be able to promote her next album with a tour. Indeed, Phyllis needed to tour as much as Arista wanted her to. Without the steady paycheck from the show, which averaged about $3,000 a week over the past year, Phyllis had little money coming in.

Phyllis had gone through all of 1982 without visiting the R&B top 40. As none of her albums had yet gone gold and only three of her own compositions had appeared on her five albums, Phyllis's royalty earnings were meager. She was, by this time, greatly in debt to Arista. So any royalties she did earn were merely subtracted from her outstanding debt to the label. In short, Phyllis needed to get back out on the road immediately.

She advised the folks over at Norby Walters, her booking agency, that she was available for any dates that came in, even though her latest album – her fourth for Arista – wouldn't be ready until the spring. In the meantime, Phyllis had the time she needed to get back in the studio with Thom Bell, who was particularly hot at the moment having a few months earlier taken Deniece Williams all the way to number one with "It's Gonna Take A Miracle."

Phyllis had been longing to work again with Bell since her experience recording with him for *The Fish That Saved Pittsburgh* soundtrack. Known for his lush orchestrations, Bell developed a reputation during the Philly Sound's heyday for incorporating instruments not traditionally found in rhythm and blues, such as French horns and harpsichords, into his productions. With Phyllis, Bell played the vibraphone on the tunes "Let Somebody Love You" and "We Should Be Lovers," giving them a Caribbean feel.

While recording was always a chore for Phyllis, working with Bell made it a little less so. "He's put me onto a totally new direction," she said. "He's managed to conceptualize all my feelings and talents and put it all into one record. I've never experienced anything like this."

Bell was by far the most experienced producer Phyllis had ever been teamed with, having been one of the originators of the Philly Sound. He was also the most expensive. Arista paid him $32,000 plus recording expenses to produce eight sides on Phyllis, more than double what Mtume and Lucas had been paid to produce the entire *You Know How To Love Me* album in 1979. Phyllis thoroughly enjoyed working with Bell, particularly on the two songs he wrote especially for her – even if they marked a departure from her signature style. When she performed it live, Phyllis called "Just Me And You" her "ever so slight contribution to the country music craze," though the song was more easy listening than country and western. The other Bell original on the album was "Twenty-Five Miles To Anywhere."

"Now there's a song that I really love, and that actually has a funny story behind it," Phyllis said during an interview with *Blues & Soul*. "I was 25 minutes late for a meeting with Thom and he wrote it while he was waiting for me. In fact, he was going to call it 'Twenty-Five Minutes Late' at first. But the melody is so haunting; and working with Thom was great. He's such a wonderful man and I was so pleased that he opted to work with me."

Bell thought that Phyllis was haunting, too "She was very haunting," he said. "She had a haunting attitude and a haunting voice. Everything about her was haunting, in such a way that you could never forget Phyllis." Bell also backed up Phyllis's story about how the song "Twenty-Five Miles To Anywhere" came together. "A lot of times her mind would take her to different places, and I wrote it specifically for that reason."

While preparing to return to the road, one glaring problem with her stage show became obvious. Phyllis's biggest hit to date was "Can't We Fall In Love Again," the Michael Henderson duet from 1981. But she had only female backing vocalists in her band, specifically Krystal Davis and Janet Wright. There was also no one in the band, which at this time consisted of Barry Eastmond on piano, Bobby Wooten on synthesizer, Adam Falcon on guitar, Wayne Brathwaite on bass and Trevor Gayle on drums, capable enough vocally to duet with Phyllis. Charlene Powell, Phyllis's assistant, had seen Miles Jaye perform around town, where he was a regular at clubs like Mikell's, Phyllis's old stomping grounds, and Seventh Avenue South. Charlene called Miles and set up an audition.

"I remember that first day, man; it was like boot camp," said Miles, who recalled waiting for an introduction to Phyllis when she arrived at the rehearsal hall. Instead, Phyllis, with a new pupil, administered her latest test and gave the order to start into the song as soon as she arrived. "I don't know what frame of mind she was in, but she started the tune. We hadn't met and she started the song, and I remember thinking to myself, 'I don't think we've been introduced yet.' So when I'm talking about intimidating, *I'm talking about intimidating*."

Miles jumped in like a trouper and sang the song with Phyllis, who had warmed very little by the time the rehearsal ended. "She was still somewhat aloof, you know. I think it was probably her version of professional, no fun and games, 'Let's just do this. C'mon, let's see what you got,' which I respected. It scared the crap out of me, but I respected it."

The Miles/Phyllis version of "Can't We Fall In Love Again" only vaguely resembled the original. Miles' husky baritone was in stark contrast to Michael Henderson's silky smooth tenor and soaring falsetto. But he did have Michael's height – making him a good physical match for Phyllis – and his rugged handsomeness was the perfect compliment to her feminine beauty. The two had a natural chemistry and made for a very sexy pairing.

On February 4th, Phyllis and the band opened for Billy Paul in Philadelphia. The next night, they opened for B.B. King at Carnegie Hall. Two days after that, Phyllis headed home to Pittsburgh, where the city council passed Resolution #102 making the week of February 7th Phyllis Hyman Week. Phyllis made various appearances throughout her hometown before capping off the week with two shows at Club Heaven.

Reviews were favorable for Phyllis's shows as her tour continued to wind its way across the country. "Hyman has never had the killer hit record that would put her in the commercial class of a Roberta Flack or Dionne Warwick," said a reviewer for the *Los Angeles Times*. "Her Palace concert indicated that, vocally, she is their equal – and possibly destined to be pop music's next reigning diva."

Phyllis finished recording the new album during a tour stopover in San Francisco. It was there, in the Automatt recording studio, that she cut three sides with Clive Davis' latest protégé, Narada Michael Walden. Though Arista was paying Thom Bell a significant amount to produce eight sides on Phyllis – theoretically a complete album – Clive had called in Walden after listening to the Bell-produced tracks.

"The reason that Narada was called in by the company is because they felt that there were no hit singles in the tunes that Thom did, and I'm the kind of person who is always open to suggestions," said Phyllis. "Actually, working with Narada was great, too. He's a lot of fun. In many ways, they are similar people – both are serious, hard working guys but they are both a lot of fun and relaxed in their job.

"We laughed a lot and there were no fights," Phyllis finished, possibly referring to her heated studio exchanges with Mtume and Lucas.

Like Norman Connors, Walden's instrument of choice was the drums. He was playing in the renowned Mahavishnu Orchestra at 21. His recording career as a solo artist began on Atlantic Records in 1977, but he had little chart success with the five albums he recorded there. At Arista, Walden had begun to fare better as a producer, and Clive quickly matched him up with Phyllis's rival, Angela Bofill.

In fact, as Phyllis was in the studio with Walden, his latest Bofill production, "Too Tough," was climbing the R&B charts, where it would make its way to number 5. Ironically, Walden had written "Too Tough" specifically for Phyllis. It may have very well have been Phyllis's second top ten R&B single had Clive not heard it and recommended Walden record it on Bofill instead.

Phyllis was, in essence, a stepchild at Arista by this point, constantly at odds with Daddy Clive. Both blamed the other for the fact that her career had not taken off, and for the failure of the *Can't We Fall In Love Again* album. "Her relationship with Clive did get contentious," recalled Milton Allen. "Phyllis was the kind of person who would speak her mind. She would say things that were very, very inappropriate. She was certainly not a diplomat by any stretch of the imagination."

"She made it very unpleasant for him, calling him a plantation owner and all this stuff," added publicist Barbara Shelley. "And that's too bad, because he would have loved to make a star out of her." According to Shelley, Clive could not understand why Phyllis didn't want to play by his rules. After all, his way had worked for so many others. "She scared him," Shelley said. "He thought, 'Why give all the energy there if it's not wanted?'"

If Phyllis scared Clive, it's because she was deeply frightened herself. Control equaled comfort to Phyllis. It was what she needed to feel safe, and she could never feel that with him. She had asserted a certain amount of control over her siblings. She did the same with Larry and, in the years to come, she would succeed in doing the same with not just her romantic interests, but also her close friends and staff members, who were often one and the same.

But her tactics would not work on Clive. Unlike her siblings, lovers and personal assistants, Clive had no emotional attachment to Phyllis. Without that, none of Phyllis's standard control mechanisms could succeed. So acting out – lambasting Clive in the press, showing up late for meetings or blowing off commitments altogether – was the only option, the only hope, Phyllis saw of exerting some form of control.

But this strategy backfired on Phyllis. The more she acted up and acted out, the less attention Clive actually paid her. Until, finally, he paid her none at all. Phyllis needed control to feel safe. It was just that simple. She knew what she needed, but she miscalculated the best way to go about getting it. You catch more flies with honey, they say, than with vinegar. The harder Phyllis tried to regain control in her relationship with Clive through emotional outbursts, the further it slipped from her reach.

Like the Thom Bell sides, the three Walden-produced tracks, "Riding The Tiger," "Goddess of Love" and "Why Did You Turn Me On," were pure pop. But unlike the Bell tracks, "Riding the Tiger" and "Goddess of Love" were heavily overproduced, much more suited for discos than the drive-at-five radio slot. "Tiger," the song selected to be the album's first single, was an upbeat dance number that began with synthesizer-produced sounds of the jungle and a Tarzan yell before Phyllis spoke the opening line "You want to ride?" After a couple verses of lyrical gibberish, Phyllis speaks once more. "In a forest of rain, you'll feel the fear of my name," she says, unleashing a maniacal laugh as the chorus repeats.

Phyllis had done dance music before, and done it well. "You Know How To Love Me," however, was merely a Phyllis-type ballad put to a track with a much faster tempo. Phyllis was still allowed to emote on the song, its instrumentation was light and airy, and her voice was still the focal point. In contrast, "Tiger," with its early '80s special effects, featured a heavy-handed accompaniment to Phyllis's vocal performance, which was restrained and unexpressive. For perhaps the first time, you could listen to a Phyllis Hyman song and not feel she believed what she was singing.

"Oh God, did I hate it!" said Gerry Griffith, Arista's head of A&R, and he was not alone in his thinking. "'Riding the Tiger' was not it, and that was a good example of deferring to the producer for single selection," said Milton Allen. It was also a good example of preferential treatment and proof that Phyllis's rank had been lowered. Even working with the same producer as

Angie, it was obvious that Phyllis was receiving second-hand material. "His work was much, much, much better with Angie at the time," said Milton.

When Phyllis added it to her stage show, "Tiger" proved to connect no better with live audiences than it did with radio listeners. "I was there," recalled musical director Barry Eastmond. "I can tell you for sure, we were playing it on stage and the reaction from the audience was like, 'What is she doing?' It wasn't the high point of the show. The high point was when we went back and did all the songs from the Buddah days.

"The audience just couldn't understand why she was recording a song like 'Tiger,'" Barry continued. "It just didn't fit her at all. It was an attempt at a dance hit. But you can't fool the audience. They love you for a certain thing and they really want to hear that from you."

Phyllis considered her collaboration with Norman Connors on "Betcha By Golly Wow" to be the real start of her recording career, and she appreciated the prestigious note it started on. "I wanted to get in the serious area of the music business, not in the fly-by-night, hit or miss, one-time-out-and-you're-gone," Phyllis said back in 1979. "People took me very seriously."

But how seriously would anyone take her after listening to "Riding The Tiger?" Phyllis was clear on what she wanted to record and how she wanted to build her career. "Positive thoughts, love and happiness – as long as my lyrics have something good to say, I'm satisfied with it." The problem here was that Phyllis was unsure what the message of "Riding The Tiger" was, or if she was even delivering a message at all.

Phyllis, it should be stated, was not in control. So the fault for "Tiger" must rest with her boss. Though Clive Davis was already by this time an incredibly powerful music industry mogul, his A&R man's instincts, particularly as they related to his black artists, were not always infallible. This is graphically illustrated by his approval of the Walden-produced tracks. "He just sometimes didn't get it," said Gerry Griffith. "It's like, 'Clive, this is just not right for the market. It won't resonate. It won't sell records.' But a lot of times, he'd go with the writer and the producer. And Narada was a guy who could convince anybody.

"Clive never had a feeling for black music," Griffith continued. "That music resonates in our souls, and he never got that. He didn't understand the black cultural connection of jazz and R&B as it relates to black folk, as we relate to it emotionally and how we feel it. He couldn't make that connection. That's why he had to have people around him that understood it; and most of the time, in the early days, he didn't listen to us either."

Andre Perry saw the same thing during his days at Arista. "I give him the highest praise for publishing some of the best songs that were ever recorded," Perry said. "But that doesn't mean you know all music. Clive didn't have his finger on the pulse when it came to R&B."

Even if the Walden tunes clearly missed the mark, there was still gold to be mined from the album. Phyllis recorded eight songs with Bell. Here, tunes like "Your Move, My Heart," "Let Somebody Love You," and "We Should Be Lovers" appeared tailor-made for her. Perhaps that was why Clive could overlook them so easily. Despite working with various producers and trying on several different types of songs, Phyllis's signature style – her pleading, passionate, angst-filled love ballads – was already well established. But five albums later and it had repeatedly failed to connect with both radio and the record-buying public in a powerful way. Clive, giving Phyllis one last if not very concentrated shot, determinedly steered her 180 degrees in the opposite direction.

Only six of the eight tracks Bell produced would ultimately make it onto the album. "I'm Not Asking You To Stay," a real rocker that could have easily been done by Steve Perry of Journey or Mike Reno of Loverboy, and "Is This Love, Must Be Love," a tune that Bell had originally meant to record as a duet between Phyllis and Teddy Pendergrass for *The Fish That Saved Pittsburgh* soundtrack, were passed on by Clive.

Another song that did not make it onto the album was the track that Phyllis cut for her new movie. When Phyllis signed with Maurer Management, Inc., Sid told the trades that he would work to create music and television production companies in tandem with Phyllis. She was already a promising actress, as *Sophisticated Ladies* had proven, and Phyllis was anxious to explore other acting opportunities.

Sid secured a role for her in a film called *The Doorman*. The movie marked the feature film directorial debut of Tony Lo Bianco, who had made a name for himself directing television series such as *Police Story* and made-for-TV movies. *The Doorman* starred Mike Connors, from the TV series *Mannix*, along with Leon Isaac Kennedy and a stiff Anne Archer in her film debut. *The Doorman* was a slasher flick, and Phyllis's role was not even a bit part. She was, essentially, a walk on, with no lines, much like she had been in 1974's *Lenny*, filmed while she was living in Miami.

This time, however, her character did have a name. She played a fashion model/call girl appropriately enough named Phyllis. She was seen in exactly two scenes – one in which she was smoking a marijuana cigarette – and on screen for a total of about three minutes. All in all, the day's work earned Phyllis less than a hundred dollars, scale for extras at this time. But she did live through the end of the film. "I don't get murdered," she said. "Not for $92.50. Actually, it's hard work for relatively little money but it's great experience. Just being around people like Dustin Hoffman and Valerie Perrine in *Lenny* and Mike Connors on this movie teaches you a lot. I was like a kid in a candy store."

The Doorman was not a very prestigious follow up to Phyllis's Tony-nominated debut on Broadway. The film, in fact, was so bad that it never made it to a theatrical release, and Lo Bianco never directed another feature film again, returning, instead, to television.[5] Phyllis, of course, did not yet know the film's fate when she contracted to contribute some songs to the movie's soundtrack.

On May 13, following a show at the Greek Theatre in Los Angeles, Phyllis recorded "I'll Be There," a song written by the film's musical director, George Garvarentz, and Charles Aznavour, and a second one called "Never Say Never Again," which Aznavour, the French actor and composer, wrote with Richard Falcone. In traditional cinematic fashion, the songs were dramatic love ballads, much in the vein of Maureen McGovern's "The

---

[5] *The Doorman* was released on video in 1985, renamed *Too Scared To Scream*.

Morning After" from *The Poseidon Adventure* or Barbra Streisand's "Prisoner," the love theme from *Eyes of Laura Mars*.

According to Phyllis's contract with Doorman Productions, Arista had first rights on "I'll Be There" should the song be released as a single. This didn't happen. Films that don't have theatrical releases don't generally have soundtracks culled from them, and *The Doorman* was no exception. The songs that Phyllis recorded for the movie showed another side to her and proved she was quite capable of moonlighting as a pop princess much the way urban acts like Deniece Williams and The Pointer Sisters were doing with great success at the time. But, sadly, few people would ever actually hear them. For those who saw the video release, "I'll Be There" played over the closing credits while "Never Say Never Again" wasn't featured at all.

Dismal as the film was, Phyllis was upbeat about it in interviews, saying she hoped it would lead to bigger things. "What I would really like to do is some comedy," she told the *Philadelphia Daily News*. "I'm always laughing, and I'd like to be able to make other people laugh."

"Riding The Tiger" entered Billboard's Black Singles chart in late May and managed to make it no farther than number 30 in its 13-week run. That it didn't make it past 30 was not a surprise; that it made it that far was the shocker. The tune was pure pop, but Phyllis had no base there; and without some semblance of R&B success the song could not cross over.[6]

The new album, *Goddess of Love*, was released in June. Keeping with the company line, Phyllis acknowledged the boss in its liner notes, saying "Thank you, Clive Davis. Well, you were right, as always." Phyllis also singled out A&R man Gerry Griffith for special praise. One of the few executives at Arista that Phyllis felt was in her corner, Griffith had pitched Phyllis a new song by

---

[6] Arista must have known, at least in retrospect, that this was the wrong direction for Phyllis. In 1989, when they released the greatest hits package *Phyllis Hyman – Under Her Spell*, the two Narada Michael Walden-produced singles were the only two of Phyllis's charting singles not to be included on the album. One of the Thom Bell-produced songs from the *Goddess* album, "Your Move, My Heart," was included, despite the fact it was never released as a single.

the writing duo of Terry Britten and Graham Lyle. Feeling it wasn't quite right for her, Phyllis passed on "What's Love Got To Do With It," the song that launched Tina Turner's solo career into the stratosphere the following year. As the single went gold for Turner and she picked up a Grammy for best pop performance off of it, Phyllis and Griffith were both deeply disappointed. For Griffith's part, he would soon find redemption at the label with a new discovery.

Griffith got his first glance at Whitney Houston in 1980. Joining her mother, Cissy Houston, on a number at New York's Bottom Line, she was only 17. Impressed with what he heard and saw, Griffith, nevertheless, felt she wasn't quite ready for the majors. But by late 1982, when he caught her once again performing with her mother, this time at Seventh Avenue South, he knew the time for action was now. "I was completely floored," he told *Billboard*. "She was mesmerizing."

There are dueling versions of how he brought her to Clive's attention – some accounts cite Clive attending a show at Sweetwater's supper club at his insistence, while Griffith, himself, recalls setting up a showcase for Clive at Top Cat Studio – but no one disputes that Griffith did bring Whitney to Clive's attention. Whitney was no prettier than Phyllis, and arguably no more vocally gifted. But she was young, not yet 20, and Clive saw in her someone he could mold into a superstar, someone who would play by his rules, someone who would appreciate both his position in the industry and the benefit of his knowledge and experience. Phyllis, in Clive's mind, was difficult, testy and unreliable, and she withheld from him the one thing he craved most: respect.

These were hard times for Phyllis, but she didn't have to weather them alone. In the liner notes to Goddess, Phyllis acknowledged the companionship of her new beau, though the cryptic message didn't mention him by name. "A special thanks to my special friend in Philadelphia who has kept my spirits up and made me happy through this tough time," Phyllis wrote.

That special friend was Nate Robinson, an optician Phyllis had met through her road manager, Craig Hentosh. "I felt like Nate was a very good spirit, a good human being," recalled Craig. "He had a good sense of humor and physically he was a very handsome guy.

He had his own business and I felt that he would be a good person for Phyllis to meet."

Phyllis and Nate hit it off instantly, and soon Phyllis was spending a great deal of time in Nate's West Philadelphia apartment. "I think it was kind of a novelty for Phyllis to just pick herself up out of the madness out of New York City and move herself in West Philadelphia, on this sort of tree lined street with this guy that she was involved with," said Craig. Phyllis enjoyed having dinner ready for Nate when he came home from work each day, doing the laundry, keeping house and just being normal people. "She was really into this whole setting up house and this little domestic scene," Craig continued. "It was sort of a breath of fresh air for her and she was enjoying the diversion."

But Phyllis could only be diverted for so long. There were still steep expenses and rent was due in New York each month, even if she wasn't spending much time there. Phyllis was glad, for the most part, to be back on the road and singing her own songs. Her favorite dates: "Jazz joints, where there are only two or three hundred people and I can feel completely relaxed. Where I can be a comic, a dramatic actress or the consummate singer. But, above all else, where I can touch people. I can feed off of them. That's how I get off."

On July 6, 1983, Phyllis celebrated her 34th birthday with a lavish party in Philadelphia, attended by such celebrity friends as Patti LaBelle. Nate was by her side throughout the evening in a black tuxedo shirt, white bow tie and dark, oversized sunglasses. Phyllis, who had recently cut her hair drastically short, was wearing a black jacket over a gold, sequined halter-top. Guests, including her band, staff and assorted industry friends, partied until the early hours of the morning.

The next week, Phyllis was back on the road, but she barely made it there. She had no money, and Sid's wife, Barbara, had to personally loan her $1,275 to enable the tour to continue. Phyllis was growing increasingly unpredictable, partying hard both at home and on the road – basically anytime she wasn't in Nate's presence. While she would drink in front of anyone, Phyllis rarely indulged in anything more serious in front of her staff or friends.

Percussionist Mayra Casales, though, was an exception, and Phyllis and Mayra would often share a room while on the road.

The exact dates and locations are a blur to Casales, but the incidents themselves, and the wild times she shared with her former employer and friend, are embedded in her mind forever. Once, the two had stayed up half the night. Phyllis awoke the following morning before Mayra did, and ordered breakfast from room service. Not yet dressed, Phyllis asked that her breakfast tray be left outside in the hall. When Phyllis stepped out to get it, though, the door to the room slammed shut behind her. Dressed in only a silk nightgown, Phyllis started pounding on the door. Finally, a hotel guest in a nearby room called the front desk, and someone was dispatched to help the scantily clad singer gain reentry to her room.

"We had hung out and I was passed out," Mayra recalled. "When she got back in the room, she shakes me and wakes me up and she goes, 'Mayra, I've been knocking on that door, girl, and you're passed out, you can't hear me and I got locked out.'

"I looked her up and down, and I go, 'You got locked out like that?' I started laughing, and then she started laughing. I laughed so hard I nearly peed in my pants."

Another time, Phyllis and crew were staying in a hotel with a beautiful pool and spa that Phyllis wanted to take advantage of. Between soundcheck and the show, however, there was little opportunity, and by the time they would return to the hotel after the performance, the pool would be closed. "She said, 'Mayra, do like you do. Call the front desk.'" So Mayra, pretending to be Phyllis's personal assistant, called and spoke to the hotel's manager. She told him that Ms. Hyman, who was paying for more than a dozen rooms in his establishment, would like the exclusive use of the pool area after her performance. The manager agreed, and following her show, Mayra and Phyllis changed into their suits and headed for the sauna, a bottle of white wine in tow.

There was a red light on outside the sauna, so Mayra and Phyllis assumed it was already on. Inside, they talked and drank until the bottle was history. Then it dawned on them – they weren't even sweating.

"So we came out and realized we had been sitting in there for an hour, talking shit and drinking this wine, and the sauna wasn't ever on."

Phyllis's unpredictability and Sid's deteriorating heath demanded a change in their business relationship, and in late July Sid called Phyllis to tell her he needed heart surgery. "I said, 'Phyllis, listen. I gotta go away. I gotta into the hospital. I'm sick.'"

With Maurer out of the picture, Phyllis promoted her personal assistant, Charlene Powell, to the post of manager. Charlene, no longer earning a salary but instead five percent of Phyllis's earnings, did the best she could. But soon it became apparent that additional assistance would be needed. "Charlene had really bitten off a little more than she could chew," Craig Hentosh, Phyllis's road manager, remembered. "She just really wasn't up to the task at hand." Craig had been friends with Glenda Gracia for some years; and Glenda had made a good impression on Phyllis when the two met after Phyllis's Philadelphia concert. Brought on as a consultant, Glenda wasted no time in making some drastic changes around the Command Performances office, a.k.a. Phyllis's one-bedroom Manhattan apartment.

Glenda helped disentangle Phyllis from her booking agent, Norby Walters, and took her to Associated Booking Corporation, where Oscar Cohen agreed to a $10,000 advance to be used in connection with Phyllis's "artistic development." The contract also specifically stipulated that ABC would use their "best efforts" to obtain bookings for Phyllis in Europe, Japan and at "first class hotel rooms" in Las Vegas, Lake Tahoe, Reno and Atlantic City.

Phyllis also wanted to find bookings in Africa, but was adamant about not performing in South Africa. She had recently lent her name to the Artists and Athletes Against Apartheid group, which was co-chaired by Arthur Ashe and Harry Belafonte, and felt strongly about the anti-apartheid movement. In 1981, Phyllis had reportedly been offered $100,000 to visit the country and turned it down flat. "I could not tour South Africa under any circumstances," she said at the time. "I have a moral commitment that supercedes money. My manager put the proposition to me when he got the offer. I believe he was hoping I would say no, but he left it up to me."

Phyllis began thinking a little less about her career and focusing more on her love life as Glenda began to take on more responsibility. Things with Nate Robinson were really starting to heat up and Phyllis realized her feelings for him were quite serious. "I live, breathe, think and eat music, but I am happy because my mate understands me," she said. "I feel relaxed with him because he's the first man I have ever known – ever – who has no hang-ups about my job because, after all, it's only a job. You won't hear me singing in the shower, for example. When I'm at home, I do the laundry and take care of my man. In fact, I really enjoy doing the household chores.

"I'm completely in love and enjoying every minute of it. You see, all of the career success is fine. But it doesn't mean an awful lot unless you've got someone to share it with. I don't hang out any more and it's meant an end to all of my bad habits, except for one – I still love eating. It was time for a new lifestyle for me and I thank Nate and Philadelphia for giving it to me."

In an interview with *Class Magazine*, an off-start of *Right On*, Phyllis elaborated on her relationship with Robinson. "I am involved with the most terrific guy," Phyllis started. "I have finally found an adult. I have finally found someone who I don't have to raise, who I don't have to lead. I am not that great at leading myself. The last thing I needed was a man who was not quite sure."

Of her celebrity, Phyllis said that Nate "handles it better than anyone else that I have ever associated with. That is one of the reasons I decided I would like to put more time in with this man. We are building our lives together. It just seems like we got a nice start. We understand each other and each other's work. Taking care of my home, cleaning, doing the dishes, and planning meals – as funny as it may sound, that has been one of the high points of my life.

"I had been denying that subconsciously. I didn't think that it was the worst thing in the world. I just wasn't into it. Then all of a sudden, with him, these things came very naturally to me. I am enjoying it. My biggest kick is going to the store and figuring out what I am going to make exciting for dinner. It's fun."

Friends say the secret to the relationship's success was Nate's no nonsense approach. Born and raised in Birmingham, Alabama, Nate was from the old school. "He didn't take anything from her," said Tina Stephens. "He was a southern boy, a cave man, you know. He was like 'You're my woman and you're going to do as I say.'"

What Phyllis would never admit is that she actually needed and appreciated such a dominant partner. Men were too often intimidated by her height and celebrity status, and she was happy to have found a man secure enough in himself to call the shots. "She used to talk about leaving the business and settling down with him," Stephens continued. "She was the happiest I'd ever seen her when she was with him." So happy, in fact, that she even began considering starting a family, something she had often questioned her desire to do. "If I get pregnant this time, I'm going to keep it," Phyllis confided to Tina.

Phyllis upped the ante on the relationship with Nate in September, when she agreed to co-sign on an apartment he was leasing in the upscale 2400 Chestnut building in Philadelphia. Now with both her man and her management in the city, Philadelphia was becoming a second home. The move produced a multitude of mixed emotions for Craig Hentosh, Phyllis's road manager. Craig, who lived in Philadelphia, had first met Phyllis at a Valentines Day concert in 1980 in Wilmington, Delaware. Like many of those who would enter Phyllis's inner circle through the years, Craig had started out as a fan. As her employee, his loyalty was total, and his relationship with Phyllis boundary-less.

"As I look back, there were times when I probably should have asserted myself and put my foot down and said, 'You know what? I need some space and I need some time for me,'" said Craig. "But that line between friend and employee, it became very blurred and that was a big problem that contributed to our relationship being rocky at times."

Though he was only paid for the dates he actually worked on the road, Craig was on call day and night. With Phyllis in New York, this wasn't quite as bad. More than an hour away by train, she wasn't likely to call him to run a quick errand. But once she moved to Philly, and with Craig only a few minutes away by car, his responsibilities greatly increased and he became not only Phyllis's road manager, but her personal assistant, valet, friend and confidante all rolled into one. Once she had secured an employee's devotion, as in Craig's case, Phyllis, perhaps out of fear of losing it, was unwilling to share. "She became very possessive," said Craig. "She wanted to control you and keep you for herself."

When Phyllis was especially irritable, or when her insecurities bubbled over and she exploded at Craig, the two would ultimately always reconnect. She'd wait until she knew he was out, then call and leave a message on his answering service. "I love talking to your machine," Craig recalled Phyllis saying. "She would leave me these long rambling messages apologizing and telling me that she missed me and wanted to hang out. She was famous for leaving me these messages on my machine. I guess it was much easier for her."

Arista released a second single from *Goddess* on September 24th. Once again ignoring the Thom Bell sides that made up the bulk of the album, Arista chose the Narada Michael Walden-produced "Why Did You Turn Me On" to service to radio. Radio wasn't buying, though, and the song flopped. It peaked at only number 74 and disappeared after a mere four weeks on the charts. It was the final blow for Phyllis at the label, of this Milton Allen had no doubt. "We pretty much knew when *Goddess of Love* died that that was it," Allen continued. "It was not likely that she was going to be re-signed."

A mere year ago, Phyllis Hyman had been the talk of the town. But by the time 1984 rolled around, the talk was cheap. Something had happened, and Phyllis's star, which had been on this slow upward ascent for years, had begun to fall. Charlene Powell didn't know how to help Phyllis – she had never managed anybody before – and so she decided to remove herself from the situation entirely. Glenda Gracia, already assisting Phyllis with several personal business matters, was the obvious choice to step in. To demonstrate her commitment to restoring Phyllis to personal and professional health, she agreed to temporarily take only three percent of Phyllis's earnings as her managerial cut.

"I wanted to contribute my part to helping her sort of dig herself out and, wisely or unwisely, I didn't feel that burdening her with the normal percentage would have been a prudent move for the beginning of our relationship," said Glenda. "I felt that there would be opportunity down the road – because I was betting on her *and* myself – to enhance her overall financial profile."

"Glenda and I formed a bond because we were both trying to keep Phyllis consistent," recalled Sheila Eldridge, Phyllis's publicist, and one of the few folks Glenda kept on. In addition to switching booking agents, Glenda had also switched Phyllis's accounting firm. "When Glenda came she inherited a very fragile situation, and she was just trying to keep Phyllis working and keep her afloat," said Sheila. "She inherited a tall order. Sid let Phyllis do as she pleased. He didn't really go there with Phyllis like Charles did. Charles used to go there with Phyllis. I mean, she didn't mess with Charles. Then Sid came and he just kind of let her go. Then when Glenda came in she had a lot of cleaning up to do."

For a time, Phyllis was in negotiation to reprise her role in *Sophisticated Ladies* for a European tour. But that never materialized. So the show was now definitely a part of her past. She had, however, incorporated some of the Ellington songs into her stage act. The two years Phyllis gave to *Sophisticated Ladies* was time well spent, and she had learned a lot from it.

Since the close of the show, Phyllis had spent a fair amount of time on the road. But without a hit, she had been forced to reduce her nightly rate substantially. For years, she had lived off of the advances for her records. Now, there were no more of those. The $10,000 advance from ABC was long gone and the bills were mounting. She was bouncing checks to both her creditors and her staff with alarming consistency. All told, Phyllis started 1984 with over $50,000 in past due bills.

Glenda looked to Arista to solve Phyllis's financial crisis, believing that the key to a turnaround was in producing a hit record. She initiated a series of meetings with Arista to ascertain the prospects. But what she discovered was by no means encouraging. *Goddess of Love* had sold a mere 80,000 copies, and Phyllis owed Arista more than all of her creditors combined. Her debt to the label, including all advances and album-related expenses to date, was the sobering sum of $429,466 – nearly half a million dollars.

If Phyllis distrusted Clive Davis before learning this, she now loathed him. Phyllis was furious; at Clive, who no longer paid her any attention, at Whitney Houston, who was now getting all of Clive's attention, at the record industry in general and at the entire world around her. Her anger ate at her, and gradually it began to spill over onto her stage show.

Phyllis had always been direct with her audience, quaintly candid. But now anything that crossed her mind could find its way into her show. Though she hadn't even officially filed for a divorce from Larry, she began attacking him from the stage. "Some of you know that I used to be married," Phyllis told an audience at the Beverly Theatre in Los Angeles. "I used to have a husband. Well, believe me, it wasn't all that bad. I'm sure there are many of us out there who had husbands and thank God we ain't got 'em no more. Same goes with you guys now. You had some tacky wives and you got rid of them, too. I won't lie to you or tell you that he was a bad guy. He was really a nice guy. But what happens in so many relationships, after a long period of time, is that somebody, or both parties, ceases to communicate. You know what I mean, girls and guys? Well, I married a deaf mute. I mean he wasn't handicapped or nothing. The nigga just couldn't talk!"

Phyllis then sang a song she said she had written for Larry to drive home the point. Titled "Give A Little More," it was a pleasant mid-tempo number that dealt rather eloquently with the sensitive subject matter of relationship problems without carrying the emotional weight that many of her later songs would.[7] By now, Phyllis's band has grown accustomed to her onstage tirades, even if they still made them uncomfortable. But there was nothing to be done about it. Phyllis had a special way of sharing what was on her mind with her audience. "Sometimes she would share it and sometimes she would knock you over the head with it," said Miles Jaye. "She would take on anybody, and what a formidable

---

[7] NOTE: "Give A Little More" had actually been released on the *You Know How To Love Me* album in 1979, one year after Phyllis married Larry. On the album, Phyllis and Larry shared writer's credit on the song along with Howie Schneider, Phyllis's one-time pianist.

adversary. I mean, listen, you better have your game face on or else you back down. And I've seen many an individual, male, female or otherwise, back down."

Barry Eastmond agreed. "It was always unpredictable with Phyllis. That was just the way it was. She had quite a personality and sometimes it got a little tense on stage because we just didn't know where she was going to go or what was going to happen. But it kept it really interesting. And, musically, it was phenomenal. She pushed the band and really made us all better musicians. She was unpredictable in that she might say something that might shock everybody. Then she'd go back and do the show. It was just the way Phyllis was and we accepted it."

After Phyllis finished berating her estranged husband from the stage, she continued with the show as if nothing out of the ordinary had happened. Her singing throughout the evening was particularly heavy, though, and she dragged "Somewhere In My Lifetime" out into an eight-minute gospel-infused testimony.

"I never sang in church, you know," she told the crowd during an interlude in the song. "But I bet you what, when you black you can fake it."

Chapter 9

There were some nice records, but I'd say 70 percent of the time being with Arista was a nightmare.

Phyllis spent most of 1984 on tour. Except for her semi-annual stints at Blues Alley in Washington, D.C., and Fat Tuesday's in New York, most of Phyllis's concert dates were one-nighters, which made the road that much more grueling. She was earning $5,000-$7,500 a night, but her overhead was high. ABC took 10 percent of this fee, Glenda, who had generously reduced her rate from that industry standard, an additional three percent, and out of the balance Phyllis had to pay the band and pick up the tab on the travel and lodging for the group. This could be quite costly when you consider that Phyllis often traveled with an entourage of 12, including an eight-member band, soundman Ethan Orlovitz plus an additional tech, a road manager and a personal valet.

As a cost-cutting measure, Glenda convinced Phyllis to reduce the size of her staff. "When you are restructuring and reorganizing financially, you cut your costs, period, on every level," Glenda explained. For most of 1984, Phyllis performed with only a trio – Terry Burrus on keyboards, who acted as musical director, Tracy Wormworth on bass and Kyle Hicks on drums – behind her. On occasion, Mayra Casales, who first started with Phyllis in 1979, would join in on percussion. Burrus, who had left Stanley Turrentine to come play with Phyllis, initially left her after only a few dates.

"I didn't like her," said Burrus. "I thought she was wonderful to look at, but I didn't like her. It was something in the way she treated her assistants. I wasn't quite used to that. She was very bossy. I had just come on board, and usually if I start to see something like that I leave, because there were too many other artists I was working with and I didn't need that kind of headache."

Burrus bowed out of Phyllis's band and took a job with Lena Horne whose one-woman show, *A Lady and Her Music*, had just finished its Broadway run and was now playing in Europe. Soon Burrus was set up with an apartment in London. But when he called his New York apartment to check in for messages, there was a familiar voice on his answering machine. "I'm sorry if I bothered you or whatever," said Phyllis. "Please come back." Burrus didn't even return the call. But Phyllis was persistent. She knew that Burrus was just what her band needed, and on a trip home to visit his family, Phyllis tracked him down at his parents' house. "She said, 'Please come and play with me. I'm sorry if I upset you.'"

Phyllis's persistence paid off, and after the two had a heart to heart, Burrus agreed to return to her band. "It's so funny," he said. "She never bothered me again. We had a great time. At least, I had a great time. I really, really enjoyed performing with her. In the beginning, I didn't want to be around her. But when I came in the second time, you know, you had your rocky roads, your rocky moments, but she became like my big sister."

Cutbacks or not, road manager Craig Hentosh still traveled with Phyllis, and she wasn't ready to part with her personal valet, Carlos Suarez, either. The group was at LaGuardia Airport on March 24 en route to a show in Miami when their flight was canceled. Standing in a massive line at the ticket counter trying to book another flight, Phyllis was recognized instantly by Tymm Holloway, an employee of Piedmont Airlines. Tymm approached her and asked if he could be of any assistance, and soon he had them rerouted onto another flight and on their way. In return for his kindness, Phyllis invited Holloway to come to her show the next time she was playing New York. "She gave me all her info, and of course I took her up on it the first chance I got."

That chance came in early May when Phyllis was at Fat Tuesdays for a week. After the show, Holloway was delighted to be invited back to Phyllis's apartment. Once there, though, Phyllis found her cupboards bare and the best she could rustle up were bacon sandwiches with barbeque sauce. If Holloway was expecting more from the visit – in the way of cuisine or the décor in the modest one-bedroom apartment – he gave no indication.

"We were woofin' those sandwiches down like it was White Castle," he said. "I wasn't like, 'Is this is all you have?' or "I can't believe you can't afford something more.' We ate those sandwiches like little kids. Other people might have been like, 'This all you got? No hamburgers or steak?' But that's what she conjured up and from that point on there was no drama; there were no issues."

Following their little barbeque bacon sandwich fiesta, Holloway and Phyllis became fast friends. In fact, he soon started calling her "mom" and she, in return, affectionately referred to him as her son. "What I liked was we could talk about, and be candid about, anything," continued Tymm. "It was never forced or strained."

ABC did an excellent job of promoting Phyllis. They secured her a spot on the Kool City Jam Festival summer tour, and that combined with the additional bookings they brought in barely left Phyllis a chance to breathe throughout the season. Even with its size drastically reduced, Phyllis's band was tight. "The trio, musically, had gotten so strong," said Burrus. "A lot of groups at that time really couldn't touch us. There was just something magical about that Phyllis Hyman voice. The shows were fantastic."

Glenda was also proving handy and was kept busy with the task of bringing order to Command Performances. "It was wonderful," Craig Hentosh recalled of having Glenda at the helm. "She brought a real sense of organization and a lot of structure into the scene." More importantly, her experience as an attorney allowed her to help extricate Phyllis from the legal muddles she could not seem to escape. The latest of these came about when her landlord in New York, R.W. Kern, Inc., tried to evict her for falling behind in her rent.

If this wasn't enough, Phyllis was being audited by the Internal Revenue Service. The IRS, known for the watchful eye it kept over entertainers, had found discrepancies in her 1977 income tax returns. With Glenda's help, Phyllis had to scramble to locate all the musicians who had played for her in 1977 and get them to sign affidavits attesting to the cash payments she had made to them that year.

Financial difficulties aside, Phyllis was nothing if not generous. "Phyllis was the type of person that she would see a homeless person on the street and give them money," said Tina Stephens, her friend and former production coordinator. "She was one of the most generous persons you could meet. She would give somebody her last dime. There was not a time when I needed something that I didn't know I could call Phyllis, and if she had it she would help me.

"Phyllis would never go in a store with you and not buy you something, even if it was just a tube of lipstick," Stephens continued. "I mean, anybody that worked with her. That was just how she was. She was generous to a fault."

Indeed, in the midst of her fiscal crisis, Phyllis continued to send a monthly allowance, which ranged from $200 - $500, to her mother in Pittsburgh. Phyllis also regularly sent money to her father and grandmother, and could be counted on to bail out her siblings when they were in need. When her sister Jeannie left her husband and relocated temporarily to Kansas in September 1983, Phyllis loaned her $500. This when she could not even afford to pay her own rent.

Nate was another one she often had to help out financially, and this proved to be a genuine problem in their relationship. Phyllis was looking for someone to make her feel safe – physically, emotionally *and financially* – and unfortunately Nate only scored at two out of three. When she'd co-signed on the apartment, it was with the understanding that Nate would pay the rent. But by the summer of 1984, Nate was depending on Phyllis to cover him. An entrepreneur, Nate was trying to get his own optometry business off the ground. Phyllis, believing that if the business succeeded perhaps so, too, would their relationship, loaned Nate more than $3,000 to keep it going.

Glenda believed the answer to Phyllis's financial problems was a hit record. She also wisely understood that there was damage control to be done at Arista and, to that end, arranged for a lunch meeting with Phyllis, Clive and Gerry Griffith. "I knew that she and Clive Davis were not on the greatest terms because she felt that he wasn't really seeing her," Glenda recalled. "I knew that it created great conflict for her because, of course, Clive was just trying to do what he thought was important for her career and his company's bottom line, which was to develop an artist that would be very popular and sell lots of records.

"Phyllis admitted that she hadn't been as cooperative, perhaps, as she needed to be at times," Glenda continued. "I think that's what drove us to have the reconciliation meeting with Clive. She was very interested in reconciling with him. They had reached, for all intents and purposes, a creative impasse, and potentially a professional impasse. So the purpose of the meeting was to create this sort of new relationship and to move it forward and to demonstrate to Clive that there was a new intention – a new feeling, if you will – that Phyllis wanted to demonstrate that she trusted him, that she would for all intents and purposes allow him to do what it was that he felt was best for her and her career."

Glenda recalled that Clive responded positively to the meeting and she thought that Phyllis and the label were finally on the same page. Following the lunch meeting, Glenda began speaking with the label about plans for the next album. Showing up for what she thought was to be an A&R meeting with Gerry Griffith, the executive dropped the bombshell: Phyllis was being dropped from the label. Glenda had been blind sighted. "I was flabbergasted," she recalled.

For his part, Griffith said he had nothing to do with the decision to let Phyllis go, and that Clive came up with that one on his own. "I got stuck in the middle of that thing. I would never have dropped her. Never, ever, in life – if it were up to me – would I ever have dropped Phyllis Hyman from my label. I loved her too much. She was just so amazingly special in so many ways."

Phyllis had her own theory to explain why she was being let go. Clive, she believed, had never forgiven her for accepting the role in *Sophisticated Ladies* against his wishes. "I got that role by myself," she said. "Clive Davis didn't like it. He said the show was going to fail. I said, 'Watch.' And, of course, it didn't fail. It was a huge success. I don't think he ever forgave me for that. Instead of buying the soundtrack to *Sophisticated Ladies*, they bought *Woman of the Year* with Lauren Bacall. They ignored me. Shunned me. But Arista taught me a lot. If anything, I'm grateful. I won't ever let other people push my buttons again."

No sweat off her back, Phyllis said she was glad to be gone from the label. "There were some nice records, but I'd say 70 percent of the time being with Arista was a nightmare."

Ironically, for all its inability to produce a real hit on Phyllis, Arista was a haven for soulful female heavyweights at this time. In the early '80s, the label had effortlessly revived the careers of Dionne Warwick and the queen of soul, herself, Aretha Franklin. Now, by all indications, they were primed to take a newcomer, Whitney Houston, who was actually Dionne's cousin, straight through the roof. Her duet with Teddy Pendergrass on the Asylum label, "Hold Me," entered *Billboard's* R&B chart, where it would eventually peak at number 5, the same week the label sent Phyllis her walking papers. Arista also paired Whitney up with Jermaine Jackson on a song called "Take Good Care Of My Heart" for his self-titled release on the label. This strategy – introducing a newcomer by featuring them on the releases of established stars – was not uncommon. Yet they'd never employed the tactic on Phyllis, which might have been the best way to introduce her to the pop market.

Clive once explained his knack for creating hit records as such: "You gotta find artists who are unique; you gotta find material that could become standards." He also said that vocalists who do not write their own material "have to bring songs to life in a manner never thought of." Phyllis, obviously, was a unique artist, and she could breathe life into the dullest of compositions. Yet a fair share of her material, which all received the green light from Arista's A&R department, was obviously not destined to become standards.

Surely Clive knew this when he heard songs such as "Goddess of Love" and "Riding The Tiger." When Clive signed Whitney Houston in April of 1983, while Phyllis was very much still on the roster, he spent months finding the right material for her debut album and even went on a nationwide search, conducting bi-coastal showcases with his new discovery to solicit material for review. When you consider the concentrated effort Clive put into Whitney, compared to the relative nonchalance with which Clive treated Phyllis, it's easy to understand why Phyllis came to resent them both so deeply.

When Clive offered Whitney an album contract, he set the budget for the album at $175,000, more than double the amount Arista had allotted for the recording of *Goddess Of Love*. Clive planned to pair Whitney up with four different and in-demand producers who would record songs he hand picked with Griffith and his A&R team. Still, insiders say that at this point Clive wasn't convinced that Whitney was as much a great talent as she was a great package. She was a young, professional model with a solid reputation and a pedigree that included her mother, respected vocalist Cissy Houston, her cousin, Dionne Warwick, who was Clive's favorite vocalist of all time, and Aretha Franklin for a godmother. So how could he lose?

"At this point, the executive was still not all that wowed by her voice, but he told himself and his staff that with all these marketable ingredients there was no reason in the world why they couldn't turn Houston into a household name," wrote James Robert Parish in *Whitney Houston: The Unauthorized Biography*. "The more he talked about the challenge, the more he became convinced that he had a winner in the making."

In Phyllis's case, Clive was confident in her voice, but he obviously felt that her stubbornness and independence proved too great a challenge to conquer. Clive could have made Phyllis a superstar, but at a cost she was unwilling to pay. She needed to feel that her input and opinions mattered. She needed to be shown that she was valued and respected for who and what she was, not just what some record mogul thought he could make her into. But her independence and integrity came at a high cost. Many think that Phyllis could have today been the household name that Whitney became had she been willing to do it Clive's way.

"Without a doubt; without a doubt; without a doubt!" exclaimed Sheila Edridge. "I have always said that Whitney got the songs, she got all the hit-making that Clive would have put into Phyllis."

Despite her inordinately busy schedule and her pressing financial difficulties, Phyllis still found time to host her teenage nieces – Jeannie's daughter Tamani and Ann's daughter Tamyra – for a visit in the summer of 1984. Phyllis's maternal instincts were not very finely tuned, and even as she shared small living quarters with her nieces, her contact with them was limited. "Really and truthfully, there weren't that many hands on experiences," said Tamani Eldridge.

There were chats, though, and those were always special. "We'd talk. We had an open forum. That was something I can honestly say. We could get in her bed and talk." Jeannie had encouraged her older sister to talk to her nieces about their career choices and to get them looking toward the future. But Phyllis didn't take much time with the topic. "Basically, when she would bring things like that up, she would be like, 'This is what you need to do. Do it. Don't let no man get in your way.' Then we could go back to the mundane. She wasn't parenting us. So if we came home and we bought something she wouldn't be like, 'Those are poor choices that you're making.' She wouldn't do that. She'd be like, 'That was stupid. Don't do that tomorrow. See if you can take it back,' and we would move on."

Phyllis spent a significant portion of the summer on tour with the Kool City Jam Festival, which was paying her $7,500 a night. Combined with the independent bookings brought in by ABC, Phyllis was on the road more than she was home. At the end of August, Phyllis had her mother join her for a date in Columbia, South Carolina. After the concert at the Township Auditorium, the band flew back to New York, while Phyllis and the elder Ms. Hyman boarded a plane bound for Greensboro, North Carolina, where the annual Hyman Family Reunion was taking place. The following evening, Nate flew in from Philadelphia – at Phyllis's expense – to join them. Phyllis's mother had met Nate some months earlier when she visited with Phyllis in Philadelphia and taken an instant liking to her daughter's beau. She even went so far as to start referring to herself as his "adopted mom." Now, in North Carolina, Phyllis's sisters – indeed her whole family – became enamored with Nate and his southern charm.

Despite the Hyman family's affection for him, things between Nate and Phyllis cooled shortly after the trip to Greensboro. Phyllis's celebrity, and her frequent touring, inevitably took a toll. "At first, I think he enjoyed being in the limelight with her," said Craig Hentosh. "But I think it wore thin rather quickly." In addition, as time wore on, it became impossible to ignore the magnitude of Phyllis's personal struggles, and if Phyllis wasn't ready to address them, what could Nate do? "Nate didn't have the full capacity required to be committed to someone such as Phyllis, given the nature of many of her issues," explained Glenda. "I think her issues just wore their relationship thin."

As the relationship came to a close, Phyllis instructed Glenda to set up a meeting with Nate to formally make arrangements for the repayment of all the loans she'd extended. Phyllis was feeling the need to tie up the loose ends in her life and for a while they began to come together. The day before Glenda's meeting with Nate, Phyllis received word that the arbitration on the Manhattan apartment had been successful and that R.W. Kern would issue her a new two-year lease.

Two days later, her divorce from Larry finally came through, which had been held up while the two talked money. "Larry was her manager and husband, and so I guess he felt that she was obliged to support him in some way," said Glenda. "I didn't feel that she was obliged to do that." In the end, Phyllis agreed to cough up $5,000, a small price for her freedom.

Phyllis was also trying to broaden her professional horizons and find new ways to make a living. *Sophisticated Ladies* was still close enough in the rearview mirror to win her the opportunity of a lifetime, and soon Phyllis secured an audition with Steven Spielberg. The veteran director of such epics as *Raiders of the Lost Ark* and *Close Encounters of the Third Kind*, Spielberg was beginning work on his adaptation of the Alice Walker novel *The Color Purple*. Phyllis, because of her vocal ability, was being offered the chance to read for the part of Shug Avery, the saloon chanteuse of the film.

Glenda and her partner Sydney Francis could not get Phyllis to read *The Color Purple*. So Sydney did the next best thing. She read it to her. "I couldn't believe I had to read a book to an adult, but I did it," Sydney recalled. "I read it to her line by line and page by page. I helped her get a sense of the character."

Phyllis auditioned for casting director Reuben Cannon in Chicago and New York, and he was duly impressed. "He called Spielberg and said, 'I've found Shug Avery. The search is over,'" said Glenda.

When the time came to audition for Spielberg, Sydney traveled with Phyllis to Los Angeles. At the Hollywood Sheraton, Phyllis met up with Whoopi Goldberg, Oprah Winfrey and Danny Glover. Together, they all traveled by van to Spielberg's compound. Goldberg was particularly impressed with Phyllis. "She was thrilled to see her," Sydney said. "She told Phyllis, 'I love you. I'm so glad you're here. I wanted you to be in this.'"

Once at Spielberg's place, the hopeful actors were ushered into his ensemble room. Sydney was not allowed to accompany Phyllis inside, and instantly she grew worried. She had traveled to California to hold Phyllis's hand. Now she had to release her grip. Sydney knew that Phyllis was nervous, and that when she became anxious, anything could happen.

Shortly before lunchtime, the doors to the ensemble room opened. "Whoopi was the first one out," said Sydney. "She didn't even look at me. She walked right on past me." Next out was Danny Glover. "Your girl acted out," he whispered to Sydney. "She was trying to run the audition. She was ordering Steven around."

Sydney was mortified. Still, she was not surprised. "That was Phyllis's M.O. When she got scared, she tried to take over things so she could regain control. She lost the part because they could not wrap their heads around being with Phyllis for five months in North Carolina while they shot the film."

Later, when she spoke of the incident, Phyllis did so with indifference. "I tried my best, but I didn't see myself in the part," she said. "I live in the real world. I'm my own manager and agent. I knew I wasn't right for it."

Not so, said Sheila Eldridge, Phyllis's publicist. "She wanted that part. She was devastated. She knew that part was for her." Instead, the role went to Margaret Avery who, not being a singer, had to have her vocals in the film overdubbed by Tata Vega. It's difficult not to imagine Phyllis in the role, and consider what it could have done for her career.

It's also tragic to see the pattern that was forming. For as much as she craved it, Phyllis was scared of success. Totally terrified. Glenda and Sydney were working hard to take Phyllis to the next level. But every time they reached the brink, Phyllis sabotaged herself and her chances. Just as Phyllis would pull back in her personal relationships when someone managed to get too close, she did the same when it came to her career. She just could not tolerate succeeding beyond a certain point. The risk was too painful. The pressure too intense.

As the holidays arrived, Phyllis's baby sister Anita arrived in New York for an extended visit, her four-year daughter Qiana in tow. Anita had recently separated from her husband and needed some time to find herself. Phyllis was supportive, but the close quarters of her one-bed room apartment afforded Anita a view of her sister's life that she'd never seen before. It was a healthy dose of reality. "I looked at her life as glamorous until I lived with her and I realized it wasn't," Anita said. "She worked hard."

One of Anita's fondest memories from this visit is the time the two ventured out in the bitter winter weather and were in the back of a warm taxi when Phyllis spotted a homeless woman on a street corner without a coat. "She made the cab driver stop and she took her coat off and gave it to her."

"Now you ain't got no coat," Anita told her big sister, clearly shocked.

"Do you know how many fucking coats I have?" Phyllis answered.

"Oh, OK. Why don't you give *me* one of them damn coats then?" Anita joked, and the two shared a special laugh.

"There were two sides of Phyllis," Anita said. "I've seen some real good times. But she had a mean streak, too. She had another side to her. If you crossed her, it was hard for her to forgive you."

Chapter 10

There's a certain depth of understanding that comes from keeping it all the family.

As the search began for a new recording home for Phyllis, Glenda didn't have to look far. She had known Kenny Gamble since she was in law school, and had worked for him while at the Black Music Association. Gamble, along with Leon Huff, owned the Philadelphia International record label. Together, and often with the aid of writer/producer Thom Bell, the pair created what came to be known as the "Philly Sound," "a multi-layered, bottom-heavy brand of sophistication and glossy urban rhythm and blues, characterized by crisp, melodious harmonies backed by lush, string-laden orchestrations and a hard-driving rhythm section," as described by John Jackson in his 2004 book *A House On Fire: The Rise and Fall of Philadelphia Soul*.

Jackson maintained that Philadelphia International was "pop music's last great independent 'hit factory.'" By 1985, however, the factory had long since shuttered its doors. The label had spent the past two years without a distributor, and the only viable act still on its roster was the O'Jays. Now, though, they had finally succeeded in inking a new distribution deal, this time with Capitol-EMI, the third largest power in the recording industry behind CBS and WEA (Warner-Elektra-Atlantic). The news was music to Glenda's ears. Once she learned of Kenny Gamble's interest in Phyllis, she passionately pursued a deal. In so doing, Glenda overlooked a crucial fact about the Philadelphia International Records empire. The label's historical strongpoint was male recording artists, and their track record with female vocalists was less than stellar.

"In my mind, women weren't his forte," said Joe Tarsia, the owner of Sigma Sound, PIR's recording studio of choice, and the man who engineered most of PIR's hits. "Kenny didn't know how to cut women." According to Jackson, Gamble was "a chauvinist at heart." The son of a Jehovah's Witness, in 1976, Gamble converted to the Nation of Islam, taking on the name Luqman Abdul-Haqq. Soul singer and one time PIR recording artist Jerry Butler claimed that Gamble's focus in songwriting was "for the male ego. It was kind of his personality that he was writing."

Nelson George, in his book *The Death of Rhythm & Blues*, said that Gamble's personal message, "a tough, male-dominant, anti-materialistic perspective," could be found in his most of his music. But that didn't scare off Glenda, who knew Kenny better than most. "I felt that if he could write one hit on her first album like he wrote for Teddy Pendergrass, I was going to be a happy camper."

Philadelphia International wasn't the only offer on the table – Glenda was also speaking with Larkin Arnold, who had moved on from Arista to CBS Records, and Bruce Lundvall of Capitol/EMI – but the deal with PIR was the frontrunner from the start. Phyllis felt Arista had been too big for her. There she was forced to compete with many other female artists for songs, producers, marketing dollars and, perhaps most importantly, the attention of the label's head. The same would not be so at PIR where, like she had been at Buddah, Phyllis would once again be a big fish in a little pond. She needed that personalized attention to make her feel safe. "Kenny Gamble's offer seemed to be the most appealing," said Glenda. "Not only in terms of his huge success as a producer, but his boutique independent label was very, very appealing to me, Sydney and Phyllis."

There was also another factor that played heavily into Glenda advising Phyllis to sign with PIR. "Kenny said something to me that was for all intents and purposes the key to making the decision about where to go, and it was that he heard a 'tear' in Phyllis's voice," Glenda said. "I knew, based on him saying that, that he was compelled to capture that in her recordings, that he was really onto something. It was my hope that he would be able to tailor-make and produce songs for Phyllis's voice unlike anyone else had."

The deal was not fantastic. Kenny would go no higher than a $50,000 signing advance, the same amount Phyllis had received for signing with Arista back in 1978. But there was one major perk: PIR was willing to give Phyllis a two-album deal. "At that time, most labels only wanted to give you a one-album deal, and then they wanted options to give you additional albums," said Glenda. "But coming out of the Arista episode, a one-album deal would have made Phyllis feel really skittish because if the first album didn't do all we hoped it would, there was the risk of her not getting picked up."

Financially, it was not the deal that Glenda was hoping for. But most important, it was a deal. And while the PIR contract was not as generous as Arista's, that wasn't necessarily a bad thing. There was no guarantee that Phyllis's albums for PIR would sell any better than her Arista albums. Thanks to Arista's "front loaded" contract, Phyllis had never quite been able to catch up to her advances, part of the reason she was still heavily in debt to the label. It was a pattern she did not need to repeat at PIR.

It was, for the most part, a good period for Phyllis. She was once again a signed artist and, perhaps most importantly to her, she was once again keeping company with an attractive man. Phyllis had met Tad Fennar while on a rare excursion to the supermarket, an errand that was generally delegated to one of her assistants. "I met him over the tomatoes," she laughed. "He has great teeth. He's a joy to me. I can be testy, but he stands up to me and I like that."

Fennar, a full thirteen years her junior and only 23 at the time, was working for a Philadelphia television station when he met Phyllis. Like Nate and Larry, Tad was tall, relatively light-skinned and had at least part of the requisite facial hair – in this case a mustache. With Nate out of the picture, as well as the Philadelphia apartment, Phyllis had been lonely and was relieved to once again find companionship. It was also another reason to spend more time in Philly, where she began working on her debut PIR album in July. Ironically, one of the first songs presented to her was a tune co-written by Kenny Gamble, Dexter Wansel and Cynthia Biggs, called "Living All Alone." "I said, 'OK, who told 'em? Who told 'em Nate left?'" Phyllis said of receiving the song. "I was so pissed."

Though Phyllis had a very deep well of internal pain she could draw from to deliver a convincing performance on this and any other lyric put before her, Phyllis was actually falling in love when she recorded this, one of the saddest songs ever to find a place in her repertoire. That irony is understandable to Phyllis's nieces, who returned in the summer of 1985 for another visit. "She was lonely," said Tamani. "Even in the midst of when she would have boyfriends, she was lonely, moody and sad. A lot of times, even as a teenager, I realized that when she was acting out it was because of her loneliness."

Most noted a distinct change in Phyllis's overall personality when she was involved with someone, yet she could still find herself in love and despair at the same time. "She could love in a very deep, deep way," explained Glenda. "She had the capacity to love so deeply that she would become empathic, meaning that she was so sensitive that she could actually *feel* the feelings and the pain of others."

Her play son Tymm recalled a visit to Phyllis's apartment when he had parked his car in a garage on Broadway. On the phone with a friend, Phyllis was oblivious to Tymm until the precise moment he started to panic, pondering how long he'd been in the apartment. "I was thinking, 'Wow, I better get going, that thing is by the hour,' and she turned to me like, 'What's wrong.' She was already in my thought. She was like, 'Why is he so pensive?' She's all in her conversation on the phone, yet she was also in my head. I think most people didn't know that she had those capabilities. She was very intuitive. So she knew where you going before you did."

On average, Phyllis's nieces were spared her outbursts. When they did get caught in the mix, it helped to have the other to commiserate with. "That was our buffer," Tamani said. "We knew that if she was having a bad moment or staff was having a bad moment – because of her, usually – we had each other to bounce it off of. When she would have her moments, usually she stayed in her room. She didn't bombard us with always being mean to us or things like that."

By their second visit, the realities of Phyllis's existence were becoming harder to ignore. "The surprising thing to me was that things weren't that grand," said Tamani. "She lived pretty much a boring life. I couldn't understand how things could be so extreme: from the stage to wanting to be in her bed the majority of the time. That just seemed kind of strange. Now that I'm older it seems bigger than that. I can't imagine being that old and not really having a sense of self."

For Phyllis's first PIR album, Kenny Gamble paired her up with some of the staples of the Philly Sound, including, of course, himself. "Everyone was excited that Phyllis was going to be walking through those halls and going into that studio – everyone, from the receptionist to the people in business affairs," recalled Glenda. "All of the musicians, all of the writers, were just like, 'Wow, can I get on Phyllis's album? Can I write one of her smashes? C'mon, Gams, give me a turn.' It was electric there." Abuzz as the place may have been, not everything Kenny brought to Phyllis sizzled with the sound of a hit.

"They brought me some things at first that just weren't right for me and what I appreciated was that they went back to the drawing board to come up with some music that did fit," said Phyllis. In retrospect, Gamble is not sure he made the right move. "I think I might have messed up a little," he said. "I should have made her do some of those things. But she was a big baby and I went along with her because she was my main girl. Normally, I would have convinced an artist to do those songs. I would have bargained with them. But I was really trying to find out how to make her happy, because then I thought we could get the best performance out of her."

Gamble also brought in Thom Bell, whom Phyllis had enjoyed working with on *Goddess*, and Dexter Wansel, PIR's head of A&R, and his writing partner Cynthia Biggs. Together, Wansel and Biggs had penned Patti LaBelle's number one record "If Only You Knew."

Wansel and Biggs began writing with Phyllis in mind as soon as word came down the pipeline that she had signed to the label. "I remember Dexter was sitting at the piano in our office and he was basically working out the chords to the verse and the pre-hook and the chorus of a new song," Biggs recalled. "Gamble happened to be strolling by and heard the music playing, and he stopped and gave us the hook line. Then he told me to finish the lyrics. Thus, you had 'Living All Alone.'" The candid tale of a woman pining for her lost love and remembering the joy she knew when they were together, the undercurrent of loneliness struck a chord with Phyllis immediately.

When the time came to record the song, which was produced by Dexter, Phyllis "was not in a good mood at all," said Biggs. "I remember her saying, 'Here I am again recording another album that's not going to go gold.' She just felt like, 'Why do I keep trying?'" Phyllis was scared. Thoughts that the album would be another commercial failure or that it would be a commercial smash were both equally frightening to her. Here, her fear manifested as agitation, and she took it out on Biggs, who was wearing jeans and a Philly International T-shirt.

"She called me a refugee," Biggs remembered. "Glenda, who was in the studio at the time, immediately read Phyllis the riot act. Then Dexter took her outside of the studio and reprimanded her because he felt that was unfair for her to attack me like that. But we could see beyond it, and see that she was reacting to something she was going through about being in the studio."

At Glenda's suggestion, Dexter cut the third verse from the song to make room for Phyllis's haunting whistle. "Phyllis's ad lib during the tag of the song was so powerful that when Dexter edited the song he made a production decision to feature that," said Biggs, who didn't mind if a few of her words ended up missing from the final cut. "Phyllis had one of the most beautiful voices I've heard in my lifetime, just a magnificent instrument."

One newcomer on the scene was Nick Martinelli, a newly-signed client of Gracia, Francis & Associates. Martinelli, himself a Philadelphia native, had started out on the local club scene as a deejay. Soon enough though, he was producing records for the independent Philly World label. His breakthrough effort was his work for the British group Loose Ends. Martinelli had recorded a song on the group, "Hangin' On A String (Contemplating)," in Philadelphia's Sigma Sound Studios that had just made it all the way to number one on the R&B chart as work on Phyllis's new album began.

That work was grueling at times. Phyllis was not a fan of the recording studio, and at times her fear and doubt – of success and whether she deserved it, of being happy in life and love and whether that realized happiness would look anything like how she envisioned it – overwhelmed her. When this happened, Phyllis coped the only way she knew how, by looking to alcohol and cocaine to take her out of the moment when she couldn't bare to be alone with her thoughts a second longer.

The drinking was no secret, but Phyllis tried to keep her cocaine usage under her hat. Inevitably, though, those in the inner circle would discover it one way or another. Glenda had become aware even before she took over managerial duties from Charlene Powell, when Powell told her Phyllis had "a problem" she did not know how to address. Slowly, as Glenda took the reigns, a pattern began forming. Phyllis would come off the road and completely shut herself off from the world for a day or two.

Being on stage, for Phyllis, was the ultimate high. When she left it, when she relinquished that special connection she had with her audience and returned to the isolation of her apartment, Phyllis came crashing down. Unable to regulate her emotions, to modulate her affect and transition from the road to home peacefully, Phyllis looked to cocaine to replicate the high of the stage. In so doing, Phyllis never addressed the pain of this transition or sought an authentic way to make it easier on herself. Instead, the drug helped her to avoid making the transition all together. She simply replaced the adrenaline high of the stage with the synthetic high of cocaine until she exhausted her stash and hit rock bottom. Then, the following weekend, the cycle would begin all over again.

In the first year or so of their professional relationship, Phyllis would always resurface within 48 hours. But now, she was spending more and more time with her addiction, and her erratic behavior was threatening to blow the best career opportunity to come her way in some time. Punctuality had never been Phyllis's strong suit, but now she was blowing off commitments entirely, including recording sessions. "Phyllis's behavior was getting ready to track her for disaster, and that was not on the agenda, as far as I was concerned," said Glenda. "I wanted to make sure that she didn't hurt herself or her opportunities. So I stepped in."

Glenda, with the help of her partner Sydney and Phyllis's boyfriend Tad, planned an intervention. "The three of us basically ambushed Phyllis," recalled Glenda. "We just confronted her." Tad kept Phyllis at home, in her apartment at 2400 Chestnut, and Glenda and Sydney made an unannounced house call after leaving the office for the day. Once there, the foursome sat cross-legged on the floor, the issue laid out before them. "It was very, very powerful," said Glenda. "Phyllis cried, and then we all started to cry, and then she thanked us." The result of the meeting was that Phyllis agreed to go into therapy with Dr. Portia Hunt, a psychologist Glenda recommended.

Phyllis began seeing Hunt regularly when she was in town – sometimes several times a week – as her touring schedule allowed. Hunt diagnosed Phyllis with multiple disorders, including substance abuse disorder with a connected eating disorder and bipolar disorder, also known as manic depression. The options for treating bipolar disorder were not nearly as sophisticated when Phyllis was diagnosed in 1985 as they are today. Lithium was the drug of choice at that time. Lauded for its mood stabilizing effects by the medical community, the bipolar patient, on the other hand, often felt robbed by the drug of the intense highs that mania can produce. Phyllis was no exception.

"What happens with a lot of bipolars is once they start to stabilize, and start to feel normal, it frightens them," said Hunt. "They think the manic piece is tied to their creativity."

The illness, therefore, makes the patient believe they do not need the drug, leading many to instead self-medicate with alcohol and other substances, as Phyllis was prone to do. Lithium also frequently comes with the side effect of weight gain, something Phyllis was not willing to risk.

Phyllis opened up to Hunt about many of her issues, including her frequent suicidal thoughts. Suicidal ideation, as it's called in psychological terms, is a common symptom of bipolar disorder, and one that would plague Phyllis throughout most of her life. It wasn't unusual for the topic of suicide to come up in casual conversations with Phyllis. "She would say, 'Could you commit suicide?'" her play son, Tymm Holloway, recalled. "I would say, 'Yeah, I could, but I don't think I would.' And she said, 'I could too. I could kill myself.'" Like most who found themselves in this heavy situation, Holloway tried to lighten the mood. "Then who would sing your songs?" he asked. "I'd have to sing your songs and then your whole career would be in vain."

Phyllis played along. "You're gonna sing my songs? Oh, Jesus! I can't do that then."

Cynthia Biggs, who following her work on the *Living All Alone* album went on to tour with Phyllis briefly in 1987 as a backing vocalist, was also privy to many such conversations. "She would always threaten to do that. It had gotten to the point where people just thought it was like the boy who cried wolf. But she had a serious depression problem. I mean, she was probably one of the worst cases of depression that I have ever witnessed."

A signed artist once again, work on her debut album for Philadelphia International was progressing slowly, and on January 2 Phil Asbury, a vice president at PIR, granted Phyllis an extension on its completion date. The album, which had originally been due to PIR on October 20, 1985, was now due January 30, though it ultimately wouldn't be finished by then either. Phyllis did spend a good deal of January in the studio though, recording songs such as "You Just Don't Know," "First Time Together" and "Slow Dancin'."

One standout from these sessions was "Old Friend," in part because it was obvious that the melancholy tale told in the song was a perfect fit for Phyllis's voice. But even more so because of who had penned it. The wistful words were among the last to be written by Linda Creed, producer Thom Bell's longtime lyrical collaborator. Creed, who had co-written "Betcha By Golly Wow" with Bell, had been a part of Phyllis's career from the beginning. Now, as Phyllis stood in the sound booth of Sigma Sound Studios, where Creed had helped bring so many Philly Sound classics to life, the 37-year-old songwriter was dying. Creed, who unbeknownst to many was actually white, had been writing soul classics since 1971. For the past decade, however, she had been doing so while simultaneously battling breast cancer.

"I spoke to her shortly before she died and she told me she knew she wasn't going to get any better and she didn't have long left," said Phyllis. "I recorded that song with her in mind. For a year after I recorded it, when I performed it live I couldn't sing it without crying."

Creed would succumb to the disease on April 10, just days after the favorite of all her compositions, "Greatest Love Of All," which had originally been a number 2 R&B hit for George Benson in 1977, entered the charts as the fourth single from Whitney Houston's debut album. Creed would never know that Houston's remake would go on to be even larger than the original, reaching number 3 R&B and number 1 pop.

But Phyllis knew. She watched helplessly as three of the four singles from Whitney's debut album on Arista reached the number one spot on both the R&B and pop charts, and as her album went on to sell millions of copies. Phyllis watched with great frustration, determined to somehow get even, to prove to Whitney and Clive – and to the world – that she had what it takes to be a star – even if her tenure at Arista wasn't a testament to that fact. With her new album, Phyllis wanted to prove that she still had the goods, and that Clive had goofed by letting her go.

Kenny Gamble and Leon Huff had a few things to prove to Clive, too. PIR's first distributor had been Columbia Records, led at the time by Davis. It was Clive, in fact, who OK'd the distribution deal in 1971, and watched the following year as four of Columbia's nine gold singles proved to be PIR releases. But the partnership suffered irreparable damages four years later, when Davis, Gamble and Huff were among nineteen record executives indicted in the Project Sound payola scandal. By the time it was all over, Clive had been forced out of the presidency at Columbia, and the last years of the Columbia-PIR distribution pact were a dismal failure.

But for as much as Kenny and Clive had in common – they were both strong-minded businessmen determined to do whatever it took to make it to the top of the music business – it was their differences that interested Phyllis. "Kenny Gamble wanted to record me, and he said something very important to me, and that was he thought I was very special," said Phyllis. "Clive had never said any such thing to me. Clive thought he was special, because everyone in the industry knows that Arista Records is Clive Davis. He's the star and everyone else is just there. I mean everyone knows that. That is not a secret.

"In Kenny's position, I'm not sure that he thinks any less of himself, but he also thinks a lot of his artists as well. He's not afraid or ashamed to speak that. That was one of the reasons I decided to go with PIR at the time. Because it was Kenny Gamble, the way he talked to me, the way he let me talk to him, the way we communicated, the fact that it was an East Coast-based company and, without a doubt, because it was a black-owned and run company.

"There's a certain depth of understanding that comes from keeping it all the family," Phyllis continued. "I talked to other companies. But the record industry in 1986 is not like it was when I first entered it a decade ago. It's geared more toward record sales, not so much toward creativity. Kenny Gamble was interested in capturing my music as it really is, as opposed to taking the attitude of saying, 'Let's get Phyllis to sing a lot of crap tunes and sell a lot of records.'"

As work on the new album progressed, and as Phyllis continued to sing Kenny Gamble's praises to the press, Glenda, likewise, could not help but be pleased. Even if the money was not what she was hoping, she was still thrilled with Gamble's enthusiasm for working with Phyllis. "To him, she had that sort of blaze glowing from within that builds the sort of career you have with, say, Barbra Streisand," said Glenda. "That's how Kenny thought of her. That big. That spectacular."

But what neither Kenny nor Glenda took time out to realize was that the industry was no longer building the sort of careers that Streisand had known. Barbra's career had always been about more than hit records. She got her start in theatre, on Broadway in the show *I Can Get It For You Wholesale*. In fact, her first single, 1964's "People," came from her starring role in *Funny Girl*. But after its release, Barbra would have to wait seven years for another pop smash. In the interim she continued releasing records, mostly show tunes, and she continued to hit big on the adult contemporary chart. Barbra did have her commercial periods, most noticeably the '70s, but by the time Phyllis joined PIR, the era of Barbra Streisand as pop star was long over.

In stark contrast to Streisand, Phyllis's entire professional career had been orchestrated with one goal in mind: getting a hit record. No one had attempted to cultivate a trademark sound for her. No one had worked to capture the charm of her popular stage show on vinyl. And even though the critics had heaped mountains of praise on her for her turn on Broadway singing the songs of Duke Ellington, no one had contemplated recording an album of standards with Phyllis. That's what Streisand was doing at the time. Her *The Broadway Album* from 1986 would eventually sell more than four million copies, making it one of the most successful albums of her entire career.

Gamble toyed with the idea of recording an album of jazz standards on Phyllis, but he saw that as something to be done down the line, after the hits had come. "I love the idea," said Phyllis. "I'd want to do an album that covers all areas of jazz – bebop, fusion, swing, contemporary – because I think jazz is the only true American music form." But first, Phyllis still felt she had something to prove – to Clive Davis, to Kenny Gamble, to herself – and the only way she knew how to prove it was to get a hit record. By now, there was a nagging need in Phyllis to hit the top of the charts. Phyllis was so concerned by the number of lesser talents topping the charts that she never took time out to consider how many of the greats never did.

While Phyllis continued to work on the new album she toured as she could. Phyllis was doing a week's worth of shows at the Blue Note in New York in December of 1985 when she found herself performing in front of Bill Cosby. Impressed with what he saw, Cosby approached Terry Burrus, Phyllis's musical director.

"Hey, you think Phyllis would want to open up for me in Lake Tahoe and then the following week we'll come to Atlantic City?" Cosby asked Burrus, who suggested they pay Phyllis a visit in her dressing and find out.

"She was hesitant about doing it, although no monies had been discussed yet," Burrus recalled. "I think the fact that Bill Cosby was a big, big star, and sometimes Phyllis would get intimidated if the star was too much bigger than she was. In the beginning, she was like, 'No, no, I don't want to do it.'"

Another reason that Phyllis was hesitant was likely the ultimatum that Cosby had laid down. He wanted her to drop some significant weight before they played together. "Television puts 20 pounds on you, and I want you to be as beautiful as I see here," Sydney Francis recalled Cosby saying. "I want to make you a star."

No matter how sweetly he phrased it, Phyllis still took the statement as a demand. And she didn't respond well to those. "I remember her telling me she wasn't going to do this Cosby thing because he had the nerve to tell her she needed to lose weight," recalled psychologist Portia Hunt. "She said she wasn't going to let anybody tell her what to do."

For their part, Glenda and Sydney were not exactly thrilled by Cosby's prerequisite either. But they knew that opening for him would be a great opportunity for Phyllis. So they set about convincing her that she couldn't turn the offer down. They reminded Phyllis that she'd been trying to get to Vegas since 1980, when she accepted the part in *Sophisticated Ladies* in the hopes it would lead to such offers. Lake Tahoe wasn't Vegas, but it could certainly lead to a booking there.

By this time, Phyllis's bassist, Tracy Wormworth, had left to work with Sting and had been replaced by Ron Richardson. Doug Nally was now on drums and Mayra Casales joined in occasionally on percussion. The band rehearsed for a week straight to learn all the new material. "We rehearsed, we rehearsed, we rehearsed, because there were going to be a lot of Vegas promoters there," said Burrus. "We knew that if we could pull the whole show off she could get big contracts with some of the Vegas hotels."

Phyllis opened for Cosby at Harrah's February 21-27, 1986, but her shows did not go over well. "She was very much an unknown to many of the people there," said Burrus. "But Cosby was finding a lot of acts that were not well known in the pop sector and trying to expose them to that market. So now it's up to you, the artist, to run with that, and she didn't quite run with it. I don't think she took to that type of an audience and it showed."

It was not only the audience she didn't take to. Phyllis still could not get past Cosby having the nerve to tell her to lose weight. She had, of course, taken off the pounds as requested. But the whole scene was off-putting. Though Cosby couldn't have known it, Phyllis had struggled with insecurity issues surrounding not only her weight but also her height and, indeed, size in general, since adolescence. To be told she had to look a certain way was no different than being told she had to sound a certain way. It was all an attempt to put her in a box, to treat her as a commodity.

Phyllis hadn't let Clive Davis define her, and she wasn't about to let Bill Cosby do it either. The sheer audacity of Cosby's command offended and infuriated her. She obsessed over it, and replayed the conversation in her head over and over again each time she put down the fork and pushed away the plate. It got under her skin, and by the time she arrived in Tahoe, Phyllis had scratched herself raw.

Clive had wanted Phyllis on his label. But for whom she could become, not who she was. Now it was the same thing with Cosby. The comedian wanted to work with Phyllis, but only if she was willing to fit into his package, and allow him to put the wrapping paper on her that he picked out. Not surprisingly, Phyllis reacted as she always did when someone tried to box her in. She busted out.

Following the second show, Phyllis was supposed to have dinner with Cosby at his favorite Lake Tahoe restaurant. The plan was for Cosby, who was excited to be working with her and hoping for a lengthy partnership, to introduce Phyllis to some of the Tahoe bigwigs. But as often happened with Phyllis when the stakes were too high, she panicked. She stepped out of her dressing room, saw Cosby with his entourage and, feeling outnumbered and outgunned, turned back around.

When she finally emerged again some minutes later, it was a different Phyllis that showed up. "She was like a kid having a brat attack," said Sydney. "She immediately developed an outrageous attitude."

Phyllis, in her rattiest robe and most tattered pair of slippers, started heading to the elevator. Cosby saw her walking away and called to her.

"Where are you going?" he asked. "We're supposed to be going out to dinner."

"I don't eat with people I don't know," Phyllis answered.

"She didn't even turn around and look at him," said Sydney. "She spoke to him over her shoulder. I didn't know what to say or do. She'd taken months of preparation, years of good will and thrown it right in this man's face."

Once again, as it had with *The Color Purple* audition, Phyllis's fear had gotten the best of her. Her Vegas career was over before it began. "Cosby stuck to his word and we did Atlantic City the following weekend," said Terry Burrus. "Then that was it. It was no more Bill Cosby and no more of that type of crowd for her."

Though Phyllis had ruined another major opportunity, she had done so on her own terms. She had called the shots, even if she called the wrong one. "It was the illusion of control," explained Portia Hunt. On the precipice of success, Hunt said that Glenda and Sydney were both good and bad for Phyllis. They had the potential to really launch Phyllis's career, which she both wanted and was afraid of at the same time. "All of a sudden, it's on you," said Hunt. "I think she was terrified of not being able to live up to the expectations.

"She had a love-hate relationship with her career," Hunt continued. "Everything in her life was a love-hate relationship for her."

Chapter 11

The kindest thing Clive ever did was to let me go.

Phyllis's signing to Philadelphia International was not seen by the label as a singular occurrence. Rather it was part of a bigger plan, the proposed second coming of the label. At the time that PIR inked their new distribution deal with Capitol-EMI, the only act still signed to the label was the O'Jays. Without a doubt, the O'Jays were to Philadelphia International what The Supremes or The Temptations were to Motown – they were the flagship group. But one group does not a successful label make, so Kenny set out to build a new stable of stars.

In addition to Phyllis, Kenny signed Shirley Jones, who with her sisters Brenda and Valerie had recorded as The Jones Girls since 1979, when their hit "You Gonna Make Me Love Somebody Else" had gone to number 5 R&B and number 38 pop. Rounding out the new PIR roster, Kenny signed The Whitehead Brothers, two teenage sons of John Whitehead from the duo McFadden & Whitehead of "Ain't No Stoppin' Us Now" fame, and billed them as PIR's "second generation of hit makers."

The label began sending out a single publicity glossy that featured pictures of all three of its latest acquisitions – Phyllis on the left, Shirley on the right and The Whitehead Brothers in the middle – in an effort to set the stage for what they hoped would be a very successful summer of hits. Phyllis had enough material in the bag for a complete album already, but there was one more song she wanted to contribute to the project.

"We decided to re-record 'What You Don't For Love' by Bobby Caldwell," said Phyllis. "I've always loved that song and I kept telling the company I wanted to do it. Terry and I agreed that we'd go in together and I'd never done that before. I don't even like being in the studio. But Terry and I work real great together."

As Terry recalled, Phyllis walked into the rehearsal studio one day to find him playing the song on the Fender Rhodes. "Hey, that might not be a bad idea," she said. Terry and Phyllis cut a demo version of the song at his home studio and forwarded it on to Glenda. She approved and the song soon found its way into Phyllis's live act. It was during an engagement at the Blue Note in New York that Kenny Gamble heard it for the first time and he was impressed; so much so that he invited Terry down to Philadelphia to record it. "He said, 'We'll bring you down to Philly and we'll do that and see what it turns out to be.'"

When it came time to go into the studio, Phyllis was sick. "She had a cold," recalled Terry. "She came over to the studio and she was running her assistant around, 'Get my tissues, get my water, get me this.' I'm in the middle of it, like, 'Phyllis, will you please just sing the thing already?' It's already like 1, 2 o'clock in the morning. And Phyllis being Phyllis, she nailed it. Oh baby, did she nail it."

"What You Won't Do For Love" marked the first time that Phyllis shared co-producer credits on one of her songs. "That was Glenda's idea, which I thought was a good move, to try to get Phyllis into some kind of a production area," Terry said. "So we sat and co-produced that thing, sat behind the board together and people came in and took pictures for the newspapers." Without the cameras in front of her, Phyllis's attention wandered. "We gotta order food," Phyllis insisted in the thick of session. "In the middle of each word, it's time to eat. But even with all of this, at the end of the day, you accomplish what you came in there for and it's truly amazing."

Kenny Gamble was eager to see the album released, and he quickly went about making a big fan out of Phyllis. He became more than just a label head to her, more than just a boss. Phyllis felt she had a true partnership with Kenny. "He oversaw the procedure. He co-wrote some of the tunes. He produced a couple of the tunes. But he never pressured me and he never bothered me.

"Anything I did not like, I did not record," Phyllis continued. "That's why this album is what it is. It was the first time that I have participated in the total concept of music, the whole ball of wax. That's why it feels so good to me."

The timing was right for artists like Phyllis and Shirley Jones, whose own album featured primarily the same personnel as Phyllis's and material she could just as easily have done. Radio was rife with female vocalists and ballads were once again en vogue. If ever there had been a time to release a Phyllis Hyman record, it was now. Meli'sa Morgan ("Do Me Baby"), Rene & Angela ("Your Smile"), Stephanie Mills ("I Have Learned To Respect The Power Of Love") and Patti LaBelle and Michael McDonald ("On My Own") had all made it to number one since the start of the year.

Phyllis, at psychologist Portia Hunt's urging, had decided to begin this new phase of her career with a clean slate and entered a rehabilitation facility to help her kick drugs and alcohol. "I told her I wasn't going to see her anymore if she didn't go," Hunt recalled. "She was doing the vodka, the cocaine and all of that stuff. She was cycling in and out of it. I felt she was really about to hit rock bottom. I told her, 'Phyllis, I'm not helping you. You really need to be in treatment.'"

In early August, just as PIR prepared to service her first single from the album, "Old Friend," to radio, Phyllis traveled to Ephrata, Pennsylvania. There, using her middle name, she checked herself in the ARC/The Terraces residential addiction treatment program as Linda Hyman. "It devastated her that she was treated like everyone else," Glenda said with a laugh, recalling Phyllis's first days in rehab. "It devastated her and at the same time refreshed her. She was almost childlike when she would make her phone calls to report on her progress and her sobriety, and her understanding of some of the stuff that she was dealing with."

Glenda kept her up to speed on the record's status during her month in rehab. So far, PIR's second coming was being met with mixed results. The Whitehead Brothers first single, "I Jumped Out Of My Skin," had only maintained a position on the charts for a mere six weeks, making it no further than number 79. Phyllis's friend and former PIR recording artist Jean Carn, now billing herself as Jean Carne, was enjoying the biggest success of her career on the Omni label. Her "Closer Than Close" managed to top Billboard's R&B singles chart, until Shirley Jones's "Do You Get Enough Love" toppled it. Both Jean and Shirley's songs spent two weeks in the number one spot. Phyllis was encouraged by these marks. It seemed as though artists of her caliber were finally being recognized; and if Shirley Jones could get a number one hit, Phyllis had no doubt that she could, too.

She was doing well in rehab. For the last week of her month-long treatment, Phyllis was asked to invite her family to her therapy sessions. Phyllis's relationship with her mother, in particular, was one that would never cease to confound her. Phyllis, in many ways, had fought to create a persona for herself that was the antithesis of all that her mother represented. What was Louise Hyman? A mere housewife who had never worked, whose only job was to change the diapers and wipe the noses of seven children? And the ultimate insult, after playing the role of the dutiful wife to the best of her ability for nearly 20 years, Louise was then forced to watch helplessly as her husband walked out the door. Phyllis viewed her mother with equal parts pity and fear. She felt sorry for what had become of Louise's life and was simultaneously terrified that it would happen to her.

What's more, in her clear moments, Phyllis felt yet something else toward her mother: guilt. She knew she had followed in her father's footsteps and continued in his tradition of verbally abusing her mother, of taking her for granted. Louise had never learned to stand up for herself, and her own battle with depression precluded her from teaching her children how to properly communicate with her. Phyllis and Louise hadn't shared any long, storybook mother-daughter chats. They, in fact, didn't even know how to talk to each other. So even if Phyllis wanted to make a new start with her mother, to clear the air and turn over a new leaf, the truth is she was painfully ill equipped to do so. Phyllis had trouble saying sorry.

Her relationship with her siblings was, for the most part, similarly complex. Like Phyllis, two of her siblings would eventually be diagnosed as bipolar/manic depressive. A third would suffer from chronic chemical depression and a fourth suffered from schizophrenia. Phyllis grew up surrounded by mental illness and alcoholism and as she matured, these two debilitating traits would continue to factor largely into her communication with her brothers and sisters. Long before they realized they were self-medicating – that there was anything to self-medicate – three of Phyllis's sisters began experimenting with alcohol and drugs. Eventually, their teenage curiosities turned into full-fledged addictions. The result is that Phyllis had trouble talking to her siblings, and the channels of communication were often corroded by the combination of mental illness and substance abuse.

Phyllis's solution to the dilemma was to seek out surrogate families, people she felt were more emotionally stable than her own kin that she could attach herself to. She learned this trick during *Sophisticated Ladies*. The long working hours and close quarters made her castmates practically family already, so Phyllis took it a step further and adopted her castmastes' biological families. "She would glob onto other's people's families and my family was one of those," said Mercedes Ellington. "She called my mom her mom. One of my sisters is a federal judge, and Phyllis came down to her to her induction at the courthouse. Also, when my stepfather passed away in Philadelphia, she came down to the funeral and turned the funeral out. She didn't care. She had her own way of doing things." Phyllis did the same when castmate Leslie Dockery's mother died, too.

Closer to home, Phyllis employed the same technique when it came to hiring assistants and assorted staff members. Most of them, including road manager Craig Hentosh, office manager Jim Lewis and valet Carlos Suarez, had started off as fans, transitioned to friends and, finally, ended up on the payroll. "For most of us who started out as fans there was that devotion, and I think Phyllis sensed that and she tuned into it and tried to create a surrogate family," explained Craig. "She created this group around her that she felt loved her and respected her and that she could rely on."

It's not surprising then that for the family portion of her therapy at ARC/The Terraces, Phyllis opted not to invite either of her parents or any of her siblings. Instead, Phyllis asked Glenda and Sydney to join her, as well as her assistant Jim Lewis and her boyfriend Tad, who stayed at the nearby Treadway Resort Inn for the week on Phyllis's tab. Completely clean and sober, Phyllis left rehab ready to recommit herself to her career. "She took from rehab the realization that she was powerless over her addiction, that she had a disease that she had to be on top of, and that she had to really change her lifestyle if she was going to heal herself," said

Glenda. "She was so refreshed. By her own admission, it was the first time that she had been sober for an extended period of time in years. So she had new eyes, basically, and was really excited about those new eyes. She saw great opportunity to do what she had never done before in her entire life: embrace success successfully."

To be sure, Phyllis loved her surrogate family, and in clear moments realized they contributed to her success, supporting her both personally and professionally. "She would introduce me as her brother and people would do a double take, because I'm Caucasian and she was African-American," said Craig. When she felt up to shopping, and perhaps out of some degree of guilt over how she treated them on her dark days, Phyllis would lavish gifts upon her assistants and insist on treating them. But it wasn't the repayment they wanted. They wanted her respect.

"They always say that you hurt the ones you love the most," Craig said. "I would see her lashing out at members of her inner circle and the people that were busting their chops for her and it just didn't make sense to me. But someone will only abuse or mistreat you as long as you let them. If you don't stand up to that person then you're partially to blame for it, and I'm willing to admit partial blame for that."

As she returned to Philadelphia, "Old Friend" was sitting at number 59 with a bullet on the R&B chart. She was optimistic about the possibilities and very much in love with Tad, who was spending a great deal of time at her Philadelphia apartment. She began accepting limited dates to keep some cash coming in, and to allow her to promote the album in the various cities she played. Phyllis flew a day early to Detroit, for example, and did stopovers at all the major radio stations in the city.

Early indications were that *Living All Alone* was a hit, and the album received almost universal praise from the critics. The *New York Daily News* called it "unquestionably a masterpiece" and *Stereo Review* said, "Let the word go out ... that Phyllis Hyman has found her true element ... *Living All Alone* plays up the finest qualities of Hyman's lusty, full-throated voice and sensual delivery with songs that reflect a full range of moods in tasteful, rhythmically varied arrangements."

"I definitely think this it the best album I've done since my very first one for Buddah because, like that one, it reflects Phyllis Hyman – not what producers think I am or should be musically," Phyllis said. "Most of the records in between have been fragmented. They've had great moments but no consistency. I can be fully responsible for this one. This is definitely my record."

Clearly, time hadn't mellowed Phyllis's feelings for Clive Davis. Smart or not, Phyllis relished the opportunity to be able to publicly attack Clive. The spotlight was once again on her, and she didn't mind sharing it with Clive in this context. She considered it payback for all the times she'd try to speak to him and he didn't listen. "You know, Clive Davis would say, 'This is the tune,' and I never had the nerve to say differently," Phyllis said. "Consequently, you had knots in your stomach, you were stressed out, you abused yourself and you did things you didn't want to do. Today, I don't do that. This last album just turned my whole life around."

Yes, now that they were listening once again, the whole world would get to hear exactly how she felt. "Whitney's the only one they took time with," Phyllis told one reporter. "She got all the attention. Gil Scott-Heron didn't get any. The Average White Band got pushed aside, and so did Gino Vannelli. Myself, Angela Bofill, none of us did very much there. I can go on and on about the artists who suffered [while Houston got all Davis' attention]. The kindest thing Clive ever did was to let me go and leave me free to do whatever I could."

Phyllis blamed Clive for momentarily stealing her self-esteem. "For a while, it played a lot on my psyche," she said. "I had a total lack of confidence and self-worth. The thing that kept me going was the fact that I had live performances, that I could get a job." Phyllis failed to realize that while stabbing Clive Davis with her words felt good to her at the time, it was she who would do the bleeding.

"Obviously it hurt her, and probably more than we realized at the time," said Sheila Eldridge. "Who would have thought that Clive, quite honestly, would be around and Phyllis would be gone? But at that time we always said Phyllis should have been Whitney. Clive focused on Whitney because Whitney was younger and he could better control her. That was bitter for Phyllis. She put a lot of energy into that. She was not going to bite her tongue.

"The thing about Phyllis is that you could start a conversation, and the conversation would go way too far," Eldridge continued. "There was too much said. With Phyllis, she would do interviews and if I was not there to kind of cut it off, she would go and tell way too much. I'd have to go back and say, 'Well, could you not write about that?' So that was always a concern. If you let her start talking about something, Lord knows what she'll come up with."

In psychological terms, Phyllis had problems with impulsivity. "What happens is that when you have a thought, you can't regulate your emotions around it," explained Portia Hunt. "So you have a variety of emotions that shoot out at people. And once it's out there, you can't take it back."

Clive and Whitney weren't the only ones Phyllis took on in a public forum. Time and time again, she said what others only dared to think. She called it self-confidence, and perhaps, at least in part, it was. Still, if she truly believed she was as gifted and talented as she led on, many wondered why she had to belittle so many others to make that point.

In a radio interview promoting an upcoming engagement in Chicago, Phyllis explained the difference between natural talent and learned talent for on-air personality Al Beard. "Personally, I think Liza Minnelli's a studied talent, Jody Watley's a studied talent. There are a lot of people out there that are not natural talents. They have to go to class. The Vanitys, the Apollonias, I'm sure those girls are in dance class every day, vocal classes every week. But they're not naturals. Hello! Hello! Let's talk about it. Some of those girls are making grand theft dough and don't have the talent of a two-dollar bill."

In some cases, Phyllis could probably find a host of critics to agree with her. But that is a critic's job after all. Phyllis, though, was not a critic, and her constant attacks toward other artists often came off sounding like sour grapes. "Oftentimes, there'll be some aspect of the attack that's accurate," said Portia. "But it's usually distorted in a way that's exaggerated."

The impulsivity issue Phyllis struggled with was likely caused by a biochemical response that affects the physiology of the brain. But to solve the problem, to regulate the emotion and modulate the affect, "the person must have some sense of the impact of their behavior and be motivated to look deeper at what they're doing," Portia explained. "Phyllis could not allow herself to do that. She would only go so far and then she would recant and go back to being abusive."

Phyllis "couldn't understand at first why people cared about her because her vocal talent was effortless and she felt she was cheating," explained her manager Glenda Gracia. "When she finally became gracious enough to accept her gift, Phyllis would listen to the other voices who'd sold more albums than she did and it would confuse her, agitate her, frustrate her. She never reconciled not getting her props."

It's easy to see how this could confuse Phyllis. But pointing out the shortcomings of her fellow recordings artists so blatantly made her sound vain and mean, though those that knew her best can attest that wasn't her intention. Still, if the Vanitys or the Jody Watleys of the world were selling more albums than she was, it wasn't exactly their fault. Phyllis would have been wiser to aim her anger more directly at a recording industry that valued youth and beauty over talent, or perhaps at a record-buying public that bought into that. But Minnelli, Watley and all the rest were just trying to do the same thing Phyllis was – sing a song and make a buck.

"Phyllis was bitter," said Sheila Eldridge. "She was hurt. She knew that she could sing rings around the Jodys and Lizas. She knew that she was as good as or better than most of them and they were having far more commercial success. They represented everything that she wanted that she wouldn't admit that she wanted. They represented that. And Phyllis had never been a person that did anything in moderation. It was, 'I'm going for it, all or nothing.' From the men to the business, the drinking, the drugs, everything. That's what it was. So she didn't know how to not talk about somebody if that's how she felt."

Phyllis was uniquely Phyllis and she knew how to be no more or no less than just that. Sometimes this was quite charming, her wicked sense of humor absolutely delicious. But what Phyllis lacked was perspective, the foresight to know what was appropriate to say and to whom, and, most importantly, when to merely keep quiet. Phyllis could not stop herself from saying whatever came to mind, and often long before her mind had even processed the thought.

Racing thoughts is another symptom of bipolar disorder, and the short of it is that Phyllis's mouth just couldn't keep up with her overworked mind. True, Phyllis was real and genuine, both admirable qualities. But in the recording industry – as in life in general – there are times when it's appropriate to merely nod and be polite. A verbal response is not always required, but it was for Phyllis.

That response, of course, was determined by where Phyllis was mentally, whether she was in the midst of a manic episode, a depressive episode or caught somewhere between those two extremes. During her manic periods, Phyllis was prone to be easily agitated and exasperated by the fact she was not receiving the attention and acclaim she felt she rightly deserved. In a depressive state, Phyllis doubted herself and her craft, and felt she did not deserve the acclaim at all. "It was a very inconsistent kind of mixed signals behavior," said Craig Hentosh. But it was also par for the course for someone afflicted by bipolar disorder.

Even harmless situations could quickly turn awkward in the wake of Phyllis's mouth, like the time Gerry Griffith brought Sal Licota, the president of EMI, to see Phyllis at Fat Tuesdays in New York. Fearing he would never get the recognition he deserved at Arista for finding Whitney Houston, Griffith left for EMI as Whitney's debut album was still being recorded. EMI, through their Manhattan Records division, was now distributing Philadelphia International, Phyllis's new label. As the show came to a close, Licota decided he'd like to meet Phyllis and asked Griffith to take him backstage. Licota, Griffith recalled, "was not a creative guy; he was salesperson. So whenever we would introduce an artist to Sal he was always very uptight." Griffith went in first and found Phyllis, in a robe and slippers, curling her hair. Phyllis was happy to see him and quickly told him to bring Licota in. Just as the record executive walked through the door, however, Phyllis's finger slipped on the curling iron and she burnt herself.

"Cocksucker, motherfucker, what the fuck is wrong!" Phyllis screamed as her finger started to sting.

"She went bananas," said Griffith. "I'm laughing, but Sal had this look of horror on his face. He did a very gentleman like, 'Nice to meet you' kind of thing and left. Now, to any of us in the business that had been around artists for a while, this would be a funny thing." But it wasn't to Licota, who was expecting a more ladylike reception.

As Phyllis began giving interviews to support the album, Glenda encouraged her to speak about her recovery. But Phyllis only did so in generalized terms and never specifically addressed her month-long stay at ARC/The Terraces. "Nobody under pressure should touch anything that is mood altering," she told *EM* magazine. "I realize that I have a choice – to choose a better way to live. It's not easy, but it's more exciting. I can spend these next years of my life exploring my new lifestyle."

"I used to drink too much and use drugs," she said in another interview. "There is no place in my present life for that. Now that I no longer indulge in those things, I don't like being around it. It drives me crazy. I now work with God in my own perspective and there is a partnership. I'm no born again Christian, but I am adamant about having God in my life." She also mentioned another type of partnership that she longed for. "As a woman, this field is isolated and lonely. I want what most women want. I want to marry and have children. I'm looking for Prince Charming. But I'm told men are threatened by me. I can't understand why."

Quotes such as these made it sound as if Phyllis was alone and continued her tradition of advertising her pain. But she was in a committed relationship, and though she said she wanted to marry and have children, that claim is suspect. Phyllis, in fact, had always been adamant about not wanting kids. Now, as her new album climbed the charts, Phyllis discovered she was pregnant once again.

On October 28th, just as "Old Friend" entered the top 20, Phyllis went to her regular physician, Dr. Victor Zachian, and received a second abortion. Later that day, Phyllis's friend Julie Aponte passed by. "She was in a lot of pain," said Julie. "She was very sad after she had that abortion. I really felt bad for her."

There were a lot of reasons for Phyllis to decide not to have the baby. She wasn't ready for the responsibility, certainly not so early in her recovery. It was bad timing, her rejuvenated career was on the upswing and demanding 100 percent of her time. Then, there was the matter of money. Phyllis had no savings. Her only consistent method of generating income was to stay on the road, something that wouldn't be possible for a while if she decided to have a child. So how would she support it? Tad was young and without the financial resources to take care of either Phyllis or a baby. So who would care for the baby while she went on the road every weekend to bring home the bacon?

Then there was the simple truth that Phyllis didn't really want a baby now. In fact, she never had. Just days before the abortion, Phyllis shared her feelings on pregnancy with *Rhythm & News*. "I can't relate to my body being in that shape," she said. "I still feel that way. I think many other women do also. Women are programmed to believe that motherhood is the ultimate area of life. And that's a lot of B.S. For centuries, it's been a tradition that since women had the reproduction equipment, that's what we're supposed to do.

"That's a crock!" Phyllis continued. "Women are supposed to be people first and foremost. And for those who want to have children, have them because we have that option. I just can't relate to being in that sort of physical condition, whereby there's something growing inside of me, and my stomach is sticking way out. To me, that's bizarre. Nor can I relate to the labor pains. I've had enough pains with menstrual cramps over the years. But I do relate to children. I think they're wonderful, especially when they're somebody else's.

"I'm not necessarily saying I won't have a baby," Phyllis went on. "Just because I don't relate to the process of carrying one doesn't mean that I won't change my mind. But I haven't thought seriously about having children, period. Children to me are very special. Unfortunately, I've seen too many women have babies just because they felt it was 'the thing to do.' They really didn't want those babies. Statistics prove that. Just look at the cases of child abuse and neglect. I know that I would never be that kind of person. But at this stage of my life I'm very impatient, very self-consumed, busy and don't think it's fair to do that to a child."

Phyllis said she had felt that way "all my life. Most women I know would like to state that opinion. But they've already had their babies, and many of them are disappointed but they won't say it. It's a subject you're not supposed to speak out on. So many women just grin and bear it. But I don't believe in that because it hurts the child, and that's wrong. I'm also against me having a baby because I'm a single woman and I believe a child should have two parents to raise him or her."

Tad, of course, would have gladly married Phyllis. But she stated that she now took marriage very seriously – though she didn't the first time around with Larry. "I believe that marriage should be a strong and moral area between the man, the woman and God. I didn't get married with that in mind, and I regret that because I think we made a mockery of the situation. I promised God that I wouldn't play with him in that area again. I do believe in the institution of marriage, though. But to me, marriage is a lot more than two people getting together and hanging out with each other."

Three days after the abortion, Phyllis returned to the road as the opening act for a series of Al Jarreau shows. The dates provided good exposure for Phyllis; and while she was the opening act, she was playing in 10,000-seat arenas. Generally, she preferred much smaller houses – and her material was much better suited for them, as several reviewers pointed out – but it was a good booking. On the road, Phyllis was tense. She tried hard to maintain her sobriety, but with nothing to take the edge off, she was operating on a short fuse. She was still drinking champagne from time to time. It wasn't hard liquor, after all, and she didn't think it could hurt her. Though it almost hurt her road manager, Craig Hentosh, once. Or at least the *bottle* did.

On her way to a date at the Park West in Chicago on December 14th, Phyllis picked up some dinner. She purchased two orders of ribs from a favorite rib joint, ate one before the show and saved the second for after. But during the show, her new lighting director, Justin Edgerly, wandered into her dressing room and, thinking the ribs were for the band and staff, proceeded to eat them all. Following the show, Phyllis returned to the dressing room, ready to throw down. But soon her hunger had turned to rage.

"When she opened up that container and saw just the bones, she was livid," recalled percussionist Mayra Casales. Musical director Terry Burrus was there, too. "One little thing can tick Phyllis off and it's like a mini-earthquake is about to happen,"

Terry said. "She's yelling at Craig Hentosh, 'Craig, where the fuck are my ribs? Where's my food?' Now, mind you, the concert just ended. People in the audience are getting their coats and walking out. You can hear Phyllis all the way behind the stage yelling and cursing at Craig for the food disappearing."

A few VIP fans were lined up backstage, waiting to meet with Phyllis. One woman, standing in the doorway to her dressing room, tried to solve the problem. "We know a better place," she told Phyllis. "We'll get you more."

Phyllis looked at them with fury in her eyes. "Do I tell you what you do?" she asked coldly.

Casales turned to the lady and put her arm on her shoulder. "She didn't mean that," I told her. "She really didn't mean that. She's upset."

So upset, that seconds later she launched an empty champagne bottle across the room at Craig. "It missed him by an inch," said Mayra. "It wasn't the jewels or the furs she was worried about locking up. It was the food. Those ribs were as valuable as diamonds to her."

Days later, the band rolled into Denver, and Craig realized he had reached the end of the road. "She just acted out, and I felt like I can't do this anymore. I can't take this kind of behavior," said Craig, who stated that his time on the road with Phyllis had brought him to the brink of a nervous breakdown. "She could be loving one minute and just as generous as she could be. But she could turn in a moment's notice and just cut you to the quick.

"I felt like I was working very hard because I believed in her craft and I believed in her as an artist," Craig continued. "But it seemed to me that when things started to go well she would, either consciously or subconsciously, throw a wrench into things. I was putting all this time and energy into her career, into helping her, and then for her to thwart things, or try to throw a wrench into things, it just didn't make sense to me."

Phyllis left more of her famous phone messages for Craig, extending her apologies and expressing her regret, and even sent a telegram. But the weary road manager had made his decision. He would not return.

Shortly before the end of the year, Sheila Eldridge secured Phyllis's first booking in support of the album on national television. Phyllis was out running errands on the morning she was scheduled to appear on *Late Night with David Letterman*. Returning home to prepare for the show, dressed in a big hat and wearing no makeup, she found her building surrounded by a SWAT team and was refused entrance. She called her assistant Jim Lewis, who was in her apartment, to apprise him of the situation. Finally, she worked up the nerve to approach a police officer and explained the situation. She promised him tickets to the taping, and was allowed to return to her apartment to get dressed.

For all her trouble, Phyllis's appearance was brief. The third and final guest, she followed Hollywood legend Ann Miller and comedian Jeff Altman on the show. She wore a full wig and a denim dress and matching jacket – made by her favorite new designer, Cassandra McShepard – and sang "What You Won't Do For Love" live, backed by Paul Schaefer and the Letterman house band. But after the performance, which was powerful, she was given less than two minutes with the host before the close of the show.

Following the Letterman taping, Phyllis went on to make appearances on *The Today Show*, the regional *Made in New York* and on the newest national show to hit late night television, *Night Life with David Brenner*. On Brenner, Phyllis sang "Living All Alone," which PIR had just released as the album's second single. She appeared to be crying toward the end of the number, and Phyllis blew Brenner away with a bit of whistling she inserted into the end of the song, which she told the host she'd learned how to do from her mother. Once again, Phyllis was the last guest. The interview following her performance was brief but poignant.

"As a child, I fantasized that I would be a very successful woman, but I didn't know what that meant," she told Brenner. "A lot of that's come true today. I run my own business. I employ a staff of eight people and it's really wonderful."

"It hasn't let you down?" Brenner asked. "It is what you thought it would be?"

"Well, I thought that along with the success and money would come a husband and kids, and I don't have either one of those."

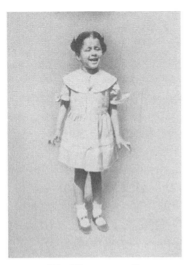
Phyllis at age 7.
The Hyman Family/Estate of Phyllis Hyman

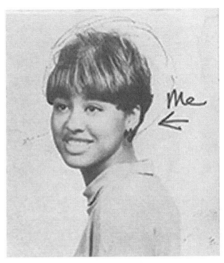
Phyllis's 1967 senior photo.
The Hyman Family/Estate of Phyllis Hyman

New Directions, the Dick Morgan-led band that was Phyllis's first professional gig. *The Hyman Family/Estate of Phyllis Hyman*

Larry Alexander, who would become Phyllis's husband and manager, as he was when she met him aboard the MS Skyward.
The Hyman Family/Estate of Phyllis Hyman

The P/H Factor: Hiram Bullock, Billy Bowker, Mark Egan and Clifford Carter.
The Hyman Family/Estate of Phyllis Hyman

Phyllis's first publicity shot.
The Hyman Family/Estate of Phyllis Hyman

Sultry, sexy and stylish: Phyllis was the Sophisticated Lady long before she landed a part in the Ellington review.
The Hyman Family/Estate of Phyllis Hyman

The Buddah family. Phyllis appreciated the easygoing managerial style of label president Art Kass. From left, Kass and his wife, Melba Moore, Allan Lott, Phyllis, Norman Connors and various members of the label's staff.
The Hyman Family/Estate of Phyllis Hyman

Arista's supermodels: Phyllis Hyman and Angela Bofill, two stunning beauties with sensuous voices. When he found she wouldn't roll over, label head Clive Davis turned his attention toward Angela and let Phyllis languish, for which she would never forgive him - or Bofill.
Ray Avery Collection/Chansley Archives and Arista Records Archives

During Sophisticated Ladies' Washington tryout, Phyllis visited the Duke Ellington School for the Performing Arts. Listening attentively on the far left is a young student named Tony Terry. He would go on to have his own recording career and actually play Phyllis's love interest in a posthumous play based on her life.
Copyright © Oggi Ogburn

Phyllis poses backstage in Washington. She said that this costume, which was designed for the "Rhumbop" number that was cut from the show before it made it to Broadway, looked like something Judy Jetson would wear.
Courtesy of Ken Hanson

Though Clive didn't want her to do it, Sophisticated Ladies turned out to be a good career move for Phyllis. It earned her a Tony nomination and a Theatre World award.
Courtesy of Sondra Gilman

Sophisticated Friends: Phyllis poses backstage at the Lunt-Fontanne with, from left, castmates Gregory Hines and Gregg Burge. Hines died of cancer in 2003 and Burge passed in 1998 from complications from a brain tumor. *Courtesy of Ken Hanson*

That's what friends are for: Stevie Wonder feeds Phyllis lyrics as the two do an impromptu duet at a birthday party Stevie hosted for his wife at Greene Street in New York. Stevie suggested from the stage that the two record together.
Copyright © Laura Levine

Nate Robinson brought a lot of joy into Phyllis's life for a few years.
Courtesy of Tina Stephens

Phyllis with, from left, trumpeter Donald Byrd and Melvin Lindsey, the Washington-based disc jockey credited with creating the Quiet Storm radio format. When Melvin became the latest of Phyllis's friends to die of AIDS in 1992, Phyllis flew to DC to sing at a memorial concert.
The Hyman Family/Estate of Phyllis Hyman

The *Oui* photos were not entirely flattering, and did substantial damage to Phyllis's career, causing her to lose endorsement deals.
Copyright © Princeton Media Group

Phyllis models a Tony Chase creation as part of a profile on the designer for US Weekly. *Copyright © Mark Weiss*

Phyllis snuggles up next to actor Leon.
The Hyman Family/Estate of Phyllis Hyman

Phyllis is shocked to find she towers over television star Tony Randall.
Courtesy of CancerCare

Phyllis was always respected and admired by her peers. This photo, taken at Phyllis's 34th birthday party, shows her deep in conversation with Patti LaBelle. *The Hyman Family/Estate of Phyllis Hyman*

There was more to Phyllis than her pain. When in good spirits, she loved to ham it up. At right, she does so with friend and personal assistant Ann Gore.
Left: The Hyman Family/Estate of Phyllis Hyman, Right: Courtesy of Ann Gore

When Arista stopped recording her, touring became more important than ever to Phyllis's livelihood. Life on the road, as this photo illustrates, wasn't always easy. *The Hyman Family/Estate of Phyllis Hyman*

Welcome to Philadelphia: Phyllis poses with her managers, personal and professional partners Glenda Gracia and Sydney Francis, along with members of the Philadelphia International Records staff, including label head Kenny Gamble on the far right.
The Hyman Family/Estate of Phyllis Hyman

Phyllis lost many friends to the AIDS epidemic. When she learned her backing vocalist, Eric Jones, was HIV-positive, she vowed he'd have a job "even if he has to be wheeled on stage."
The Hyman Family/Estate of Phyllis Hyman

Phyllis had a fondess for younger men. Two of those she was particulary taken with through the years were (left) Tad Fennar and (right) her one time fiance Dante James. Phyllis took these Polaroid images herself. *The Hyman Family/Estate of Phyllis Hyman*

Phyllis and gang hanging out in New York. From left to right, Phyllis' personal assistant Martha David, musical director Terry Burrus, Phyllis, vocalist Rachelle Farrell, who got her start in Phyllis's band, and singers Lori Fulton and Veronica Underwood. *The Hyman Family/Estate of Phyllis Hyman*

Phyllis was thrilled when director Spike Lee asked her to appear in his film School Daze. *Courtesy of Ann Gore*

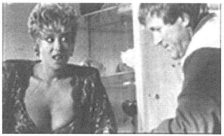

Phyllis showed she had potential as an actress in Soda Cracker, released on video as The Kill Reflex. *Po' Boy Productions*

Singer Miki Howard, Leo Lord, Phyllis's right hand man, Phyllis and actress Phyllis Stickney. *Copyright © Castro*

Phyllis backstage with two members of the Smokey Joe's Cafe crew in May 1995.
Courtesy of Ken Hanson

Phyllis shortly before her death. Her weight had ballooned up to nearly 300 pounds.
The Hyman Family/Estate of Phyllis Hyman

Phyllis: A timeless beauty with a voice that will live on forever.
The Hyman Family/Estate of Phyllis Hyman

"Would you give up the money and success for the husband and kids?"

"Forget it," Phyllis said without missing a beat. "No, I wouldn't."

These performances were nice, but the crème de la crème of Sheila Eldridge's promotional campaign was a spot on *The Tonight Show*. Johnny Carson was still the reigning king of late night, and he remembered Phyllis fondly from her performance to promote *Sophisticated Ladies*. By the time Phyllis, wearing another sensational Cassandra McShepard number, appeared on the show February 4, 1987, "Living All Alone" was slowly climbing up the chart. Glenda and Sheila were both sure that her appearance on the show would push it all the way to the top.

Living All Alone, the album, had yet to go gold. The album reached number 11 R&B/number 78 pop, while Shirley Jones's *Always In The Mood* managed to reach number 8 R&B/number 136 pop. The Whitehead Brothers album failed to even chart at all and the biggest winner on PIR/Manhattan-Capitol-EMI would be The O'Jays, when their *Let Me Touch You* album was released in March 1987.

At the time of the Carson taping, only 226,000 units of *Living All Alone* had been sold, or in other words, it was still less than halfway to gold status. Glenda monitored sales closely following the taping, anxious to see what *The Tonight Show* appearance would do for the record. An additional 45,000 copies of the album was moved in the month following Phyllis's appearance on Carson. But gold was still a long way off. From a historical perspective, it was still a good showing for Phyllis, and *Living All Alone* was already one of her best-selling albums, second only to 1979's *You Know How To Love Me*.

"Living All Alone," the single, did only two points better than its predecessor, reaching number 12 R&B. Again, from a historical perspective, 12 was either Phyllis's lucky or unlucky number, depending on how you looked at it. Her two biggest solo hits, "Somewhere In My Lifetime" and "You Know How To Love Me," had both made it to number 12. But none of her singles had ever managed to make it any further than that, save for her duet with

Michael Henderson, "Can't We Fall In Love Again," which climbed to number 9.

With *Living All Alone*, Phyllis, Glenda, the powers at PIR – everyone – was hoping for number one, and at the least a top ten single. But it was beginning to look as if that obviously was not in the cards. Glenda blamed Phyllis's inability to top the charts on Philadelphia International's distributor, Manhattan Records. Manhattan's relationship with PIR was rapidly deteriorating by this time, and it was obvious that the two labels would not enjoy the lengthy and successful partnership that PIR had known with CBS.

In fact, Manhattan-Capitol-EMI let it be known that they had no intention of renewing the agreement, which expired at the end of the year, and that meant that Phyllis's recording career would be dead in the water until such time PIR managed to enter into a new distribution pact. The O'Jays, meanwhile, decided not to renew their contract with PIR and signed with Capitol direct. "The wind had gone out of the sails of the big ten-year Sound of Philadelphia thing and it was winding down," said Thom Bell. "Just like the Motown sound, the Memphis sound, just like anybody's sound, anywhere, it starts from nothing, it becomes something, it gets big, it lasts for a while, it fades and it goes away." By this point, the Sound of Philadelphia was merely an echo.

Songwriter Cynthia Biggs, a longtime insider at PIR, concurred that promotion on the album was lacking. "PIR was never really good at promoting material, and especially during the last days," she said. "They just didn't find it necessary to engage in those expenditures. Now, in the early days, when CBS was the distributor and PIR was given a budget to cut all those acts, promotion was not an issue – ever. But I think the more self-contained PIR became, the more discriminate they became about what their expenses would be. So consequently, there were not tremendous promotional campaigns and I don't remember a whole lot of hype and promotion around the *Living All Alone* album, not even around Shirley's."

Number one or not, *Living All Alone* was still doing wonderful things for Phyllis and her career, and she was working non-stop. Upon returning to New York following the *Tonight Show* taping, Phyllis had dates in February 1987 in Philadelphia, Boston, Hartford, Connecticut, Richmond, Virginia, and Washington, D.C.

before the close of the month. She also had to go into the recording studio in New York to work on a very special new project.

Spike Lee had asked Phyllis not only to sing a song for the soundtrack of his new film, *School Daze*, but also to actually sing it in the movie. "When I performed at Morehouse College, Spike, Mr. Lee, came down for homecoming," said Phyllis. "He came to my dressing room and as he was leaving I got up enough nerve to ask him to consider me if he ever had another movie where he was going to have singers. I said, 'Please, Mr. Lee, think of me.' I got a call. I didn't have to audition. The job was mine."

On February 19, Phyllis laid down the vocals for "Be One," a song that Spike's father, Bill Lee, Sr., had written for the film. The song had a smoky, jazzy feel to it and a melancholy lyric that was right down Phyllis's alley. "When I was asked to do the soundtrack for this movie I was pretty excited," Phyllis said. "Then its director, writer, producer, Mr. Spike Lee, he called me personally and said, 'We're going to do the soundtrack and you're going to be in the movie,' to which I almost had a coronary, 'cause I didn't know I was going to be on the screen. I said, 'Ohhhhhh.' But you don't tell Spike Lee you're not going to be in his movie."

By this time, Phyllis had decided to take Tad on the road and anointed him her new road manager. Though inexperienced, he was proficient at the post if initially naively unaware of the strain his role as Phyllis's employee would put on him in his role as Phyllis's lover. "I told her it was going to be the destruction of her personal relationship with him and that it was the worst thing that she could ever do," Glenda recalled. But Phyllis had made up her mind. "Too bad," she told Glenda. "I'm doing it."

Members of the band, too, were skeptical of the decision. "Bad move," said Terry Burrus. "They were lovers for two or three years. In the beginning, everything is nice and rosy, even her attitude changed onstage. You could see the lover in her coming out on the stage, and just the fact that Tad was there and very supportive in her life at that time. It was great when he was a spectator and just came to see the show.

"But once your lover starts working for you and she gave him a job, it got to be a problem," Terry continued. "I'm not saying that those relationships can't work. But that's a little extra pressure on you because now you're working for your lover. As a road manager he seemed to be working OK. But after a while it started getting on his nerves, because it's not an easy business. When you start dealing with the monies and there are a lot of eggheads in between you and getting paid. It wasn't an easy job.

"Then after that he had to take care of Phyllis," Terry continued. "Then it became pampering Phyllis. Then it became babysitting Phyllis, and suddenly he had a big problem. Then he had to be road manager, too? It was a bit too much for him to handle."

Cynthia Biggs, who toured briefly with Phyllis, saw this, too. Having him on the road "was a control mechanism, keeping him close to her and under her watchful eye. They fought a lot, and here's the other thing: Tad was a number of years younger and it was obvious, in appearance and even in his conduct and behavior. There were times when I saw them very affectionate toward each other, and there were times when they were really going at each other's throats."

Tad hit the ground running and had no time to reconsider his decision to join Phyllis's road crew. Phyllis was booked solid. In March she opened for the Temptations in Birmingham, Alabama, before moving on to Columbia, South Carolina, Chicago and back home to play the Westbury Music Fair on Long Island. Then, on March 28th, Phyllis flew to London, where in a few days she would give her first real British performance at the Hammersmith Odeon. Glenda and Sydney worked in tandem with EMI's London office to plan a publicity and promotional tour for Phyllis while she was in England. And on April 5th, Phyllis's show at Croydon's Fairfield Hall was broadcast live on the BBC.

Back in the states, Phyllis flew to Atlanta where *School Daze* was being filmed. "I had a chance to witness something that I don't know if many of us will witness, and that is the entire crew, I'm talking about stagehands, lighting people, cameras, actors, the entire crew – excluding a few people, invited people – were all black folks, and the most wonderful bunch of people to work with," she said. "I thought I'd died and gone to heaven. Yes, I did, honey."

In May of 1987, Philadelphia International released a third and final single from the *Living All Alone* album, the Nick Martinelli-produced "Ain't You Had Enough Love." Regardless of whether or not she'd reached number one or gone gold, Phyllis was by this point far and away the most successful of the three most recently signed PIR acts. The second coming of the legendary label hadn't gone very far. Despite her chart-topping debut single, "Do You Get Enough Love," Shirley Jones' subsequent singles failed to gain radio's interest. "Last Night I Needed Somebody," another emotional ballad that was right down Phyllis's alley, barely made its way to the R&B top 40, sneaking in at number 36. Her third single, "She Knew About Me," didn't do half as well, stalling out at number 80. The Whitehead Brothers fared even worse. Their second single, "Stylin'," got no farther than their first and once again only made it to number 79, effectively ending their career with the label. Sales-wise, Phyllis was undoubtedly the star of the show here as well, and gold or not, she had outsold the other two acts combined.

But neither the label nor Glenda would consider it a real victory unless the album sold 500,000 copies. It was a benchmark that had eluded Phyllis for a decade now, and Glenda not only wanted it for Phyllis, but she wanted to be at least partially responsible for giving it to her. Glenda was hoping that Phyllis would be presented with her first gold record during Phyllis Hyman Week in Philadelphia, a promotional campaign she had put together with Sheila Eldridge to correspond with Phyllis's scheduled performance there on July 31. The mayor was lined up to present Phyllis with the Liberty Bell Award, and she was also going to receive the Congressional Award of Merit.

But there would be no gold record presented on this prestigious occasion. "Ain't You Had Enough Love" made it only as far as number 29. PIR briefly considered releasing a fourth single from the album, "You Just Don't Know," for which Glenda wrote a video treatment, but those plans were scrapped when the label's distribution deal abruptly came to an end.

Though no one in the PIR camp has publicly spoken about why the Manhattan-Capitol-EMI deal fizzled so quickly, Cynthia Biggs believes that albums sales of the label's new roster was simply not enough to sustain it. "I think the sales just were not there," she said. "*Living All Alone* was not gold. I think it capped out at maybe 465,000, which, I don't know why Kenny didn't buy the other 35,000 and push it to gold status. I mean, they certainly could have done that for Phyllis, and it could have done wonders for her. Then Shirley had a number one record, "Do You Get Enough Love," but it wasn't a strong number one record, and she didn't have many sales."

For any markers it may not have reached, *Living All Alone* was by this time already a monumental recording for Phyllis. It had produced three top 40 R&B singles – a definite career first for Phyllis – and by the summer of 1987 it had outsold all her previous releases and become her most successful album to date. ABC booked Phyllis on an extensive summer tour for $10,000 per show or $12,500 for two-show, single night engagements – more than double her pre-PIR rates.

And there was another perk. Phyllis had finally and undeniably received full star status. While she was playing the tour with several others acts she'd been playing with for years, Phyllis received above the title billing. In other words, Phyllis was not a part of the Jazz Explosion Jam tour, but rather the tour was her opening act. Per her ABC contracts, the billing for all engagements was to read "Phyllis Hyman and the Jazz Explosion Jam featuring Jean Carne, Ramsey Lewis and Stanley Turrentine."

To Phyllis, the billing meant that she had arrived. Before the tour started, Phyllis opened for The Whispers at the Beacon Theatre in New York. Following soundcheck, she and her play son, Tymm Holloway, stepped out for a bite to eat. "We went to Marvin Gardens to get some chicken fingers, and she told me that her career was going to change," he recalled. "She was going to start being a headliner instead of an opening act, and she was very excited about that change."

"Times move on, and so do I," Phyllis said. "I have moved in such incredible ways. Now I'm the star of the show – I'm not opening up for anyone. This one's mine."

Chapter 12

The way I see it, if the toilet's going to be flushed, I might as well flush it myself.

In September of 1987, Phyllis's baby brother Michael came to stay with her for a few weeks. It was the first time the two had spent any considerable time together since the summer of 1975, when Phyllis had flown him and Mark down to visit her in Florida. Now, both siblings were all grown up and both had changed. Phyllis let Michael tag along to her weeklong stint at the Blue Note, and told Tad to pay him $300 for assisting her. "Tad, pardon the pun, was a tad young," said Michael. "But I liked him, and I thought he was good for her."

Michael liked New York, too, and decided to move to the city. Phyllis agreed to let him stay with her while he got situated and looked for work, but there was an obvious distance between the siblings. "Look," she said finally, "you're not going to understand this. But even though you are my brother, I don't know you."

Michael was taken aback, but resolved to remedy the situation. "I took that very hard. I understood what she meant. She was not very family oriented. But I made it clear that I wasn't going anywhere. I used to say, 'Just think of me as a piece of gum on your shoe, 'cause I'm not going anywhere.' I let her know that she was going to get to know me, whether she cared to or not."

Staying in Phyllis's apartment, Michael slept on the sofa in the living room, which was actually the office of Command Performances, where Jim Lewis worked, by day. Soon, the two were fast friends. "Jimmy was a such a beautiful person. Jimmy was just the sweetest person and I have to say this honestly: my sister walked over Jimmy. I watched her treat people in a way that I really thought was unnecessary. As we got closer, there were times when I started voicing my opinion and saying, you know,

'You need to check yourself.' But by that time, you couldn't tell her anything.

"She would come and go," Michael continued. "She had good moments and bad moments. I think the bottom line was Phyllis called all the shots. A lot of people caught so much hell from her. She was brutal. I never understood why she was so tough on people." Michael credited his sister with inspiring him to take up the saxophone, but after relocating to New York he had no ambitions of playing with her. "Someone asked me, 'Would you ever want to work with her?' I immediately said, 'No way.'"

For all its many plusses, one thing *Living All Alone* hadn't done for Phyllis was help her make any headway on the pop charts. As with all her previous singles for Buddah and Arista, the Philadelphia International singles had failed to cross over. This is just one of the reasons that the invitation to appear on Barry Manilow's new duet album was so appealing. "Barry called and said, 'Phyllis, you're the girl for this tune,'" she recalled. "I said, 'Why me? And why haven't you called me in six years?' I was very curious. I wanted to know. There are a whole lot of singers who've come and gone since my time – especially those who have gone – and I hope they stay gone. But anyway, he did call me and I said, 'Barry, send me this song and we'll talk about it,' and he sent it to me and I thought it was so fierce."

The album Barry was working on, *Swing Street*, was designed to be the industry's first "techno-swing album." It was a risky proposal, combining traditional swing music with the synthesized instrumentation that had become so popular in the '80s. Reviews were universally awful. "The album seems like music made for an audience of mannequins," wrote a reviewer for *All Music*. "It certainly swings, especially on tracks like 'Big Fun.' But it does so in a cold, canned sort of way, suggesting jazz-pop if it was painstakingly recreated by futuristic robot musicologists." The *Miami Herald* called *Swing Street* "a pale shadow of true jazz." The album made it no higher than number 70 on the *Billboard* 200, and the two singles released from it, "Brooklyn Blues" and "Hey Mambo," fizzled at number 13 adult contemporary chart and number 90 pop respectively.

Good move or not, Phyllis had done as she wanted. And that's what mattered to her most. That she had that freedom. That control. "I've prepared myself so I'm knowledgeable about the business," she said. "Why pay someone a percentage when I can do it myself? I manage myself in partnership with GFA. I've been bilked by high-priced managers and agents. I've had to sing in front of drunks and people who've fallen asleep from too much to eat. I've sung in places where waitresses make a habit of dropping trays and audiences don't know any better than to talk during a song. I didn't particularly care for it then, and I have no intention of going back to it now. I'm honest with others and I expect them to be honest with me."

But Phyllis wasn't being honest with herself. She wanted – *needed* – people to believe that she was her own manager, the master of her destiny, an astute businesswoman who wielded a certain amount of power in the industry. But the reality is that Phyllis wasn't any of those things. "She wasn't doing any of that because she could not tolerate doing any of that," said psychologist Portia Hunt. "She had major problems being focused. She couldn't work her way through a deal because she'd become too emotional and erratic, and she ended up alienating the very people who were trying to do business with her."

Phyllis, in a strange turn of a metaphor, said, "The way I see it, if the toilet's going to be flushed, I might as well flush it myself." She meant this statement to project that she made all final decisions regarding her career on her own. But more often than not, the only final decision Phyllis made was the subconscious choice to sabotage herself and her chances when she wandered too near the precipice of major success. It was her fear of succeeding that did the flushing; it was her opportunities that ended up in the toilet.

On a rare night off from the road, Phyllis was being seated at Jezebel's, a trendy soul food restaurant not far from her Manhattan apartment, when she passed by the table of Lionel Hampton. The legendary vibraphonist and bandleader was in the middle of an interview with a music writer for *The New York Times* when she approached. After the two exchanged pleasantries, Hampton resumed his interview – but not before commenting on Phyllis to the interviewer. "She is going to be one of the next greats, in the Ella Fitzgerald and Sarah Vaughan tradition."

If anyone believed that Phyllis truly had the potential to achieve such legendary status, it was Glenda. By the fall of 1987, Glenda was busy at work planning the follow up album to *Living All Alone*. But Philadelphia International was currently without a distributor. The label, now a complete independent, had launched a new subsidiary, Gamble and Huff Records, just as the distribution deal with Manhattan-Capitol-EMI ran out. For their first effort, they teamed up with Lou Rawls, whom they had produced with great success in the mid '70s, and released *Family Reunion*. The album made it only to number 73 on the R&B chart and its single, "I Wish You Belonged To Me," stalled at number 28, proving that the industry veterans lacked the proper network to distribute their own material.

As work started on the album, Phyllis began pouring through the boxes of songs tapes that had been submitted to her and picked out favorites for possible inclusion. Making the list were songs such as "Someone To Love," "Hottest Love Around" and "One Good Reason." Phyllis also found songs through other methods as well. In September, she was doing backing vocals on some demo sessions for her friend Carri Coltrane. One of the songs Phyllis sang on rang an instant bell with her. Coltrane had composed "Meet Me On The Moon" with veteran singer/songwriter Gene McDaniels, the lyricist responsible for Roberta Flack's smash "Feel Like Makin' Love."

"I heard it, and this is a song that I was supposed to do backgrounds on, and I fell in love with it and wanted the song for myself," Phyllis recalled. "I remember hoping that this song was never going to be released by her and she was a good friend of mine. But two or three weeks later I found out that she wasn't going to release it." Relieved, Phyllis immediately asked if she could record it and was thrilled to find out she could.

Nick Martinelli had a good ear for what worked for Phyllis, and the two shared a special connection. Phyllis felt she could be herself around Nicky, as she called him, and he went out of his way to make her comfortable. "She would come right out and tell you she hated the studio," said Nick, who recalled that Phyllis felt "lonely" in the sound booth. "I was the first one who said to her,

'Well fuck it! You don't want to be alone in the sound booth and you don't like somebody looking at you from the next room. So just come in here and sit with us, and you'll sing right here. We'll wear headphones and we'll all just be here, right in one room.'

"That's how we recorded from there on in," Nick continued. "She never went behind the glass again." Phyllis was thrilled, and the new arrangement definitely made her feel more at ease. "I thought, 'If it's that doggone easy, how come I didn't record the other six albums this way?'"

Phyllis and Nick initially cut four songs, a smooth ballad written by his friends Jon Rosen and Karen Manno, "I Found Love," the gutsy mid-tempo numbers "Prime of My Life" and "We're So Good Together," and the up-tempo "Hottest Love Around." Phyllis also cut an updated version of "Set A Little Trap." One of the songs she had originally recorded for *Living* with Bunny Sigler, this time around Phyllis co-produced it with Terry Burrus. "Hottest" and "Trap" quickly found themselves in Phyllis's stage repertoire. She would sing them and then ask the audience whether she should include them on the new album, conducting a field test of sorts.

By now, percussionist Mayra Casales was tired of dodging dynamite on stage and decided to call it quits with Phyllis. "At one point at the Blue Note she twirled her mike around my cymbal. She knocked the cymbal down and it almost crashed on someone's head. She spilled water on people in the audience. She claimed she wasn't drinking anymore, but she was taking pills, which made her look as bad as if she was drinking. It was embarrassing. I wanted to hide behind my drums.

"Phyllis was so great," Mayra continued. "She would give me goose bumps every night when she sang 'Somewhere In My Lifetime.' Nobody I've played with ever gave me goose bumps every time I played with them. Nobody but her. Phyllis was a singer's singer. She could give you such emotion that she would shake you inside. She would make your heart melt. Every single night she would give her all and kick ass. Once she would cross the border and get on that stage, she would turn it out. Up until the time when she was getting inebriated on the stage. Then it was awful. But when she wasn't high, it was the best experience I've had playing with anyone."

With each passing year, Phyllis grew both bolder and more vulnerable onstage. While performers frequently pepper their between-songs patter with polite exchanges with the audience and short stories, Phyllis began to lose focus. Or rather, her singular focus on whatever she was feeling at the moment, or whomever she was thinking of, often overshadowed for her the fact that she was standing in front of an audience that had paid to hear her sing. Like with the *Jet* cover story, wherein Phyllis confessed that she wanted her love life to match her professional success, Phyllis told all to whomever was willing to listen. And as her professional success began to fluctuate, and her personal unhappiness grew, the captive audience she found at her concerts became a sounding board for all her hurt and fear.

Glenda was going for an image of refinement, but that was never going to be accomplished so long as Phyllis could not control her mouth. Phyllis was aware that her bluntness made her management – Glenda and Sydney – nervous. "They don't always feel comfortable with the things I say, but they don't pay me; I pay them," she told the *Greensboro News & Record* during a tour stopover in North Carolina. "I decided a long time ago that real honesty is very important. It may hurt me down the line. But I say, 'Phyllis, you can still learn shorthand and type. Don't worry about it.' I will always have something to do."

To be certain, Phyllis had a natural down home charm that when kept to an appropriate level was delightful. "I'm sweating so much I'm swimming," Phyllis told one audience while trying to catch her breath and regain her composure. "People always say, 'Oh honey, you look OK.' You should be up here and see this. You know how you say, 'Oh she's a star, honey. She's a real star.' Yeah, she's a mon-star!"

By the end of 1987, Phyllis's relationship with Tad was winding down. "I thought he was good for her, but Phyllis was hard to be good for," said her friend Ama Ward, who Phyllis had first met during her run in *Sophisticated Ladies.* "I think when she realized that she could have found something good, she sabotaged it." If Phyllis feared anything more than success, it was intimacy. Consequently, it was in her interpersonal relationships that Phyllis fought the hardest to maintain the illusion of control. Phyllis, said

Portia Hunt, was "counter-dependent. She fought being dependent and yet she craved being dependent, and she hated it. The reality was that she really was dependent."

Anyone who managed to get truly close to her, whether as a lover like Tad, or as a fan-turned-friend-turned-employee like Craig Hentosh, would eventually begin to see behind the mask she wore. But Phyllis's couldn't risk exposure. So every time a hand reached out to remove the mask, Phyllis smacked it away.

"She was unable and unwilling to learn the tools that would allow her to be able to communicate more effectively," said Portia. "In some ways, she never grew up emotionally. She was stuck at 13 or 14, at that rebellious stage. So her identity, as she developed as an adult, was sort of a fragmented identity. And that's a hard place to be in."

Stuck emotionally at adolescence, it's not hard to understand why Phyllis was so attracted to younger men. Men her own age were more often than not her emotional elders. Be that as it may, even the younger men she chose would eventually surpass Phyllis in emotional maturity and, as they did, begin to pull away from her. Things with Tad had pretty much wrapped up by the end of 1987, even though he stayed on several months afterward as her road manager. By putting him on the payroll, Phyllis's attempt at exerting even greater control over him had only served to drive them farther apart.

In late December, Phyllis began spending significant time with a young woman named Martha David, whom she had first met some months earlier at a boat party thrown by Clive Davis. Martha had been an admirer of Phyllis's for some time and wrote to Phyllis telling her she'd like to work for her. Phyllis was taken with Martha but initially unsure of what role she could best fill in her company. Martha's passion was dance, having served as co-director of Smith College's Celebrations Dance Company while she earned a degree in math, and initially she started off as Phyllis's latest personal trainer. But that plan of action was abandoned after only a few sessions.

While they waited for the right opening to present itself, Phyllis began inviting Martha to hang out with her frequently, and even brought her on the road for company. Then, as luck would have it, Phyllis's valet Carlos Suarez called in sick for what Phyllis felt was one time too many, and she asked Martha to fill in. The arrangement worked, and Carlos did not return.

But it was not just a professional relationship the couple shared. The two became intimate at about the same time Martha came on the payroll. Hanging out in Phyllis's apartment one night, watching TV and lying on the bed, Phyllis took things to the next level. "What would you do if I came onto you?" Phyllis asked nonchalantly. "I said, 'What do you think I would do,'" Martha recalled. "I thought it obvious that I was attracted to her."

Though Phyllis was deeply attracted to Martha, she was not entirely comfortable pursuing a relationship with another woman. "I think Phyllis was very conflicted early in our relationship about her feelings for me," said Martha. "She would feel she was in love with me one day, and the next she wouldn't."

Phyllis didn't actually flaunt Martha around as she would a boyfriend, but there was no denying to the band that they were a couple. "I wasn't shocked," said Terry Burrus. "With Phyllis Hyman, after a while you can't be surprised at too many things." And the band and crew were always grateful for anything that kept Phyllis occupied and entertained. Plus, as an added benefit, Martha was actually a good assistant. "Martha's extremely reliable," Burrus said. "She was there when you needed her. Even for the band, certain things we would need and it would be like she'd read our minds."

Still, Martha was having trouble gauging Phyllis's emotional investment in their relationship, which wasn't surprising. Phyllis's manic behavior, the result of her untreated bipolar disorder, confused many. She was prone to mood swings, laughing and joking one moment, yelling and screaming the next. "One thing that Phyllis said to me early on was that people took things that she did too personally and that she didn't mean things personally," recalled Martha. "That helped me along the way. There were a few things that altogether contributed to my staying around for all of it, and a lot of it was that I didn't take it personally. Although a lot of times it was hard not to, and hard not to get angry about it anyway."

"No matter what the reason, someone should not be allowed to behave that way," Martha continued. "But I did know that it was nothing personal and that it had nothing to do with the way that she felt about me personally or professionally. You couldn't expect to be around Phyllis and not be exposed to that behavior, and in direct proportion to how close you were to her and how much time you spent together."

On stage, Phyllis's moods were as volatile as they were behind the scenes. Tears were a regular part of any Phyllis show. She could be laughing, joking with members of the audience as she stole shrimp from their plates. And the next minute, a thought would strike her and the tears would fall. Sometimes, even the things she joked about were no laughing matter. In 1988, Phyllis added a new monologue to her stage show. In complimenting herself for losing weight, Phyllis took it upon herself to put down her old rival from the Arista days, Angela Bofill.

"For those of you who have seen me before, I wonder if you've noticed a major change in my appearance?" Phyllis asked an audience in Richmond, Virginia in May. "Oh yes, darling, I took off some pounds. You know what happened? I started going to the supermarket. I'd go to the movies, and people would say, 'Is you Angie Bofill?' I said, 'Oh no, wrong.' Oh no, no, no, no. I will be Aretha Franklin. I will be Patti LaBelle. I'll be Jennifer Holliday. But I will not be Angela Bofill. Totally out of the question."

It was almost childlike the way that Phyllis said whatever came to mind. A little girl in spirit, she was laughing one minute and crying the next. And in 1988, the pendulum was also regularly swinging back and forth between the vulgar and the spiritual. At the same show in Richmond where Phyllis took on Angela, she took on God. But before she took on either of them, she took on Ethan Orlovitz, her longtime soundman. Phyllis's microphone was not completely cooperating throughout her opening number, "What You Won't Do For Love," and figuring that Ethan had made some last minute adjustments with the levels following soundcheck, Phyllis let her displeasure be known at the close of the song.

"Ethan, I told you guys not to fuck with this," said Phyllis for her opening line. "I cannot get it up. You promised me, man. I can't get it up." Then, as an afterthought, "Sorry guys for the bad language."

To Terry, this behavior was not surprising. "She's yelling through the audience," he said. "Now see, in my mind, I've done hundreds of concerts with Phyllis Hyman. So by this point, I'm laughing. We're all laughing." But Phyllis wasn't. "I'm serious," she screamed. "I'm serious and you all are laughing at me."

Minutes later, during the audience request portion of the show, Phyllis broke down. Phyllis felt all losses profoundly, and the death of Linda Creed was no exception. Creed's songwriting skills had played a major part in Phyllis's career. She had co-written "Betcha By Golly Wow," the song that gave Phyllis her first taste of chart success. And Phyllis had chosen one of her songs, "I Don't Want To Lose You," for inclusion on her first album. Of course, Creed's biggest gift to Phyllis was "Old Friend." It had proven to be a big hit for her. But it hadn't come without a price. Released the same year of Creed's death, it – like all of Creed's tunes – caused her to revisit the songwriter's passing each time she sang it.

"I have a great fondness for this song because it was written by a young lady from Philadelphia by the name of Linda Creed," Phyllis said, in the middle of "I Don't Want To Lose You." "I can't tell you how much I miss her."

Phyllis had a hard time finishing her tribute as the tears rolled down her cheeks. "I have to believe that because of my new knowledge of the Lord and the little that I've learned in such a short time, that the body is the only thing that leaves this earth and the soul will always remain," Phyllis continued. "And knowing Linda the way I did, I guess I just believe, in my imaginative mind, that she's somewhere in the audience, sitting back, going, 'Go ahead, girlfriend. Sang.'"

In April of 1989, Phyllis traveled with Martha to Washington, D.C. to take part in the fight for women's abortion rights. Joined by such fellow celebrities as Cybill Shepherd, Jane Fonda, Melissa Manchester, Penny Marshall, Glenn Close and an eight-month pregnant Susan Sarandon, Phyllis marched with nearly 300,000 others through the streets to a demonstration on the steps of the Capitol. Avid television fan that she was, Phyllis was particularly excited to meet Michele Lee and Donna Mills of *Knots Landing*. But making their acquaintance did not distract her from the serious cause that had joined them together.

"It's just something I felt strongly about," Phyllis reflected in an interview later that afternoon. "I think the rights of people have to be kept intact and a relatively small group of people should not be able to dictate to the masses. They can't tell me what to do with my body."

While Phyllis had always been a vocal supporter of causes she felt strongly about, the abortion march, following on the heals of her endorsement of Jesse Jackson's presidential campaign, displayed a stance decidedly more political than she had taken in the past. And she boldly took the stance knowing it might not be a wise career move. "It's the kind of issue that may mean you lose record sales," Phyllis told *USA Today*. "I'm hoping my audience has the education and sophistication that they'll understand – at least enough to say, 'She has the right to her opinion.' That's what this is about – making our own choices."

From Washington Phyllis headed back to Philadelphia, where she was scheduled to start a six-night run at the intimate 400-seat Theatre of the Living Arts. Phyllis was born in Philadelphia, and she'd kept an apartment in the city for six years now, so she was very much considered a hometown girl, her appearance generating a great deal of press. Here, Phyllis laid into a whole new crew of popular performers.

Paula Abdul took a particularly hard hit. "She's a big-time joke," Phyllis said. "How are you going to take a choreographer and tell her she can sing, and give her black music to sing on top of that? It's really a hoot." Not stopping there, Phyllis was on a bitter role. "I saw New Edition and Bobby Brown on *The Arsenio Hall Show* and I had to turn it off," she continued. "It was horrible."

Phyllis told the reporter she no longer listened to the radio at all. "Why should I?" she asked. "They're deliberately looking for people who can't sing. It just gets in the way of my creating. There's so many of these new, little fly-by-night acts coming and going." And many of them were selling much better and charting much higher than Phyllis, a road-tested talent, which was probably her main problem with these acts to begin with. The industry is all about marketing and packaging; and Phyllis – to both her creative delight and career detriment – refused to be put in any box.

Chapter 13

*I'm sabotaging my career
with my addictions.*

After her weeklong engagement in Philly, Phyllis did a week's run at Yoshi's in Oakland, California, and then another at the Blue Note in New York. Sometimes performing twice a night, Phyllis had done nearly 30 shows in just under a month. The pace was grueling and not scheduled to let up anytime soon. Phyllis had only one day off after the Blue Note engagement before she was scheduled to fly to Washington for yet another week's worth of shows at Blues Alley. Exhausted, Phyllis didn't feel she could do it.

"She was very worn out, worn down and depressed," said Martha David, who recalled that Phyllis said she was going to cancel at least the first night of shows in Washington. As Phyllis began making the necessary phone calls, Martha left the apartment to run some errands. When she returned, the situation had worsened. "Jim Lewis, who was working, told me that while I was out Phyllis had called several people, including family members, telling them she was going to commit suicide. She'd discussed suicide before but I hadn't heard her say she was going to do it imminently. Whenever she discussed suicide she always got angry with anyone who tried to talk her out of it, like me. She felt it was her right to take her own life, and I think needed to know she had an ultimate escape from her pain when all else failed."

As Martha went about preparing for the Washington engagement, Phyllis continued to behave strangely. She asked Jim and Martha to leave, telling them she needed sleep. But Martha was skeptical. From the other room, Martha phoned first a suicide hotline and then called Phyllis's business manager, Glenda, who in turned called Portia Hunt, Phyllis's therapist, and together they decided the best course of action was to dial 911.

"Phyllis seemed so lonely and alone and sad, and she didn't seem to want anyone to comfort her," said Martha. "I wanted to make her feel comforted, loved and safe. But she wouldn't let anyone in. She usually wouldn't accept that kind of help when she needed it most." If Phyllis would not let Martha console her, Martha would, at least, save her life by whatever means necessary. Before she left, Martha unscrewed the chain lock from the door and put it in her pocket.

Martha hoped to intercept the authorities on their way to Phyllis's apartment and planned to wait for them in the lobby. She wanted to seek their advice and, if they felt they needed to speak to Phyllis, she wanted to alert her to their arrival. "I was protecting her and I didn't want to scare her if she was just going to bed to rest. But by the time we got down to the lobby we had crossed paths in the two elevators. They were on their way up as we were on our way down."

When Phyllis answered her door and found a barrage of law enforcement authorities and medical personnel, her anger toward Martha was instantaneous. With five policeman and two paramedics crowding around her, Phyllis picked up the phone. Reaching Martha's voicemail, she patiently waited for the beep before letting her have it. "How dare you!" Phyllis shouted. "It's my personal fucking life to do what I want with."

Phyllis also called Glenda, who once again conferenced Portia Hunt. The psychologist, whom Phyllis hadn't seen in some time, encouraged her to go to the hospital. "I can't go," Phyllis told her. "I don't have my makeup on and I haven't taken a bath. I don't want anybody to see me like this." Hunt made Phyllis promise to immediately resume therapy, and then convinced the authorities not to force Phyllis to leave the apartment.

By the following day, Phyllis's anger had subsided. "She called me to come back over the next morning and said that we were going to Washington to proceed with the performances," said Martha. "She was a changed person towards me and was apparently very thankful and appreciative that I'd called 911. In the moment, as all those people showed up at her apartment, I'm sure she was angry and shocked. She was angry that I was trying to prevent her from doing something that she felt was her right – to take her own life. When she was in a different frame of mind the next day, she knew I had done it only because I cared so much and I think was appreciative for having been stopped."

The day before, Martha had left the apartment briefly to run some errands in preparation for the trip to Washington. While she was out, she picked up a small stuffed teddy bear for Phyllis. Finding her in her bedroom with the door closed when she returned, she simply left it outside her door. The next day, Martha didn't pack the bear – she didn't think Phyllis would have a use for it on the road – but once in Washington, Phyllis asked for it. When Martha told her she had left it in New York, Phyllis called Jim back in her apartment and had him FedEx it to Washington immediately. "That was very Phyllis," said Martha. "Her way, I think, of showing her appreciation without knowing really how to find the words."

During this period, Phyllis split her time – when not on the road – evenly between Philadelphia and New York. Considered a hometown girl in both cities, Phyllis had managed to build a life for herself in Philly even after the relationship with Nate Robinson – her reason for moving to the city – had fizzled. Now, with her relationship with Tad Fennar also in the rearview mirror, Phyllis was once again looking. She enjoyed her time with Martha. But she still desired male companionship.

Songwriter Ann Gore had met Phyllis a year or two earlier and the two would often hang out and club hop together. Once or twice, their escapades even ended up inspiring a song, such as the time the friends both found themselves in an intimate relationship with the same man – at the same time. "'Boyfriend You're Busted' was a tune that we wrote about a singer named Christopher Williams that we both had a relationship with," Gore recalled.

Williams, who was nearly 20 years younger than Phyllis, was a nephew of the legendary vocalist Ella Fitzgerald. Managed by Cassandra Mills, sister-in-law of singer Stephanie Mills, he released his debut CD, *Adventures in Paradise*, which featured a track produced by Phyllis's frequent producer and friend Nick Martinelli, in 1989. The album spawned two R&B top ten hits – "Talk To Myself" and "Promises, Promises" – and set the stage for

Williams to go all the way to number one with "I'm Dreamin'" with his sophomore set.

"He had a good voice," said Gore. "We both were seeing him and we both knew it. But he didn't know we knew it. He thought he was being sly, but we had the laugh."

The song actually turned into a detailed account of the set up:

> *When we first saw you*
> *we laid it on the line.*
> *Both of us thought you were hot,*
> *we like that young, sweet kind.*
> *So we made a deal,*
> *we became partners in crime.*
> *He's all yours tomorrow,*
> *but tonight he's all mine.*

"Phyllis and I did a lot of that," said Gore. "We both were attracted to the same kind of guys so that happened several times. Not at the same time. But you know, one of us would get done with him and throw him to the next one."

Phyllis first met Ann after hearing a demo of singer Spencer Harrison singing one of her songs. Phyllis liked the song, "Love Is (So Hard To Find)," so much that she asked to do a demo of it herself. The song tells the story of a woman who has found success in all but love, a theme that Phyllis could definitely relate to. She asked Ann to remove a reference to drinking before she recorded it – she was on the wagon and hoping to stay there – and the line "I've sipped champagne over Tokyo" became "I've tasted fame but it takes its toll."

The recording went so well that Ann asked Phyllis to demo several other songs she had written. Phyllis, obviously believing in Gore's talent, graciously agreed. "She would come over and sit in my living room and do it for free," said Gore. As the friendship progressed, Phyllis invited Gore to join her at several high profile events. "She took me to a lot of really cool things," said Gore. "She took me to Ashford & Simpson's taping at the 20/20 Club. Cissy Houston was behind me. Patti was right next to me. She opened up a lot of doors for me and gave me a lot of opportunities."

Phyllis, Gore remembered, relished in being a down-home diva. "I remember one time she got a limo in Philly and we drove to my mother's house in New Jersey. That was really funny. But she did things in a grand way. She enjoyed that, and I enjoyed going places with her. It was fun and exciting."

For years, Phyllis had dreamed of branching out into acting. *Sophisticated Ladies*, and the Tony nomination and Theatre World Award it resulted in for her, was a good start. But Phyllis had made little headway since. Despite her relative inexperience, she had ambitiously auditioned for the roles of Shug Avery in *The Color Purple* and Clair Huxtable on the television sitcom *The Cosby Show*, but lost out on those parts to Margaret Avery and Phylicia Rashad, respectively. In 1989, however, a less auspicious but no less legitimate role literally fell into her lap. Phyllis was in the midst of a weeklong run at George's in Chicago when one of that city's leading citizens dropped in to catch her show.

Fred "The Hammer" Williamson had been an All-Pro defensive cornerback for the Oakland Raiders and the Kansas City Chiefs, for whom he played in Super Bowl I against Green Bay. After a decade in football, Williamson cleverly parlayed his fame into a respectable acting career, beginning with a recurring role as Diahann Carroll's love interest, Steve Bruce, on the series *Julia*. Moving on to film, Williamson was a major player in the "blaxploitation" craze of the 1970s, starring in such films as *Boss Nigger*, *Black Caesar* and *Mean Johnny Barrows*. Williamson established his own film company, Po' Boy Productions, in 1974. By the '80s, Williamson had moved on to mainstream action movies, in which he could usually be found playing a cop.

"I had always wanted to work with Phyllis," Williamson recalled. "I saw a great quality in Phyllis. She was a very warm person, a very voluptuous person. She had something that hadn't been tapped on screen before." Visiting with Williamson backstage, Phyllis was skeptical. "I don't think she thought I was very serious. And I said, 'Hey, this is me, darlin'. I want you and I'm the boss. I'm the guy who writes the checks. So if I say you got the part, you got the part.'"

The film in question was *Soda Cracker*. Williamson, in the title role, once again played a cop and, this time, one whose partner was killed in a mysterious assassination. Phyllis was to play the role of Irene, girlfriend to the film's proverbial bad guy, Ivan, which was originally to be played by Tony Franciosa, but later changed to Bo Svenson, a regular in Williamson's films.

Phyllis was unaware of the change a few nights later when she mentioned her new project to the crowd at George's. "Tony Franciosa, one of my favorite actors, is going to be my boyfriend. Maud Adams is going to be Mr. Williamson's girlfriend. I think that's a little screwed up there. She's a white girl. I'm a black woman. I think I should be Fred's girlfriend and Maud should be Tony's girlfriend. Keep it in the family. Aside from that, I think Fred's cute. Well, I think Tony's cute, too. So I should have them both and Maud should have nothing. I'm going to propose that when we go over the script."

Just from his viewing of her show and his brief backstage encounter with her, Williamson was aware of how vulnerable Phyllis was and took to directing her with a gentle hand. "She was a very, very sensitive woman. But I guess that is what you need to bring reality to a song, so people can believe that you're feeling the words to a song. That was definitely one of her qualities, bringing a song to the audience and letting the audience feel that she experienced whatever it was that she was singing in the song. Her sensitivity was definitely on the surface. You could really bruise her feelings. You could elate her. You could make her sad within five seconds. She was a very sensitive person. I knew that when I met her, so I gave her her own way.

"A sister can do a whole lot with a look," Fred continued. "Sisters don't have to do a whole bunch of dialogue to get their point across, whether it's positive or negative. They can do it in looks and shoulders and shrugs. They can most definitely communicate with you without giving you a whole bunch of dialogue. So I gave her that freedom to use expression, to use her sensitivity in expressing how she felt at the moment and what was happening."

In what was perhaps Phyllis's most serious scene in the film, Irene is seen snorting cocaine. Phyllis discussed with Williamson her own addiction to the drug and the battle she had waged to quit it. "We discussed that and that the way to beat demons is to face them. So this was a pretense moment, and a pretense moment, to make a separation between what was pretense and what was reality, was something that she enjoyed very much, pretending that she was doing this. She thought it was funny and comical. I think she got a kick out of it."

Soda Cracker showed in theatres across the world – Williamson had a large following in Italy in particular – but it was a direct-to-video release in the States. Renamed *The Kill Reflex*, the film was in video stores by the fall. Domestically, the film came and went without a whimper. But Phyllis was pleased by a positive write up in *Variety*. The entertainment bible said that Phyllis made "a strong impression" in the film.

In July 1989, Phyllis once again teamed up with Bill Withers and Pieces of a Dream on the road as a sort of sequel to the previous year's successful Quiet Storm tour. Rounding out the bill this time was newcomer Regina Belle, who had just finished recording her sophomore album and was on the verge of breaking out. The tour opened in Philadelphia at the Mann Music Center. Phyllis didn't have far to travel from her apartment and was pulling up to the venue when she noticed unauthorized vendors selling T-shirts with her likeness on them in front of the Mann. Phyllis ordered the driver to pull over and flew out of the limo to confront the vendors. They tried to run and Phyllis gave chase. When she finally returned to the limo, it was with the bootleg T-shirts in hand.

She was in a foul mood after the incident, and brushed by Bill Withers without greeting him properly. Despite the snub, she was actually a fan. Phyllis used to sing his songs "I Wish You Well" and "She's Never Lonely" when she was still an unknown performing at clubs like Rust Brown's and Mikell's. Two days after Philadelphia, Phyllis walked into the Sunrise Musical Theatre in South Florida for soundcheck and happened upon Withers. She walked right up and hugged him. But Withers was apparently still hurt.

"Oh you know me today?" he asked.

Phyllis tried to explain she had just had a bad day in Philadelphia and meant no offense.

"It must have been PMS," Withers said, which set Phyllis off.

"Well, if you're not in a good mood should I blame your little dick?"

Once he recovered from the shock, Bill's anger threatened to boil over.

"Oh go ahead," Phyllis said, egging him on. "You gonna beat me like you did Denise Nicholas?"

The reference to Withers' ex-wife set Regina off into a fit of laughter and she ran to the back of the theater. Withers and his band left to allow Phyllis to do her soundcheck. But despite another full month on the road, the relationship never really recovered.

Between the touring, Phyllis continued working on the new album as she could. Gene McDaniels, who had co-written "Meet Me On The Moon" with his personal and professional partner Carri Coltrane, had asked to produce the song when Phyllis decided to record it. Phyllis had known Gene for years, and got the proper permissions in place for him to take her into the studio. "She used to tease me a lot," said McDaniels. "Carri's white, and she used to say, 'Why do you like white girls?' I said, 'I just like people, you know. Racial prejudice is a divisionary process. It's just a way they distract us and keep us busy so we don't see them stealing money from us and changing our democracy, and stuff like that.' And, conversely, she loved Carri Coltrane. She loved her. She said, 'Carri Coltrane, girl, you can sing.'"

When the two finally met up in New York's Clinton Studios, the recording session proved to be an interesting event. McDaniels' old friend, Miles Davis, was recording down the hall in Studio B, while Phyllis was recording in the larger Studio A to accommodate the orchestra, three trumpet players and four trombonists, McDaniels had hired. In between takes, McDaniels ran down the hall to visit with Miles, but all was not fun and games.

"Phyllis was a very fiery woman," said McDaniels. "She was an imposing figure. She was a very beautiful woman, one of the greatest voices that I ever heard in my life. As far as distinctive voices, Sarah Vaughan, Roberta Flack, Gladys Knight – very distinctive voices – Aretha Franklin and Phyllis. She ranked right there with the best that ever opened their chops to sing."

The session was not easy for Phyllis. For the benefit of the orchestra, McDaniels had drawn up charts of the song. Sheet music was a foreign language to Phyllis. She was deeply insecure about not being able to read it. This issue would, said Portia Hunt, frequently trigger minor manic episodes in Phyllis. It made her feel she could not communicate with those around her, and that she was inferior as a musician. "She was extremely talented and also extremely insecure," said Portia, who had often encouraged Phyllis to go to school to learn to read music. "It was sort of a narcissistic injury. She didn't want anybody to see her as being human. She would try to hide that behind this false sense of self. So the narcissism – the self absorption – was pretty intense at times."

Not being able to read the sheet music, Phyllis could not understand what McDaniels was asking of her and, as a result, producer and singer argued over how to record the song. "She wanted to do it more in an R&B style, and we fought about that. I kept trying to tell her that she was one of the greatest voices that ever sang a song, so why try to sound like teenagers and hardcore R&B singers when she had the greatest voice in the country at that time? Why not just do that? I tried to get her to do a jazz album, something jazz based, with high quality and taste and practical values. But she wouldn't listen to me. What she didn't understand was that the black audience would have loved it. They loved 'Meet Me On The Moon,' and they would have loved the rest."

McDaniels was upfront about not sharing Phyllis's obsession, which was learned from Clive Davis and kept burning by Kenny Gamble, with recording contemporary-sounding material. "The thing is, you only need one commercial tune. You don't need a whole album full of them because they sound like attempts at getting a hit. That's not what an artist should put forth. An artist should be like Erykah Badu. You put the stuff forward that fits your soul, and let them buy your soul, because that's what they really want anyhow."

McDaniels was convinced that Phyllis had a powerful message. "I think she just wasn't cut properly. I think the songs just didn't measure up to her voice. She needed first-class material, and she could have been an international star. No question in my mind. She was a character, on top of everything, but most assuredly one of the greatest voices that ever existed."

Eventually, McDaniels convinced Phyllis to do it his way. But she fought him right up to the bitter end. "She tried to put an R&B

ending on it and I wouldn't let her do it. We were out in the hall fighting. I said, 'Phyllis, please, don't ruin this. We got this now.' She gave me a hard time. She would blow takes on purpose. It was nuts. She wanted her way." But despite the struggle, McDaniels finished the session with as much admiration for Phyllis, if not more, than he'd had when he went into it. "She was a good person. She had a beautiful soul. She was just insecure."

As Phyllis continued to work on the album, Glenda searched for ways to keep her in the spotlight. The easiest way to do that was through duets. Grover Washington, Jr. had a long and successful duet history. A shrewd businessman, Washington, a saxophonist, knew that his instrumentals, no matter how great they were, could only make it so far up the R&B charts, if they charted at all. Washington had released 20 albums in 20 years and they always reached the upper echelon of the jazz albums chart. But *Billboard* had no jazz singles chart and he was lucky if his instrumentals cracked the R&B top 40. In 1981, Washington hit pay dirt. He teamed up with Bill Withers, who provided the vocals on "Just The Two Of Us," which rocketed to number 3 R&B, number 2 pop – a spot it held for three weeks. The following year, Washington and Patti LaBelle made it to number 14 R&B with "The Best Is Yet To Come." Patti's soaring vocals proved the perfect compliment to Washington's screamin' sax, and though the song failed to make the pop charts it became an R&B standard.

When Washington approached Phyllis, Glenda was happy to recommend that she do the duet. Phyllis made herself available to promote the duet whenever possible, appearing on *The Arsenio Hall Show* with Washington, as well as on a *Showtime From the Apollo* taping. A good move, "Sacred Kind Of Love" was well received at R&B radio, reaching a respectable number 21.

Phyllis's pairing with pianist Lonnie Liston Smith was not quite as successful. Produced by her musical director, Terry Burrus, and featuring her bassist, Ron Richardson, and a special appearance by saxophonist Najee, Phyllis wrote the lyric to "Obsession" herself, and Terry the music. "He brought me a vamp and I did all the basic changes and lyrics," Phyllis said. "I like writing with other people. I just haven't spent that much time at it. I have all these things I feel that I could write about. But you can't be lazy. And if there's a TV in the room, I am not gonna write a song – bottom line. I'll watch anything: fishing shows, cooking shows, the daytime stories."

Of all the things Phyllis could have written about, she didn't need to look far for inspiration this time out. "My initial reason for writing it was because of an ended love affair, and then I used all of the drug addiction terminology and feelings about drugs and connected that to the song as well," said Phyllis. "Although I wasn't actually talking about drugs, particularly, you surely can consider and relate to drugs being as obsessive and addictive, and even more painful than a broken love affair 'cause you can always move on to the next affair and hope for better results. But you can't move from one drug to another and expect better results. It's always going to do the same thing, kill your spirit and ruin your life.

"I know those lyrics sound very serious and they sound angry, and I tried to figure out a way to not be so angry," said Phyllis, who had written the song following her breakup with Tad and now found new meaning in it having just ended things with Martha David. "I wasn't as angry as I was hurt, and dealing with what I consider to be a real situation. Each time I had ever fallen in love it became a real sickness for me. I couldn't think for myself. I had no real sense of self. I became so obsessed that I couldn't really function as an individual. That's one of the reasons the last guy left. He said, 'You're too centered on me. You don't have anything for yourself.' So I decided I needed to get with Phyllis."

The album that "Obsession" was featured on, *Love Goddess*, was a critical failure, but it charted decently at number 40 R&B and number 10 on the contemporary jazz albums charts. As she had with Grover Washington, Jr., Phyllis teamed with Smith to promote the record, appearing on BET's *Video Soul*. But "Obsession" made it no further than number 79 R&B. A video was made of the song, and Phyllis was displeased by the fact that the director inserted a drug-related storyline throughout. That was not the song she had written.

If Phyllis wasn't yet an international superstar, she certainly had her pockets of popularity across the globe. She remained wildly popular in the United Kingdom, even if her records weren't always readily available there, and Japan was proving to be another major market. For the second time in one year, Phyllis traveled with the band to Japan in December of 1989. She played a private party in Osaka on December 22, and then opened for a week's run at the Tokyo Blue Note on Christmas Day. No one in the band was particularly thrilled to be out of the country over the Christmas holiday. But Santa knew where to find Phyllis, and on opening night her gift was waiting for her outside the club.

Dante James was an American living in Tokyo and teaching English to Japanese students. He was a full decade younger than Phyllis's 40 years, but also undeniably mature and disciplined. He had signed on to spend a year in Tokyo not only to teach, but to learn as well, studying martial arts from the masters. James had begun studying karate while still in his teens. Now, at 30, he was a third degree black belt who had left behind a thriving TaekwonDo academy in Denver to train in Japan.

A cousin of saxophonist Pharaoh Sanders, Dante had been brought to the club by a friend. "I was just out in front of the club and up pulled this van and out came Phyllis and the entourage," he recalled. "They saw me and Phyllis, Leo, just everybody, thought it was funny that here's this black man in Tokyo standing outside the Blue Note." The group shared a laugh with Dante before ushering him inside the club. "They just befriended me and said, 'C'mon in and hang out.'"

The next day, Dante returned the club and partied with his new friends once again. He spent a lot of time with all the guys, but it was Phyllis that had really caught his eye. "When she was there, the entire time she was in Tokyo, we just spent a lot of time together. We just really hit it off. We had dinner and just sat up and talked."

Phyllis was definitely impressed by the handsome American who spoke Japanese and practiced the martial arts. When it came time for her to leave Japan, the couple pledged to keep in contact and despite the distance between them did just that. "I had a hell of a phone bill. We just called back and forth, wrote back and forth. Email wasn't happening back then. So I made a lot of late night phone calls because of the time difference."

Dante, like Larry and Tad before him, was light-skinned. He also had another one of Phyllis's favorite physical attributes: facial hair, wearing a complete beard. He was an inch or two shorter than she, but tall enough that the two still made an attractive couple. Phyllis began to contemplate her weight once again. After years of martial arts training and practice, Dante was a finely chiseled fighting machine. Phyllis was not as svelte as she had been at the start of her career, and endeavored to regain a shapely figure of her own. She experimented with products such as Ultra Slim Fast® and Omnitrition International's Omni IV® to achieve this goal, but the results were mixed. Much like the practice of karate, losing weight requires a mental and physical discipline, something that Phyllis had struggled with for years. Working the road meant you kept strange hours. After exerting so much energy on stage, she was often hungry afterward, which led to countless late night meals before succumbing to exhaustion.

Through the long distance phone lines, Phyllis's relationship with Dante developed quickly. "She was an artist and the opportunity to get to know her better was intriguing, certainly," said Dante. "But she was funny, she was smart, she was gregarious, she was all the things for all the reasons you'd want to get to know somebody better, aside from being, you know, gorgeous."

In late February, the two rendezvoused for a weekend in San Francisco. Phyllis fell hard for Dante and soon was talking marriage. Glenda insisted on having a prenuptial agreement drawn up. "I don't think anyone had proposed at that point," said Dante. "I think we just started talking about being together."

The talks only intensified as winter turned to spring. In March, Dante flew to Philadelphia to see where Phyllis lived. "It was a chance to go and be where she was and be where she lived, and a chance to be in her place," said Dante. "She enjoyed being in Philly. She felt comfortable being in Philly." But as Dante learned during the trip, she didn't always feel comfortable in her own skin. "The one thing about her apartment, which reflects on kind of her discomfort with her place in the world in some sense, is she had all of her awards, all of her certificates, all of her albums, all of that in a closet. And I had asked her about it and she just said she didn't put them up."

Impressed with these physical symbols of her success, Dante thought they deserved some space in her two-bedroom apartment.

He found himself looking at them one afternoon after Phyllis had gone out, and one thing led to another. "I am a pretty good decorator, so I put them up around her place. I took my time. She had some really, really beautiful memorabilia."

Dante was pleased with the redecorating job he had done. But when Phyllis returned she didn't share his enthusiasm. "She came home and was livid that I put it up. We just had a big fight about it and I took it all down. So it was just disappointing to me that she wasn't comfortable with who she was."

The trip was not without its highlights, though. The two went out for a night on the town to see *Sarafina* at the Forrest Theatre. And before he left town, Phyllis took Dante home to Pittsburgh to meet her family, where he officially asked Phyllis's father for her hand in marriage. With the senior Hyman's blessing, the two celebrated back in their room at the downtown Pittsburgh Ramada. There wasn't a ring yet, but the two were now officially engaged.

"She wanted to marry him," recalled her musical director Terry Burrus. "Dante, he was the man. And we were happy. We were like, 'Somebody, please calm her down,' and Dante, every time he came around her attitude changed. So we said, 'Well, maybe this is the one. Maybe this is it. Maybe this will do it for her.'"

When Phyllis was performing in Toyko in early 1989, she told the audience that her new album would be out "sometime in 1990. I don't know when, only the record company knows when." By 1990, however, four years after *Living All Alone* had breathed new life into her career, Phyllis and her fans alike were tired of waiting for the next breath – and the next album – to be released. Her live shows included long segments full of material recorded for the album, which she referred to at the time as *Phyllis Hyman in the Prime of Her Life*. Among the songs featured in her sets were "Living In Confusion" and "What Ever Happened To Our Love," the latter of which her musical director Terry Burrus had co-written and co-produced with Kenny Gamble, as well as "I'll Never Do You Wrong," "Set A Little Trap," "Hottest Love Around," "Walk Away," and "Meet Me on the Moon."

Following a performance of the latter at Blues Alley in Washington, D.C., in June of 1990, several members of the audience began calling out, asking when the new album would finally be released. "Don't ask me," Phyllis told the crowd. "Am I a mind reader? Do I look like a record company? I don't have a clue."

Phyllis did, however, announce that Philadelphia International had found a new distributor at last. PIR's latest distribution deal was with Zoo Entertainment, a new BMG-owned label that was branching out into distribution. The deal came along just in time, as Phyllis's enthusiasm for the project was dwindling. In 1989, Phyllis was deeply dismayed to find out that "Walk Away," the song she had recorded with producer Marti Sharron in January 1988, was coming out as a new cut on Dionne Warwick's latest greatest hits package for Arista.

Phyllis took this one in stride, but she was stopped dead in her tracks when she discovered that the song she called her "masterpiece," "Meet Me On The Moon," was being released by a new jazz artist, Kimiko Itoh, on Columbia Records. Though the release was somewhat obscure – the album it was featured on, *Follow Me*, was distributed primarily in Japan and few of Phyllis's fans likely heard Itoh's version of the song – Phyllis was furious, and considered the release an act of treason. Her anger aside, the bottom line was that Philadelphia International's delay in finding a proper distributor was costing her.

"We did the best that we could," Kenny Gamble said of this dilemma. "During the days when Philly International was doing very well, we had a tremendous distribution arrangement with CBS and Sony. It just so happened that when Phyllis Hyman came along, we were at the descent of Philly International, and we did not have those relationships."

Gamble pointed out that the lengthy delay technically meant that the label was in breach, and that Phyllis could have left had she wanted to. "But we stuck together and we tried to figure something out. I'll always remember that. How loyal Phyllis was. I think we had a real good understanding as it relates to our friendship."

While Phyllis continued to prepare for the new album, she was also breaking in a new band. Her musical director and keyboardist of the past several years, Terry Burrus, had exited earlier in the year. His replacement, Vince Evans, was a talented young graduate of the prestigious Berklee College of Music in Boston. Evans was just a teenager when he first met Phyllis while playing some dates with Pieces of a Dream, with whom she was touring on one of her many Quiet Storm-themed package tours.

"I remember, she invited me to come backstage to her dressing room and we were talking," recalled Vince of that first meeting. "I was really impressed with Phyllis because this is like my first chance to really talk to a performer who was so professional and had her career going and all this. It felt like a big sisterly kind of talk; you know, keep your nose clean kind of thing."

Less than a week later, on one of the tour's next stops, Vince encountered Phyllis in the lobby of the hotel both bands were staying at.

"Hey Phyllis, how are you?" Vince said, happy to see the vocalist once more.

"Do I know you?" Phyllis asked, looking him in the eye.

Confused, the young pianist tried to explain.

"Well, yeah, I'm Vince Evans, the keyboard player. We were just …"

"Honey, I don't know you," Phyllis said, cutting him off. Then she promptly walked away.

With Burrus out, though, Phyllis apparently had no problem remembering Vince, and he was asked to join the band without auditioning. Vince took the train from his home in Silver Springs, Maryland to New York, and joined the band where they were rehearsing at Boo Studios. Phyllis didn't have much to say to him during rehearsal, but at the conclusion of it, she invited him to join her and some of the guys for lunch. The group went to a nearby Benihana steakhouse, a favorite of Phyllis's, and she waited until she was seated directly across the table from Vince to engage him in conversation.

"So, do you eat pussy?" Phyllis asked him.

"Excuse me?" Vince asked politely, appalled to be asked such an intimate question in front of the group.

"Do you like to eat pussy?" Phyllis repeated.

Vince decided to take a stand from the outset, wisely calculating that if he rolled over this time he would be setting a dangerous precedent.

"I said, 'Well, frankly, Phyllis, that's none of your business.' I just really felt like it was really outlandish and really distasteful."

With new members came a new act, or at least a few updates. Most prominent was a tribute to the legendary Sarah Vaughan that featured a medley of her hits, including "Sophisticated Lady," "Old Black Magic," "Smoke Gets In Your Eyes," "Lullaby of Birdland" and "Body & Soul." Vaughan, who had received a Grammy Lifetime Achievement Award a year ago, had died just months earlier. But not before coming out to see Phyllis during an engagement at George's in Chicago. "I don't know why she came to see me but for whatever reason I was grateful," said Phyllis. "No one told me she was coming. But I could see her in the audience and I knew it was Miss Vaughan and I freaked. She came, she sat at the end of the bar, she's really cool. The audience gave her a standing ovation and I was so flabbergasted. I was so honored.

"So I thought, 'Phyllis, you know in your entire career you've never really sung a segment in your show that featured jazz and standards. You may sing one or two. You've never recorded more than one standard.' I did record 'Here's That Rainy Day.' I don't recall recording anything else. So standards are not what I do normally. But it is something that I can do musically. So I decided, 'Phyllis, let's pick some real serious music. Let's pick some of Sarah's music. Let's sing about Sarah. Let's sing for Sarah. Let's sing to Sarah.'"

Phyllis rehearsed the new band for several days in advance of a week's engagement at D.C.'s Blues Alley. The only veteran of the group was bassist Ron Richardson, who had joined in 1986. In addition to Evans, Lionel Hamilton joined the band on saxophone, replacing John Valentino. At the end of 1989, backing vocalist Rachelle Ferrell left to work on her first solo album. She took with her fellow backing vocalists Lori Fulton and Veronica Underwood, as well as her boyfriend, drummer Doug Nally, who was replaced by Dennis Alston. Eric Jones came on board then and was the sole backing vocalist until just before the Blues Alley engagement when Phyllis brought on Bobby Lovett and Douglas Powell to join him. It was the first time Phyllis had employed all-male backing vocalists and the trio, supplemented by Evans, was quite dynamic.

She was a hard taskmaster, the band quickly learned, and not in the best of spirits. "Sometimes there was so much drama going on off-stage that we weren't always sure that she would make an appearance," recalled Douglas. One of his early shows with Phyllis was a particularly trying engagement at the Long Beach Jazz Fest in Long Beach, California. "I remember praying in the wings with Kirk Whalum that somehow, someway, the storm would pass and we would give the people the show that they anticipated."

A worrisome moment during the performance came at the start of the Sarah Vaughan medley. Phyllis was relying on lyric sheets on a nearby music stand to be her first line of back up should she forget the words. "For weeks, Phyllis had refused to learn the lyrics to 'Body & Soul' and was still depending on us to help her through the song when the lyric sheets would inevitably blow off stage. When the time came for the Vaughan medley, and in the mood she had been in, we knew this wasn't going to be one of her better performances. But never count Phyllis out. Not only did she sing every note and nuance, she sang the lyric like she never had before. I remember how I cried that night on stage, marveling at the genius of Phyllis that under duress she was often better than most in perfect conditions."

Yes, Phyllis was at home on the stage, perhaps more so than any other place in the world. "Phyllis was at her best and most comfortable there, kicking off her shoes, talking to the people," said Dante, who was with her that night in Long Beach. "Her performances were an opportunity to talk to each and every individual in front of her. I just have different pictures of her in my mind at different times in front of people on stage, just being comfortable, just singing with her eyes closed with a hat on, just loving it. Just loving it. She was complete on stage."

Phyllis was still doing select dates with Grover Washington, Jr. – and summer was generally her busiest touring season – when the offer of an extensive fall tour with Jonathan Butler came in. Phyllis was not pleased by the prospect of opening the shows, especially considering the fact that the South African Butler had only released his first album four years ago. But she would technically be co-headlining the tour and, most importantly, Stageright Productions was offering a total of $200,000 for 25 shows.

It was a deal too good to pass up. But money aside, Phyllis was in no shape to take on such an extensive tour. She was drinking heavily and using once again, happy to once again be in love but tormented by the fact that her lover was living thousands of miles away in Japan. She was testy and impatient, her fuse shorter than ever, and despite the tour offer, the bad news was still billowing. Though Phyllis had completed the new album, a release date was nowhere in sight. Four years after *Living All Alone* was released, PIR had only submitted a single royalty statement to Phyllis, and in August Glenda had been forced to threaten PIR with litigation. Due to Phyllis semi-annually, PIR was over six statements behind. And as recording costs for the new project mounted, Phyllis had no idea what the last album had earned, and what her financial picture with the label looked like.

The pressure soon grew to be too much for Phyllis. Amid her troubles, there was still much to be optimistic about. She was engaged to be married. She had a record in the bag that, once released, was sure to be as big a success as the last one. But the combination of the disappointments and anxieties floating around in her head proved too potent for Phyllis. In July 1990, Phyllis decided that she wanted out.

"For Phyllis, suicide was always an option she thought she should be allowed to have," said Dante. "She made that very clearly known to those who were around her that were in an intimate enough relationship. She would have that conversation. She and I talked about it on numerous occasions, at length, because it was an option that she believed she had the right to exercise."

As a result of those conversations, Dante was not completely surprised when Phyllis called him in Japan to say she was about to end her life. The call was agonizing for Dante, but he did not threaten to call the authorities or attempt to order her not to do it. "If you love someone, and for them, their belief system says suicide is an option ... she was like, 'So if I choose to do that, I need you to allow me to have that option.' So if I love her, do I allow her to exercise the option or do I overrule that because of my own belief system? For me, I have to respect somebody's choices."

Tearfully, Dante said goodbye, and once off the phone with him Phyllis swallowed a handful of pills. She had failed to cancel the plans she'd made with Glenda for the day, however, and when after repeated attempts Glenda was still unable to reach Phyllis on the phone, she caught a cab to 2400 Chestnut to check on her. At the door of apartment 2210, Glenda once again received no answer. She had her own key and tried to gain entrance, but the chain lock was on the door. She called out to Phyllis, but yet once again, there was no answer.

Glenda feared the worse, and rushed in search of help breaking down the door. Once inside Phyllis's sparsely furnished apartment, Glenda's fear reached fever pitch. "The place was a wreck," she recalled. "There was a path of pills leading from the living room back to her bedroom and stuff was strewn everywhere. It looked chaotic." In her bedroom, Phyllis lay unconscious. Glenda called 911, and once the paramedics arrived Glenda joined them in the ambulance as they rushed Phyllis to the hospital.

Learning she was there, Phyllis's personal assistants, Denise and Razz, began notifying the appropriate people. One of those to receive a phone call was Phyllis's brother Michael in New York. Michael caught the first train out to Philly and rushed to the hospital. Phyllis's sister Ann also took the first flight out from Pittsburgh, unsure of Phyllis's fate. "When Phyllis woke up, I was standing there and she grabbed me and held onto me for dear life," said Glenda. "She was glad to be alive and she thanked me for saving her. It was a very powerful moment. She realized that she had been saved. Because I think that's really what she wanted more than anything. To be saved. Saved from herself. And the experience sort of matched her fantasy."

Is it at all possible then that Phyllis attempted to take her life to live out her fantasy, believing she'd be saved? She did, after all, have plans with Glenda and knew she'd come looking for her. "It's possible," Glenda admitted. "It's very possible."

Shortly after regaining consciousness, Phyllis began lobbying for her release. Despite the fact that suicide attempts generally require a 48-hour stay for observation, Phyllis was able to convince the medical personnel on hand that she was no danger to herself and they allowed her to leave. But once back at her apartment, she let her true intentions be known.

"I'll give you a year, maybe two," she told her brother and the staff that had gathered. "But I don't want to be here."

"I was crushed," recalled Michael. "I mean, God, what do you say to someone like that? How do you respond to something like that? How do you respond to someone who has given up? It was a crushing blow to me, to everyone. I knew the pain she was going through. I witnessed it."

Relieved to still have his fiancé alive, Dante met with Phyllis in Denver in August. Dante introduced Phyllis to all of his friends before the two took a trip to the mountains. There, they stayed in a lovely loft at the Glacier Lodge just enjoying each other's company. Dante was planning to once again settle in Colorado after returning from Japan, and he was pleased that Phyllis seemed to enjoy it. "She loved it. She loved the people. She loved my friends. We'd go to jazz clubs and sit in on different sets with folks that I knew who were playing."

But by now, Dante had seen first hand just how troubled Phyllis was. It wasn't just the pain that she couldn't handle. It was also the joy. "Good things can cause their own fear about how good they really are or how long they'll last, or are they going to be as good as I want them to be?" Dante explained. "So they can cause their own difficulties. I think a lot of that type of thought process is what kept Phyllis from being able to take that step over her issues. She could let herself love only so much before it scared her. She could only let herself hope so much before it scared her. She could only let herself feel good so much before it scared her.

"For Phyllis, sometimes, getting up was just too hard to do," Dante continued. "Those were her words. 'Sometimes getting up is just too much.' And that's not because, I don't think, there were insurmountable difficulties. I think sometimes life was scary for her on its good days as well."

When she was with Dante, Phyllis tried to be on her best behavior. But separated from him, her loneliness got the best of her and her behavior was unpredictable. "Her fears were so intense that they could trigger anything from very aggressive behavior to other techniques that she would employ to feel like she was in control – procrastination, no shows, just issues around punctuality all together – in an attempt to sort of regain her control over things," said Glenda. Phyllis had a few weeks off from the road in September, and too much free time meant too much time for her mind to run wild. To occupy herself, Phyllis, who was staying predominantly in her Philadelphia apartment, went out on daily shopping binges, often spending several hundred dollars a day on clothes and costume jewelry. At home, she was going through half a gallon of her favorite Russian vodka – Stolichnaya – and several bottles of white wine per week.

By the start of September 1990, the Jonathan Butler tour was beginning to disintegrate. Advance ticket sales were dismal and Stageright Productions took on a sponsor to offset the "financial burdens" of the tour. In select markets, the tour was billed as the "Hennessy Jazz Series" thanks to the sponsorship dollars of the popular cognac brand. In others, Stageright added a third act to the bill, jazz keyboardist Alex Bugnon. None of these adjustments proved enough to ensure the tour's success, however, and ultimately dates were canceled. The tour was trimmed and the price tag reduced from $200,000 to $144,000, meaning Phyllis was making only $9,000 per night, a great reduction from her average nightly take at this time, which was about $15,000. The tour, which Stageright Productions had christened the Sweet Deliverance Tour, was beneficial to Phyllis only because of its bulk, the 16 dates would take place over the span of a single month.

After her 1986 stint in rehab, Phyllis had managed to go a year or so without drinking alcohol. When Martha David came on the scene at the end of 1987, Phyllis was still on the wagon. "I asked her early on if it bothered her when I drank alcohol around her," Martha recalled. "At first she said no, and then maybe about a week later she said yes, it did bother her. I said, 'Fine, I won't drink around you,' and for a long time I didn't, even when she started drinking again. I thought that in some way it was at least not encouraging her so I wouldn't drink alcohol."

Without seriously addressing her mental health issues, it was inevitable that Phyllis would start drinking again. Alcohol, cocaine, pills, food, sex, shopping – Phyllis binged on all of these things in an effort to self-medicate and make herself feel better. Once Phyllis was sober and her mind clear, the thoughts Phyllis had tried so long to run from – the deep core of her pain – were suddenly knocking on her door with great force. The only real chance Phyllis had to stay clean of illegal drugs and unhealthy habits was to start a medicinal regimen to treat her manic depression and continue with talk therapy to explore and excise her pain. It is no coincidence that Phyllis stopped her therapy sessions with Portia Hunt at about the same time she resumed drinking.

Phyllis's problem with therapy was the same problem she had in every other facet of her life. She could not risk vulnerability. Therefore, she fought at all costs to remain in control of the sessions. "There was a real avoidance type of reaction to me because she didn't know how to place me, between being a lackey and a mother figure," recalled Portia Hunt. "That was really hard for her at times."

By its very nature, talk therapy requires the patient to be vulnerable, to explore their inner workings – what makes them tick – and discover the open wounds inside of them so that they may be healed. But just as Phyllis kept her lovers and friends – indeed, everyone – at arm's length, she did the same to Portia Hunt. Phyllis would only drop her mask so far. Then, once Portia managed to get too close to the real Phyllis, she pushed the therapist away, shut down and closed herself off.

While Portia's office represented a safe place to do so, Phyllis did not want to confront her true self. She did not want to look deeply inside herself. She did not want to revisit the past and unlock the hurts she had sealed off so securely. Phyllis may have feared judgment from Portia. But more than anything, Phyllis was her own judge and jury and she imposed a stiff sentence on herself.

"Phyllis had a deep sense of shame that ruled her all of her life," said Portia. "Even though she had gotten a lot of accolades, if you don't feel good about yourself, if doesn't matter what other people tell you. In fact, if they tell you the opposite of what you think about yourself, you experience more shame because you can't live up to what you think other people think about you."

As Phyllis resumed drinking, Martha did what she could to discourage her. "Once we went across the street and into a liquor store on a break from the recording studio. She didn't have her wallet with her and wanted to buy something. She wanted to borrow money from me and I wouldn't lend it to her to buy liquor. I was saying, 'If you want to do it, you're on your own.'"

More often than not, Martha was unsuccessful in her efforts to keep Phyllis off booze. Phyllis was good at finding a way to do whatever she wanted, and drinking was no exception. "Another time we went to Japan and I got to her room ahead of her and I grabbed the mini-bar and ran it down the hall and put it in someone else's room. Then she walked in with bottles that she had bought downstairs."

Slowly, as she resumed her love affair with liquor, Phyllis gradually began adding cocaine and pills into the mix. Phyllis's brother Michael was at the apartment once when she received a drug delivery. "I always knew when food was coming because she'd give me the money. Phyllis was a generous tipper. Those delivery guys loved her. They knew when they came to apartment 33-C they'd be taken care of. But I knew this was not that kind of delivery, just by the way it was going down."

Phyllis waited anxiously, pacing about the apartment. When the man delivering the package arrived at the door, Phyllis made the tradeoff without inviting him in. Then, she quickly closed herself off in her tiny kitchen. Minutes later, she retreated to her bedroom, once again closing the door. Michael had no doubt that Phyllis was freebasing cocaine. "That was the first time that it hit me that she had a very serious problem," he recalled. "I felt so helpless. I just felt so bad."

According to Phyllis's friend and sometimes-assistant Julie Aponte, Phyllis said it was her ex-husband Larry Alexander that had first introduced her to cocaine. In the late '70s and early '80s, when it was fashionable for blow to be served on silver dishes at special parties, Phyllis had occasionally snorted cocaine. But cocaine was something she preferred to do privately. It was not a party for her, and Phyllis didn't invite anyone to share the experience. If fact, even if other staffers were aware of what she was doing, she actually addressed it with very few people. Julie, however, was one person she confided in. "That was her escape," Julie said. "Phyllis used it as an escape. I don't think she enjoyed it."

"I'm going to go get fucking high," Phyllis would tell Julie when something would upset her greatly. "It just makes me not feel."

For Phyllis, whose emotions ran rampant and whose pain threatened at times to engulf her, not feeling was the ultimate goal. Not feeling, not fearing, not having to worry or wonder about anything. Phyllis fought to be in control at all times, but while freebasing, Phyllis could just let go and let the snow drift over her and wash her cares away.

"It wasn't a party for her," said Julie. "It just made her not feel and she wanted to be in her own world. Phyllis did not do it for fun."

More than self-medicating, Phyllis was actually self-anesthetizing. She knew the high wouldn't last, but for a few precious moments it would numb her from the pain. But cocaine is a deceptive lover. Although freebasing actually delivers an incredibly fast rush of pleasure – the cocaine reaches the brain within seconds via this method, resulting in a sudden and intense high – the euphoria quickly disappears. And, according to the National Institute on Drug Abuse, it leaves in its wake an enormous craving to freebase again and again. The user usually increases the dose and the frequency to satisfy this craving, resulting in addiction and physical debilitation.

Phyllis was already debilitated by her mental illness, by the manic depression that made her tired mind work overtime. She had great difficulty sleeping. Her mind would not shut down no matter how badly her body needed to rest. But treating a debilitating condition with a debilitating substance was no solution. Whether she realized it or not, it only intensified her problems, giving her more she needed to escape from, and less strength to make the trek.

Martha was aware of Phyllis's cocaine usage, though Phyllis would never use in front of her. "Most of the time it wasn't something that was present during our relationship. At one point I realized that she'd started again, and it did start to interfere with our relationship because she would go off by herself. She only wanted to be by herself and she didn't want to be around anybody. She'd turn her phones off and disconnect from the world."

Though her options were limited, Martha did what she could to dissuade Phyllis from her drug usage. But she felt the wisest approach was to tread lightly. "I never put together an intervention or threatened to leave if she didn't stop. But I was always very discouraging. I thought that was the least that I could do and I tried to help at least keep her going professionally. I tried to make sure that she didn't miss appointments or anything like that. One time as I was leaving the apartment and I knew what was coming, I said to her, 'You know you're not going to ever make it to what you have to do tomorrow.' I managed to convince her to not do the cocaine until she finished what she had to do the next day.

"Some people might call it enabling, helping her keep it together," Martha continued. "But I never knew what else there was to do. I felt like I was there to take care of her, and short of threatening to leave or putting together an intervention I, day to day, did whatever I thought was best in my own way."

Terry Burrus remembered the first time he stumbled upon Phyllis doing cocaine. "I was depressed. I mean, here's this very beautiful woman, she had a great heart, a very giving and loving spirit. But she just had problems in her life. I was disturbed. But at the same time you have to understand that in the music business you're going to run into these things. All I could do at the time was come out and say, 'Phyllis, I understand, but do you need to do this?' And she would yell back, 'Yes, of course.' She was like that. She's gotta do what she's gotta do.

"There were several times that I caught her in the middle of certain things, although she liked to keep things private when it came to that," Terry continued. "But if you catch her, you catch her. She'd tell you verbally, 'Oh yeah, this, that and the other, I was with my good friend and we were doing this.' But she tried to never let you see her doing it. But to actually catch her, if you open up the door to the room and she's doing something, it's like, 'Phyllis, Phyllis' ... but what can you say?"

As Christmas, always a hard time for her, approached, Phyllis's condition only worsened. Early in the month, she had actually a missed a show at the Village Gate, representing a new low for her. She was depressed and despondent, and using potentially lethal combinations of drugs and alcohol daily to manage her manic depression. "As she got older, her disease became more and more difficult for her to manage," said Glenda. "She elected not to use pharmaceutical medication. She elected to self-medicate and her self medication distorted her disease more and more, until she felt helpless about ever being able to recover from it."

Phyllis eventually agreed to once again enter treatment. "She was definitely in trouble," Glenda continued. "She was starting to gain weight again and she was starting to slip. Her weight gain was always a tell tale sign. Between the alcohol and the drugs and not getting any sleep, she would just balloon up."

Even if Phyllis was willing to go back to rehab, there was a month's worth of tightly scheduled obligations that had to be kept before she could leave. Glenda booked Phyllis into The Willough, a high-end and highly reputable inpatient rehabilitation facility in Naples, Florida, for a 28-day stay. But first, Phyllis had a week's worth of shows to do at Kimball's East Supper Club in Emeryville, California, which began on New Year's Eve. Phyllis went on to play a night at The Strand in Redondo Beach before returning to New York, where she appeared at a DancEllington benefit given by her old friend Mercedes Ellington. The following day, Phyllis canceled a scheduled photo shoot for the cover of her new album with photographer Jean Pagliuso, stating she was unhappy with her appearance at the present time. On the 12th, it was off to Washington, D.C., where Phyllis performed for the Delta Sigma Theta sorority before finally playing the week's worth of shows at Blues Alley that had been pushed back to allow for the conclusion of the Sweet Deliverance Tour.

Finally, on Monday, January 21, 1991, Phyllis had fulfilled all her outstanding commitments and was ready for rehab. She had bought eight cartons of Marlboro Lights 100s to get her through her stay. Phyllis flew directly from D.C. to Naples and checked herself in without incident. As rehabilitation facilities go, The Willough was rather posh. It resembled an upscale hotel with a fully equipped gym, tennis courts, a Jacuzzi® and a large screened in swimming pool, where one could take a dip or merely lounge and watch the palm trees sway outside. Phyllis did well in rehab. She took fervent notes during the seminars and group therapy sessions. At night, after midnight "lights out," Phyllis wrote letters to friends until sleep overtook her.

Upon checking into the facility, Phyllis was given a large binder labeled "My Willough Journey." A personal recovery journal, Phyllis began writing in the binder during her first week. On the page labeled "What got me here?" Phyllis wrote, "I need help. My drug, alcohol and food addictions are out of hand. I began missing work. My management – Glenda and Sydney – recommended it because of my absence from work and living. I began thinking again of dying; this time through a window, 33 stories above ground. My self-worth and self-esteem were at an all time low."

In the section labeled "Crisis," Phyllis mentioned the missed show at the Village Gate in December. "I missed work. Got high and just didn't show up. I'm sabotaging my career with my addictions." A few pages later, under the heading of "Addiction defined," Phyllis was asked to describe a feeling or behavior that existed between her and her substance of choice. "Coke – freebasing ... never stopping until it's all over, not taking care of personal hygiene." Phyllis admitted that in her early days of using, cocaine made her feel "light, happy, silly, sexy," but that now it only made her feel "sad, angry." On the page called "The denial progression," Phyllis wrote that she would use cocaine "till my throat was sore, my head ached and my voice slurred" and that she used it "as often as I could." As for problems caused by her addictive behavior, Phyllis said "people didn't want to be around me ... I was called rude and harsh to people I loved."

As Phyllis sobered up and her head cleared, the therapy sessions she underwent while at The Willough caused her to become increasingly introspective. Per the suggestion of her counselor, Phyllis began carrying a notebook. In it, she explored her emotions and showed great remorse at how she had treated those close to her through the years. Completely clean of mood altering substances, she was able to clearly examine her life and her actions, at least to the extent her untreated mental illness would allow her to do so. She wrote letters to specific individuals including the woman she had chosen to guide her career for the past eight years.

To Glenda – Apology

I always resented you for your rigid health practices, your constant happy attitude and your perpetual laughter. I couldn't stand it. Nobody should be so happy. I always ridiculed you for the way you lived, you were so boring.

In reality I was jealous of what you had. If you said, "Yes, of course." I said, "No." I've lied to you and cheated myself out of the chance to learn from you the lessons on good old hate-free, resent-free living. I was always so mean to you and I'm sorry. Please forgive me.

Many of Phyllis's letters, though, were to and regarding members of her family and reflections of her childhood.

Mom – Apology

I've always been ashamed of you for tolerating my father's verbal and emotional abuse. I thought you were a fool for having so many children and not allowing anything for yourself because there was no time or money. I've also been ashamed of your lack of education and motivation for anything. I remember you just living there and that was never good enough for me. I felt women were more than these things.

I have been so riddled with shame and guilt because I treated you with disgust the same way Dad did. I ignored and belittled you at every turn. Instead of hating me, you were hurt. You could have turned away from me, [but] you loved me in spite of myself. ... You did the best you could and I will be forever grateful.

I love you, mommy.

How I was different from my family

I always wanted to be an only child. Even though there were six others I pretended that they were visiting, but of course they never went home. I always played boss to the little ones since I was the oldest and even managed to (of course with their help) [enjoy] a maid and valet service business, which consisted of my six brothers and sisters waiting on me at every turn. I would lay on the couch watching TV and call on whomever was available to do my bidding.

My father finally discovered this scam and demanded that they refuse or receive just punishment. I was now on my own.

Throughout my teenage years I set my sights on a life free of kids and [a] husband. My mom and dad had no affection in their marriage that I could see and in my mind, if that was marriage then forget it. Kids represented taking in time and money and me, being the selfish person that I was, [I] was not interested in sharing.

At an early age I knew I was different and without question special. I decided early on that my destiny was to be a rich and famous businesswoman with no husband or kids.

Perhaps most telling, though, was this letter. While Phyllis addressed it, simply, to "Anger – Disease," she is really speaking to her bipolar disorder, to her manic side and the symptoms of such that she was having an increasingly difficult time controlling.

Anger – Disease

I have hated you longer than you will ever know. You have made my every waking hour a horror. I couldn't work, make love, have friends, enjoy singing or have relationships because of you. My attitude sucks and I hate the world. Nothing ever feels good to me anymore because of you.

You ruined my marriage and kept me isolated from the world. It's a wonder I even get on stage anymore. But when I think of performing, even that's a drag. You've made me a lonely, angry person with no will to live. The only thing you didn't do was let me [die] this summer when I wanted to.

You've lied to me over and over again and I've had it with you.

I'm inviting you to do something very special for me: Kiss my ass.

Hottfully yours,

Pepper H.[8]

One of Phyllis's specific assignments was to examine the harmful consequences of her addiction. "Both my drinking and my cocaine use had begun to affect my voice," Phyllis wrote. "My

---

[8] Phyllis was christened "Pepper H." by members of her road staff in tribute to her fiery temper. The nickname was also her code name on the walkie-talkie system her road crew used.

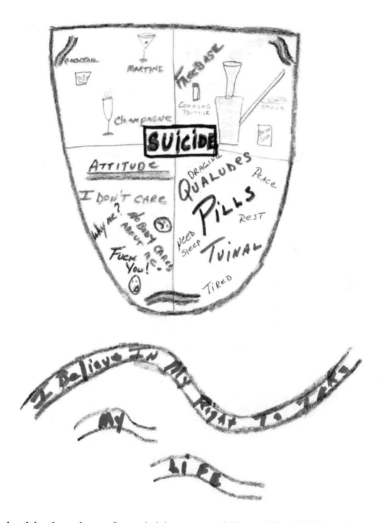

Phyllis made this drawing of a suicide crest while at The Willough. She initialed it in the top left-hand corner. (Credit: The Hyman Family/Collection of Jason A. Michael)

throat would become tired more quickly and would often feel dry and tight. I began to lose interest in performing and being in my work environment. My drinking put on extra pounds and made my face puffy. Complexion was not good. The uglier I got, the more I drank and did cocaine. My cocaine addiction caused me to spend thousands of dollars that could have been used to improve my business operations. Couldn't sleep – haven't been able to in five years. Made me cranky and short-tempered. Had little or no kind words for friends and co-workers. Was abusive to boyfriend."

On February 10, the third Sunday in her treatment, Phyllis received a pass to leave the center's grounds. She hired a limo and along with Gail, a fellow patient and new friend from The Willough, headed off to the Coastland Center mall. She dropped about $300 there, buying mostly clothes and some film for her trusty Polaroid camera. Gradually, as her release from the program neared, Phyllis began to envision a life for herself free from substance abuse. She filed an aftercare plan that listed her personalized problems and an action plan to address them. She identified potential social pressures and talked of ways to handle them. Perhaps most importantly, she admitted that she could do none of this alone. "I truly want the Lord to take away my bad thoughts," Phyllis wrote as her daily affirmation for February 13. "It feels strange. But if I say it and believe it, it will be so."

Toward the end of the month-long stay, it was time for the requisite family counseling sessions. Phyllis asked Glenda once again to be a part of these sessions. She also asked her mother and had Glenda arrange for her to fly into Naples from Pittsburgh. She considered inviting Dante, but he was in Japan, which made the plan unreasonable. She did, however, write to him from the center, thanking him for his patience and love.

On February 20, the day after she had received her degree of sobriety, Phyllis left The Willough and flew alone to Chicago. Her travel manager and all around assistant Bill Schultz met her in Chicago's Midway Airport and escorted her to the Lenox House hotel. Initially, Phyllis made Schultz promise to take her to an Alcoholics Anonymous meeting that night. But once at the Lenox House, plans changed. Phyllis got out of her clothes and into bed, then ordered up every dessert listed on the Lenox House room service menu. After eating a few bites from each of them, she passed out. When Schultz returned to her room several hours later to take her the meeting, he found her naked in bed – her half-eaten desserts spread out around her – and was unable to wake her.

Phyllis performed at Chicago's Civic Opera House the next night, and afterward asked Schultz to accompany her to a local club to see dance diva Martha Wash. One half of The Weather Girls, the group responsible for the monster hit "It's Raining Men," Martha had a predominantly gay following. Phyllis highly enjoyed herself at the show and soon had slipped backstage. It was there that Schultz found her some time later, eating fried chicken and – just 36 hours out of rehab – sipping champagne. "She was crazy," recalled Martha with a laugh. "I was surprised to see her but glad, because I don't get a whole of entertainers that come to my shows. So it's very much always a surprise when I see somebody that I know. It was fun. She was just, I guess, happy to be out. She was having a good time. She said she was doing fine."

While in Chicago, Phyllis couldn't help but indulge herself. She stayed in town for a week following the Opera House concert, going on daily shopping binges and quickly running through a healthy portion of the earnings from the show. An interesting item among her purchases was two fifths of vodka. Phyllis was officially off the wagon already.

Phyllis flew directly back to Florida from Chicago. But this time it was a recording studio rather than a rehab program that called her to the Sunshine State. Phyllis met Nick Martinelli in Miami where the two resumed cutting tracks for the by now long-awaited *Living All Alone* follow up. Since they'd last hooked up, Martinelli's career had continued to flourish. Two more Martinelli-produced power ballads – Stephanie Mills' "Home" and "Make It Like It Was" by Regina Belle – had been released and made their way to the top of the charts, bringing his tally of number one R&B hits to five. Now Nick brought two more songs to the table for Phyllis, "When You Get Right Down To It" and "I Can't Take It Anymore."

Phyllis was especially taken with the message of "I Can't Take It Anymore." "It's about a guy who's a major jerk and my attitude is 'Get out of my face; don't even try it.' Nick Martinelli wrote that specifically for me, and what I like about it is that it's saying that women – and men, too – don't have to be abused by anyone else.

It's horrendous the emotional abuse that goes on in relationships, and we need to empower ourselves rather than taking all the stuff."

Nick recorded the two songs on Phyllis in Miami's famous Criteria Studios. Phyllis was familiar with Criteria, having recorded some of her early Roadshow tracks there some 15 years earlier. Phyllis's old friend Betty Wright got wind that she was in town and called the studio, where she got Nick on the line. "I said, 'Come on in, honey, and sing,' and that's how we met," Nick remembered. "Phyllis loved Betty. Phyllis never had a bad thing to say about Betty, honey, and if anybody would ever say anything about Betty she would kill 'em. Really, she loved Betty."

Betty told Nick not to tell Phyllis she was coming. "And when I got there it was so funny," Wright recalled. "She's sitting with her legs across the chair, you know, sitting backward in the chair singing this song, and when I came to the door she just screamed to the top of her voice. We just had a great time, and then Nick said, 'You wanna sing on something?' and he handed me some lyrics, just automatically. 'You feel like singing a lil' bit?'"

Betty was happy to repay Phyllis for the favor of adding background vocals to "Give A Smile" from her 1980 album for Epic Records. Turnabout is fair play, they say, and Betty is heard prominently on "When You Get Right Down To It." But for all the fun they had, Phyllis still had a few quirks about being in the studio. "Whenever she came to the studio, she would drag a cooler with all her drinks, her wine, whatever she was wanted," said Nick. "I used to say, 'Why do you drag all this shit around? I mean, anybody will just order it for you when you want it to be here.'

"The one thing about Phyllis is she over-obsessed on everything," Nick continued. "If she ordered food, she'd order four platters. She wouldn't just order one. She was addicted to food. She was addicted to liquor. She was addicted to drugs. She just had an addictive personality, and when you have that kind of personality it's hard to function normally."

While in Miami, Phyllis visited with Julie Aponte, her old friend and sometimes assistant from New York. Julie knew all about Phyllis's addictions, and on the heels of rehab she was very disappointed to find Phyllis still drinking. "I got very upset at her," Julie recalled. "I said, 'You wasted all of this money,' because rehab is expensive. But I think the second time around she went because of Glenda, because she was pressured to." (Glenda admits this is true. "She did go at my insistence ... I could just see her sinking and I told her, 'You and I both know that you need help. We both know that. We both know that you're getting out there again.'")

Word traveled all the way to Japan that even after a month in rehab, Phyllis had not stopped drinking. Phyllis's alcoholism had long been a point of contention in her relationship with Dante, and the strain was now growing unbearable. "It created difficulties, obviously," said Dante. "We had conversations about it, some calm, some not so calm, and to her credit, a piece of the difficulty was she could function very well, quite well. She was a functioning alcoholic when we were together and that would sometimes be her answer; that she was able to function and do what she needed to do and perform and continue doing what she does and not look like an alcoholic. So it was at times quite difficult. That was a piece of the puzzle of at some point why it became just too difficult for me to remain."[9]

When he first became aware of her problems, Dante had fooled himself into believing that he could fix them. Now, he had to face the fact that he was only human. "I had a tendency to want to be the knight in shining armor. So I could see Phyllis's pain and see all the things that she could be that she wasn't, or that she wanted to be but wouldn't let herself be, and for some period of time I wanted to help her do that. And that's not always the best reason for a relationship."

Eventually, feeling crushed under the pressure, Dante called an end to the relationship. "It was a combination of things. At some point it gets to be very draining, very difficult and love gets pushed into the corner when you've got to deal with all the other negativity and demons and issues and things like that. I guess at some point I just realized that I couldn't continue on the way the relationship was, and I didn't see that there was anything that was

---

[9] To Glenda, Phyllis's description of herself was inaccurate. "For her to say that she was a functioning alcoholic, no, no, no. She was a functioning mentally disabled human being who used other things to help her function, to sort of stay in the game. Phyllis was disabled, just like anyone who has a physical disability. She was virtually in a mental wheelchair."

going to change it. At some point I just said, 'I can't do this anymore.'"

Chapter 14

'Living In Confusion' is a song about me. It's about someone who's not being honest with themselves.

On June 25, 1991, five long years after her first album for Philadelphia International Records came out, its follow up, *Prime Of My Life*, was finally released. "The title track of this album is one of the most positive lyrics I've heard in a long time," Phyllis said. "It's the way I feel about myself now because, frankly, I haven't been happy for the past 25 years. I've been through a lot of therapy, and I discovered that I'd been playing the game of life, smiling on the outside. I was a very insecure person, suffering from low self-esteem. I acted my way through my life, through my career."

Phyllis admitted that when she first recorded the song, in Los Angeles during the summer of 1988, she was faking it. "I believed in the lyric but, honestly, I wasn't living it. I really wanted to sing it for everyone else." For years, Phyllis had been on an emotional roller coaster, but now she felt she was standing on solid ground. "I guess things came to a head when I reached a really low point last year. Now I feel like I'm more secure, more comfortable with me, with what I'm doing, with who I am."

She was also more content with her voice and for the first time capable of comprehending its beauty. "Up until five years ago I didn't listen to myself that much. Now I've learned to appreciate my voice and my talent in a way that I didn't before. It's funny, because people's descriptions of me didn't mean that much to me. When people would say they loved my voice, I'd wonder 'Why are you moved?' Now I'm beginning to understand how people can be turned on by my singing. I'm starting to appreciate my talent and I feel a whole lot less uptight. I now understand the spiritual, the emotional and the physical aspects of my voice. I think people can sense that when they see me perform. I've been told that people can feel a lot more love and calm coming from me these days."

The delay between albums was a subject that came up in many interviews, but Phyllis handled the topic gracefully. "Yes, it's taken a while between records, but I'm aware that I have an audience that's made up of special people who have never stopped showing me their support and their love. Hopefully, they'll feel that it's been worth the wait."

BMG-owned Zoo Entertainment had been launched in 1990. At its helm was Lou Maglia, the former president of Island Records. Zoo's initial emphasis was rock music, and its roster at the inception of the PIR distribution deal was far from impressive. Signed to the label were such groups as Procol Harum, the band responsible for the 1967 crossover hit "A Whiter Shale of Pale," and newcomers such as Odds, Blue Train and Love Jones. A precious few singles grazed the pop and rock charts, but none of the albums they were culled from charted at all. On the R&B side of things, Zoo had Voices, a quartet of young teenage girls who reached number 14 R&B with "Yeah, Yeah, Yeah" and Dem Dames, a provocative female rap duo whose album featured such racy tracks as "Irresistable Bitch" and "The Nasty Thing." Again, neither of these albums charted.[10]

Early on, Zoo began branching out into distribution. Little is known about the details of the PIR distribution deal, but it's obvious it was a low-cost, low-risk investment for Zoo. "I wasn't privy to what the arrangement was, but I know it wasn't an expensive one," said Jesus Garber, Zoo's vice president of urban promotion, who came to Zoo from A&M Records, where he worked such albums as Janet Jackson's blockbusters *Control* and *Rhythm Nation*. "It wasn't a very, very high dollar investment."

In fact, it's unlikely that the deal, which included only Phyllis and legendary act The Dells, allowed Kenny Gamble to recoup more than a fraction of the five years worth of recording costs he had put into Phyllis. If Phyllis questioned these costs, she said

---

[10] The label would hit its stride in 1993, releasing gold albums by rocker Matthew Sweet and the group Tool. However, the ride would be short-lived as disappointing sales forced it to be sold in 1996.

nothing publicly. "I stuck with Kenny Gamble and Philly International while they were dealing with the business aspects of getting a new deal because I didn't feel comfortable with anyone else. At one point, he was putting his personal money into making my album, and he expressed just how much he really cared about me and my music. Plus, my loyalty runs too deep to consider leaving a situation. The people I have around me are there because I love them."

Phyllis felt that Gamble's commitment to her and her career afforded him a certain level of respect, so she lavished him with praise in the press. It was a subtle way to continue her digs at Clive Davis. Though in truth, there had been conflicts at PIR, too. In addition to the enormous wait period between albums there were also several missed royalty statements and an overall messy approach to bookkeeping in general. There was also the matter of how much material had been recorded for the new album. Before Phyllis recorded a single song for the new album, there was already enough in the can for a complete one.

Phyllis had sincerely hoped that songs such as "Set A Little Trap" and her version of the classic "My Funny Valentine" would be included on *Living All Alone*. When they weren't, she went back into the studio with Terry Burrus and rerecorded them hoping to see them show up on the next album. There were also new songs the two worked on and recorded such as "Forever With You." Kenny Gamble shared co-writing credits with Terry on "Forever," and Kenny co-wrote another he produced on Phyllis, "The Kids," with Bruce Hawes. Neither "Forever" nor "Kids," though, was a favorite with Phyllis.

In addition, songs like the Nick Martinelli produced "Hottest Love Around," "I'll Never Do You Wrong," co-written and produced Marti Sharron back in 1988, "Uncover Me," which had originally been recorded for *Living*, "Found Another Lover" and a remake of the Harold Melvin and the Blue Notes Philly classic "Wake Up Everybody" were all mixed, mastered and in the can. All told, in addition to the 10 songs released on *Prime Of My Life* there were at least another 10 that were fully mixed and mastered but did not make it onto the album plus a dozen or so miscellaneous extras that were in various stages of production.

The production fees and studio costs for these songs were, of course, all charged against Phyllis – even though they never saw the light of day. To illustrate how quickly they added up, consider this: The budget for *Prime Of My Life*, per Phyllis's contract with PIR, was $150,000. Yet by November 1988, with only six songs in the can, the project was already $50,000 over budget – and only three of these songs would actually make it to the album. With producer's fees, studio time, musicians, travel and other miscellaneous charges, each side – or song – was costing a minimum of $25,000 to produce. The result is that Phyllis was in debt to PIR to the tune of $500,000 or so – or more than three times the album's original budget – by the time that *Prime* was released.

"We had budgets for Phyllis, but we would always spend more than we allocated," explained Kenny Gamble. "Our intention was to try make Phyllis a platinum artist. So we didn't spare too much expense when it came to recording her."

The long list of tunes she worked on and the lengthy recording process of *Prime* – five years off and on – may have ultimately resulted in the release of a fine recording. But it also set Phyllis up not to make any money off of it. When he signed her, Kenny Gamble assured Phyllis he would take care of her. It was all in the family, after all. Clive Davis may not have given a damn about her, but black folk, Phyllis surely thought, would take care of their own.

Instead, six years after signing a far less lucrative contract with PIR, Phyllis suddenly found herself owing her new label a substantial amount more than she owed Arista when she left – again, where she had incurred the cost of five albums to PIR's two. The situation brought to mind the title of one of the songs that did make it onto the album: "What Ever Happened To Our Love?"

"The exploitation of blacks by white record company owners has been decried over the years, but it was not so much skin color as it was power that brought about such unilateral relationships," explained John Jackson in *A House On Fire: The Rise and Fall of Philadelphia Soul*. "Berry Gordy amply proved that at Motown. Kenny Gamble, Leon Huff and Thom Bell simply followed suit." The defection of the famed MFSB rhythm section and many of its other members in the late seventies is not at all dissimilar to the departure of producers Holland-Dozier-Holland from Motown in 1968. (Lenny Pakula, a member of the MSFB rhythm section who arranged many Gamble-Huff productions without receiving proper credit, recalled in Jackson's book that Gamble and Huff "were very slick on how to take talent out of people.... They sucked my talent. I'm drained from that company.")

If Phyllis realized any of this she didn't publicly address it. But she was frank about the pain the wait between albums had caused her. "You begin to think that people don't care about you anymore, and that you'll never have another record," she said. "With this album, I somewhat understood why we went through the delay. We were looking for the proper distributor and we were looking for the right songs. I had to train myself to calm down and not be so freaked out. You have to talk to yourself. It's like therapy. I've been in and out of therapy – group and private – for years. So I used those experiences. I just told myself, 'This is the way it is. You have to relax and live with it.'"

Phyllis, of course, didn't mention that she'd almost decided not to live with it and had tried to take her own life, for the second time, in 1990. But she did talk openly about her pain. "I fought against doing anything that I didn't feel down in my gut and down to my toes. I wanted songs that had storylines, songs that could be visualized in one's mind, not just a bunch of words. A lot of them are painful songs, but very realistic. Pain is a part of our lives."

Phyllis discussed several songs on the album, and the messages they conveyed. Of "I Cant' Take It Anymore," which tells the story of a woman in an abusive situation, Phyllis said, "I firmly believe that no one has to put up with someone who hurts them. This is the type of lyric that empowers people. People hear it and say, 'I don't have to deal with this. I'm outta here.'" "Walk Away" was another sad song, about a man who doesn't know how to communicate. "It says, 'Don't walk away without talking about it, because once you do, you can't come back. If there's a chance of saving this relationship, let's work through it.' I've learned that lesson."

Here, Phyllis alluded to her breakup with Dante. "It made the songs difficult to record, but the result is fabulous. The pain you feel personally is reflected in your interpretation. Expressing it publicly helps me to accept it. I'm giving the audience a chance not to make the same mistakes I have. I can save them the pain. My therapist says it's unhealthy for me to do this. But I don't want my audience to have to go through what I've gone through."

While by the time it was released Phyllis had just broken up with Dante, "Walk Away" was actually recorded in January of 1988, just as she was ending things with Tad Fennar, and began showing up in her stage show later that year. "I used to go onstage and cry whenever I did this song. It really had everything to do with communication. Neither of us in the relationship had the guts to try to save it, and our egos got in the way. I feel that if a relationship is worth having, it's worth fighting for. But we just didn't communicate fully with each other."

The current breakup with Dante made not only the sad songs hard to sing, but the positive love songs were challenging as well. "'When I Give My Love (This Time)' – I recorded it with that 'old Phyllis' attitude. My depression wouldn't allow me to feel the things that other people felt. Even the song 'I Found Love' was hard for me because I had to pretend. I really wasn't in love when I recorded it."

She also admitted she had no plans of being back in it anytime soon. "Being without a man certainly isn't the worst thing in the world. If someone who looked like Mr. Right came my way, I'd cross the street. I won't suffer like that again. It's insanity. I've been going through failed relationships for 20 years. I don't need it. Relationships require compromise, and I'm not a very compromising person. Most men aren't willing to compromise. They want the woman to make all the sacrifices. They want a maid. Changes in the workplace should bring a change in male attitudes. Let's get down to the business of forming real partnerships, based on mutual strength."

In truth, Phyllis was involved even as she made these statements. While her relationship with Dante was dissolving, things with her former personal assistant, Martha David, were again heating up. Phyllis had flown Martha down to Miami while she was recording there in March, and soon the two were very much an item once more. "It was a very intense time and we were both very happy to be together again," said Martha, who spent some time shopping with Phyllis while in Miami. "We were in a store and there were some little pewter frames that she was interested in, and I said I'd buy her one. She picked out a heart shaped frame and she put a picture in it that someone had taken of us at a club the week before, and she carried the picture around with her."

Fans and critics alike were kind to the *Prime Of My Life* album in their reviews, with one notable exception. *The Washington Post* called it the album's "most glaring error," and it was none other than its first single. "Don't Wanna Change the World" was an upbeat hip hop-ish, new jack house track complete with Phyllis and an unidentified male vocalist doing a rap duet on the bridge. Produced by Nick Martinelli and written by his friends Karen Manno and Jon Rosen, "World" was met by almost universal disproval by every critic who had a column to slam it in. "Hyman's loyal following will enjoy this album with the possible exception of one song that sounds out of place, the single "Don't Wanna Change the World," wrote a reviewer for the *Chattanooga News-Free Press*. "Leave the rap to the rappers."

It's shocking that Phyllis agreed to do the song, which sounded more like a Paula Abdul number than a Phyllis Hyman record, considering her feelings for "Riding The Tiger," which she now openly admitted to detesting. "I don't like doing that song in concert but I'll do it if they insist," she said in 1989, which wasn't always the case. "It's a tired tune, stupid. Who the hell rides tigers? Fools, junkies and crazy people. I didn't ask for it and I didn't want to do it. But I didn't have the balls to say no. If I continued my career this way, it'd be down the toilet."

For as much as Phyllis disliked "Tiger," she fell into the same trap with "World." After more than 15 years in the business, she had only reached the top ten of *Billboard's* Hot Black/R&B Singles list once. It was the realization of this fact that must have caused her to sacrifice her signature style and sophistication in an effort to be trendy, and succumb to producer Nick Martinelli's suggestion.

Mature listeners were put off by Phyllis's attempt to rap, while younger listeners thought it a weak effort. Critics one after the other let it be known that they did not particularly care for "World" and saw it for exactly what it was. "In her biggest role reversal since the much-maligned, disco era 'Riding the Tiger,' Hyman dabbles in rap on 'Don't Wanna Change The World,' an easygoing dance number with stabbing synthesizers and new-jack influences," wrote another reviewer, this time for the *Indianapolis Star*. "Hyman needn't go street just to pay the bills."

Despite such predictable – and rather valid – criticisms, "World" performed well. Urban radio programmers – a breed far different from music critics – liked the contemporary feel of the song and added it quickly to their play lists. Released in late June, "World" entered *Billboard's* Hot R&B/Hip-Hop Singles and Tracks chart and began its slow ascent on July 6, Phyllis's birthday. Two months later, it was entering unfamiliar territory for a Phyllis Hyman single, the top 10. It surpassed the only other Phyllis song to ever go there, "Can't We Fall In Love Again," which went to number nine in 1981, in September, creeping up to number four. The next week it went to number two. Then, on September 13, Zoo got word that the following week "World" was scheduled to topple "Let The Beat Hit 'Em," by Lisa Lisa & Cult Jam, and land at the spot Phyllis had been trying to reach for 15 years. When *Billboard's* September 20 issue hit the stands, "World" was going to be in the number one spot.

The staff at Zoo, who had worked the record feverishly, gathered in the conference room of their Los Angeles headquarters and began pouring champagne as president Lou Maglia dialed Phyllis at home in New York on speakerphone. "I feel just like a kid in a candy store," Phyllis told Lou and crew, and then she began to cry. "She was truly overcome with emotion," recalled Mark Matlock, a member of Zoo's promotion team. "That number one had been a long time in coming and Phyllis had finally made it. Those were definitely tears of joy, and we all knew it."

Matlock had attempted to work the record at pop radio just before it hit the number one spot on the R&B chart. Sadly, he found that Phyllis had missed the pop boat. "Phyllis didn't have any track record with top 40 so it was like working a brand new artist for them," he explained. And not only was she considered a new artist to pop radio, she was now an artist in her 40s. "Because radio was starting to skew young at the time at top 40, the mere fact that she was not a teen act, that wasn't appealing to them as well. Therefore we did not get any bites or anything like that, regardless of any favors I tried to pull or ask for."

While unable to get "World" any pop play, Matlock was able to understand Phyllis's reasoning for recording the song. "It might have seemed kind of gimmicky, kind of cheap, for her to do something that was kind of rap oriented," he said. "But if you're going to play the mainstream pop game you have no choice. You have to go with whatever the style of music is at that time, and that doesn't always take into account an artist's artistry."

Overall, reviews for *Prime* were generally quite favorable – and none as favorable as the one she received from PIR's new distributor. Zoo was thrilled with the initial response to the album and the number one single was icing on the cake. "The exciting thing about the project is that it's a deep record with at least four or five singles," said Zoo's president, Lou Maglia. "This is a project that we're going to be working for at least a year to a year and a half." Jesus Garber, vice president of R&B promotion at Zoo, also expressed his glee. "We're delighted that this is the first release with PIR and that we have a record that is making the cash registers ring," he said. Yes, it looked as though this new distribution deal was off to a better start than PIR's deal with Manhattan-Capitol-EMI.

"Zoo afforded me the luxury of doing what I felt was necessary to market and promote the release correctly," Garber recalled of the heady days of *Prime's* success. "Low and behold, it was not that difficult because it all starts with the product. So having an album full of great hit songs just made my job a lot easier. Radio accepted it, the public that listens to radio stations accepted it. So for a couple of years it was a magical period. The stars lined up in her favor, and it was a real divine blessing for her at that time."

Greatly appreciative of all Garber's efforts, Phyllis invited him to dinner with friends at Benihana while she was in Los Angeles. "I was such a big fan of hers, and I experienced the delight and joy she enjoyed at that place," Jesus said. "I remember saying I had to go because I had a meeting I had to go to. I walked out, and before I knew it she came out behind me and she said, 'Look, I just want to thank you so much for believing and doing such a great job on my album.' She gave me a little peck on the lips, just a little soft kiss, and she had the most incredible, beautiful lips. I thought I'd died and gone to heaven. It was a very innocent peck, but I got star struck at the moment, and got weak in the knees and said, 'Shit, boy, I'm lucky.'"

Phyllis said in interviews that she felt she had surpassed *Living All Alone* with the new album. "I listened to a lot of songs before we recorded this album and there are a lot that didn't get on there. But I do feel that I got the best record I could from all the material we had, and I'd say this record really stands up to and goes beyond the last album. It's much more well-rounded than some of my previous records. This album also represents the growth I've undergone not just as an artist, but as a human being, during the last few years."

Still, many would continue to herald the 1986 album as the mark by which all her other recordings would be measured against. The controversy over Phyllis rapping on "World" probably playing a part in this – and in the overall feeling that *Prime* didn't flow quite as nicely because of its inclusion.

"World" aside, *Prime* was a very sophisticated album, with distinct undertones of jazz in the arrangements and very grown up lyrics. "My masterpiece on this album is 'Meet Me on the Moon,'" Phyllis said. "Kenny didn't really hear it so I fought for over a year to record that song. It's a real tearjerker, and when I did it, it made me realize that I didn't have that special person in my life."

Now, though, she was no longer looking for anyone to fit that bill. "That is not my purpose in life – to be with someone. My purpose is to be with me. I haven't learned how to do that as yet. That's what I'm working on: How to be with Phyllis. How to make Phyllis happy. How to make her a better person. For many years I had been a very insecure person. Plus, I probably had a reputation. My mouth could be deadly, and I could curse you out and feel OK about it. I didn't know any better. Now that all feels very ugly, and I've discovered I have a choice in how I deal with people."

But just because she knew she had a choice didn't mean she always made the right one. The folks over at Zoo would have readily agreed that Phyllis needed to work on her issues. Her odd behavior had already shown up clearly on their radar by this time. When Phyllis was scheduled to perform a concert at the Wiltern Theatre in Los Angeles following the release of *Prime*, they brought in back up. Bud Scoppa, Zoo's vice president of A&R, had worked with Phyllis's old publicist Barbara Shelley back at Arista. He knew how much Phyllis liked Barbara and hoped she could have a calming effect on her if she showed up at the theatre.

"It was odd that someone from another record company would ask you if you would take a day off work from your own job and come over and help out with Phyllis," said Barbara. "And of course I would because I loved her." Once there, though, Shelley wished she'd stayed at home. "She was drinking like I've never seen her drink. Every time she turned around there was like some kid, or some assistant, who had a glass of wine for her, and she was being really uncooperative to the label people."

Phyllis was asked to pose for a photograph with the staff from Zoo before the show started. But every time the photographer tried to corner her, Phyllis made a beeline in the opposite direction. "She would go outside and talk with the people who were in line waiting to come into the concert," said Shelley. "So it was cool the things that she was doing. But she wasn't doing the things that they needed her to do."

Eventually, Phyllis did pose for the photo, which ran a few weeks later in *Billboard*, and Zoo hosted a brief press reception backstage after the show. "It was hard," continued Barbara. "I had been in AA at that time. I had gone through the crazy '80s and I decided to clean up and get sober. I could see that she did not want to talk about that subject at all. But I mentioned it, and she said, 'Oh yeah, I went to one of those meetings once and it didn't work for me. But I'm really glad it worked for you.'

"So she gave me her number and I called her a few times in New York," Barbara continued. "She just never returned my calls. I thought maybe I'd have a little bit of a chance with her because she and I used to do everything bad together. When I worked with Arista we were doing everything. We were doing blow. We were drinking champagne like it was water. We were staying up all night and dancing and partying and carrying on. So it wasn't like I was coming to her from a place of being a goody two shoes. She knew that we were both little devils back then. I thought it might help, and my friend at Zoo Records was really hoping that I could work a little magic with her."

Sadly, the only magic potion Phyllis was looking for at the time came in a champagne bottle. "Honestly, she was nothing more than an alcoholic at that time," said Barbara. "That's all I saw. All the goodness and the sweetness was covered over by the fact that her main purpose was to get the next drink."

With her new album finally out, Phyllis once again called on publicist Sheila Eldridge to deliver the television exposure essential to promoting it. The five years between albums made it a bit difficult to stir up media interest initially, and Phyllis started locally, appearing on a new show called *Night After Night*. Phyllis spent a brief few moments chatting with the host, comedian Allan Havey, but it was still a full and fascinating exchange, especially when Phyllis revealed to Havey that she didn't listen to music other than her own.

"I do not own a record player," she said. "I don't own a CD player, and I have one very battered tape player that I take on the road because I have to study."

"But you don't like to listen to other people's music?"

"I like music, but for me to put on music instead of the television, that's not going to happen in my house."

"What about oldies? You were in *Sophisticated Ladies*. You ever get in the mood to listen to some Duke Ellington?"

"No, I didn't listen to Duke Ellington before I learned his music. I just don't. I mean, I appreciate it now that I've been exposed to it. But I've never been one to seek it out. Music is not my center, music is not what makes me ... performing makes me feel very centered. But going after music – especially music from other people – no."

"Don't you feel, though, maybe if you got out, listened to some music, if you got out and away from the TV you wouldn't be so damn depressed?"

"Depression ... I don't think it's so bad. I'm not crying about it. I'm not trying to make you feel sad for me."

"I'm not sad for you."

"No, I don't think it's so bad," said Phyllis, mulling it over. "It really helps to make me the colorful person that I am."

One of Phyllis's first national television appearances was on BET's *Video Soul* as part of the show's Divas Week, where Phyllis talked about the type of music she recorded to host Donnie

Simpson. "I don't have an easy time singing about love. 'I'm in love. I'll always love you. We're always going to be happy together.' I have a difficult time with that kind of lyric because that's not true.

"Although there's one song on the album called 'I Found Love.' It says, 'when I looked into your eyes there it was.' *That is such a lie.* What I had to do is reach into my acting chops to pull it off because there is no such thing in my life, and it makes it difficult to portray that feeling if you're not feeling it."

"You've never felt that?" Donnie pressed, obviously finding it hard to believe that Phyllis had never known love.

"On occasion, very seldom," Phyllis answered. "I don't do good in relationships."

Following the taping of the show, Phyllis hung around BET's studio. Patti LaBelle was taping an episode of the show for part of the same Divas Week presentation, and in the middle of her taping, Phyllis tiptoed on stage and presented her with a bouquet of flowers. Patti didn't mind the intrusion. "She could interrupt me anytime," Patti said.

"I just didn't want to come out on the spot, but I had to," Phyllis told Patti afterward.

"Girl, if you hadn't, I would have pimp slapped you," Patti shot back.

"Seriously, she was a wonderful woman," said Patti, who first met Phyllis through her sister Jackie while she was recording in her hometown of Philadelphia in 1980. "We ended up going across the street to this corner bar and just having fun. We sat at the bar. We were like bar flies, and we just had girl time."

When Jackie died of brain cancer in 1989, Phyllis stepped up. "She was there when my sister passed to support me. We cried together. We did a lot of things together. I never knew that she was so depressed. Whenever she was around me she was making me feel good. She was always lifting me up, if I was going through some stress issues or whatever. She was like a big ole, beautiful yellow sister."

As her interview on *Video Soul* demonstrated, Phyllis was again riding the seesaw on the issue of love. Her comments on the subject went back and forth from wondering why she couldn't find a relationship to not wanting one at all – despite the fact that she, in truth, was still seeing Martha David at the time. Just weeks after the *Video Soul* appearance, Phyllis told another interviewer that she was through with love for good. "My career is my life," she said. "Some women want to have marriage and kids. That's all relevant and wonderful. I'm just not willing to sacrifice Phyllis for that. I'm truly an equal-opportunity girl. Yet when I have fallen in love, I have always given in. I've been a real sucker, a sap. I don't like that feeling. I like loving. I don't like being in love. It's a very addictive, obsessive state."

Martha explained Phyllis's comments – indeed her unique take on interviews as follows. "Sometimes in interviews I think she would go into another persona that wasn't even related to where she was in life. She would combine real things about how she was really feeling with how she wanted to feel. But I think she was always being sincere, even when she wasn't telling the truth." Phyllis wanted folks to believe as she did, that she was a victim of love gone bad; that men were threatened by her celebrity and intimidated by her success and stature.

But a few sentences later, the truth slipped out, whether or not Phyllis was aware of the revelation or its significance to the failure of her relationships. "Happiness, to me, means being in control," Phyllis said in a rare moment of complete clarity. It's possible, perhaps even likely, that Phyllis, herself, wanted to believe she was a victim as much as she wanted her fans to. But Phyllis had also done her share of victimizing. The layers of Phyllis's emotional complexity were thick, and she was caught in a vicious cycle. Those who are abused as children grow up to abuse others. In Phyllis's case, she had been taught as a child to verbally abuse her mother, by emulating her father; as young children are want to do. As an adult, Phyllis followed in Philip's footsteps, often verbally abusing her own life partners.

She admitted to liking younger men. But what she didn't say is that she pursued them by design. Younger men were easily influenced. More importantly, they were her emotional peers. But stuck somewhere in emotional adolescence, Phyllis could not contribute to building the type of union she sought. "Phyllis had a fantasy of the ideal relationship she wanted to have," said Portia Hunt. "She was looking for something out of a TV movie, something like the Huxtables. She put on this bravado of being superwoman. Yet at the same time, the stress and pressure of being an adult was too much for her. So she got trapped between developmental stages."

She complained of not meeting men who could offer financial security, but secretly she relished in the fact that her boyfriends' financial dependence helped keep them in line. Bringing Tad on board as her road manager may have ultimately played a role in the relationship's demise, but for a time it had also allowed her to always know where he was and it gave her an excuse to demand loyalty and obedience from him outside the normal boundaries of intimacy between couples. The pattern continued during Phyllis's tumultuous relationship with Martha David, but with Dante, living on another continent, it was harder to exercise that type of control, though she did try.

"Her demeanor was very powerful and I think, in short, most people could not deal with the power that came with her," explained Tymm Holloway. "She could compartmentalize different emotions and when she's fun, she fun. But when she's business, she's business; and when she's singing, she's singing. I think brothers had a problem trying to figure out who she was and sticking around long enough for that. It was a hard sell. I think that's primarily why if you didn't have a strong sense of who you were, you may have had a fear of what could be next with her. She had a strong personality. She was very strong-willed. It was not 'what I can add to your table,' but 'what can you bring to mine?' I think a lot of people got turned off by that kind of boldness. She wasn't the okie-dokie kind of woman."

It's fitting that at the same time Phyllis was making these disjointed statements about love, the second single from *Prime*, the aptly titled "Living In Confusion," was making its way up the charts. The origins of the song date back to about 1988 when Terry Burrus was sitting in Kenny Gamble's PIR office. "We could see that Phyllis went through a lot of stuff in her life," said Terry. "Kenny's the one who said, 'Sometimes she seems confused about this and that.' Then we both said, 'Confusion. Let's try to write something about confusion.' So we came up with these lyrics in his office, and we put them down and we let Phyllis hear them. Then

Phyllis came up with some words toward the end of the song and we cut it with her voice on it and boom!"

Boom, indeed! The song rapidly made its way up to number 9 on *Billboard's* R&B chart and would go on to win an ASCAP award for its trio of writers. "She was the perfect person to sing such a song at that time because she felt every word," said Terry, and Phyllis agreed. "'Living In Confusion' is a song about me," she said. "It's about someone who's not being honest with themselves."

Just days before Thanksgiving, Phyllis flew to Washington, D.C. to tape another edition of *Video Soul* with Donnie Simpson. She wore a long, very full-bodied wig and thanks to the efforts of an unkind cameraman who repeatedly shot her from a lower angle, her face looked puffy and her double chin was prominently on display. If Phyllis was feeling self conscious about the weight, she didn't show it on this appearance. It was the holidays, and Phyllis had food on the brain, even going so far as to sing an impromptu line from a song she called "Chitlin Kind Of Christmas."

"You know why, because Eric is making me chitlins for Thanksgiving," Phyllis told Donnie, gesturing toward her background singer, Eric Jones. "Some friends of mine, the Bundys in Philadelphia, they're making me chitlins as well. I have double duty chitlins on Thanksgiving. So when I said 'Chitlin Kind Of Christmas,' I'm gonna freeze 'em and have them for Christmas.

"I go crazy for chitlins. I truly do. So for those of you out in the audience who make chitlins and would like me to have some, please ship them to the BET office. Make sure they're sealed very tightly. They'll freeze them and ship them to me in New York or Philadelphia. Thank you so much."

"Oh boy, I can imagine what they would look like when they go through the mailroom," said Donnie.

"See most of the group won't even talk to me because they don't eat pork. A lot of them don't eat pork. But I eat anything that doesn't move, as long as it doesn't move or talk. Where is the knife and fork? Let's cut it and let's eat it."

Phyllis used humor as a coping mechanism to help her deal with her fading glamour. Three short years ago, Phyllis had stood up on stage and told her audience that she'd drastically slimmed down for fear of being mistaken for Angela Bofill. But following rehab and throughout her struggle to stay clean, Phyllis had put on a large amount of weight.

By now, Phyllis had recognized a need to shed some pounds and get back into shape. To assist with this goal, Phyllis hired personal trainer Duane Adams. "I work out three to four hours a day," Phyllis said proudly. "I was inactive for so long. Then I focused my attentions on recording a great record and over the last couple of years I just let my body go. When you're overweight your knees begin to hate the rest of your body. Now I want to be skinny again."

Adams was actually the latest in long line of personal trainers Phyllis had worked with through the years. "She went through personal trainers like other people go through pencils," recalled Glenda. Phyllis lost as much as a dozen pounds working with Adams before she grew tired of the exercise routine. She was smoking heavily during this time, which didn't make things any easier on her. Finally, the exercise sessions ended all together.

In interviews Phyllis tackled the subjects of weight and food as she did most others: no holds barred. "I can't sit down and write about love. I really don't know what that feels like anymore. But I can sing about love of people, love of God. I could do a song about the love of food. I'll eat anything that doesn't walk and isn't talking to me.

"I'm recognizing the need to lose weight, not so much for looks as for health. I tire more easily. It's harder to move around when you're carrying extra weight. The overeating is partly to keep men away, which is sick. They tend not to approach me anyway, because I'm six feet tall and I'm an executive. They want somebody who's tiny and subservient. I've always felt insecure in that way. I didn't go to my prom. You begin to feel inadequate when you don't function in a male-female society the way other kids do."

Relationship issues were always a subject that Phyllis was up for. Just months ago Phyllis had declared that she was through with love and fine with it. But for her December cover story in *Jet*, Phyllis was frank about her loneliness. The headline read, "Phyllis Hyman Says 'The Man I Wanted, I Made Him Not Want Me And Now I'm All Alone.'"

"It was shake-your-head crazy," Dante James said of the article, which was essentially an ode to him. "I didn't call her. We didn't communicate about it. Of course, I got enough phone calls from all around the country because folks knew it was about me, even though my name wasn't mentioned." Phyllis spoke at length about the failed relationship. "He was one of the most gracious of men – a man I respected more than any other man I have ever met. He is brilliant. He's well read, well educated and he is a man I could really talk to about things of substance. I had never met a man like that before, ever."

Phyllis went on to say for the first time ever she had "really imagined having a home and kids. I had never, ever thought about that before in my life. That never, ever crossed my mind, to be in the kitchen cooking food and wiping our baby's nose. That was never on my agenda. But this man and I had planned to marry, and I am most hurt that the relationship did not work out. I destroyed it because I was afraid. I just did anything and everything to put him off, to make him not want me any more. I had never been that happy and it scared me."

Chapter 15

What else is the point of having cake if you're not gonna eat it?

Phyllis was still enjoying renewed interest in her career as 1992 rolled around. *Prime* had managed to peak at number 10 on Billboard's Hot R&B Albums chart, and in addition to her first number one single, "World," and the number nine "Confusion," in February the album's third single, the Nick Martinelli produced "When You Get Right Down To It," went to number 10. It was quite a coup for Phyllis, a top 10 album with three top 10 hits, including a number one. Phyllis had also been voted best female vocalist by Britain's *Blues & Soul* magazine, another real coup considering that PIR had no European distributor and *Prime* hadn't even been released in the UK.

Even as *Prime* continued to soar, Phyllis was down. She found herself unable to maintain the optimism she conveyed to the press upon her album's release and the "personal transformation" she spoke of then was proving to have been only temporary. Slowly, Phyllis reverted back to her old ways. She was growing ever unpredictable onstage, often showing up late for performances and not in the best of shape when she got there. "It's important to remember that the bipolar disorder really encourages such behavior," Glenda offered. "The perception of someone who doesn't have an understanding of this disease, or an appreciation of some of Phyllis's deep seated fears, would only see her coming off as aggressive or irresponsible. But that was not her true intent."

Glenda thought that a stronger band would help better support Phyllis onstage, and encouraged her to start fresh. Phyllis offered a compromise, opting to keep backing vocalist Eric Jones and bassist Ron Richardson, but dismissing the rest. Actually, most band members weren't so much dismissed as they were simply ignored.

When they called road manager Larry Kendricks to inquire about new dates, he simply told them there were none.

With dates continuing to pour in, there was little time to put together and rehearse a new band. Glenda called on a new client, Steven Ford, to help out. Ford had been referred to Glenda while working as musical director of *Don't Get God Started*, a gospel play that ran on Broadway for a short time. Ford was a minister and an unlikely match to work with Phyllis, something she commented on when he traveled to New York and met with her for the first time at her apartment.

"Her statement to me was, you know, 'How we gonna put this together? You're a gospel person and I'm R&B,'" Ford recalled. "In other words, 'I ain't no gospel person. So how we gonna make this work?'"

Once Ford assured her that the arrangement could, in fact, work, the two quickly set out to make it happen. "We sat down and talked, and I heard some of the directives and kind of got to know her to see what worked and what didn't work, as far as what kind of personalities to put on stage. Because you can have some gifted and talented people, and they can be wonderful players or singers, but if the chemistry doesn't work it's just not going to happen."

Soon enough, Ford had succeeded in impressing Phyllis. "She noticed that I didn't use any profanity. She noticed the things I said, the way I walked and the way I carried myself. We established a relationship wherein she knew that I was a Christian man. And after her watching my life and watching what I did, that also gained a respect level between both of us. Phyllis didn't miss too many things. You didn't think she was paying attention. But she checked you out. So if she saw me, like, flip off or do something against what I said or preached or taught, then her respect level would change. So I think that's why I didn't see the Phyllis that many would see."

If Ford didn't see the heated side of Phyllis's personality, it was only the result of her own conscious effort to block it from him. "There were times when she had to say something, when she'd get ready to cuss somebody out," Ford recalled. "She'd say, 'Pastor Ford, Steve, Reverend, you gotta leave cause, uh, I gotta tell 'em somethin' and I don't want you to hear what I gotta say.' We had that kind of relationship."

One of the musicians Ford brought in was guitarist Jonathan Dubose. Like Ford, Dubose came from a gospel background, but he had played with acts as diverse as Tramaine Hawkins to Sheila E. Dubose was polite and mild mannered. He always referred to Phyllis as "Miss Hyman," and she returned the courtesy by calling him "Mr. Dubose." But unless they were rehearsing or onstage, the two had few face-to-face conversations.

"You would have to use a walkie-talkie to speak with her, even if we were 20 yards away," Dubose recalled. "So if I wanted to speak to her I would have to go to someone, Leo Lord or perhaps Larry Kendricks, and let them know that I needed to speak to Miss Hyman, even though she might have been in the other room. It was very interesting actually."

As a live performer, Phyllis, with a number one hit now under her hat, was in greater demand than ever. For her new stage look, Phyllis was now wearing a severe beehive sort of wig designed by Danny Wintrode that stood nearly a foot off her head. Extremely self-conscious about the weight she could not seem to lose, Phyllis thought the added height might serve to slenderize her. The high hair was often accompanied by large candelabra-style earrings – anything to take the emphasis off her expanding waistline. The pace she struggled to keep at this time was so dizzying that Phyllis was destined to stumble. And in January, while onstage at Universal Amphitheatre in Los Angeles, she literally did just that.

The stage was dark and filled with smoke when she began walking backwards during "Living All Alone." Before she knew what had happened, Phyllis tripped on a monitor and went tumbling backwards. She hardly missed a beat, finishing the song – including its traditional whistling segment – from the floor. By the end of the set, though, she was in great pain and had to be taken to the emergency room. Luckily, her ankle was only sprained and not broken. Even still, Phyllis used the assistance of a wheelchair to travel for the next several days. And at the Trump Taj Mahal in Atlantic City, where Phyllis opened for The Whispers for two nights, she alternated between using a stool and a cane for support.

For her first solo appearance on *The Arsenio Hall Show*, Phyllis chose an almost somber ensemble. She wore a black pantsuit complete with a flowing, cape-like jacket that managed to cover up most of her ample cleavage. As was her usual preference, she once again wore a hat. This time, it was covered in multicolored jewels and matching accessories completed the outfit. Phyllis sat in with a combination of her band and Arsenio's for the entire hour, singing an assortment of tunes such as "Don't Wanna Change The World," The Stylistics' "You Make Me Feel Brand New," and The O'Jays "I Love Music" and "Back Stabbers" on the way in and out of commercial breaks. Steven Ford, her musical director, sat in the front row watching with rapt attention throughout the proceedings. Finally, Phyllis sang "When You Get Right Down To It" before heading to the couch to chat with Arsenio.

Phyllis had recently begun seeing yet another younger man, Jay Love, whom she met through one of the actors in her "Living In Confusion" video. But she was also still involved with Martha David, who was again acting as her personal assistant and accompanying her on the road. "Things with our relationship were disintegrating at that point and had been on and off for a while," Martha recalled. "There were periods of our relationship that were monogamous and periods that were not. It was tumultuous. It wasn't always a healthy relationship. Yet the love and attachment between us, I felt, always remained. But there was a lot going on at times that wasn't good."

As long as Martha remained close by though, the relationship would continue in one form or another. Having accompanied Phyllis to the *Arsenio* taping, Martha feared that the new man in Phyllis's life might find his way into the on-air conversation. In the dressing room before the show, Martha shared her concern with Phyllis. "I brought it up that it bothered me that she probably was going to talk about Jay on the show," Martha recalled. "After our having been together for such a long time, and considering the depth of our relationship and everything that had gone on between us, the whole thing just galled me a bit. It just felt so unfair. I knew that things with Jay were still very new and pretty superficial."

Phyllis didn't care for being told what she could or could not talk about, though, and things got a little out of control backstage. "She got very angry, and we had a fight about it before the taping," Martha said.

On Arsenio's couch, Phyllis did, in fact, talk about Jay when the host inquired about her love life. "We went out and he had a limousine and he brought me a little black teddy bear and he had a bottle of champagne. So I decided to go on a – what do you call it – a double date? See, I didn't do these things when I was young, girls. I didn't go to the prom. I didn't do any of that stuff. So I'm old, and I'm doin' it all now.

"I liked him," Phyllis continued. "He was fun. He's young. A lot younger than me. I don't like nothin' old but money. He's 25, owns a restaurant, black. What more could I ask for?"

Remarks such as these made Martha, who was standing backstage, cringe. She felt a special bond with Phyllis, and this line of conversation seemed an affront to it. Martha knew that to be involved with Phyllis she would have to make certain concessions. But she also hoped that Phyllis would make some, too. "I didn't expect ever that she should mention me," said Martha, "but that perhaps, out of respect for me, she might not have to mention him."

After the taping, the argument between Phyllis and Martha continued. Glenda tried to de-escalate the situation with limited success. Though she understood why Phyllis had done it, Martha could not help but feel slighted. Phyllis had failed her once again; treated her as less than. But treating someone badly was not an indication from Phyllis that she had no genuine feelings for that person. Indeed, the opposite was often true. Those closest to Phyllis often got the brunt of her bad temper, and Martha, like all those who traveled with Phyllis, was a convenient punching bag.

"I think Martha just kind of took all that with a grain of salt," recalled Terry Burrus. "It just went in one ear and out the other. She was just there for Phyllis; she was at her beck and call. I think she took more abuse. But when you become that close to Phyllis as a personal assistant, Phyllis turns on this abuse button. It's just like a natural thing for her. If she had a bad day, she's going to take it out on the person that's closest to her, and that was usually her personal assistant. So that's what they went through. But they became lovers and they did love each other. Phyllis loved Martha and vice versa."

Knowing a bit about how Phyllis operated helped Martha to hold on when Phyllis's temper flared. "Phyllis was very loving towards me, treated me very, very well, respected me, trusted me and relied on me to take care of her," said Martha. "If I had felt that Phyllis didn't deep down really love me and trust me, I wouldn't have stayed. As much as anyone could, I felt understood her – as did all the other people in her life who stayed by her side. With Phyllis you had to take the good with the bad. I knew no one could help her change and heal until she was ready. The only other option was to leave. I loved her very much, and I chose to stay and make the best of it for her and for myself for as I long as I felt I should."

Martha was smart enough to realize that the outbursts had little to do with how Phyllis truly felt about her. To stand close to Phyllis was to stand close to a flame, and you had to be prepared for it to flare up at any moment. "I was aware that there would be some rough days for me and many times there were people on stage that would be recipients of her rough days," said Steven Ford. "I'm not saying that in a negative tone. If you knew Phyllis, you just knew her. That was part of her and you had to learn how to embrace her. That all came with the package."

Aside from key dates like the *Arsenio* appearance, Steven Ford didn't travel with Phyllis. He appointed guitarist Jonathan Dubose as musical director in his absence. Away from the frantic pace of the road, Ford learned that Phyllis was rarely ambivalent. She was either incredibly pleased or amazingly put off, and either way, he was bound to hear about it. "I can remember phone calls where the band really did well on stage and she would call, just excited on the telephone, saying, 'Reverend, they knocked 'em dead last night, yeah, yeah.' It was like, 'OK, Phyllis, great.' And then, of course, there were other times when things may not have gone too good and she'd come on the phone and say, 'Where you at?' and I'd say, 'I'm home, you called me at home.' 'Well, you need to come to Cincinnati cause they just wasn't poppin' tonight. So you need to come.'"

On the road, Phyllis generally played to smaller theaters and clubs like the Blue Note in New York and Blues Alley in D.C. And while by her own admission she preferred these type of venues, where she was "able to see the people" and "put them in the act," the type of extended engagements she would enter into with them

– often doing two shows nightly for a week or longer – could be grueling. Often enough she played larger houses, like D.C.'s Constitution Hall or the Fox Theatre in Detroit, as part of a package show. But in April of 1992 she received an interesting offer to play a few much larger venues for a much larger sum of money.

G&L Productions of Columbia, Maryland entered into an agreement with Phyllis's booking agent, Associated Booking Corporation in New York, to bring four of their acts together for two shows in the D.C. area. In addition to Phyllis, the shows would feature Regina Belle, Keith Washington and former Manhattans lead singer Gerald Alston. For these two dates, Phyllis would earn $20,000 a night. The shows, at the D.C. Armory/Starplex and the Hampton Coliseum in Hampton, Virginia – both 10,000 seaters – were supposed to be only the start. G&L, led by Gerald Boyd, Jr., was hoping to add an additional nine dates to the itinerary and produce a mini-tour following the D.C. shows. But this was not to be.

On May 15th, the date of the first show, Phyllis was scheduled to do a soundcheck at the Armory/Starplex at 3 p.m. But according to Phyllis's road manager, Larry Kendricks, Boyd was inexperienced and things at the venue were not set up according to the specifications in Phyllis's rider. Kendricks did not arrange transportation for Phyllis until such time as the stage was properly set up, which resulted in her arriving at 7:30 p.m., the scheduled start time of the show. This meant a delay in the start time of over an hour.

Following soundcheck, Phyllis learned that there were not enough dressing rooms in the venue and sent the band back to the hotel to change. This meant that at 10 p.m., when Boyd went backstage to tell Phyllis he was ready for her, she was not able to go on. Boyd, citing the fact that the Armory was a union hall and he would be billed for overtime if the show ran past midnight, wanted to put Keith Washington on immediately. But Phyllis's contract stated that Washington was supposed to follow her, and she was not having it. Phyllis countered that if Keith went on before her, she wouldn't play at all.

Boyd was then forced to wait for the arrival of Phyllis's band, and was horrified when, just after 10:30 p.m., Phyllis, disconcerted over the treatment she'd received from the novice promoter, took the stage just long enough to tell the audience that she would not perform because of her dispute with him. The response to Phyllis's announcement was fast and furious. Fans stormed the stage and began threatening anyone wearing a G&L identification badge. Boyd was told by members of the Metropolitan Washington Police Department assigned to the event that they did not have sufficient manpower to control the building riot, and dozens of police officers had to be sent as reinforcement.

When order was at least partially restored in the auditorium, Washington took to the stage to begin his set. But the crowd wasn't having it. Before he could complete his second song, the audience began booing him loudly.

"So, what, y'all don't want to hear me sing?" Washington asked, to which the crowd responded soundly with loud shouts of "No!" Flustered, Washington quickly left the stage.

Desperate to regain control of the crowd, Gerald Boyd pleaded with Phyllis to perform. She did, and by the time her set was completed and the stage refreshed for Regina, it was well past midnight.

"By the time I came out it was almost 1 o'clock, and I was supposed to go on at 10," recalled Regina. "It was ugly. It wasn't cute. When I first came on I said, 'Before I sing a note I would like for you to give Keith Washington a round of applause. Everything that you see is not always what it seems. I'm backstage so I know what's going on.'"

The audience, though certainly more receptive to Regina than they had been to Keith, was still focused on Phyllis – if for no other than reason than she was walking throughout the auditorium and amid them the whole time Regina was onstage. Heads were turning and everyone was mumbling as the crowd tried to figure out what she was doing.

"She came out in the audience and was walking around, which was kind of interesting," said Regina. "But Phyllis was always kind of interesting. I didn't take it to heart. My thing was, let me do my show so I can get paid and we can get up out of here. In fact, I didn't even know she was in the audience. Somebody told me. So when I went back to my dressing room, I was like, 'Wow, she would do that, huh? Like totally be a distraction while I was onstage?'"

The next night, things "just got progressively uglier and worse," Regina remembered. Following Phyllis's performance the night before – both on and offstage – neither Regina nor Keith were none too pleased at the prospect of having to take the stage after her. In response to this, Boyd approached Phyllis and asked her to close the show. Phyllis and Regina were being paid equally. But Phyllis had not been contracted to be the headliner. Therefore, she let it be known that she'd only close the show if given an additional $5,000.

Boyd felt he had the right to arrange the show. But Phyllis, through Larry Kendricks, pointed out that her contract said otherwise. When the promoter did not waver on his demand that Phyllis play last, she prepared a handwritten statement, had it photocopied and then assembled her staff outside the Coliseum to distribute copies. As a result, nearly 500 patrons who arrived with tickets demanded refunds, and, according to Boyd, an additional 500 or more who arrived planning to purchase tickets decided not to in response to Phyllis's statement.

Boyd had already paid ABC for Phyllis's services – as well as those of the other performers – well in advance of the shows. So in the days following the fiasco, when ABC made it clear they would not return the monies paid to them for Phyllis's performance, Boyd initiated a $1 million lawsuit against Phyllis, and in conjunction Command Performances, Inc, ABC and Keith Washington. Glenda determined that Boyd had attempted to change the terms of the contract that were the "essence of the agreement," namely Phyllis's position on the bill. Her Temple law school skills showing through, Glenda was right on the money and Boyd's attempt to bump Phyllis to the closing slot cost him his case.

If Phyllis felt any remorse for her part in this incident, it was in how her actions may have affected Regina. A few months later, when Regina was in New York for the All Stars Talent Show Network, an annual fundraiser Regina regularly took part in that benefits the Community Literacy Research Project, Phyllis took the opportunity to set things right with her and asked their mutual friend and producer Nick Martinelli to go with her to the show.

"Before she got there I got these flowers and a card from her," said Regina. "She wrote to me basically saying, 'I would never ever do anything to hurt you or your show.' It was just really, really heartfelt and I really appreciated that from her. She didn't need to do that because I loved Phyllis, and I just accepted her as she is. Then she came backstage with Nick, and that made my day."

Regina had long admired Phyllis. In her college years at Rutgers University, Regina had booked concerts for the school's African Student Congress. One of the first shows she put together had been a joint bill with Phyllis and Peabo Bryson. Later, when she set out to build a performance career, Regina looked to Phyllis for tips on pitch and control. "In terms of anything concerning my lower register, I learned all of that from Phyllis," said Regina, who remembers practicing to Phyllis's classic "Somewhere In My Lifetime." "Her lower register was so rich. Patti and all of them, I love what they do, but nobody could get down in the basement like Phyllis. She had a resonance in the lower register that just filled the room."

Often, when Regina found herself on the same bill as Phyllis she would sit backstage and take in her entire show. "Phyllis had some idiosyncratic moments and at those points you never could tell what you were going to get. But whenever I had the opportunity to perform with her, which was on many occasions, I would always sit right backstage. After you've seen a show, a lot of times you'll sit and you'll watch some of it but then you'll kind of move on. But for her show, I always sat in the wings because I always wanted to hear everything. I remember times when she would cuss the band out. You know, just ridiculous, just really go off. So those were some of the not so nice moments. But then there were those times when she would sing 'Living All Alone,' and I remember one time she sang that song and she was crying, and I was crying and oh my God! I was giving her a standing ovation from the wings."

In June, *Blues & Soul* ran a lengthy interview with Phyllis. Reminiscent of the *Oui* article from 1983, Phyllis was even more candid than usual and at times downright graphic with reporter Jeff Lorenz. It had been a year since her breakup with Dante, and

Phyllis shared that while she had given up sex for a time she had never stopped physically pleasuring herself.

"I realized I don't actually need a man in my life to make me happy. I actually had a one-year celibacy mission.

"I won't print this if you don't want me to but I'm just curious," Lorenz started. "Didn't you miss sex?"

"Ha! Let's just say I didn't have physical human contact for a year, but the electricity bills were paid. You know what I mean."

"I'm not sure I do."

"A vibrator, Jeff. And you can print that."

The celibacy mission was over, though, and Phyllis talked about her new male love interest, Jay Love, though she was insistent that the relationship was not serious.

"I'm too selfish and too independent for a steady relationship right now. The guy I told you about is 17 years younger than me. I like younger men. The time we spend together is fun for what it is and that's how it should be. But I've got my own independence because I'm not in a serious relationship. Because he's younger, it's fun helping him discover things and grow."

"So, basically, you've got your cake and you're eating it, too," Lorenz said.

"Of course I am! Why else would I want my cake if I couldn't eat it? I never understood that saying, you want your cake and you want to eat it, too. What else is the point of having cake, if you're not gonna eat it?"

For her 43rd birthday in July, Jay threw Phyllis a birthday party with the help of her staff. The happy couple was all smiles and Jay doted on Phyllis appropriately throughout the evening. Phyllis's friend Julie Aponte was living in Miami at the moment, but knowing how Phyllis was about birthdays, she was sure to send her best wishes – and a gift. "Phyllis was a child at heart," Julie said. "When it came to her birthdays, you had to celebrate. If not, she would get very upset. She would say, 'I want this and this for my birthday,' and you had to make her birthday special. There was a child in Phyllis and that child used to come out. I think what kept me around for many years is that child. I felt I had to mother that child."

Sometimes, the roles were reversed and it was not the child in Phyllis that shone through but her own maternal instincts as well. If Phyllis told her brother Michael five years ago that she didn't know him, by this point, she was feeling the need to look out for him. More than once, Michael had become involved with someone Phyllis thought was using him to get closer to her. Now, word leaked out that Michael was about to get married and Phyllis was not at all happy. Melinda Gilliard, who preferred to be called Razz, had worked for Phyllis as a personal assistant in 1990. She eventually left to return to a job with BET and Michael pointed to her resignation as the root of the animosity Phyllis felt for her. "Phyllis just had a problem with people leaving," he said. But other staffers say that Phyllis's issues with Razz began while she was still in her employ.

Whatever the reason, by this point in time, the consensus, bluntly, is that Phyllis deeply distrusted Razz. When she found out that Michael was planning to marry her, Phyllis was livid. Her distrust for Razz went deep, and she was convinced that her former personal assistant had only pursued her baby brother for the Hyman name and associated celebrity.

"Man, did I catch hell for that," recalled Michael. "I think for her it was an act of betrayal that I was seeing someone that she was dead set against. She was so angry with me. I was grown. I said, 'Well, you can be how you want to be because it's my life, not yours.' And at the time, I couldn't see what everyone could see. These guys worked with Razz. I knew a different side of her. So I didn't see anything until later."

If Phyllis felt strongly about Razz and her efforts to enter into the Hyman family, she wasn't alone. "Phyllis had a lot of opinions about a lot of people and she wasn't always right, but she was right about this one," said her sister Jeannie, who shared that all of Phyllis's sisters developed an immediate distrust of Razz. "She was on the money. When I met her, me, Ann and Anita were in different parts in the house, and within 15 minutes we were all talking about the fact that we had this terrible feeling of evil spirits coming from this woman. I had been a completely open book to this woman when I met her. But after being around her for a few minutes I had a real bad impression of her."

Phyllis was so incensed by the marriage that she stopped speaking to her brother. "She didn't want nothing to do with me," Michael said. "She was very clear." She also wanted to make her intentions clear to Razz. "She left a nasty message on Razz's home phone in Maryland. 'You will never be a Hyman. Never! You think just because you're marrying my brother you're a Hyman? Think again!' That's something I will never forget."

Chapter 16

Men are not my problem.
I'm my problem and
I have to work on me.

In 1993, Phyllis again teamed up with another well-known instrumentalist she had worked with before. But Phyllis's reunion record with Norman Connors was not greeted with the same enthusiasm her groundbreaking early efforts with the drummer/producer had garnered. Connors was no longer a commanding presence on the R&B charts, having graced the top 40 only once in the past decade with a song called "I Am Your Melody," which featured the vocals of newcomer Spencer Harrison.

Now, Connors had a new contract with Motown's jazz arm, MoJazz, and he was counting on it to bring him a comeback. It was only fitting, then, that he had asked Phyllis to join him on this effort. She had become, without rival, the most successful of all the vocalists he had employed throughout the years, and she was just coming off the most prosperous period of her career. Phyllis was reluctant, but agreed for old time's sake.

But it was the '90s, and the meshed jazz/R&B genre that Connors had mined so thoroughly in the late '70s was now an empty tomb. This was the "New Jack" era, and even Phyllis had had to go that route to get her number one. "Remember Who You Are," which employed all of Connors' traditional techniques, was a throwback to a simpler era of music. Further limiting the song's prospects was the fact that Connors treated the rich and powerful lyric to a firmly adult contemporary arrangement that lent little resemblance to the music making the R&B charts at the time. Perhaps because of this, the single stopped far short of the top forty and after a mere three weeks stalled at an embarrassing number 86.

Even as Phyllis was coming off of the most successful period of her recording career, she was coming down. Phyllis had floated through all of 1992 on the momentum of *Prime's* success. By 1993, however, that wave had reached the shore and the ride was over. Phyllis was continuing to perform, if somewhat less frequently, and her shows were growing continuously more unpredictable. When food was in the room, Phyllis had always been known for nibbling off her fans' plates – and they loved her for it. But at an April performance in Philadelphia, Phyllis began eating popcorn on stage as the band played the intro to "Old Friend." She continued to do so for a full three minutes while the band kept playing. "Gotta get all the kernels out," she finally sang, to the tune of "Friend." "This is so tacky. But this is what fat people do. We just eat and act stupid. Some of my band members are new. Most of them are going to quit after this."

Indeed, the band Steven Ford had assembled for her in late 1991 had begun to come apart. Keyboardist John Working was the first to make his exit, in mid 1992. He was replaced by a succession of pianists, including Will Boulware, Doug Jordan, Darryl Grant and, finally, Alec Shantzis. Ron Richardson remained the greatest constant on bass, and guitarist Jonathan Dubose continued to act as musical director on the road and was responsible for the new hires. Paul Mills replaced Jeff Davis on drums, and Lance Bryant replaced Ray Gaskin on saxophone. Eric Jones, on vocals, was the other holdover. Joining him at various times were the duos of Charlene and Paula Holloway, Michelle Kornegay and Donna Nadsen, and Michelle Kornegay and Millie Rodriguez.[11]

In early March, Phyllis was attending a Harambee festival in Washington, D.C., where she was to present an award to the African ambassador to the United Nations, when a nine-year-old boy approached her table and asked for an autograph. Phyllis was so impressed by her young admirer, whose name was Jason, that after signing a photo for him she escorted him back to his table

---

[11] By mid-1993, Phyllis felt she could no longer afford a trio of backing vocalists and cut back to just Eric Jones.

where she spoke to his parents, Brenda and Skip Barry. "I want you to know your son has more personality than most men I've dated," Phyllis told them. Then she asked if Jason could sit at her table for the rest of the night and help her sign autographs. At the end of the evening, Phyllis handed a Jason a business card and told him to call her anytime.

A few weeks later, little Jason, who lived with his parents just outside Baltimore, asked for permission to give Phyllis a call. Brenda Barry assured her son that the number he had been given likely belonged to Phyllis's fan club. But when he asked if he could try anyway, and after his mother said yes, Jason found the number he'd been given was actually the direct line to Phyllis's Manhattan apartment. Phyllis remembered the young man and was happy to chat with him for a while.

Later, she explained her infatuation with him to his mother. "She said, 'I don't have no kids and I don't want none. But if I'd had a child, it probably would have looked like Jason,'" Brenda recalled.

The following month, Phyllis was asked to be a part of a special 75th birthday celebration for Ella Fitzgerald at Carnegie Hall. Suffering from the ravaging effects of diabetes, Ella was not scheduled to attend. But the concert still promised to be a grand affair. Nancy Wilson, Diane Schurr, Nicholas Ashford and Valerie Simpson, Maya Angelou and many others were all slated to appear. The Duke Ellington Orchestra would be playing, and current New York City Mayor David Dinkins would be in the house, too. The stage manager and assistant director for the production was none other than Ken Hanson, Phyllis's former stage manager and confidant from *Sophisticated Ladies*. The director and crew of the show were reluctant to use Phyllis, as her reputation for unpredictability had fully penetrated the New York theatre circle. But Hanson prevailed. "I told them I knew her and she was a friend of mine and I could control her," said Ken, who soon enough began to wonder just how true those statements really were.

Ken tried to dial Phyllis at home, but was never put through to her and instead got sidetracked by friend Julie Aponte, who, standing in as Phyllis's valet, started issuing a series of Phyllis's demands. Ken was not impressed. "I told everyone, I said, 'Look, I don't know what Phyllis's problem is. But when she gets here, we will rehearse her and send her on her way.'"

Phyllis's problem was that she was racked with fear. She was terrified of playing Carnegie Hall, of sharing a stage with her idol Nancy Wilson and a host of other superstars. Phyllis was afraid that she did not belong on such a prestigious bill, at such a prestigious venue, paying honor to such a prestigious American icon as Ella. As often happened in such circumstances, when Phyllis was this desperately frightened, she sabotaged herself. She began drinking and turned to other substances to calm her fear as well. She showed up for rehearsal hours late, with a bad attitude and an angry agitation in tow.

"She was just high out of her brains, just sweating and carrying on," said Ken. "She was out of control. I remember, Mercer Ellington and others were there and they were all like, 'Oh my God, look at Phyllis.' This was the lowest I had ever seen her." Complicating matters further, Ken was horrified to find out that despite the fact he had sent Phyllis a tape of the song she was scheduled to perform a month earlier, she had failed to learn any of it.

"This was a simple little song, 'I've Got The World On A String,' a famous Harold Arlen song, very simple and she had a long time to learn it and she didn't know one word," said Ken, who was shocked when he heard Phyllis screaming at a stagehand to get her cue cards.

"I said, 'Cue cards? This is Carnegie Hall and you're carrying on about cue cards?' She was talking about how she wanted somebody sitting in the front row of Carnegie Hall holding up cue cards." Ken vetoed that idea immediately.

"So then it was decided that they were going to tape the words to the stage so the audience couldn't see someone holding them up but if she needed them they'd be there," said Ken. "So I wrote them out myself on big pieces of white paper."

Following the rehearsal, Ken was direct when he spoke to Julie. "Look, Phyllis is around the corner, just let her go and stay around the corner. I will call you before she has to go on," which, of course, he did. "All I remember is that when she came to the theatre that night it was very obvious to everyone that she was blasted out of her brains. You could tell that the people in the industry that were there knew what was going on, that Phyllis was out of control and she was high on drugs, and you could see the sympathy in them. I remember Nancy Wilson just sitting on the side with her, almost like a mother. She was a pitiful site that night."

If things were going bad for Phyllis, they were not about to get better any time soon. Phyllis was doing a series of dates in California opening for The Whispers when she received word that her maternal grandmother, Louise Lively, had died at age 88. Phyllis's grandmother had lived with the family off and on through the years, and full-time since her father left. Phyllis wanted to go home, but she was scheduled to perform at a benefit concert for the People With AIDS Coalition at Webster Hall in New York. Unsure of whether or not to cancel the engagement, she called her sister Jeannie. "I told her, 'If you're asking my opinion, I don't think you need to come back.' I felt like my mother was not going to be far behind, so she was going to be making another trip real soon."

Phyllis was still being booked by ABC, though the dates weren't coming in as they once had. There were often several weeks between shows now, which, if nothing else, made it convenient to begin work on the new album. Phyllis flew with her right-hand man, Leo Lord, to Los Angeles on May 23, where she met up with producer Nick Martinelli. Five days later, it was back to Manhattan and back to the grind. She gave two shows on May 29 at Club Bene, in nearby Sayreville, New Jersey. Then, on May 31, Phyllis received devastating news. Just 26 days after the passing of her grandmother, Phyllis's mother was dead at the age of 70.

She did not immediately travel to Pittsburgh. Phyllis was scheduled to appear the following day at a Kennedy Center benefit for St. Benedict the Moor School, a school for troubled teens, in Washington, D.C. Her sister Sakinah, who was living in Philadelphia, called and offered to travel with her. "I took off from work and we met up on the same train," Sakinah said. "I went down and stayed with her for the performance." Sakinah was intent on keeping her sister clean and out of trouble. "I didn't let her get high. I didn't let her drink. She wasn't out of my sight for a minute."

Onstage, Phyllis was a trouper. But as always, she was honest with her audience and told them about her loss. "She told the audience that her mom had passed away the day before," Sakinah recalled. "She said, 'My sister came down to hold my hand.' Everybody took to that." Sakinah was proud of her sister for being so strong, and shocked at how devastated she was by their mother's death. "The emotion that she showed, it was kind of a surprise. Then she sang that song 'This Too Shall Pass Away.' So here I am down there being strong for her, and she played this song and I found myself in the bathroom with the water running, boohooing, crying. We cried and we hugged and we got through the thing."

Sakinah, a Muslim, was hoping that Phyllis would take something meaningful away from one of the gospel acts on the bill. "This was a Christian benefit. There were a lot of gospel and spiritual groups that were there and Phyllis was the headliner. It was beautiful because my thing is if you choose another faith, then that's between you and your Lord, and we'll all find out at the end. But grab onto something. So I was hoping this was something that she could hold onto. But obviously it wasn't."

The next morning, Phyllis hired a limousine for the ride home and dropped her sister off in Philadelphia before returning to New York. Phyllis waited until June 5th, the day before the funeral, to go home to Pittsburgh. Phyllis chose not to stay with any of her siblings and instead checked into the downtown Ramada Inn for two nights. Relations between Phyllis and her sisters were particularly contentious as they each struggled to deal with their grief in their own way. Each of them had their own special lingering resentments toward their mother, and though they all genuinely loved her, they still mourned for the lost portions of their childhood that her depression had claimed.

At the funeral, Phyllis "was acting out," said her sister Jeannie. "I don't recall ever feeling the way that I felt towards her that time ever before or since, and I now believe it was her addiction. When I look back on it, it was her addiction. But she just was so full of herself she made me just want to get up and slap her right across the face and tell her, 'Listen, calm down.' It was her voice inflection, her mannerisms. She was not herself."

Julie Aponte, who had traveled with Phyllis to assist her, recalled that Phyllis did not want to have to deal with extended family and friends. "She kept telling me, 'Don't leave my side. Don't leave me. Stay next to me. Stay next to me. I don't feel like talking to this one. I don't feel like talking to that one.'"

As her firstborn, Phyllis was greatly distraught by her mother's death. She knew she had been cruel to her mother as a child and had tried to compensate for that in adulthood with her generous financial assistance. But money is no substitute for communication. For years, Phyllis's guilt and confusion had made it impossible for her to grow close to her mother. And now, with so much still left unsaid, her mother was gone.

"It was just too painful," recalled Phyllis's sister Anita of this time. "I mean, she cried the whole time." Anita agrees that Phyllis was grieving not only for the loss of her mother, but for the loss of the hope that their relationship would ever be repaired, that there could ever be understanding and healing brought about. Phyllis wasn't the only one who lacked the ability to share with her mother, even if she felt as though she was."

"We didn't have two loving people sharing their love with us in our family," said Anita. "So it was hard for us to interact. There was a lot of bickering. Yes, we ate together and all that, but there was a lot of distance growing up. Now that I'm an adult, I see. Because there weren't two loving people who loved each other and shared their love with us, it affected us. They tried. Honest to God, I know they tried. But they were lacking stuff. When you don't feel loved by the two people that are providing for you, it's real hard to give it to other people."

The following week it was back to Los Angeles for more work with Nick Martinelli. Phyllis, at Glenda's urging, was taking a more active role with the new record than she had with any of her prior releases. While she had, since signing with PIR, always chosen songs she could personally relate to, she was now contributing to their creation. "It was the only way that she was really going to be able to express what was on her mind, craft her own brand identity as an artist, and kind of get her groove on," said

Glenda. "She had written some stuff in the early days with Larry and other people. But there was this stretch where she hadn't really written anything."

One of the first songs Phyllis wrote was "It Takes Two," with Noel Cohen and Daryl Hair. When she was finished with it, Phyllis called Glenda to check in. "She was as excited about writing this song as some little girl coming home from school with a great report card," Glenda recalled. "She was bitten by the bug again." Phyllis credited her recent losses, particularly the death of her mother, as her inspiration. "That's the only thing I can attribute it to," she said. "I just started to write. I didn't think about it. It rekindled my ability to write."

Phyllis didn't necessarily co-write songs in the traditional sense. Rather, Phyllis would sit down with the songwriters and tell them what she was feeling, and they'd translate her thoughts into song lyrics. But as Phyllis began to delve into the inner realm of her emotions and commit her feelings to print, they possessed her and held her tightly in their grip. Many writers write to exorcise their pain, but Phyllis could not release hers. Stirring up these emotions only confused her more, and made the recording sessions painfully difficult.

"'I Refuse To Be Lonely' was basically her talking about her life and what she wished her life would be like," said Martinelli. "The message she wanted to send out was that she refused to be lonely. But in real life, no, that's not the way it was. She was lonely and she didn't want to send that message out. It was a very grueling writing experience and she was crying through a lot of it. She was an emotional wreck."

At the end of June, Phyllis returned to her home away from home – Blues Alley in Washington, D.C. – for a week's worth of shows, where she remained one of the few artists who could pack the house for such an extended run. Here, Phyllis felt comfortable and it showed. She was hysterical between songs and the enthusiastic crowds laughed as much as they clapped. Her birthday was approaching, and for 12 shows she never let the crowd forget it. "I'm accepting all cards, presents," she said. "I got a king size bed at home that's desperate for some linen. I need linen, nothing frilly, nothing flowery, sexy linen only. I figure if I ain't gettin' any, I might as well pretend. King-sized pillowcases. I need a comforter cover. Not the comforter, it's a little cheaper for you. Some glasses and some cookware. You see I like to eat. I need some new pots and pans. You think I'm joking? I'm oh so serious. When you get to be my age, you have a nervous breakdown when you get no gifts. Just remember that, if Phyllis Hyman has a nervous breakdown because she can't change her linen."

One fan knew it was her birthday already and had brought her a card, which Phyllis read on stage. When she got to the end she looked out at the crowd and said, "I don't know how to pronounce your name." Suddenly it was shouted out to her.

"Co – leev – ee – uh."

"Colevia, I have a very short question for you. How long was your mother in labor?"

"Thirty minutes," the fan, happy to be acknowledged, called out.

"She was in just for a half hour and she came up with this name? Deep name, Cole. Colevia. 'Co-le-via,'" Phyllis called with a heavy southern drawl. "'Come here girl.' No, seriously, what would possess her to name you this?"

As was her custom, Phyllis stepped off the stage often and nibbled from the plates of those sitting up front, making sure to point out that Blues Alley had a house dish named after her, Phyllis Hyman stuffed shrimp. "Anybody eatin' me tonight?" she asked. "Oh, that is so tacky."

Phyllis closed each of her shows with "Old Friend," and, not surprisingly, for this run the song served as a tribute to her mother. She was candid about the strain on her relationship with her siblings, speaking to her audience as if they were all 'old friends,' which, in a way, they were. "We still have some things to discuss because I think there's some healing that has yet to begin; and, for me, for sure, there's probably a great deal of grieving that has still not been done," Phyllis said, while singling out her sister Anita, who lived with and took care of both her mother and grandmother for years, for praise.

Phyllis even managed to be funny while talking about her mother's funeral. "The Delanceys were there, and that's the family I used to go to church with. Mrs. Delancey, I thought she was dead. Shows you how old we are. She was there and looked the same, too. And she brought her daughter along, and she's still ugly. Yeah, she's still ugly."

Turning serious, Phyllis said of her mother, "The one really cool thing about her being gone is that she no longer has to suffer, because she was not in such great shape. And as good as my mother was, I know girlfriend's got a special space in Heaven. I'm gonna have to rent me a spot. Me and God gonna have to do some bargaining for my place, somewhere near Heaven, like on the outskirts, in the suburbs. Gabriel's gonna say, 'No, Miss Thing, you'll have to wait a while, about 3000 years before I let you near the gates.'

"But my mother, I don't get it; I don't know how anybody could be so nice. It's real weird. But I like to think of all of the good things. I've changed a few habits. I'm really trying to work on some things that she really did not like. I could not do that while she was alive. I couldn't do it. And for some reason, some of those things are beginning to change and I know it's the grace of God, and I know it's her blessing on me. So, mom, I love you."

Then, finishing both the song and the show, she sang, "Talking 'bout the power, the power of her love, everything she gave to me, she gave willingly. She always gave with love. And she taught me, she taught me the power, taught me the power, the power of my Lord, of my God, Jesus. She taught me, taught me the power. Welcome back into my life again."

Blues Alley was one of Phyllis's favorite places to play. It was where she felt most at home, in part because the intimate venue allowed her to see her fans – her friends – up close and personal. Still, it was grueling to perform 12 shows in six days, and Phyllis, who had begun putting on significant weight, was not in the best shape. Tired or not, Phyllis was jovial and in good spirits considering all she had been through as of late.

Following her reworked ending to "Living All Alone," where Phyllis boldly declared "I'm gonna make it on my own," Phyllis was ebullient. "I sang that song for years cryin' the blues. 'Oh God he left, oh what am I gonna do? Woe is me!' It's like you don't have no idea how happy I am to be by myself. I have no cats, dogs, kids, and if they visit, go home. Your vacation is over. You keep a boyfriend through part of the weekend. He don't stay for Sunday breakfast. And please don't bring a toothbrush. Get a washcloth, put some toothpaste on it and rinse your mouth out with Listerine and leave."

On the Saturday of this engagement, Phyllis accepted an invitation from Jason Barry, the young friend she made some months earlier, and his family to attend a birthday barbeque in her honor at their home outside Baltimore. Phyllis and assorted members of her staff took a van out to the Barry home. There, Phyllis found a cake with her name on it, and a feeling of familial warmth she was unfamiliar – yet immediately comfortable – with. At the end of the day, Phyllis turned to Jason's mother Brenda. "Girlfriend," Phyllis told her. "You're going to see me again. I like this house."

While Phyllis was working with Nick Martinelli in Los Angeles in June, she took time out to connect with Sunny Hilden. A songwriter who worked a lot in film and television, Hilden had recently lost her grandmother. On the way to her funeral, Hilden wrote a song to memorialize her called "All That Reminds Me Of Love." Hilden submitted the song to Phyllis who, having just lost her own grandmother, as well as her mother, immediately related and agreed to put a vocal on the demo. Phyllis met up with Hilden in her West Hollywood apartment. Phyllis was impressed with the song, and with Sunny, and encouraged her to look her up if she was ever in New York. "She said, 'I'm thinking of starting to write and I'd like to write with you,'" Sunny recalled.

Though Phyllis may have made the remark casually, it was all the invitation Sunny needed. Just a week or so later, she flew out to the East Coast and surprised Phyllis with a phone call. Pleasantly surprised – and knowing Sunny was low on funds – Phyllis invited the songwriter to crash at her place for what was supposed to be a few days.

Sunny had a previous invitation to collaborate with fellow songwriter and socialite Denise Rich, and invited Phyllis to tag along to Rich's posh penthouse apartment. "I thought it would be fun to have three women writing something together because Phyllis really wanted to write about issues that were from a point of strength for women and being independent," said Sunny. For her part, Rich had been wanting to write for Phyllis for some time. "She was one of the most beautiful voices in the industry," Denise explained. "She was so classy and such a lady, and she reminded me of someone from the 1940s, like Ella Fitzgerald. I thought she was such an incredible persona, just to be around her."

Of the songwriting session that produced the song "Strength Of A Woman," Sunny said, "Phyllis was having a hard time with men at the time and I had found this to keep coming up when I write with artists. If they're going through something negative, some of them just want to focus on that and write a painful, painful song. I like to ask, 'Is that what you want to continue to feel or, if a girlfriend of yours was going through the same thing, would you advise her to keep feeling that or would you want to come up with a way to say how can we look positively at this or learn from this and turn it into something that comes from a point of strength?'

"Her eyes just lit up, and I said, 'If you feel weak physically you have to feel pain to get stronger. If you're going to pump iron, if you grab one of those 10-pound barbells and pull it, pull it, pull it, you're going to have to feel pain to get stronger. But it's not the pain you focus on. You focus on growing stronger.

"She was very happy by the end of that day, just really loving the process of writing," Sunny continued. "When you have a talent that's as profound as hers was, I think you have a responsibility innately to use that gift to help empower other people. It greatly moved her to be doing that. She got swept up in the energy of that and it really colored all that she had envisioned for the next CD. A lot of the things she had released before were about pain. Now, Phyllis was very excited to make this the title of her next CD and have all the songs on the CD reflect that kind of stance of independence and feeling good about your life, and not being dependent on anyone else for feeling good about your life."

Following the success of the "Strength" session, Phyllis asked Sunny to stay a while longer to help her work on additional songs. "Everyday she would say, 'Stay another day. Stay another day.'" But Phyllis wasn't always up for the task of songwriting. "There were days while I was there, especially in the first couple of weeks, where we were supposed to write and she'd say, 'No, I can't do it today,' and she'd just stay in bed all day with the TV on. That happened several times, which is another reason I stayed. She'd say, 'Don't go. Maybe we can do it tomorrow.' She had an enormous well of pain. It was just profound."

Sunny, who stuck to a strict health food diet, would leave the apartment everyday to jog and purchase food. "Phyllis would never leave the apartment," Sunny recalled of this period. "Whenever I went out to get something to eat she would give me a list of what she wanted, and it was always huge portions of Chinese food and liquor. She wanted liquor every day." But before long, Sunny started feeling awkward about supplying Phyllis with these things. "After two of those days when she just couldn't get out of bed and had me bring her Stoli and takeout food – and it was always really bad for you food and lots of it – I told her that I felt strange getting her these things. Even though this is what she wanted, it just felt strange to me.

"I felt a little guilty and we had a long talk about that and just what all of these things meant. She would eat the food and drink the drink and then not be able to work the next day. I told her, 'I can work any day. I can write whenever and wherever and I have so many ideas in my head that sometimes I can't get them out on paper fast enough.' I was feeling like maybe she had so much emotion in her and maybe there were a lot of ideas in the back of her mind, too, and it's just so much that you just want to stop them and this is your way of stopping them, like numbing them. It was self-medicating and she didn't even realize that she was doing that. The combination of all those things together just clogs up your soul so that you can't get your emotions out and you can't get your ideas out, and then I think that made her feel even worse.

"Another thing that I thought was very detrimental to her was that she would always have the TV on in the background, even when she slept. The TV was on 24 hours a day and I tried to get her to turn it off and not be afraid to be within her own self. I think that TV was almost like another drug. It was all those talk shows where people are yelling at each other."

Having lost 70 pounds herself, and having kept it off successfully for several years, Phyllis was willing to listen to Sunny. "I had lost it and never gained it back and she said, 'How'd you do it? How'd you do it?' I told her that I thought dieting was an important part but that it was also important to realize why the weight was there in the first place. Why did I need that wall around me? I felt like it was my protection against men. And once I figured out why it was there, I decided I didn't need it anymore. So she said, 'OK, well, today get me health food, too.' So for the last couple weeks that I was there, she only ate what I ate, and by the end of the month she went jogging with me every day and she got out of that apartment.

"I think sometimes if people live alone and they live in a tiny, tiny cramped space, even though it was in the middle of the busiest city in the world, it was a lonely existence if you don't leave every day and connect with the world outside you. Every day that she went to Central Park to jog people would wave and would stop and chat, and it always affected her and made her feel loved, which she was. But if you just stay alone in your apartment all the time, you forget.

"She started on a whole other path by the end of that month and it was remarkable to watch. Trying the health food and the water and all the other things was a way to try to unclog her emotionally. But then I guess it was too hard for her to stay in that unclogged place. I could tell a huge difference in just the couple weeks that I tried it. It was quite a difference and she got to the point where she didn't have to have the TV on at all and she said it was a very different kind of experience. She could feel her feelings, but it was easier to focus on what they were exactly, which is what you have to do when you're writing. But it was hard to get her to finish things. She had a lot of distractions in her own mind."

Still, after having stayed with her a month, Sunny hoped she had made an impact. "Now and then she would call me, and she'd say, 'I'm sliding back. I'm back on the Chinese food and I just needed a pick me up.' I visited her several more times and stayed with her and I could tell it was getting harder and harder for her to stay in that place. But every time she went back to it, it always made her feel better."

In August, Phyllis hosted Jason Barry and his family in New York in celebration of her young friend's 10th birthday. Phyllis had Leo pick the Barrys up from the train station and, later, had him take the family to the mall and buy Jason a pair of roller blades. When they returned to the apartment, Phyllis had balloons and a cake waiting.

Throughout the summer and into the fall, Phyllis continued to work on the album – and continued to write. Though there was no release date for the new album in sight, she quickly began talking up "Strength Of A Woman" to the press. A logical lyrical successor to "Prime Of My Life," Phyllis, who compared the song to Helen Reddy's classic "I Am Woman," was hoping the song would be the title track to her next album. "I want to call it that because the album is about strength and choosing strength," she said. "This will be the first time in years I've heard a song that speaks directly to women. It makes a great statement, and women need to spend more time concentrating on their inner feelings and building our nation of women. We could be a powerful force if we didn't dicker over little things, like men, who are going to be gone next week anyway.

"Girls cry too much," Phyllis continued. "Women need to learn that their existence isn't defined by a man. A man is a gift, not a need. I'm not man bashing. Men are not my problem – I'm my problem and I have to work on me. That's the kind of songs I'm writing now."

Through her pain, Phyllis became increasingly introspective. Glenda had brokered a deal for Phyllis to be featured in a new book by Lenora Fulani. A co-founder of the All Stars Talent Show Network that Phyllis was introduced to through Regina Belle, Fulani's book was to be called *Women Who Don't Sell Out*, and the chapter on Phyllis was appropriately enough called "The Strength Of A Woman."

"I respect women and I definitely try to nurture them the way they have always nurtured me," Phyllis's chapter read. "I strongly believe that women of all colors and religions have far more similarities than differences. We have to learn to be there for each other. That's what my song 'Strength Of A Woman' is about. I think it's time women stopped looking for someone other than themselves to make them feel whole. Don't get me wrong, I'm not trying to get you to think that I haven't been lonely and wouldn't have preferred a wonderful person in my life. We're told we're supposed to have partners. Whether we're partners with women or men, we're supposed to be a partner. It's sad. I would love to be in a relationship. I really would. But that's not my focus right now.

"Recently I have begun to focus on allowing my feelings to surface. What I have learned to do in my life is put up emotional walls that keep pain out. I have not really learned how to have a relationship, to be vulnerable, to be intimate, to be a real friend. Now, I want to be a real friend, especially since I have been blessed with so many beautiful people who have loved me without conditions or restrictions. I want to learn how to love them back. After that, I'll go for the biggie – a relationship with that 'special person' who I can be there for, as a lover and a friend."

"In many ways, Phyllis did not feel that she deserved to be loved," said Glenda. "So she would partner with people who could ultimately disappoint her and make her feel as if she was not being loved by them. Almost the self-fulfilling prophecy concept, you know? What this boils down to is this: underneath it all, Phyllis was a very warm, special, loving and tender woman who really just needed to know that someone special would be there for her no matter what; that they could handle her – all of her – and love her unconditionally. But to receive unconditional love, each of us has to first love ourselves unconditionally. This way, we really know it when we find it because we do it for ourselves. This was Phyllis's greatest challenge."

But Phyllis couldn't see this. She was tired, worn out and growing increasingly glum. She had remained in contact with her little fan and friend, Jason Barry, and asked his mother Brenda if she could visit the family in Maryland for a few days. Phyllis told the Barrys she needed to get out of New York, and when they picked her up at the train station, they found her in quite a state. "She was suffering from depression," explained Barry. "She really was. The next day I was waiting for her to get up, and I knocked on the door and she told me she was having a bad day." Phyllis had to fight to get herself out of bed. But day by day she began to get more comfortable and cheered up somewhat. One day, she asked Brenda to take her to the store to buy lobster, which she later cooked for the family.

Phyllis was astounded at how well Brenda and her husband Skip got along. "She was amazed that I cooked dinner and then Skip got up and washed the dishes," recalled Brenda. "We just work as a unit, and she said that was impressive to her because not too many people in her circle worked like that." Phyllis called the

Barrys the Cleavers: Skip was Ward, Brenda was June, Jason was the Beaver and his older brother, John, was Wally. "She just really liked that home unit. I told her one day that I was just mesmerized by her life and the excitement of the music industry. She said, 'Girl, you got the best life. Don't you ever wish my life upon yourself.' She said, 'You have the perfect life. Believe me, this is not as glamorous as it seems.'"

For years, Phyllis had been on the road constantly. Now there were larger gaps between performance dates. This would have been a blessing for Phyllis save for the fact that she had no other real sources of income except touring. "It's nice to be employed," Phyllis told a crowd during her weeklong engagement December 28, 1993 – January 2, 1994 at Kimball's East in Emeryville, California. "Let's get real. Unemployment's a bitch! I'm not real fond of it." Weeklong engagements were most difficult of all, though. Doing two shows a night, by the end of the third day, Phyllis's voice showed signs of severe strain. The request portion of her show was hugely popular with her fans. But Phyllis couldn't fill every request this time. "That's all I can sing of that, OK?" Phyllis said, after cutting short an acapella version of "I Found Love." "The voice gets weak after this many shows."

Phyllis did talk a lot during these shows, and she sounded cheerful and upbeat, not to mention hysterically funny. After putting a particularly defiant ending onto "Living All Lone," Phyllis had the crowd in stitches. "Ain't it time we changed those lyrics, girls? You can cry the blues but so long. He left? So what? Buy something else. That's my answer to everything. Just buy another one. So he was cute. I got more money. I'll buy a cuter one."

Phyllis had also begun talking tenderly to the crowd. Much as she had in "Gonna Make Changes," Phyllis was delivering a message to the world through "Strength Of A Woman," and she really enjoyed introducing the song to her audience. "I really needed to direct some energy toward my female comrades. I noticed just from being on the street and watching talk shows that women have a lot of problems with one another, jealousies, competitiveness, a lot of dumb stuff. Competing for some man. Why? When he leaves your ass it ain't nobody but me and you anyway. I don't get it. Why don't we stick together? Why can't we be friendly toward one another, love each other? Do not compete for those petty things. Jobs, men – all of that is temporary. Friendship is forever. So I wrote this song. I thought that maybe it would heal some of our wounds, make us think about loving each other because truly, truly women need to be connected."

As each year passed, the portrait that Phyllis painted to the press looked less and less like the reflection she saw in the mirror. She wrote songs about who she wanted to be and what she wanted to experience, and actually sang them to herself. "For the first time, I think some of you are really going to get an insight into how I've been feeling, at least for the last few years," said Phyllis. "I've decided to write about empowerment, write about ways I really wish I was. And I figure if I keep talking about it, and I keep reaffirming that I can be this way, that I can have these things, then I'm gonna have 'em."

Phyllis had the right concept. But inside her bitterness grew. The writing had unlocked certain pains she had kept hidden for so long, and unleashed a flood of unwanted emotions. It was too much for her contain, so Phyllis began acting out, growing ever more unpredictable, even sometimes childish and mean. Creative types are known for being free spirits, and most rhythm and blues bands are pretty loose. But Jonathan Dubose, a devout Christian, headed Phyllis's band; and, as he began hiring new members, he often looked for fellow brothers in Christ. Dubose tried to set a good example, and there's no denying he was a positive influence on Phyllis who, surrounded by a band full of Christians, tried to explore her own spirituality.

In addition to turning "Old Friend" nearly into a full-out gospel song, Phyllis had begun speaking about Christianity on stage and claimed to be a Christian. "There is nothing better and more powerful than prayer," Phyllis told one crowd at Blues Alley. "You can have anything; do anything; be anybody in the name of God. I do a lot of praying on a daily basis. I'm surrounded by prayer. If I were an atheist I'd be in trouble. Prayer is everywhere in my midst, in my group, and in the people I work with. And it's a very good thing. It calms my soul."

But Phyllis's soul, in truth, was anything but calm. She had gained a tremendous amount of weight, was no longer exercising, and was drinking as heavily as ever, going through a fifth of vodka and a couple bottles of wine every few days. Clearly adding to the unpredictability of her live performances was the fact that she was drinking backstage before the show began. When not on the road, Phyllis was spending more and more time in her Manhattan apartment. "She'd say, 'I'm gonna tell you right now, I'm gonna die in that goddamned bed,'" recalled fan turned friend Larry Atello. "She'd get up, watch TV, eat in the bed, whatever; she'd wait for the car to come to take her to work, and then come back home and go to bed."

She had assistants make trips for her to the liquor store and market, and she ordered in most of her meals from nearby restaurants, her favorite being sautéed chicken livers with onions and gravy from the Carnegie Deli. In bed she would sleep, eat, talk on the phone and read voraciously. Her assistants were frequently being sent down to the newsstand to pick up the latest copies of the *New York Post* and the *New York Daily News*, as well as magazines such as *People*, *Jet* and *Ebony* and assorted tabloids, which would remain in stacks throughout the apartment until Phyllis was sure she was finished with each one. Through it all, the television remained on and Phyllis would often tell friends on the phone to hold while she watched a particularly interesting on-screen moment.

The losses in Phyllis's life continued to unravel her emotionally. AIDS remained an important cause to Phyllis, and it wasn't hard to understand why. The number of friends she lost to the virus increased each year, and the latest one added to the list was that of Jehri Terrell. Phyllis first met Jehri while working in *Sophisticated Ladies*. Like Danny Wintrode, he was a talented make-up artist and hairstylist. After the production ended, Jehri and Phyllis kept in touch. For the last year, Jehri had worked frequently as Phyllis's valet and traveled with her extensively. Now, he was gone.

Phyllis continued work on the new album. As for its creative direction, Phyllis was blunt and to the point. "I don't sing happy, lovey-dovey stuff 'cause it's not my lifestyle. Love and relationships go wrong and that's something I know about. I would never have recorded songs like 'Somewhere In My Lifetime,' 'Old Friend' and 'Meet Me On The Moon' if I hadn't gone through that pain. That pain has brought out some of my best work."

Glenda actively encouraged Phyllis to be as involved as possible, writing as much as she could. Through Andre Harrell, Glenda arranged for Phyllis to collaborate with Dave "Jam" Hall. Hot at the moment, Hall had recently co-written and produced the debut track for a young vocalist named Mary J. Blige. The song, "You Remind Me," sold gold and went to number one.

Hall was worried that Phyllis was not a strong enough writer on her own and brought in backup in the form of Gordon Chambers, a young entertainment editor with *Essence* magazine, who had been making a name for himself by writing songs on the side. But Phyllis didn't like surprises. When she arrived at Hall's place and found Chambers waiting in the basement, she was not pleased. Phyllis quickly excused herself and went upstairs to use the phone, placing a call to Glenda in Philadelphia.

"She's yelling at Glenda on the phone," Gordon recalled. "'Glenda, who's this producing? He's got this little young kid songwriter here and I want to write these songs myself.' And while she's upstairs cussing everybody out, the track for what would become 'It's Not About You (It's About Me)' was playing and I just wrote the hook of that and just started laying down the hook. It seemed like what her personality was."

When she'd finished venting, Phyllis rejoined Dave and Gordon in the basement.

"What's this?" she asked, as the young songwriter continued to sing.

"Gordon just wrote this hook," Dave told her.

"You must have written this before you got here," Phyllis said accusingly.

Hall answered for his friend. "No, he just wrote the damn hook just now."

"Hell no!" Phyllis said. "No fuckin' way."

Then she scrutinized Gordon a little more closely.

"Don't I know you from somewhere?"

"Yeah," Gordon said. "I've been to some of your shows."

Slowly, Phyllis began to warm to him. "I'm there petrified thinking the woman was going to throw me out of the studio. She said, 'You just wrote this?' She was amazed that I had actually wrote this hook that fast and that's how she kind of became aware of my gift."

Phyllis was so impressed that she called Gordon the following day and invited him to join her for a writing session with her former musical director, Barry Eastmond, who she had recently reconnected with at an ASCAP event. Phyllis asked Gordon to pick her up and drive her. In the car, "we were driving and talking about songs and music and she said, 'I like you because you write the good quality stuff. I need more stuff like this.' And we were talking about songs and how she always fought with different record labels to find her more stuff that was substantive but commercial, that struck the right balance." Then, right in the middle of the conversation, Anita Baker's "Sweet Love" came on the radio.

"You hear this motherfuckin' song," Phyllis said, pointing to the radio. "This is what I'm talking about. This fuckin' song should have been my hit."

Once at Barry's Tarrytown house, Phyllis heard a track he had been working on with her in mind. Eastmond had been reflecting on Phyllis and how she had changed in the decade since they had last worked together. "She seemed sad," he said. "We got to sit and talk here at my house. We sat and had lunch, and she saw my house and she felt like she had wasted time and that she should have something like this."

Phyllis had been in the business a decade longer than Eastmond, and she could barely afford the monthly rent on her Manhattan apartment. The Philadelphia apartment had been given up the year before as a cost-cutting measure. Now, surrounded by the spaciousness of Eastmond's digs, Phyllis could not help but feel envious.

"You know, I should have my house," she said. "I should have a family."

"She felt like she just did things in her life that she later regretted, and wished she had just focused more on her music and family," said Barry. "And, actually, a lot of this came out in the songs that we wrote, especially 'Why Not Me.' That's exactly what she was talking about. Anybody can find happiness in their lives, why not me? It truly touched me while she was writing this lyric and knowing that this is what she was going through at this point in her life.

"Then she mentioned to me how she had tried to commit suicide twice before, and that just blew me away. I was shocked. I had no idea. But she told me she was in a great place and she was really happy and things were coming together."

Eastmond turned on his tape recorder. With the track playing in the background, Phyllis sang the title line over the bridge and then began talking about how she felt.

"I want a relationship just like everyone else, but I'm not willing to give up who I am," Phyllis started. "I'm in the limelight, so to speak. I'm easily recognizable by voice and by figure. That can be a problem for men. Having money, what they consider money – believe me, I have no money, OK – having money is a problem for men and mainly because I deal with younger guys and younger guys are just starting out so that's a problem for them.

"I really don't know how to be quiet. I don't know how to shut down and shut up. I couldn't sit for five minutes quiet, not in front of somebody. I couldn't. So compromising, I don't really know what it is. But I haven't been involved in almost a year, and I mean on any level. I'm trying to keep the bitterness down. Men and women get bitter so quickly. They blame everything on somebody else. I don't want to do that.

"It's so easy to say, well, 'Later for men. It's their loss.' I still say it's their loss, but I say that in jest and I say that in all reality because, well, when I have a boyfriend he's well cared for. Boyfriend, if he sneezes, that Kleenex is in his face before the sneeze comes out. But I guess I'm like a guy. I want to be in control. I think I'm sometimes better equipped to take charge, and that's probably not the best place to be. But that's the place I've always been. Most executive women that I've been meeting lately have been very honest. They've said, 'We're looking for a wife.' The first time a girl told me that I was like, 'What? Looking for a wife? I ain't looking for no wife.' What she meant was as an executive, you put the man beside her and she's looking for the same thing the man is looking for, someone to take care of her."

This sort of free-flowing thought exchange was typical of a Phyllis Hyman songwriting session. "In our sessions, Phyllis would be a storyteller," said Gordon. "She would share about her life and her thoughts and I would interpret what she said in lyric form. I tried to make sure I captured her feelings. She was passionate about not singing anything superficial." The entire experience was a thrill for Gordon. In just under 24 hours he'd gone from being a nuisance to a new and valued friend.

"That was the side of her that I saw very often, the really generous, giving, loving side," he said. "But I also saw a lot of the alcoholism. When we would go to the studio, she liked to drink Alize. So she'd bring a cooler and there'd be Alize and Kentucky Fried Chicken. She set the studio up like a little mini cabaret, a couple of tables and a couple of friends there. And that's how she recorded the song."

After working with Dave "Jam" Hall, Gordon Chambers and Barry Eastmond, it was back to the West Coast and to Nick Martinelli. When working with Martinelli, Phyllis always stayed at Le Parc in West Hollywood. During this trip, Phyllis spent a good amount of time with Lorraine Feather. Phyllis had first met Feather in 1987, when they were both guests on Barry Manilow's *Big Fun on Swing Street* television special, Phyllis as a solo guest and Feather fronting the group Full Swing. Shortly after the taping, Feather had forwarded to Phyllis some songs she'd written for her consideration. Phyllis liked one in particular, "This Too Shall Pass," which had been co-written by Joe Curiale, and finally the time had come to record it.

"The record company might fight me on it, but this will be a special song to me like 'Meet Me on the Moon,'" Phyllis told Feather, who was in the studio when Phyllis cut it. Kenny Gamble had encouraged Phyllis to reconnect with her writing, as had Glenda. But as the head of the company, Kenny had to be a bottom line kind of guy. Phyllis had gone to number one for the first time with the last album, and followed it up with two additional top 10 singles. Gamble was hoping to repeat the same feat or even best it with the next effort. But as he started hearing the songs Phyllis was turning in, he wasn't convinced there were any number ones in the lot.

Barry Eastmond was incredulous. "Not to fault anyone at the label, but when she was writing these songs, especially a song like 'Why Not Me,' in which she was really basically telling her story ... I remember playing it for the record company people at the time and they were just saying, 'Well, we're kind of looking for hits and we're not really interested. It's a nice song but we really need singles right now.'"

To Phyllis, such statements amounted to no more than another rejection, and this time from folks she considered family. "It kind of hurt her, because she's like, 'Guys, I'm telling my story, this is my life. I'm putting my heart and soul into this album and you're just kind of almost dissing it in a way and saying, well, it's not important because you need a single,'" Barry recalled. "In that way, it was really disappointing to her. I know she was really hurt by that.

"She kept telling me, 'Barry, don't worry, these songs are going to make the album. They're going to be on the album because they've always wanted me to write about myself and how I felt and what I've been through over the years.'" Inside though, Phyllis was not completely convinced. The little girl in her was confused once again. She had done as asked, and had still not made the grade.

Dejected, Barry watched Phyllis wilt. "Not that I know what she went through during the first two times that she had attempted suicide, but I think that there was something that would happen to her that would hurt her in a way that she felt, 'You know what? It's not worth going on.' It's funny because when she was telling me about the suicide attempts, she almost made it a joke. She was really funny about it. She said, 'You know the second time I tried to commit suicide I thought about jumping out the window and I said, Ah, with my big ass I'd probably take a bunch of people with me. So I decided not to do that.' It was hilarious. It was like something really funny to her. I just sat there like, 'Oh my God, I don't believe what she's telling me.' It was so deep."

Soon, Phyllis's dismay with her record company had worked its way into her live show. At a January 1994 appearance at the Caravan of Dreams in Fort Worth, Texas, Phyllis mentioned it in her introduction to the crowd. "It has been almost a year since we were here last," she said. "I've started to work on a new album.

Hopefully it will be out sometime soon. We don't want to wait another five years. My finances cannot stand it. I have no man. I have to take care of my own self. I need all the cash that I can get my hands on. So please, record company, consider that as you decide when this album is to be released. Needless to say, the IRS will be on your behind."

Chapter 17

I don't know if I really believe in God.

Even as she worked on her new album, with all its powerful and passionate lyrics, Phyllis was feeling defeated. The lyrics she was helping to write were strong declarations of faith and strength, but they were not representative of the life she was living at the time. She was in search of a peace that seemed elusive, and unable to find it, her nerves were constantly on edge, her patience painfully thin, and her moods swinging as if suspended from some imaginary pendulum in her mind. Not even performing held the same thrill for Phyllis as it once had, and like most of her other responsibilities as an artist, it was becoming a chore, a means to an end, and the only method she had of paying the bills.

Onstage, though, she continued to strive to project an image of strength. As she had after the breakup with Dante, Phyllis reworked the ending to "Living All Alone" once again, this time taking a page from her recently recorded though as of yet unreleased new song. "I refuse to be lonely," she sang over the repeating melody. "I have a choice. It's on me. I finally learned the difference between being alone and being lonely." Then she took a break from singing and spoke directly to the audience over the music. "On the real side, being alone ain't that bad."

Since 1992, Phyllis had been alluding to a new spiritual awareness with her traditional closing number, "Old Friend." The ending differed a little each night, especially in the beginning as she struggled to perfect it. But the monologues she delivered during her two-night run at Washington, D.C.'s Constitution Hall in April 1994 were especially moving. "I now understand that all that I am is because of the power and glory of God. I really took that for granted for many years. A lot of us have lost a lot of folks in our life in the last few years. The sadness is there, the pain is there, but there's also a lot of gladness because when my mother went, she left me with some very good things. She left me with the strength to do some things now that I could not do when she was alive. I did not know how to do it. I didn't care to do it. I didn't want to do it. But when she died, God said, 'You will do this. It is done.'

"It's changed my life, because I realize that her presence is everywhere and all of the people I've lost, I keep feeling their presence, cause see the body goes away but the spirit keeps hanging around and gives you that strength."

Phyllis's relationship with God had always run hot and cold. Raised by a Catholic mother and a Protestant father, neither of whom attended church regularly, as an adult she did not attend church or ascribe to any particular religious theology. But at various times in her life, such as during her two trips to rehab, she revisited the possibility that a stronger connection with a higher power might provide a well of strength she could draw from.

"She was searching for answers and I think having a hard time finding them for herself," said her former assistant and girlfriend Martha David. "She was struggling to find something that touched her, that really was meaningful to her and made sense to her."

Continuing her quest to depict herself as a victim of Arista, she blamed the record company and its head for jeopardizing her career and stealing her soul. "During that time I developed a terrible attitude," she said. "I was angry, controlling and self-destructive. I wouldn't let people get close and I wasn't a very nice person. Then one day I woke up and said, 'Phyllis, you're such as asshole. You've not been nice to people. You've got to change. You've got to be a better human being. You cannot go through life like that. God does not like ugly, and someday you're going to have to pay the piper.

"I now try hard every day to become a better person. There are a lot of things that still tick me off. But rather than taking it out on other people, I've learned to control any spontaneous reactions and selfish desires. I say to myself, 'Who cares if you don't like it, Phyllis? Who died and left you in charge?' Now, I'm trying to be more conscious of other people's feelings."

It is not difficult to believe that the rational, reasonable Phyllis never meant to hurt anyone. But the other Phyllis, altered either by alcohol or drugs, the adrenaline of a manic period or the anguish of a crushing depression, she was another creature.

Phyllis's own awareness of her duality fluctuated. Though she often attributed her outbursts to righteous indignation, her awareness was great enough that she realized she had not always helped her own cause. "Has my outspokenness cost me? Sure. Would I live my life differently if I could do it all over again? Not a chance!"

On the flipside of her fury laid a totally soft and tender side. Phyllis could be incredibly generous. She felt empathy for those who were suffering, taking their pain on as her own, and she gave of her time and her money to many causes. In the spring and summer of 1994, Phyllis participated in two high-profile charity events. In May, it was Light Up The Night Against AIDS in Philadelphia. Phyllis had lost many friends to AIDS by now, and had participated in several fundraisers. For this one, she sang the song "The Streets of Philadelphia," from the Tom Hanks movie *Philadelphia*, backed by a choir assembled and directed by Steven Ford. Phyllis, like fellow performers Bea Arthur, Tommy Tune, Tony Randall and others, appeared for free at the event, which benefited Elizabeth Taylor's American Foundation for AIDS Research (AmFAR) and two local organizations, the Philadelphia AIDS Consortium and the Minority AIDS Coalition.

The following month, Phyllis was part of an all-star line-up for the closing ceremonies of Gay Games IV in New York. The ceremonies took place in Yankee Stadium, and following such talent as Cyndi Lauper, Taylor Dayne, and Dianne Reeves, Phyllis performed "Old Friend" just before her own old friend Patti LaBelle closed the show. Phyllis had also lent the use of her song "Strength Of A Woman" to the games. It was released as a special cassette single dedicated to openly-gay tennis star Martina Navratilova.

"Over the past 20 years of my career, the diversity of my audience has grown," Phyllis said. "Young, old, different races and people from all walks of life, but what has fascinated me the most is how the gay community has gravitated toward me. I guess my involvement with raising funds for AIDS-related causes and for the human rights of the gay community in general has created a bridge of endearment between us. As I've gotten to know this community,

I feel like I've found a new friend, a new source of energy that I didn't know existed. Now I know. As human beings, we're all going in the same direction. We're supposed to be there for each other. The only difference between us is our sexual preference, and that's not a reason for me not to be there for them when I'm needed."

One person she felt a need to be there for was her backing vocalist since 1989, Eric Jones. A talented singer, Jones was one of only two band members who had survived the mass band reorganization of 1991. By 1994 though, he was not looking well and beginning to lose weight. Phyllis was no stranger to AIDS, having lost countless friends such as hairdressers Danny Wintrode and Jehri Terrell to the disease. Now she feared Jones may also be HIV positive. Afraid to confront Jones directly, she asked Bill Schultz what he knew. Schultz was aware that Eric was HIV positive, but didn't feel it his place to share this information.

"Well," Phyllis started, "if Eric is sick he will have his job even if he has to sing from a wheelchair."

Between the charity events and concert appearances, Phyllis was still working on the new album. In June and July, she was once again back and forth between New York and Los Angeles, working with Nick Martinelli. "The last time we worked together, it was very, very difficult," said Nick. "She didn't want to focus. It was like she would have rather watched *Oprah* or something."

While on the West Coast, Phyllis turned 45, and she asked Nick to throw her a party. "She wanted a birthday party so we threw her one," he remembered. "It was a strange party. Just about 10 or 15 people showed up. She told everybody what gifts to bring if they were going to bring something. It was a weird list of stuff, like if they couldn't afford something it could've been paper towels. There were ridiculous things on it. I'm looking at it myself and saying, 'Now what is she gonna do with paper towels? Carry them back to New York?' I mean, this don't make sense to me."[12]

---

[12] Bill Schultz explains, "She'd create lists with everything on them from Gucci bags to a bar of soap. I remember she'd say, 'You've got to have a gift for every budget, that way no one can say they couldn't afford a gift.'"

Nick was aware of the decline in his friend's mental health. Never having liked the recording studio, Phyllis was never particularly easy to produce. But it was now nearly impossible. "It was really getting hard to work with her," Nick said. "The last couple sessions were nightmares. When it was done, I remember distinctly saying to Glenda and Sydney, 'Phyllis will not be here for another album. I will be surprised if she's here for another album. I'm telling you right now, I'll be very surprised.'"

One highlight of Phyllis's time in Los Angeles was a trip to the House of Blues with Nick and Jane Eugene (who had co-written "I Refuse") to see her old friend Betty Wright. "I remember Nick saying, 'She says she coming, we'll keep our fingers crossed,'" recalled Betty, who knew by then that her friend had become quite unpredictable. "She showed up and I promise you, the eyes across the room lit up. People loved that girl. People were so astounded to see her. It's like everybody knew but her – everybody knew that she was just a phenomenon."

Betty had just released a new album, the title song of which had been produced by Martinelli. A powerful ballad Wright had penned herself, the song says, "For love alone. I'd risk anything I own. Anything. For love alone. I live for love alone."

"I turned around to look at Nick's table and Phyllis was just hanging on every word," said Mark Matlock, formerly of Zoo Records, who was also in the house that night. "When Betty broke out with the chorus, Phyllis just closed her eyes and leaned back as if she knew every word – as if she'd lived every word – of what Betty was singing."

Phyllis took a few moments to catch up with Betty after the show and shared her sadness at having never received a gold record. "I said, 'What do you mean you never went gold? Did you call RIAA? Did they tell you that you never went gold?' And she said every time it went near 400,000 it would just stop."

In mid-August, Phyllis was invited to perform at an inaugural international jazz festival in Bahia, Brazil. The promoter was inexperienced, and while Phyllis accepted the date, she did so with reservations. To start with, Phyllis had always feared international travel. The differences in culture, language and money were confusing issues to Phyllis, and, as such, she could not feel completely in control and have the safety net she needed.

"The whole trip started with Phyllis being very apprehensive about going and we couldn't understand why," said Robbie Todd, a young screenwriter she had recently befriended, who joined Phyllis on the trip. "She just had this whole vibe. She kept saying it was a gut feeling."

Larry Kendricks, Phyllis's road manager, was not available, so Leo took over those responsibilities and Robbie assisted. "After a 12-hour flight, a two-hour layover in San Paolo and then another hour and a half flight to Bahia, we were all whooped," said Robbie. "Then when we got there they had vans with no air conditioning." Phyllis, whose rider called for a limousine, knew immediately that her gut feeling had been on the money.

Once at the venue, it was debatable whether the show would go on at all, as the sound technicians were refusing to work until being paid. As a result, Phyllis did not participate in a soundcheck. Her spirits were lifted when she ran into Gordon Chambers, who was covering the festival for *Essence*, for whom he was now arts and entertainment editor. When she learned that she would, in fact, be taking the stage, Phyllis invited Gordon to join her on it. Unfortunately, Phyllis had been drinking, and her voice throughout the show was heavy and dragging, sounding much like a record playing at the wrong speed.

Phyllis and Gordon had not rehearsed. "We don't have a clue what the hell we're doing, nor do I care," said Phyllis as she brought Gordon out onto the stage. "I suggest that if you have another drink, you won't either." After adding backing vocals to "Meet Me on the Moon," Phyllis called him to the front of the stage. "Gordon and I are going to fake some stuff. We've written some great stuff for my new album. I have a new album coming out like yesterday. If it doesn't, I'm going to kill somebody, cause I need this record because I need to pay my bills."

Though the dates were not coming as frequently as they once had, and while it's undeniable that the length between album releases was hurting her, the truth is that Phyllis was largely to blame for her poor financial situation. When money did come in, Phyllis ran through it. Shopping was clearly another of her coping mechanisms. But Phyllis's bank account suffered the most when she went shopping for drugs. Phyllis's binges had nearly bankrupted her. Her addictions were destroying wonderful opportunities and alienating a lot of potentially powerful allies in the business. As one observer noted, "Phyllis Hyman was invited everywhere – once."

Two days later, Phyllis and her band were scheduled to return to the States. At the airport, Phyllis asked Robbie to carry her tote bag. In it was what Robbie thought was a bottle of water packed with ice. It didn't take airport security long to figure out otherwise, though. "I don't speak Portuguese and I'm like, 'Oh, it's water.' It was in a water container. So I was like, 'Aqua, aqua.' The guy's like, 'Oh no, no, no, no.' I said oh shit. Here comes the government guy and he's smelling the bag because someone had alerted him. Luckily, Tito Puente's manager, he spoke Portuguese, so he chilled out everything. I remember getting on the plane and just giving Phyllis this look. I said, 'Thank you for almost getting me thrown in a Brazilian jail for carrying vodka and I'm telling them it's water.'"

Back in New York, Phyllis took Robbie, Leo, personal assistant Lennice Molina, Gordon and her brother Michael out to breakfast at the Park Café. If there were any hard feelings between Robbie and Phyllis, they were soon forgotten. Gordon didn't see much of this, blinded by the starlight that Phyllis radiated. "It was so overwhelming to be on stage with Phyllis Hyman singing in front of all these people. I mean, a lot of my relationship with her, you have to remember that I was almost a kid. So most of the time that I spent with her, I was really quite in awe of her. A lot of my relationship with her at the time was kind of like an out-of-body experience."

Gordon recalled a time he passed by Phyllis's apartment to drop off a tape of a song they'd been working on. "I had some of my friends in my car because we were going out. So I went to drop off the thing and I was going to just leave it with her doorman. She was like, 'Oh, no, no, come up.'"

Double-parked, Gordon rushed upstairs to deliver the tape.

"Where you goin?" Phyllis asked as he tried in vain to make a hasty exit. "I haven't been out of this house in two weeks? Where you goin? You leavin' me already?'"

When Gordon told Phyllis he had friends waiting for him in the car, Phyllis didn't bat an eyelash.

"Bring 'em up, bring 'em up, bring them damn friends up here," Phyllis ordered. "Don't be embarrassed. I'll clean this house up a little bit. I'll order some food from the Shark Bar. They'll deliver for me."

Gordon was moved. "I think loneliness is a state of mind," he said. "I think there are individuals who can just be lonely in a crowd of people, and Phyllis was one of them. My observation of her was that she was somewhat of a people pleaser and an attention grabber, very often to her own detriment. She needed to be around people to have an audience."

As Gordon's own star began to ascend and his reputation as an excellent songwriter grew, he began receiving an onslaught of songwriting inquiries at his *Essence* office. When he confided in Phyllis that it was starting to become a problem, he was shocked at the depth of her generosity and her suggested solution.

"Gordon, I'm home all the time. Give those people my number. I won't answer the phone and say, 'I'm Phyllis Hyman.' You know, I'll tell them it's Gordon Chamber's office and I'll be your secretary. I'm always home. When I'm here I answer the phone CPI. For all they know CPI can be the Gordon Chambers office. They won't know."

Glenda had for years been looking for a proper theatrical property for her charge. Phyllis had never fully capitalized on that line in her resume that read "Tony-nominated actress." So when Glenda found the script to *Blues Bar* on her desk, she was sufficiently enthused. In the tradition of *Ain't Misbehavin'*, *Blues Bar* was a musical celebrating the great institution of the blues. The play was written by Curtis King, who was also to direct it.

The founder of the Junior Black Academy of Arts and Letters in Dallas, King based the story on a little juke joint he had frequented while studying at Jackson State University in Mississippi. "I don't remember the name of the place," King told *The Dallas Morning News*. "But friends and I would go to a place on Lynch Street that had a two-piece band and a singer. We'd listen to 'Wang Dang Doodle' and the whole place would be dancing to it. I'm trying to recreate that same kind of feeling, only embellished."

King had founded the JBAAL in 1977 and modeled it after the American Negro Academy. Its goal was to increase awareness of black artistic accomplishments, rooted in the African culture, among the races. *Blues Bar* was the JBAAL's first original production, and King had high hopes for the production. "I'm 42," he said at the time. "It's time for me to make some money. I'm not going to wind up like Zora Neale Hurston or [Dallas blues piano great] Alex Moore. I had to help raise money to bury him, you know. I don't plan to die that way."

Phyllis was one of a few names discussed to play the critical lead role of Etta Pickens, a fictional blues singer who, after making it big in Europe, returns to the states for her first domestic concert tour in over a decade. Upon returning to her hometown, Etta learns that the club she first sang in is about to close. As she plans a benefit to save the struggling club, Etta is forced to confront the reasons she left Mississippi in the first place, and more than her fair share of personal demons. While the show had a supporting cast, Etta carried the lion's share of the lines.

The blues and Phyllis seemed for some an unlikely pairing. But something in the character of Etta and her struggles touched a chord in Phyllis. "In spite of the circumstances being different, this is so much like my own life that it's scary," she told *Jack The Rapper* magazine. The show was scheduled to open and run for one weekend in Dallas. From there, it was scheduled to tour and was booked solid through the end of the year.

Rehearsals took place at the Dallas Convention Center, where JBAAL was housed and began only three weeks before the opening of the show to accommodate Phyllis's Brazilian commitment. The supporting cast of the show included singer Billy Preston, who played Etta's bandleader, Antonio "Huggy Bear" Fargas (best known for his role on the television show *Starsky & Hutch*) and Roger E. Mosley (from the television show *Magnum, P.I.*) Phyllis flew into Dallas one week before the rest of the cast and began rehearsals with King on August 22.

It didn't take King long to realize he had a problem on his hands, "probably about two hours into the first rehearsal," he recalled. "I knew she was going to have problems because I could tell the way she was reading. As long as I've been out here, I could tell. She was a singer, not an actress. She was a singer who could do the work, but she didn't know how to process the story in a way that could help her memorize it."

While Phyllis had earned a Tony nomination for her role in *Sophisticated Ladies*, it's important to note that that show was a review. Phyllis had no dialogue to remember – no lines at all outside of the lyrics to the songs she sang. And while she had done some acting through the years, most notably in Fred Williamson's film *Soda Cracker/The Kill Reflex*, that was a movie, which is filmed a scene at a time and could be re-shot as many times as needed to achieve perfection. *Blues Bar* really marked Phyllis's first foray into live theatre, the first time she would be expected to learn huge pieces of dialogue and deliver them flawlessly night after night.

Sadly, by this time, she wasn't up to the task. Her substance abuse combined with her crippling insecurities made the memorization process virtually impossible. As early as 1990 she had begun using a music stand and lyric sheets to help her through new songs as she performed them in concert. But in this arena, that wasn't possible. There was no room for a teleprompter or cue cards. It was all on Phyllis here, who was far from operating on full capacity.

There were, however, promising moments. "When the rest of cast came and we did the roundtable reading, Phyllis was so on it was unbelievable," said Curtis. "When she was on, she was on; and when she was off, she was off. She had so many different things that she was trying to sort out in her mind. She was a very troubled sister."

Glenda was hopeful and confident that Phyllis could pull through when she flew to Dallas to check on the production. "She called Oscar Cohen with ABC and said to him, 'I think we have a show,'" Curtis said. "This show was going to be the show that was going to get Phyllis back to Broadway." But first, Phyllis had to memorize her lines. Rehearsals for her were tortuous affairs. She traveled with two personal assistants, Lennice and Leo, who had a hard time getting Phyllis to show up on time – not to mention sober.

"It was rough," recalled Darrell Craig Harris, a member of the show's band. "Phyllis was having some personal problems and it affected her ability to learn lines. That was kind of making it hard for Billy and those guys, because they wanted to get that stuff happening as tightly as possible, and of course before they went out on the road. The thing with Phyllis is that she was drinking, and that's what was kind of causing her problems."

"Phyllis was frightened because it meant working like she worked in *Sophisticated Ladies*, in a medium that she hadn't been in for a while," said Glenda. "In this role, she had to really act and sing and it scared her. She had to really be in character. She had to really learn her lines. She had to take direction. And she had to sing in an idiom that she wasn't all together familiar with. So she really had to professionally hunker down and stretch herself. It was challenging to her, and she wasn't sure she could do it. So she sought comfort from the usual suspects."

Phyllis was caught in a vicious cycle, and the patience of the cast and crew eventually began to wear thin as opening night drew near. "It was contentious at times," said Darrell. "I think Billy liked her and he appreciated her talent. But he really got frustrated with having to repeatedly go over stuff that, in his mind, they should have already been done with."

Billy was no stranger to substance abuse issues himself. He was, in fact, on probation at the time stemming from a 1992 plea agreement on charges of assault with a deadly weapon and cocaine possession. He was trying to get his act together, though. And onstage he was the consummate professional. "Billy definitely has his issues," said Darrell. "But when it comes to music, he didn't mess around."

Curtis King didn't mess around either. It was not only his theatre and production company's reputation that was on the line, but as writer and director, he had everything riding on the success of the show. Phyllis and Billy worked to promote the show and its opening in the Dallas market, appearing on local television shows, including *Good Morning Texas*, and on radio broadcasts all across the country. Radio was always safe ground for Phyllis, but her television appearances likely did little to entice area theatergoers. The camera, they say, adds ten pounds, and Phyllis was already well over 250 pounds, the largest she had ever been in her life. The extra weight obviously made her physical work in the play that much more difficult, and she was beginning to look noticeably unhealthy.

"She was grossly overweight and trying to perform on stage," recalled Cynthia Biggs. "She was just literally round front and back. I knew that was bothering her because that was part of her depression. When she was depressed she would just eat, eat, eat, eat, eat and, consequently, she would put on the weight. I really believe she just hated looking at herself in the mirror because she had allowed herself to get that disfigured from excessive eating and, I'm sure, the alcohol."

On *Good Morning Texas*, Phyllis wore what had become her standard offstage uniform by this time: a black pantsuit with a mud cloth shawl. She appeared without one of her trademark hats, though, and her short hair was blond. Her face was extremely full from the weight gain, her double chin and the folds on her neck prominent. She was hoarse when she spoke, undoubtedly from all the rehearsing, but quite jovial.

"It's about a blues singer who becomes very famous and goes back to her roots," Phyllis said, explaining the storyline of the show. "It's set in a bar where we do some of the finest gospel music and blues tunes that I've ever heard."

"A lot of blues singers start off in the church singing."

"Not me," said Phyllis. "I never sang in church. Millie Jackson came in to see us while she was here rehearsing her show. She said, 'Where'd you learn how to sing like that?' I said, 'Well, I don't know, but it took me two weeks to get it.' And with Billy playing the way he does, and I've never worked with anyone like him, you just follow along. You really do."

When asked about performing live on stage without the safety net the recording studio offered, Preston said the stage had its advantages. "It's a little scary but it's also fun. You've got the crowd there and you vibe off of them."

"He's lying," Phyllis said. "It is scary. It is frightening. I have all these lines to deliver. I'm not sure what city I'm in, what year this is and Mr. Curtis King has written a fabulous piece and I've just never done anything like this before. So aside from being extremely nervous, I stay a little confused. But I think one reason they hired me is because they know that girlfriend will find a way to pull through."

If Phyllis could depend on nothing else, there was always her voice. Despite the awful abuses she had subjected her body to in the past decade and a half, despite the pills and booze and binge eating, despite it all, hers was the still the voice of satin and stardust. And when the notes began to travel from the depths within and were released into the atmosphere of her audience, her faults were forgiven. She was still the sophisticated lady of song, and for as long as she was singing, the show worked.

There was little original music in *Blues Bar*. Instead, the show featured several standards as well as a few songs made famous by its stars. Billy sang his number-one hit "Will It Go Round In Circles" and the traditional hymn "Amazing Grace," which was featured in his regular concert act at the time. Phyllis, for her part, requested that her recently recorded but not yet released "I Refuse To Be Lonely" be inserted into the show as well. Other blues and soul standards she performed included Jimmy Reed's "Baby, What You Want Me To Do," Aretha Franklin's "Dr. Feelgood," Leon Russell's "A Song For You," and "This Bitter Earth" (made famous by Dinah Washington and written by her longtime producer Clyde Otis).

The undisputed standout of all of Phyllis's numbers was Bessie Smith's "Wasted Life Blues." "When Phyllis would do that piece, I tell you, the people would stand up and scream," said Curtis. "It was so real. Phyllis said that song was literally like her whole testimony. She would wear that song out. It was very eerie the way she delivered it, because she delivered it like it was almost her eulogy, like she had passed away and her spirit was delivering it to her body."

The song came at the end of the first act, and sometimes during rehearsals Phyllis would be so worn out after finishing the number that she'd have to take 30-40 minutes to pull herself together and be able to go on with the second act. "The thing about Phyllis is that when she sang, you kind of overlooked the other stuff," said Darrell. "I think that's kind of how Curtis, the director, approached it. And the other guys just sort of said, 'You know what? She's a great singer, so we'll work around the other stuff.'"

King agreed. "When she would sing, she would sing you up out of the place. But she could never get her lines out." As opening night rapidly approached, King did everything in his power to help Phyllis get ready. He hired her a coach to help with the lines. Then, three days before the show opened, he abruptly decided to cancel all of Phyllis's further press obligations. The official word was that the media interviews were "overburdening" Phyllis, but the truth was it was painfully obvious that Phyllis needed every minute possible before the curtain went up to learn her lines.

When *Blues Bar* opened at the Bruton Main Theatre on September 23rd, Phyllis still didn't have her part down and the show suffered accordingly. Esther Rolle showed up backstage and was not particularly amused when Phyllis, ever the TV buff, repeatedly referred to her as Florida, the name of her character on the hit seventies sitcom *Good Times*.

Subsequent shows that first weekend were no better, and reviews for the play were not terrific. "Ms. Hyman is indeed a sophisticated stylist," wrote a reviewer for *The Dallas Morning News*. "When her material permits, her smoky sound can caress a ballad and make it do anything she likes. But several other performers nearly steal the show. ... Ms. Hyman, however accomplished, seems more like a conventional pop singer. It's always a pleasure to hear her perform, but she doesn't hypnotize or hold spellbound."

As the opening weekend wore on, Phyllis never did pull it together. During one show, Phyllis was nearly finished with the first act when she looked down into the audience and saw that Tymm Holloway, who had flown in to surprise her, was sitting third row center. "Oh, my son's here," she said, momentarily breaking character. After the show, "We went backstage and she was pissed at me because she got in trouble because she recited words that were not in the show," Tymm recalled. "So she didn't want to meet my friend. She was like, 'Why didn't you let me know? I would have gotten you tickets. How did you get tickets?'" Holloway quickly tried to calm her down. "Girl, stop it already."

During another show, Phyllis was seated on the stage, in the midst of a scene, when she spotted a roach making its way toward the table. She screamed, stood up and fled the stage as her co-stars and the audience watched in shock. A quick thinking stagehand scurried out and stepped on the roach, clearing the way for Phyllis's return. "That was one motherfucking cockroach," she said aloud when she finally came back out. She took her place at the table, took a deep breath and said, "Where was I?"

"Luckily, she was surrounded by some great folks," said Darrell. "Roger E. Mosley and Antonio Fargas, those guys were very experienced actors. They helped her out the best they could. But again, a lot of the problems she was having were affecting her ability to really get that going."

King developed a genuine affection for Phyllis. "When she opened the show, when she came down those steps, she was glamorous," he said. "She had some great moments, sometimes those moments would be so phenomenal. She knew what to do with it when she got it, but she just could not sustain it.

"I knew she needed a lot of nurturing," Curtis continued. "Phyllis was the type of person that would give you anything that she had. She was a very giving person. But she had a tendency to lash out. She would constantly lash out and when she did this it made people not like her. And Phyllis would cry at the drop of a hat. I mean crocodile tears. She was carrying so much stuff, rocks and bricks, from a way, way distant past. She was still carrying them."

At one point during rehearsals, Phyllis had gone to King for advice. Lennice accompanied her to his office, and once they arrived there, Phyllis instructed her to wait outside and closed the door. Seated at King's desk, Phyllis poured out her heart to him. "She said, 'I want to know, you have all this going for you. You're such a good director.' She gave me all the accolades. She said, 'How do you do all this and stay so focused.'" King's response was simple: his faith in God kept him going. "She said, 'I don't know if I really believe in God.'"

Despite what she said to King, Phyllis knew there was a higher power. But she could not build a strong connection to it because it involved a surrendering she was not capable of. Phyllis had to be in control – of her relationships, her career, her body, and her life. Her belief in and support of an individual's right to commit suicide is a testament to this theory. Phyllis believed that when one's pain became too great, it was their right to be able to remove themselves from it. To ask someone – in this case God – to take it away was a sign of weakness. Phyllis fought at all costs to be the master of her own destiny, a title she was insistent upon retaining even if it meant ruining her life, or ultimately ending it.

Phyllis's occasional spiritual meanderings most often saw her flirting with Christianity. The King James Version of the Bible reads in Luke 11:9, "And I say unto you, ask, and it shall be given you; seek, and ye shall find; knock, and it shall be opened unto you." This was a problem for Phyllis and it represented her true issue with not only Christianity but also spirituality as a whole. Phyllis Hyman didn't like to need anything from anyone, not even God.

Following opening weekend, King continued to rehearse the cast in hopes of taking a tighter production on the road. It was during such a rehearsal, on September 27th, that tragedy struck the set of *Blues Bar*. The action in the show took place at a fictional bar, and the set was designed to look like a club, complete with a bandstand, bar and tables and chairs. "There were some stairs on the stage where she would enter from and she was walking down them and she actually tripped," recalled Darrell, who watched in horror with the rest of the band, cast and crew as Phyllis tumbled. "I guess she just lost her footing. She was quite heavy and I think she may have just had a hard time balancing that."

Glenda chalked it up to a combination of the awkwardness of Phyllis's extra poundage and her alcoholism. "There was a lot happening and because she wasn't sober, she slipped and broke her ankle. That was really sad. It was devastating."

For her part, Phyllis claimed she had been distracted. "The director's talking to me and someone else is talking and I just missed a stair," she said. "I didn't fall. I just kind of slipped off a stair. I thought I'd just twisted my ankle but we had a bodyguard on the set who's a trainer who said, 'No, that's fractured.'"

Phyllis was taken to Methodist Medical Center where she was, in fact, diagnosed with a fractured fibula in her right ankle. A soft cast was put on her leg and foot, and a wheelchair was delivered to her suite at the Ramada Inn the next day. Phyllis may have been out of commission, but as the grand old theatrical saying goes, the show must go on. In this case, it went on with Phyllis's understudy, local vocalist Bonita Arderberry. She didn't offer the drawing power that Phyllis had, but she had one up on the legend whose shoes she was temporarily filling: she remembered the lines.

Phyllis traveled with the show to Alabama where it played for two days – October 7-8 – at Montgomery's Davis Theatre before moving on to Birmingham's Alabama Theatre October 14-15. She may have been on multiple medications for pain and juggling between crutches and a wheelchair, but she had enough of her senses about her that she wanted to check out the competition.

To her face, Phyllis voraciously praised Arderberry. Secretly, however, she was envious of her understudy and resented her ability to memorize the role so easily. In Montgomery, Phyllis sat in the front row with a mini flashlight during each performance. A copy of the script situated in her lap, Phyllis would make a notation of every line Arderberry missed or messed up and then deliver such to King after each performance.

"Mr. Director," she would say, waving the notated script in King's face.

"OK, Phyllis, what's the point?" Curtis pressed.

But to Phyllis, it was obvious.

"The point is, I'm not the only one missing lines."

Phyllis was in such a state that she seemed not to know that the understudy was expected to miss lines, and she was too insecure to admit that the unknown was doing a better job in the show than she had. For his part, King was excited watching Arderberry on stage each night. "That's when we knew the piece really had potential," he remembered. "The lines were finally getting out."

King was encouraged by the prospects, but not for long. It was during these dates in Alabama that producer Evans Johnson told King he had run out of money. King had to end up using his personal credit cards to help get the cast and crew back to Dallas. Phyllis returned to New York undaunted and determined to make a triumphant comeback in the show. King flew to New York to meet with her, and she even spoke of putting some of her own money behind the show. Sadly, King couldn't agree to the plan. His contract with the producers gave them a ten-year option on the show, and even though they had defaulted, he could not contractually launch another version of the show without them.

Chapter 18

*I've found that the only answer
to life is really death.*

As she recovered from her fractured ankle, Phyllis began spending more and more time in her cramped Manhattan apartment. "She was totally lost in her own thoughts," said Glenda. "She was imprisoned, because between her injury and her weight, it was hard for her." Phyllis watched television, ordered in food and spent hours on the phone with friends. "She would say, 'I'm not working, I don't have any money, I'm depressed and I can't get up and clean this house,'" recalled Ama Ward, Phyllis's longtime friend.

Ward saw Phyllis in October. Phyllis had taken the train to Baltimore to spend time with the Barry family while she recuperated. Feeling some better, Phyllis decided she was in the mood to shop. "I used to call Phyllis my glamour girl," said Ama. "Phyllis told me to meet her at Wheaton Mall. I was thinking, well, how is this girl going to pull off glamour in a wheelchair? Honey, Miss Thing showed up with a black outfit on with a mud cloth belt to match the mud cloth hat to match the mud cloth shawl. I said, 'Girl, I was wondering how you were gonna do it.' And she said, 'Didn't I do it, girl?'"

It was the same outfit Phyllis had worn on *Good Morning Texas* a month earlier, and a common look for her at the time. Phyllis had long been a fan of vibrant colors, but lately had taken to frequently wearing black to take advantage of its slimming effect. Regardless of what she was wearing, Ward was happy to see her, and to be shopping with her once again. "She liked to shop, OK?" said Ama. "And if you were with her, it was like, 'Yeah, I'm going to buy this for you.' She always was there to sign an autograph. She didn't care where we were. She always had a folder with pictures to give people if they asked her."

Brenda Barry often took Phyllis to the mall, too. "We'd go just so she could meet people," Brenda said. "We sat in the Godiva chocolate store one day and she had conversations with a lot of the shoppers. She gave out her pictures and it was a good day for her. She liked being recognized as Phyllis Hyman. It really made her feel good."

By now, Brenda was one of Phyllis's closest confidantes, and the two could talk about anything. Phyllis shared with Brenda that she had been diagnosed as bipolar, and that she refused to take any mood stabilizing medications. "I should be on lithium right now, but I'm not taking that shit," Phyllis told her, adding that she felt the medication compromised her talent and made her feel not herself. Phyllis also shared that she knew she should be back in therapy, but that she had no plans of returning. "I'm just not dealing with the shit," Phyllis said.

Not surprisingly, Phyllis also shared with Brenda, as she did with all those in her inner circle, her thoughts on suicide, and the fact that she had previously attempted to take her life.

"I tried to commit suicide and I'll probably try to do it again," Phyllis told her candidly.

"Don't talk like that," Brenda responded, unsure of what else to say.

"I'm very honest. I know myself and I don't even know why the motherfuckers woke me up. I don't even know why they did it."

"Phyllis, you shouldn't say things like that," Brenda said, growing increasingly uncomfortable.

But Phyllis was insistent.

"No, no, girl," she said. "Don't tell me about my feelings. I know my feelings."

Phyllis knew by now that the road represented a grind she could not escape. Her fuse was short, sometimes virtually nonexistent. Songwriter Cynthia Biggs was backstage at the Dell East in Philadelphia earlier in the year when Phyllis summarily dismissed a member of the band in front of a line of waiting fans outside her dressing room. "It was explosive and it was loud and it was rude and it was vulgar," said Cynthia. "I turned around and apologized to the fans. *I* turned around and apologized to the fans, that they had to see her that upset. And after that she was in no shape and no condition to do any more autographs.

"She was just out of control in everyway," Cynthia continued. "She would have a clear bottle of fluid with her onstage and it would look like water, but it was vodka. She would get smashed, and as she became more and more inebriated her behavior basically became more and more irrational."

Around her apartment, Phyllis's employees walked on eggshells. It wasn't unusual for staff members working in the apartment to be contacted via the walkie-talkies Phyllis used while on tour – from the next room – and be told they were washing dishes too loudly. On occasion, laughter even irritated her and she'd stick her head out of her bedroom to inform staff members that it was a "no laughing" day.

At her worst, Phyllis's outbursts were loud and violently disturbing. People who are bipolar often have no concept of context or proportion, so the slightest infraction is perceived as an all-out attack and a logical, rational response is not possible. Phyllis, at times, could not discern the difference between a comment made in jest and an attempted jugular slashing, and, hence, her retaliations to even humor could be heavy-handed and downright hateful.

When basketball star Michael Jordan, who had come out to George's in Chicago to take in Phyllis's show, told her jokingly backstage that she had no man because she was too bossy, Phyllis was livid. She had been about to eat some chitlins brought to her by a friend, but suddenly, and rather surprisingly, she said she had no appetite and handed them back to her valet. Back at the hotel, Phyllis was furious to find that the valet, who was new, had not put the chitlins from the plate back into the pot and had instead thrown them out. Phyllis screamed at the valet, and at assistant Bill Schultz who had been showing the valet the ropes. Then, without warning, Phyllis flung the half-empty pot at both of them, spraying them with the last of the pig intestines.

"I wonder why I allowed Phyllis to treat me as she did," said Bill. "But I always made excuses for her and I knew deep down she didn't mean it. But that's really not good for a person."

Glenda was another one who took more than her fair share of verbal beatings. It was not uncommon for Phyllis to berate her in front of anyone who happened to be around. Gordon Chambers was on hand for one such occasion, and the tongue-lashing he watched Phyllis unload on her manager caused him to feel embarrassed for her. "Glenda was just being lambasted in front of everybody," Gordon recalled. "She lashed out at Glenda awfully." Finally, Gordon's curiosity got the best of him.

"This is not really in my place to ask but I'm just curious," Gordon began. "Why do you put up with this?"

"First of all, she's my sister," Glenda started calmly, clearly undaunted. "I know that she loves me dearly, and I love her, and she really does not mean it. Second of all, I will go to my grave doing everything that I can possibly do to expose this woman's talent to the world because I just believe in her that much; and I believe that she deserves my undying devotion."

With *Blues Bar* suddenly over, Phyllis needed to get back to work as soon as possible. One of the first dates ABC found for her was at Club Bene, in nearby Sayreville, New Jersey, on November 6th. Phyllis got through the first show without incident. But before the second one began, she was visited backstage by her former percussionist, Mayra Casales. "When we got there for the second set she was already very drunk," Casales recalled. "She had a drink in her hand and she was spilling it on everybody." By the time Phyllis took the stage for the second show, she was visibly intoxicated. "She got up on stage and summoned me to come up. But there was no percussion there or anything." Mayra did the best she could, playing a set of drums sticks on the wooden floor of the stage.

Afterward, Phyllis set Mayra in a chair and sang "Old Friend" directly to her. At the song's conclusion, Mayra tried to leave the stage. But Phyllis didn't want to let her go. "Finally, I whispered in her ear, 'I've got to go to the bathroom.' So I left and then she wouldn't stop calling me back on the stage. I had to sneak out of the club."

Once Mayra was gone, Phyllis lost it completely. She took the chair Mayra had been sitting in and placed it in front of drummer Paul Mills' drum set. The chair was placed to face the audience, but instead of sitting face front in it, Phyllis straddled the chair and proceeded to sing to Mills.

"The first song goes by, and no one really says anything," said guitarist Jonathan Dubose, who stood on stage totally perplexed as the spectacle unfolded before him. "The second song goes by, and she's still sitting in the chair. This has never happened before, so ain't nobody sayin' nothing. But she's still singing. She sounds great. The band sounds good. But she's doing a Miles Davis impression."

After being ignored for two straight songs, the audience began to grow restless. Finally, someone called out for Phyllis to turn around. She did. But instead of singing, she started giving the audience member the what for.

"We're supposed to be in the middle of a song and they're arguing," said Jonathan. "Then somebody joins that guy and he starts saying, 'Turn around. You sing to us. We paid to see you.'"

Phyllis was livid.

"She said, 'Well, I got your money already, so ain't nothin' you can do about it,'" Jonathan remembered.

But there was, in fact, one thing they could do about it. Nearly 40 couples got up and left the club, insisting they be given their money back and receiving it before they exited.

"It was a total melt down," recalled Bill Schultz, who was in Phyllis's dressing room packing up with Ann Gore when the club's owner came pounding on the door. "What's wrong with her? What's wrong?" he screamed. "She's acting nuts!"

"She told everyone to 'get fucked' and left the stage," recalled Ann. "She was totally freaking out."

The next day, Phyllis remembered little of her performance. But she soon learned that nearly half of the crowd at the club had left demanding a refund. What's more, Ron Richardson, her longtime bass player and musical director, had quit. And, on top of it all, Club Bene was demanding their money back from ABC.

Phyllis, as soon as she was able, went about doing damage control. She convinced Ron to return and promised the club owner to do an additional show for free at a later date. But the damage had been done and no one could deny the obvious any longer. Something was seriously wrong with Phyllis.

"I knew it couldn't go on much longer," said Dubose. "The first thing that came to my mind was Billie Holiday. I'm thinking, here I am playing with the Billie Holiday of our day."

Not all was lost though. If Phyllis returned to New York with a fractured ankle, her heart was once again on the mend. While in Dallas, Phyllis had met William Earl Ray. A respected theatre actor who had also done bit parts in television and in films, William was five years younger than Phyllis, which made him about a decade older than her average date.

William may have been nearly Phyllis's age, but she was still able to use the same control mechanism on him as she had most of her other beaus. Money. As an actor working sporadically, William had little of it. Phyllis was once again the breadwinner and it allowed her to easily manipulate her new boyfriend. With William around, Phyllis's liquor store purchases didn't lessen any either. A whiskey man, William's favorite poison was Jack Daniels Black Label, while Phyllis still preferred her Stoli.

When William came to visit Phyllis in New York, he secured a part in an experimental theatre production in the Village. For opening night, Phyllis hired a limo and took Michael, Robbie and Lennie to the show. "I was impressed," said Michael "I remember Phyllis was impressed, too. She was beaming. I guess she felt proud. It was her man and here he was doing what he loved to do."

After the show, Phyllis took the gang out to eat. On the way into the restaurant, Robbie saw a couple of ladies on their way out and held the door open for them. "It was Naomi Campbell and Jaye Davidson from *The Crying Game*," said Robbie. "So I hold the door and they walk out with another person and Phyllis was standing right next to me."

"You gonna say thank you?" Phyllis asked when they failed to acknowledge Robbie's courtesy. "You see him holding the door."

"So Naomi rolled her eyes at Phyllis and it was on," said Robbie.

"Bitch, you ain't all that," Phyllis said as the supermodel walked on.

"She wasn't being mean," Robbie continued. "She was just like, this man's holding the door, being a gentleman, you can at least be a woman and say thank you."

Campbell and crew ignored Phyllis and looked toward her limo instead, mistaking it for their own. Turning on her heels before entering the restaurant, the last word, as usual, belonged to Phyllis.

"Stop looking at the limo because the limo's mine, bitch."

As 1994 came to a close, Phyllis's brief relationship with William was waning, and her affair with Martha David was slowly rekindling. William's show closed on December 18 and though he stayed with her through the holidays and joined her on the road in Chicago for a New Year's Eve concert, he returned from there to Texas. Phyllis stayed over in Chicago for an additional week, shopping and hanging out with friends, and then returned to New York, where Martha was waiting for her.

"After William had returned home, she and I became involved again," said Martha, who confessed she initially tried to keep the relationship light, but with only limited success. "She began giving me clues that she wanted to get back together but we were taking it slowly this time. She eventually told me that she had the same feelings for me that she had always had. I felt the same way for her, too."

Soon the two were a serious item once again. Martha had a full-time job now though, so she couldn't travel with Phyllis on the road except for weekends. Phyllis was scheduled to do a week's worth of shows at Blues Alley in D.C. at the end of January, and she was planning to fly Martha down for the weekend. But Phyllis's band and staff had a plan of their own. They didn't know that Martha and Phyllis were dating again, and thinking Phyllis lonely for William, they secretly arranged to fly him to Washington to surprise her.

"William was there in her hotel suite when she arrived, along with some of the people who had flown him in to surprise her," said Martha. "She called me right away from another room. She was very angry and upset that he was there. She knew it meant that I was not going to come down. We'd been planning it so she and I could be alone together, and they weren't going to send William home in the middle of the week."

Martha was upset, but she tried to take it in stride. "When I went back that third time with her I really decided I knew who she was and I loved her very much and I was not going to have the same kind of expectations as I had had in the past. I knew how deeply she felt about me, yet I knew what issues she was struggling with and I went back willing, initially, to accept the whole ball of wax.

"Although I knew her feelings for William were not serious, I still wasn't going to go down there that weekend and she knew that," Martha continued. "We were both upset about it because we'd been looking forward to being together. But I decided I would just stay in New York and wait till she came back."

William was an instant hit with most of Phyllis's staff. But be that as it may, Phyllis, friends say, had begun to realize that her feelings for William were not serious. Back in New York, Phyllis began to be more open about her relationship with Martha than she ever had before. But even if she would openly show affection toward Martha around those in the inner circle, she never identified publicly as anything other than heterosexual. "Phyllis would say, 'I'm not gay. I'm not bi. But catch me on the right day and I'll sleep with a telephone pole,'" Robbie recalled. Bill Schultz had heard a similar proclamation, except in his recounting it was a doorknob.

Martha, of course, had greater insight into Phyllis's sexual identity than most. "Phyllis was very connected to men and mostly connected to men," she said. "Early on in our relationship she felt differently at different times depending on how she was feeling about herself and the world, and in terms of her ups and downs psychologically. For someone who sees themselves as straight, and wants to be straight, and has being straight so ingrained in who they are, to develop feelings for someone of the same sex is a hard thing to reconcile. Just sexual feelings alone can be threatening enough – though I don't think that they were for Phyllis – but beyond sexual feelings especially.

"I think that could be one of the reasons why she resisted early on allowing herself to have and admit feelings for me. She said she hadn't had those kinds of feelings about a woman before, and I think that was always hard for her and was always a conflict. There were some times when she did feel more comfortable with the whole idea and what it meant, in terms of herself. Ultimately, I just sort of have to guess that as the relationship went on and her feelings remained and deepened, and as she began to trust me and my feelings more, she just figured forget the labels and she went with it. It eventually didn't really matter to her."

Back in New York, things between Phyllis and Martha grew more serious by the day. Near the end of January 1995, Martha reminded her that it had been seven years since the two had first begun an intimate relationship. "She said that ours was the longest relationship she'd ever had, and I said, 'Well, of course, there were large breaks in it.' And she said, 'But I've never continued to have the same feelings for a person for that long.' I think that meant a lot to her as time went on, because I think that she really began to trust how much I loved her and could let herself go a little more with her own feelings, because feeling vulnerable is a big issue for everybody, but it was major for her."

The couple decided to celebrate their anniversary on February 1st. Phyllis hired the car and she and Martha planned an elaborate night on the town. They even decided to exchange rings. "There was a ring of hers that was on the table and I put it on. It was just a little copper ring, and she said we should get each other rings. She bought me a ring and gave it to me on our anniversary. Then we went out on Valentine's Day two weeks later and she picked out a ring that I got for her then."

After that, Martha never went home. Instead, she once again began living with Phyllis, who seemed more focused and more together than Martha ever remembered seeing her. "Things were really going along very positively, very well." Until, that is, the couple decided to go out of town. Phyllis had long enjoyed staying with her friends Brenda and Skip Barry in Baltimore. They were not show business folks, and Phyllis felt like normal people when she was around them. They were calming to her, their environment stable.

"Everything was really wonderful for the whole trip until we were getting ready to go back home," said Martha. "I think she was worried about what her state of mind was going to be like when she was alone while I was at work everyday. She became agitated and suddenly started behaving unpleasantly toward me. We had a fight. She was very angry on the train ride home and when we got back to New York she took off in a cab and went back to her apartment, and I got in another cab and went to mine."

Martha, who'd basically been living out of Phyllis's apartment for the past few months, had left many of her personal items at Phyllis's place. But Phyllis had, as was her habit when the going got tough, shut herself off from the world. She would not even take Martha's calls.

Eventually the couple reconciled, but Martha suspected that Phyllis had started using cocaine again. "We resumed as we had been but she was different, very up and down in her behavior and her attitude. I couldn't understand it. I wondered if she'd started to feel too vulnerable to me, or if she'd become very depressed again, or both. I didn't know. Whatever it was, she was very moody."

On Saturday, April 1st – a day that Martha recalls vividly – Phyllis was extremely irritable and, in fact, downright mean. "I confronted her with it. Over the seven-plus year period of knowing her I had been increasing in my own psychological health and maturity and I really wasn't going to stand for it. It made no sense. Her behavior was not related in any way to anything that I was doing and I wanted to discuss it." But Phyllis was not interested in talking about it at all. "Looking back on it and learning more about people who are manic depressive, I believe, perhaps, that she was then entering a new phase of that. I was trying to force her to discuss something on a rational level but the turmoil within her was not coming from a rational place at all. But I insisted on talking about it and she got very upset and angry and I started to pack up my things."

This is when, Martha believes, Phyllis began to misunderstand her motives. "I was not planning on leaving her. But I had made up my mind to make some changes in the overall arrangement. I felt I needed to take myself back home and be based out of my own apartment; that I needed to be more in control of my environment.

"Later, I realized she'd probably thought I was leaving her. She demanded at that point to have her keys back. It probably looked like I was leaving her completely, but not knowing that when she demanded her keys back I took that as her saying, 'Get out of my life.' But maybe she was just temporarily lashing out at me in response to my actions. I don't know what was on her mind and I don't know what she thought was on mine. But she demanded her keys back and we ultimately had a very, very big fight. I took all of my things and went home to my apartment and decided that was really the end of it, that I really couldn't, no matter what, put up with anymore unless she was going to go into therapy and give up her addictions."

With Martha gone, Phyllis began spending more and more time alone in her apartment. Four years after her last album, fewer dates than ever were coming in, and as she resumed touring, Phyllis was hardly recognizable to her audiences, having piled on yet more weight during her recovery from the broken ankle. Tymm Holloway tried his best to get her out of the house. "I used to go over to her place and say, 'Let's go for a walk.'" Occasionally Phyllis agreed, though according to Tymm she was very much a "cab girl. She used to make jokes. We'd be at some beauty counter and she'd say, 'My son thinks I'm fat. He's got me walking around New York City.' We did talk about the weight, but you wouldn't want to talk about that too much because you might get bit. But she kept saying, 'I gotta get this weight off.' She was talking about getting it off, but never how it got on."

A certain spark was gone, and Phyllis was now taking less and less time with her appearance. "In the past, even if we were just going from Detroit to Cleveland to Oklahoma City, she would never wear the same thing," said Regina Belle. "Now, we'd do a couple of dates, and she'd wear the same outfit. That was the first thing I noticed."

But there were other, more obvious indicators of the trouble that was brewing. Phyllis was openly reading books on death while backstage on the road. In fact, she was reading some of the same titles, she shared with friends, that Donny Hathaway had been reading shortly before he plunged himself from a 15th floor window of the Essex House hotel in New York City – just blocks from Phyllis's apartment – to his death in January of 1979.

At an April date at the Fox Theatre in Detroit, Phyllis shared her feelings on suicide with Regina. "She had gotten so big and when I looked at her I just couldn't believe how big she had gotten." Regina was just about to start her set when she passed Phyllis on her way to the stage. "I was just talking to her, and I was saying, 'It's good to see you,' and blah, blah, blah. And she just comes from out of no where and says, 'You know, I've found that the only answer to life is really death.'

"I'm looking at her, like, 'What?' I'm trying to change the subject and she's not really responding to me. My whole thought was that I needed to get away from her, because it was making me feel creepy, and I'm trying to get my head right for the show. That totally took me out of what I was trying to do. I didn't want to talk any more, needless to say."

Regina was not the only one who took note of the carelessness with which Phyllis assembled herself. Former road manager Craig Hentosh, who had reconnected with Phyllis during her January Blues Alley engagement, caught up with her around this time at a private engagement in Philly. "There was such a change in her appearance," Craig recalled. "It blew me away. In three months I just couldn't believe the difference in her appearance. She had really gained a lot of weight."

Home in New York, Phyllis didn't leave her apartment often. But Gordon Chambers was able to entice her out of seclusion from time to time. "She was really looking sloppy," Gordon said. "A lot of times I would see her and she just looked unattended to. Her clothes didn't really look quite clean. The last few times I went out with her, she wore the same outfit a couple times during the same week. I kept thinking to myself, 'Why isn't anybody taking care of her?'"

In his chats with Phyllis, Gordon often tried to persuade her to trim down her stage show and cut back on her costs. "I would take her to jazz clubs. I was trying to encourage her to play smaller jazz rooms, rather than play with the big full band and the big entourage. I said, 'Why not play some smaller dates? You've done jazz recordings. You could do that particular part of your catalogue and cut your overhead down.'"

Phyllis wasn't having it. "She said, 'Well, no, Gordon, because my diehard fans who come to see me all the time and pay top dollar to see me want to see the full-fledged Phyllis Hyman show. They want the outfits, the band, the background singers, the whole everything.' She did not ever want to disappoint those core fans. But I think she was an artist who depended on touring and her overhead with touring was very expensive. She had the diva curse."

One frustrating and yet funny form of that curse reared its head when Gordon took Phyllis to see his friend Cynthia Scott sing in a nearby jazz club. "Cynthia did not acknowledge Phyllis in the audience and she just hit the roof," said Gordon. "She went off. She said, 'That girl can't sing.' And I said, 'No, she can sing, Phyllis. She can sing. Don't even try it. Don't go there.'

"We had a debate about that and you could tell she felt disrespected. She said, 'Gordon, listen, the girl was OK. But in the future, don't invite me nowhere if I can't get some money or some dick out of it.' She said, 'There wasn't no money and there surely wasn't no dick up in that little jazz club. But thank you. I had a nice time. Call me tomorrow.'"

By this time, Phyllis was feeling genuinely disrespected, as if after all her years in the business her place in the annals of music – and the industry – still wasn't secure. Taking this into consideration, it's easy to see how Phyllis could be particularly sensitive to any action that could be termed a snub. Phyllis was not getting along with her booking agents, who had not been able to put her back on the road quickly enough following the fiasco with the play, and as a result she felt they shared in the responsibility of her precarious financial situation. More than ABC though, by this time she levied most of the blame on Kenny Gamble and Philadelphia International Records.

"She would rack her brain," recalled Robbie Todd. "She'd say, 'I'm going to the studio. I've got all this stuff in the can. But I can't pay my rent.' She just couldn't understand that."

As early as late 1993, Phyllis had begun voicing her discontent with the status of her recording career from the stage. "I'll have a new album by 1994, we hope," she said during an engagement at Kimball's East in Oakland, California. "We heard that one before, right? I mean, people want to know why does it take me five years to make a record? Like I really choose to wait five years. I don't have shit to do with that. I do not choose to wait that long. I didn't ask to wait that long. That is the politics of the recording industry. It's full of it."

Just days after the Detroit show in April, the nation watched in shock as the Murrah Federal Building in downtown Oklahoma City was rocked by a massive bomb left in rental truck parked just outside its entrance. The bomb blew away half the building, killing 168 men, women and children in what then was the worst terrorist attack on U.S. soil in history. The disaster devastated Phyllis. "It traumatized her as if she had been there, or had a loved one in that building," said Glenda, who watched helplessly as Phyllis locked herself inside her apartment for days, glued to the television and shocked into silence.

A few weeks later, Phyllis finally emerged from her seclusion and flew to Merrillville, Indiana to play at the Star Plaza, one of her regular spots. But something went wrong, and in the middle of the show Phyllis found herself unable to catch her breath. She left the stage, and her assistant Leo Lord sat her down and fanned her furiously. Finally, she felt well enough to return to the stage and a chair was placed on it for her to sit in while she finished the show.

Three days later, Phyllis flew to Seattle for a series of dates at a small club called Jazz Alley. One fan, awed by the sheer power of her voice, called out and asked her to sing a gospel song, to which she jokingly responded that he was at "the wrong show." But she was bothered by this request, and couldn't get it out of her mind. "I don't know any gospel songs," she said, between filling the requests of other fans, and then she apologized to the crowd for not being religious. She sang a few more numbers, but kept going back to that one request than she could not fill. She told the crowd she was going to sing a song that while it wasn't a gospel song per se, had a spiritual lyric, and then she began to sing "Gonna Make Changes."

But the song, which had always had a special meaning to Phyllis, was too much to get through this night. "A light seemed to shine on her while she sang, and all of a sudden she started to break down and ran off the stage in tears," recalled a fan that witnessed the performance. "The last thing I remember was the look of terror and stark fear in her eyes as she rushed into the dressing room."

"She was in a lot of pain," said Glenda. "Phyllis was one of the most brilliant, sensitive human beings I knew. She absorbed not only the pain that she felt; Phyllis would absorb the pain of humanity."

Unable to shoulder such a burden, she looked to substances to ease her mind and bring her momentary relief. "She used things to sleep," said Phyllis's sister, Jeannie, referring to the Tuinal® Phyllis kept in stock. "And she used cocaine. Whether the addiction caused the depression or the depression led to the addiction didn't matter. You couldn't treat one without treating the other."

"You can't tell what's the true mental illness, and what's the drug and alcohol abuse," explained Phyllis's friend Ama Ward, who is a social worker. "I had offered to come to Philadelphia on the weekends and stay with her. Those are the hardest times to keep clean when you're working in show business. I said, 'All you've got to do is let me know when you want me to be there and I will come.' But she never did. She never called me."

"Phyllis's pain could have been related to anything from wars that she thinks are unfair, to people dying on the street, to her not having a boyfriend that she felt she was going to get married to next week, to feeling like she didn't have all the fans she wanted," said Glenda. "It could have been any level of that. She was extraordinarily sensitive. I cannot emphasize that enough. Phyllis felt everything."

On May 18th, Phyllis went out for a rare night out on the town, taking in the latest Leiber and Stoller review, *Smokey Joe's Café*, at the Virginia Theatre. Following the show, which Phyllis thoroughly enjoyed, she went backstage to talk to members of the cast. While she was there, Phyllis heard a familiar voice come over the loud speaker and suddenly shrieked. The voice was unmistakably that of Ken Hanson, her old stage manager from *Sophisticated Ladies*. Phyllis asked a crewmember to let Hanson know at once that she was in the house, and she was soon directed upstairs to the production office. Phyllis, pushing up on 300 pounds, scarcely resembled the young beauty she had been while starring on Broadway a decade earlier.

She told Hanson she was planning to do a one-woman show, and implied she'd like to bring him onboard as plans firmed up. "She was very bitter at this point," Ken recalled. "The one thing that she couldn't stop carrying on about was Brandy. She was just bitter about this girl's success and, 'That's what they want now. Young girls.' She said she couldn't even get arrested, and she wanted to try to do this one-woman show.

"She was sounding rather desperate," Ken continued. "The whole conversation was about these young girls in the industry and how they had really taken over."

Glenda had heard the same line, too, and recognized the pain behind it. "Phyllis was very disenchanted and disillusioned about what she felt was not meritorious attention," she said. "She was angry that because she was a maturing artist and not singing popular or urban format music she could not realize the same professional success that other younger women were enjoying. She would say, 'I think my vocal quality is better than theirs.' She would be agitated at not having a sense of popularity and not being honored for who she was as an artist.

"She was so grossly hard on herself," Glenda continued. "Sometimes when I called to tell her about projects, she would say, 'Why are they calling me? Why don't they call someone else?' I would just say to her, 'Because they love you and your voice. They want you.' And she would say, 'Really? Are you sure?'"

Phyllis was selective as to whom she could reveal her vulnerability to. But after more than a decade of working with her, Glenda was intimately familiar with Phyllis's insecurities. She had met the little girl that still lived inside of Phyllis and she knew of her hurt and confusion. "She was looking for a white knight to carry her off to that wonderful place where everything was going to be safe," said Glenda. "She had this storybook, idealized version of what that love was supposed to look like; and so if it didn't look like that it was brutal disappointment, just utter disappointment for her. The whole notion of the knight in shining armor and all of those other trappings, that stuff is brutal."

Those closest to Phyllis say that she took something away from each of her two trips to rehab. She had been in and out of therapy for years and spent a good deal of time in sessions with Portia Hunt in Philadelphia. In her clear moments, Phyllis knew that no such knight was coming for her; that only she could slay the demons she wrestled with. She also knew that her resources to fight such a battle were severely limited. Physically, financially, mentally and emotionally, Phyllis was drained.

The Internal Revenue Service was breathing down her neck once again. Her savings account was empty. She held no stocks or bonds she could cash in, no property she could mortgage. She was in debt to her record label – even still in debt to the label she had left a decade earlier. Her writer's and publishing royalties generated little income, and certainly not enough to borrow against. In short, Phyllis was flat broke.

There was no money for another trip to rehab, if she had decided that was the answer – or at least a start. Taking time off from the road – a few months or a year – to find herself or undergo extensive counseling was likewise not an option. To do so, she would have to give up her small Manhattan apartment and stay with friends who could afford to take her in. And what would become of those who relied on her for their livelihoods? She had fought to keep Ron Richardson and Eric Jones when Glenda insisted the rest of the band had to go four years earlier, and Leo Lord had worked for her even longer than those two. Not working meant leaving these people without the jobs they had come to depend on.

To save herself and her sanity, Phyllis would have to sacrifice all the things that represented being Phyllis Hyman to her, all the things she enjoyed. The stage was perhaps the one place in the world where she felt truly comfortable, and she would have to give it up, at least for a time. "She knew that if Humpty Dumpty was ever going to be put back together again she was going to have change everything about her life," said Bill Schultz. And that was something she was unwilling to do, perhaps even unable to. If Phyllis surrendered her pride and her ego, what was left?

The singing star, the celebrity, this was the one part of herself that Phyllis Hyman was sure of. So who would she be if she couldn't be that person? Yet even as Phyllis knew she could not give this portion of her life up, she realized she was losing it. At 45, and after spending more than 20 years in the business, Phyllis knew that she had peeked as a performer. This caused the resentments to grow and the bitterness to fester, which in turn manifested itself as unreliable behavior behind the scenes and ever increasing outbursts of obscenities from the stage. As one promoter in Texas had said, declaring he would never hire her again, "It's not worth it. There are other legends."

Much as Phyllis used cocaine to simulate – or create the illusion of – the high of the stage, her desperate attempts to take charge – her acting out – were about maintaining the illusion of control. It was really no more than that though. An illusion. But as Phyllis in reality spiraled further and further out of control, the illusion became increasingly difficult, and ultimately impossible, to cling to. "She could keep up this persona for so long, and then the cracks began to appear all through it," said Portia Hunt. "And then there you are, exposed." This exposure devastated Phyllis. It forced her to see the truth. To confront her vulnerability. Which is what her attempts at control were about in the first place. Her fear of vulnerability.

"She had just destroyed all her options – her creative options, her romantic options, her physical options," said Mercedes Ellington, with whom Phyllis had kept in contact and continued to do favors for long after *Sophisticated Ladies* had ended. "It's as if she went down this rabbit hole with no way out."

Yet Phyllis trekked on. She asked road manager Larry Kendricks and personal assistants Lennic and Bill if they'd be willing to join her on a six-month bus tour. She severed ties with her longtime booking agent, the Associated Booking Company. Glenda had personally led Phyllis to the firm in 1983, and they had been good to Phyllis through the years. But she faulted them for not getting her back on the road fast enough. "I got a phone call one day out of the clear blue sky and Phyllis told me she wanted to fire Oscar and Jody," recalled Glenda. "I said, 'That's pretty serious stuff. We've got to talk about it.' And she said, 'There's nothing to talk about. I don't have any work. They're not getting me any work.' She wasn't connecting the dots."

The new tour, she announced, would be put together by Sal Michaels and his Pyramid Entertainment Group. She had begun negotiating with Pyramid in March, but the contracts were not drawn up until May. A telling sign was the clause she had inserted at the last moment. It ensured that should she die during the term, that Pyramid understood her wishes.

By June of 1995, Phyllis had enough material in the can for two albums. Still, she continued to record. Early in the month, she met up with siblings Jerry and Katreese Barnes at Manhattan Beach recording studio to lay her vocals down on a song the three of them had written together in the fall. "It was very cool," said Katreese. "She came in and she was prepared. We spent an hour on her vocal and spent two hours ordering food." Jerry had great fun, too. "We laughed more than we recorded," he said. "I remember it being one of the funniest sessions I've ever had in my life. She was joking and making everyone laugh. I had to pull the reigns and say, 'OK, Phyllis, we need to get recording.'

"I knew she had problems," Jerry continued. "She was emotional about her career, her weight. But she was making jokes about all that. She was laughing, too."

June 16-18, Phyllis played three nights at the Hotel Washington in D.C., a new venue that had positioned itself to be in direct competition with Blues Alley. According to one of the local acts she shared the stage with, Christian jazz saxophonist Roy Daniels, Phyllis was in fine spirits. "She was energetic, subdued, charismatic, cool, talkative and playful," he said. "I would never have guessed she was experiencing any depression."

Offstage, Phyllis's staff was much more clued in. They watched in horror as she began to unravel. Bill Schultz recalled Leo Lord, Phyllis's all-purpose assistant, coming up to him on opening night with a panicked expression on his face. "He said that Phyllis told him she planned to kill herself after the show that night," said Bill. Quickly, the two of them put together a plan. They decided to rendezvous in her room later that night, thus affording Phyllis no opportunity to go through with her suicide attempt.

Phyllis had long ago advised her personal assistants that were they ever to find her in the process of committing suicide – having already overdosed but not yet dead – that they were not to make any attempts to revive her. Phyllis remembered all too well how Glenda had managed to bring her back from the brink the last time, in 1990, and should she try it again she wanted no such interruptions. Nowadays, as she had some years ago with then-boyfriend Dante James, Phyllis had conversations with all her staff, asking them to support her right to end her life should she decide to do so. But in this case, Shultz and Lord figured that stopping her before she even tried was not the same thing as stopping her in progress, and that it was the only thing they could do.

Phyllis's contract with the Hotel Washington called for two shows a night, and the opening night shows went relatively well.

She was in good voice, but she had trouble remembering her older songs during the request portion of the show. She was also particularly biting when someone requested the least favorite song in her repertoire, "Riding The Tiger."

"They must pay you to bring your ass in here and ask for that song," she said, only half joking. "I'm gonna ignore you, and I'm gonna come out there and find your ass and beat you with this flashlight." The confused fan thought that possibly Phyllis had heard him incorrectly and repeated his request a second time. "I heard you," she said. "We don't sing that song."

In between selections, Phyllis voiced her frustration over the delay of the new album. She apologized to her fans for the delay and assured them she actually did have a new album in the works. Then she implored them to take direct action to see that it was finally released. "It's not a lie that I have a record coming out, it's just about when it's coming out because as a concept, I have no clue. That's up to the record company and I suggest that each of you who are really concerned should call Mr. Kenny Gamble of Philadelphia International," she said, before giving out the record company's main phone number. "Call him and ask him why does Ms. Hyman not have a new album out and why does she continue to put out an album every five years. Can I tell you it doesn't take that long to make a record unless you're on drugs consistently 24/7, or sending it in from Istanbul?"

Following the second show, several members of the road crew assembled in Phyllis's suite. They ate and turned on *Jenny Jones*. Phyllis was enthralled by the real-life drama enfolding on the screen. She hooted and hollered. "This shit is so funny I can't kill myself," she remarked at one point, leading Bill Schultz to believe that the immediate threat was over, that Phyllis had just needed some attention and that he had helped supply it.

The next day, Phyllis remained on edge. In the dressing room, Schultz found her to be downright testy. The Barry family was in the audience and Phyllis had asked Bill to pick up a cake for Brenda Barry's mother, whom Phyllis affectionately referred to as her adopted mom. Bill was readying the cake when Phyllis's fuse came to an end. "You're bothering the fuck out of me," Phyllis screamed, at which point Schultz made his exit. In typical Phyllis fashion, she cornered him later that night. "You know I love you, right?" she asked.

On Sunday, the third and final day of the engagement, Phyllis took time out for brunch with her favorite vocalist Nancy Wilson. At her final show that night, vocalist Alyson Williams was in the audience and Phyllis introduced her from the stage. She also lamented about her fiscal situation, as she had nightly. "I am so happy to have been here this weekend because on the real side, I was tired of being unemployed," she said. "So we're just so happy that you have chosen to give me your cash. I suggest you keep it up because I'm desperate."

The next morning, Schultz went to Phyllis's room to help her pack up. "She was groggy and had obviously taken pills of some sort," Bill recalled. Once he had packed her up and sent her bags down with the bellman, he had to put an arm around Phyllis and literally help walk her through the hotel's lobby to the van that waited to take her and the crew to the airport. She was not talking, her eyes barely open. But after helping her into the van, and as he started to leave, she called to him. "She said, 'Mr. Bill, aren't you going to kiss me goodbye?'"

Bill kissed her and the van departed. He had succeeded in helping to avert one crisis, but he didn't know how long there'd be until the next. All he could do was call Glenda and advise her of the situation, and say a silent prayer. But Phyllis hadn't made any of these remarks directly to Glenda, and talk of suicide was not in anyway out of the ordinary for Phyllis. "Because Phyllis talked about suicide all the time, and because she became particularly melancholy around her birthday, and she also could be dramatic, I didn't get a sense that there was anything happening at the level that it was happening," said Glenda. "I don't want to say she was preoccupied with death and suicide, but it's something that she thought of often."

From Washington, Phyllis returned briefly to New York and then flew to Houston to see William. Their relationship had cooled some, but with Martha out of the picture, Phyllis once again felt the need for some companionship. While in Texas, Phyllis called Bill Schultz at home in Detroit and once again began talking about committing suicide. "Have you told William how you feel," Bill asked her, hoping her boyfriend could provide her with some support. "Please, chile," Phyllis said candidly. "I'm not telling him. He's not family."

Phyllis returned to New York on Sunday, June 25, 1995. Early in the week, she called Brenda Barry in Maryland and told her she was playing the Apollo on Friday and needed her to be there. "I'm not going to take no for an answer, girlfriend," she told her. "I want you to come." On Tuesday, June 27th, Glenda called Phyllis to check in and, more importantly, to report that Kenny Gamble had turned over the finished album to Zoo. Finally, it would seem, Phyllis had something to look forward to. Her last two albums had faired well, and indications were that this one would, too. "We had a routine business conversation," Glenda recalled. "She seemed pretty happy. We were talking about future dates, the status of things to come, what she needed for the Apollo performance. There was not a hint of anything wrong."

But if Phyllis gave Glenda no indication that she planned to take her life it was by choice. For the plan was already firmly in place and it was no great secret. She spent the week contacting friends, telling them to come to the show at the Apollo. She told them she would be disappearing for a while afterward, despite the fact that her new booking agent, Pyramid, had already secured new bookings for her, including dates with Freddie Jackson at the Westbury and Valley Forge Music Fairs July 22nd and 23rd.

To select friends she was more specific. "She spoke of giving herself the gift of death for her birthday, that she was tired of it all," said one such friend who requested anonymity from the *New York Daily News* reporter he later spoke to. On Thursday, June 29th, Phyllis phoned Danny Poole, whom she'd kept in touch with sporadically in the years following their early '80s romance. Bluntly, she told him she planned to take an overdose of sleeping pills on July 6th, her 46th birthday.

Assorted members of Phyllis's immediate family received phones calls as well. When she spoke of suicide to Sakinah, her sister was not shocked. "I've never known my sister not to speak of suicide, from the time I was probably 20 on," she said. "If every time she mentioned it somebody stopped to see if she was really going to do it, nobody would have ever had a life. She talked about suicide all the time. Most of the time I just blew it off. This last time I was kind of concerned about it because she was talking about it and I was thinking about it my damn self. I thought maybe she had the right idea. But by God's grace and mercy, I had a connection with a religious community and managed to get some assistance with that."

Sakinah encouraged Phyllis to get help, too. "I said, 'You need to get to an N.A. meeting.'" But Phyllis wasn't moved. "She knew what to do. She said, 'I know what to do, I'm just not willing.' Those were her exact words."

Speaking with Anita, Phyllis was less specific. "She said, 'Well, Anita, you're not going to be able to get in touch with me anymore. I'm going far, far away,'" Anita recalled. "I said, 'Well, Phyllis, aren't there any phones around?' She said, 'No, there's not going to be any phones.' I was trying to ask her questions. She said that she loved me, and I said, 'Well, you know Phyllis, God loves you so much and I love you, too.' And when I got off the phone I knew something was wrong."

Though they were not related by blood, Phyllis dearly loved her friend Brenda Barry and definitely considered her family. Also on Thursday, Phyllis called Brenda to confirm that she and her husband Skip were coming the next day. Brenda assured her they'd be there and that they'd be bringing her birthday present. But Phyllis told her not to.

"I'm not playing," Phyllis told her. "Don't buy me anything. I don't want anything for my birthday."

Brenda knew immediately that something was wrong. "She would always call me way ahead of time to tell me exactly what I was to buy her for her birthday. A few weeks earlier she had hinted to me that she needed a vacuum cleaner, and I had bought her one."

"I'm serious," Phyllis insisted. "Don't come up here with no shit for my birthday."

Later in the day, Brenda dialed Phyllis back to tell her that Jason, the Barry's 11-year-old son and Phyllis's little buddy, had brought home a great report card. "That's when I knew that she was really in a bad way," said Brenda. "She was crying when she answered the phone and she was very short."

Phyllis sent her best to Jason, and then went back to the timeframe.

"Be here at 2 o'clock," Phyllis reminded Brenda. "I don't want you coming at 2:15. I want you here at 2 o'clock."

Brenda assured her she'd be there on time before Phyllis continued.

"This will probably be the last time that you see me."

Brenda, confused, said nothing.

"We're going to have a good day," Phyllis went on. "We're going to have some champagne. I'm going to have balloons for you to take back to Jason. It's going to be a good day. You guys know I love you, and it will probably be the last time I'm going to see you. I don't want nobody bringing gifts up here that my big ass ain't gonna use. They'll just go to somebody else."

"I hung up and I told Skip, 'She's in a funk. I don't know what's going on but hopefully by the time we all get there and we get her talking about her birthday, we'll get her cheered up.'

"Phyllis was the type of person that if she didn't want to talk about it, she wouldn't talk about it," Brenda continued. "She would tell me in a minute, 'Girlfriend, I gotta go. I love you, but I gotta go. I'm hanging up.' And she would. She would hang up the phone. So I said, 'I'm not going to back her into a corner. I'll deal with her when I see her.'"

The show the next day, Friday, June 30th, was supposed to have been Phyllis's final hurrah. But something happened to convince her to hasten her exit. Perhaps it was the fear that one of those lucky enough to receive a goodbye call would show up and try to stop her, or perhaps she was just truly too tired to get up on stage and give one more performance. Whatever the reason, Phyllis chose not to play the Apollo Theatre one last time.

She didn't share this with Mary Flowers, the show's promoter, though. On the phone with her Friday morning, Phyllis promised she would "rock the house" that night, and reminded Flowers to have a menu from Sylvia's, the famous Harlem soul food restaurant, waiting in her dressing room.

The night before, Phyllis had spoken with road manager Larry Kendricks and confirmed that a car would be waiting downstairs for her at 2 p.m. She was due at the Apollo for a 3:30 soundcheck. Phyllis received a visitor to the apartment at about 10 a.m. It was her drug source making a delivery, though neither of her assistants,

Lennie or Leo, could know that there was no cocaine this time, and only sleeping pills in her package. At around 1 p.m., she told them that she planned to sun for a bit on the roof of her building and sent them out on errands, including picking up a birthday gift for Bill Schultz, who was on his way in from Detroit, and champagne for the soon to be arriving Barry family.

But Phyllis never made it to the roof. Instead, once her assistants had left the apartment – and knowing her time was short – Phyllis walked into her bedroom, locked the door behind her, sat down on the edge of her bed and swallowed handfuls of her favorite sleeping pills, Tuinal®. The drug had fallen out of favor with most physicians for its side effects, and no respectable doctor would prescribe them to a bipolar patient to begin with. But Phyllis was still able to keep stocked up, and she took more than enough to make sure this attempt would work.

An hour or so later, at about 2:15, Lennie and Leo returned to the Carnegie Mews. Brenda Barry and her husband Skip had made it into town right on time and were waiting in the lobby. They told Leo that Phyllis had not answered when the doorman had called upstairs, and her assistants assumed that Phyllis had not yet returned from the roof. Lennie and Leo headed upstairs alone. Inside apartment 33C the duo found a note from Phyllis saying she was napping and did not wish to be disturbed. Immediately, they grew suspicious. They knocked repeatedly on her bedroom door. When she didn't answer they tried to open it and found it locked from inside.

Leo called Glenda and she gave him the OK to break the door down. Leo was reluctant. If Phyllis was, in fact, only napping, she would be furious to be awakened by the breaking down of her door. Leo went in search of the building's superintendent to ensure that if Phyllis was found only napping the door could be immediately reinstalled. The superintendent was familiar with Phyllis – she had accidentally set her kitchen on fire more than once when, engrossed in a phone call or a television special, she had left something on the stove unattended – and he said he would help put the door back up if Phyllis was just taking a nap.

Walking back through the lobby, Leo encountered Bill and told him they had a situation. Bill accompanied Leo back upstairs where a distraught Lennie was ironing what she prayed Phyllis would wear to the Apollo when she woke up. Once again, Leo pounded on the bedroom door and received no response. Lennie began to cry as Leo and Bill worked to unhinge the door. Once opened, they found Phyllis, propped up on several pillows and dressed in a black and white one-piece bathing suit and a white terrycloth robe, on the bed, her sleeping mask resting on her forehead above her closed eyes, as if she'd wanted to see the light one last time. Her arm was extended, and a pen and notepad lay just beyond her fingers. In shaky handwriting was written a note that said merely, "I'm tired. I'm tired. Those of you that I love know who you are. May God bless you."

Bill frantically searched for a pulse while Leo ran back downstairs to get Brenda Barry who, as a dental hygienist, had a bit of medical expertise. Only once they reached the 33rd floor did Leo explain the gravity of the situation. Brenda rushed into the bedroom and, after not being able to find a pulse, told Leo to call for an ambulance and began CPR. Once on the scene, the paramedics were, in fact, able to find a weak pulse. They immediately placed an oxygen mask over Phyllis's face and transferred her to a gurney, propped up in a sitting position. Bill rode with Phyllis in the ambulance. Brenda and Skip followed behind it in their car, with Lennie in tow, and Leo stayed behind to speak with Lieutenant Dwight Cunningham of the New York Police Department.

At Roosevelt Hospital, the gang waited in the lobby for nearly 90 excruciating minutes while doctors worked on Phyllis. But it was no use. This time she apparently did know what she was doing. At 3:50 p.m. a hospital official arrived in the lobby and delivered the news. Phyllis was gone.

The Barrys and Lennie left the hospital immediately, while Bill lingered for a moment. A police officer eventually offered to drive him back to Phyllis's apartment. In the cruiser, the officer switched on the radio to ease the strained silence. Suddenly, Phyllis's voice filled the car. The song was "Living All Alone," but Phyllis, finally, no longer was.

Epilogue

God is spirit, music is spiritual, so every time you hear Phyllis sing, she lives. – **Roberta Flack**

The show that night at the Apollo did go on. But not everyone stayed for it. Many fans learned of Phyllis's death only after reaching the Apollo, where local news crews waited to interview Phyllis's fans. Some gave their tickets away; others requested and received a refund.

Those who stayed received special condolences at the start of the evening from Marshall Jones, the Apollo's general manager, and the host for the evening, radio personality Sergio Dean from WBLS. In tribute to Phyllis, her band – drummer Paul Mills, saxophonist David Lee Jones, vocalist Eric Jones, musical director and bassist Ron Richardson and keyboardist Alec Shantzis – went on as scheduled. David Lee Jones performed his saxophone solo with tears in his eyes, and Eric received a standing ovation for his version of "Old Friend," which he reworked to pay homage to Phyllis. When Eric wasn't singing, a spotlight illuminated a single microphone positioned at center stage.

"If you focused hard enough, you could almost see her, and if you listened hard enough, you could almost hear her unmistakably distinctive voice filling the atmosphere," wrote one local columnist of the performance. "Those who stayed for the tribute enjoyed an unforgettable performance for a lady that will never be forgotten."

The next morning, Glenda released an official statement to the press. "The family and management of Phyllis Hyman wish to express their deepest sorrow at the loss of their loved one," it read. "Phyllis took her life on Friday afternoon, June 30, just prior to a scheduled appearance at the Apollo Theatre in New York.

"We should all take Phyllis's death as a moment to reflect on our own individual lives and commit to reaching out to our loved ones, our communities and to the rest of the world. Phyllis's tragic death is a wake-up call for everyone in pain to know that there is no need to be alone in your pain and that you should get help."

Personally, Glenda admitted that she wasn't surprised by Phyllis's decision to take her own life. "Phyllis's philosophy about suicide was that it was an option. It was her feeling that she was in charge of her body. It was her body, therefore, it was her death."

Elaborating in another interview, Glenda discussed Phyllis's final days. "Phyllis was uncovering the riddles in her life," she said. "She was in touch with her emotions. Sometimes when you start that process, the demons that you confront may have more for you than you might have thought you would find."

When *Blues Bar* came so abruptly to an end in October, Phyllis, physically incapacitated, was suddenly forced to confront those demons – particularly her addictions and their consequences – face to face. "She saw how devastating being vulnerable could be to her," Glenda said. "I think when she looked at everything that her issues represented, how, for all intents and purposes, they blew an opportunity out of the water, how it rendered her, literally, out of work for months, how she was exposed. Vulnerable. It scared her to death."

With so much time on her hands, Phyllis's overactive mind was left to wander through the minefield of suicidal thoughts. And like so many others who suffered from bipolar disorder, she didn't make it out alive. "Her healing journey was not only difficult, ultimately, it was fatal," said Glenda.

Per her instructions, Phyllis was cremated following an autopsy, which would ultimately reveal that she had died of an "intentional overdose of pentobarbital and secobarbital." Meanwhile, the first of several recognized memorial services was in its planning stage. It took place at St. Peter's Lutheran Church in Manhattan at 7 p.m. on Thursday, July 6th, the day that would have been Phyllis's 46th birthday. Like all her shows in the city throughout the years, the memorial brought out quite a few celebrities, including Roberta Flack, who told the crowd, "God is spirit, music is spiritual, so every time you hear Phyllis sing, she lives."

Others also spoke, including Kenny Gamble, Phyllis's designer Cassandra McShepard, Eric Jones representing Phyllis's band, personal assistants Leo Lord and Lennice Molina, Phyllis's ex-girlfriend Martha David, Brenda Berry, Ama Ward and an assortment of other friends and family. Phyllis's ex-husband, Larry Alexander, showed up and asked to speak, but organizers of the memorial, including Bill Schultz who acted as the afternoon's emcee, had decided that no one would be added to their already long list of approved speakers. Of all those that did speak, none was more eloquent than Glenda.

"Phyllis was many things to me," Glenda said softly. "She was a friend. She was a client, obviously. She was a sister. But the thing that she was probably the most was my teacher. Phyllis had convictions that were stronger than anything. If she believed in something, whether she got herself into trouble for it or not, she stuck by her truth.

"That gave me courage, because I had to represent those convictions. I had to tell everyone how she felt. Do damage control for it if it happened. Just manage it all the way through. I had to have patience with people who didn't understand her convictions. I had to learn patience. Patience is really important when you represent someone like Phyllis Hyman. I had to have non-judgment. I couldn't judge anything that she believed in. I couldn't question her conviction. I just had to accept it, and non-judgment is a real blessing in this life if you can learn that lesson. But most of all as my teacher Phyllis taught me the beautiful gift of unconditional love. If you really and truly learn the lesson of unconditional love you have received all that there is to receive."

Several members of the Hyman family spoke as well. Jeannie told stories of growing up with Phyllis. Anita read a poem written by a former teacher of Phyllis's. Michael told a story of a memorial service for singer/songwriter Dan Hartman ("I Can Dream About You") that he'd attended with his sister the year before. "It was a cheerful memorial and she looked over at me and she looked me straight in the eye and she said, 'This is the way that I want to remembered. I know family and friends are going to be very sad but I want this to be cheerful because I want my life to be celebrated and I want to be remembered for who I was.' Let's not think about the bad things. She made a choice. A lot of people might not agree with that choice, but it was her choice and the important thing is she is at peace."

Sakinah was unsympathetic in her remarks. "I've been going through a whole bunch of feelings," she said. "Initially, I was angry. I wanted to go down to the morgue, pick her up and slide her one or two or three times and say, 'How dare you stop struggling. And I've got to get up every morning and struggle to put one foot in front of the other. How dare you stop forcing yourself to breathe. How dare you!'

"I was envious for the first time," Sakinah continued. "I've never been envious. I've always been proud. ... I loved my sister. I tried all I could do to help her. But see, my Lord got a plan and his plan ain't always what my plan is. There's a saying in Islam that says "all praises to the God for all circumstances." So in this there's a lesson. That lesson is to take a look at your own personal little space. Not your mama's, not your brother's, not your sister's. But take a look at your own self. Because, usually, if you're telling somebody else about their stuff, you probably need to tell it to yourself."

The last of the Hyman sisters to speak was Ann, and she thanked Phyllis's extended family for the comfort they offered. "She had a big family," said Ann. "She had her birth family, which only some of us are here. But she had family that she picked - and picked her - all over the world. All over the world she was somebody's sister, somebody's auntie, somebody's mother, somebody's daughter. There are a lot of people who can honestly claim Phyllis in their family and there are many people that she claimed as family. And I honor that because I think that helped sustain her as long as she was able to be sustained."

Ann said Phyllis had a love of people. "Phyllis was very much in love with and concerned about our community and what is happening in our community, and she hurt over what we are doing to each other. She internalized that pain. She carried it like a 1,200 pound weight, and when she said, 'I'm tired, I'm tired,' she meant it."

Following the service, and per Phyllis's written instruction, there was a party held at the Birdland Supper Club at Broadway and 105th Street. Titled "A Farewell Toast and Celebration of Life," it was her last New York gig.

Phyllis's ashes were then transported to Pittsburgh, where a second memorial took place on Friday, July 7th at the Pittsburgh Memorial Covenant Church. The largest of the memorials held in Pennsylvania, however, took place the following week as friends and family gathered in Philadelphia's Bright Hope Baptist Church on July 11th. Hundreds lined the streets unable to squeeze into the capacity-filled church.

Throughout these services, and as news of her untimely death continued to spread across the country and, indeed, the world, many would ask why Phyllis had taken her life, and an equal number would offer theories. "If anything she died of, it was probably lonesomeness," said Mercer Ellington to the *New York Daily News*. "In spite of all her bragging, she was fighting down this inferiority complex."

In her interview with *Jet* magazine, Jeannie Hyman stressed to the reporter that it wasn't over a man – or lack of one – that her sister chose to end it all. "Honey, listen, listen, check this out: Phyllis Hyman would never have taken her own life over no man. There were a lot of things that troubled Phyllis. Sure, any woman wants the companionship of a good man, but that's not the kind of stuff that had Phyllis all bent out of shape. Please, dispel that myth."

Among the better notions was this one by Phyllis's longtime publicist, Sheila Eldridge. "I don't think it was any one thing that led to this. It was a gradual deterioration of her spirit and self-esteem that led her to take her life."

Journalist David Nathan, another longtime Phyllis acquaintance, reached a similar conclusion and summed it up as eloquently as anyone. "It was the culmination of years of self-doubt, insecurity and so little self-love," he wrote in a personal online tribute. The lack of self-love, Glenda said, was key. "The mythology about Phyllis is that she never felt anyone loved her," Glenda said. "That is so far from the truth it's unbelievable. Phyllis knew people loved her. But she didn't love herself."

Two days after her death, Patti LaBelle dedicated her show at the Essence Music Festival in New Orleans to Phyllis, especially singling out the song "Somebody Loves You Baby" in her honor. In September, Norman Connors and Michael Henderson performed a series of concerts called A Tribute to Phyllis Hyman. "One thing I've been realizing," Connors said at the time, "is that I knew she was loved, but I'm starting to realize just how much. People loved Phyllis Hyman." Pharoah Sanders and others would also go on to do such tribute shows, and Jean Carne, a regular headliner at these events, would permanently incorporate a selection of "Phyllis songs" into her stage repertoire to continuously eulogize her friend.

If by the fall media coverage of her death had started to lull, the stories picked up again as the November 7th release of her third album for Philadelphia International neared. Five of the nine Nick Martinelli-produced tracks made it onto the 10-track album, including the title song, which was one of five in total co-written by Phyllis. The remainder of the album was composed of two tracks produced by Kenny Gamble, one by Dexter Wansel, one by Dave "Jam" Hall, and one by Phyllis's former piano player, Barry J. Eastmond. One glaring omission was "Strength Of A Woman." Phyllis had hoped that the album would bear that name, and instead it failed to even include the song.

Released to favorable reviews, *I Refuse To Be Lonely* sold a couple hundred thousand copies within weeks. But though the album peeked as high as number 12 on Billboard's Top R&B/Hip Hop albums chart, it soon disappeared. The album's first single, "I Refuse To Be Lonely," climbed only to number 59. A video was created for the song by compiling still shots and video footage of Phyllis throughout the years. But for the most part, Zoo had no clue what to do with the record. "It's hard to have a typical record marketing plan," said Miles Baker, Zoo's national director of sales and marketing. "We don't have a tour. We don't have an artist. And it's a sticky sort of situation. You don't want to seem like you're trying to capitalize on her just passing away."

For many, the album was just too sad to listen to. Ironically, what was supposed to have been Phyllis's declaration of determination took on new meaning in light of her death. Songs such as "One Good Reason To Stay" and "I Refuse To Be Lonely" were no longer looked upon as shows of strength, but rather as swan songs. To many, it looked like the lady who'd made a career out of singing about herself and her ongoing battles of the heart had given her fans a personal goodbye note.

Though most true fans felt obligated to buy it, few could bring themselves to listen to the album more than once. Calling *I Refuse* Phyllis's "most personal album" reviewer Ray Mark Rinaldi of the *St. Louis Post-Dispatch* poignantly explained the dilemma faced by many of Phyllis's fans. "It shows a woman facing crises and searching for peace. She was more involved in the writing than ever before and it comes through in her delivery. If she were alive today that might be a pleasant turn for her many fans. The way things turned out it's hard to feel pleasant about this work."

The album's second single, "I'm Truly Yours," barely charted, reaching number 94. *I Refuse*, however, didn't remain the only new Phyllis product on store shelves for long. They were suddenly flooded by greatest hits packages from her various labels, and others, as everyone attempted to capitalize on her passing.

In 1996, Jean Carne, Norman Connors and the Starship Orchestra and newcomer Nathan Heathman (Jean Carne's musical director and one-time band member of Phyllis's) played a week of shows at Blues Alley they called We Remember Phyllis. Jean also stepped up in May of that year when Phyllis was honored with a star on the Philadelphia Walk of Fame. In a star-studded ceremony, Phyllis was honored alongside Will Smith and Boyz II Men. Jean performed a medley of Phyllis's songs and presented the award to Phyllis's father, Philip.

By this time, another tribute of sorts was in the works. The Whispers, who went on at the Apollo the night Phyllis died, conceived a stage play they called *Thank God! The Beat Goes On*. A fictionalized and somewhat inaccurate account of the last day of her life, it was scorched by critics who called it a "show-biz biography of the Whispers" with a "flabby script." Alyson Williams played Phyllis, her costumes a poor imitation of the stunning Cassandra McShepard originals Phyllis had worn.

Today, Phyllis continues to earn critical acclaim and retains the admiration of many. "When I think of all the talents that I've known over the years, I consider Sarah Vaughan and Phyllis Hyman as having the greatest voices, greatest instruments, ever," said Nancy Wilson. The compliment would have thrilled Phyllis, as she considered Wilson the greatest voice of all time.

More than a decade after her death, Norman Connors, Jean Carne and others still continue to participate in Phyllis Hyman tribute shows. New Phyllis material continues to be released. During her life, Phyllis released a total of eight albums. Since her passing, and as of this writing, more than 15 Phyllis Hyman albums have been released (including two reissues, two albums of new material and a dozen compilations and/or greatest hits packages). Despite this, her estate still remains in debt.

Commercially, Phyllis has fared no better in death than she did in life. Her body of recorded works is not comparable in size to most of the legendary ladies of song and, tragically, her name is not instantly recognizable to today's generation of record buyers. But to those in the know, those lucky enough to have heard or seen her, there will always and forever be only one Phyllis Hyman.

"There's nobody – ever – who's gonna be like her," said Patti LaBelle. "There's no voice in the world like hers. There's no spirit like hers. When she left, like with Luther, you just don't get any more."

"Phyllis Hyman was a superstar just waiting to shine."

Discography

Singles

"Leavin' The Good Life Behind"	Private Stock 45,034	1975
"Baby (I'm Gonna Love You)"/"Do Me"	Desert Moon 6402	1976
"We Both Need Each Other" (Norman Connors featuring Michael Henderson and Phyllis Hyman)/"So Much Love"	Buddah 534	1977
"Betcha By Golly Wow" (Norman Connors featuring Phyllis Hyman)/"Kwasi"	Buddah 554	1977
"Loving You, Losing You"/ "Children Of The World"	Buddah 567	1977
"No One Can You Love More"/"Deliver The Love"	Buddah 577	1977
"Somewhere In My Lifetime"/"Gonna Make Changes"	Arista 0380	1978
"Kiss You All Over/So Strange" (12" promo)	Arista 42-58	1979
"You Know How To Love Me"/"Give A Little More"	Arista 0463	1979
"You Know How To Love Me"/"Give A Little More" (12" promo)	Arista Sp-75	1979
"Under Your Spell"/"Complete Me"	Arista 0495	1980
"Can't We Fall In Love Again" (Phyllis Hyman and Michael Henderson)/ "The Sunshine In My Life"	Arista 0606	1981
"Tonight You and Me"/"The Sunshine In My Life"	Arista 0637	1981
"Tonight You And Me" (12" promo)	Arista Sp-114	1981

Discography

"You Sure Look Good To Me"/"Just Another Face In The Crowd"	Arista 0656	1982
"Riding The Tiger"/(Instrumental)	Arista 9023	1983
"Riding The Tiger"/(Instrumental) (12" promo)	Arista SP-155	1983
"Why Did You Turn Me On"/"Let Somebody Love You"	Arista 9071	1983
"Old Friend"/"Screaming At The Moon"	PIR 50031	1986
"Old Friend"/"Screaming At The Moon" (12" promo)	PIR SPRO-9754	1986
"Living All Alone"/"What You Won't Do For Love"	PIR 50059	1986
"Living All Alone"/"What You Wont' Do For Love" (12" promo)	PIR SPRO-9910	1986
"You Just Don't Know"/"Slow Dancin'" (12" promo)	PIR SPRO-79138	1986
"Ain't You Had Enough Love"/"First Time Together"	PIR 50070	1987
"Sacred Kind Of Love" (Grover Washington, Jr. feat. Phyllis Hyman)/ "Protect The Dream"	Columbia 73234	1990
"Obsession," (Lonnie Liston Smith feat. Phyllis Hyman)/(Instrumental)	Startrak 044	1990
"Don't Wanna Change The World"/(No Rap Version)	PIR 14005	1991
"Living In Confusion"/(Album Version)	PIR 14005	1991
"When You Get Right Down To It"/ (Album Snippets)	PIR 14030	1992
"I Found Love"	PIR 17068	1992
"Remember Who You Are" (Norman	MoJazz 2201	1993

Connors feat. Phyllis Hyman)

"I Refuse To Be Lonely"/"Meet Me On The Moon"	PIR 14238	1995
"I'm Truly Yours"/"It's Not About You (It's About Me)"	PIR 34263	1996
"Funny How Love Goes "/"Forever With You"	PIR 90302	1998
"Tell Me What You're Gonna Do"	PIR 89032	1998
"Groove With You"	Roadshow RS0046	1998

Albums

Phyllis Hyman	Buddah 5681	1977
Sing A Song	Buddah 4058	1978
Somewhere In My Lifetime	Arista 4202	1978
You Know How To Love Me	Arista 9509	1979
Can't We Fall In Love Again	Arista 9544	1981
Goddess of Love	Arista 205543	1983
Living All Alone	PIR 46422	1986
Prime Of My Life	PIR 11006	1991
I Refuse To Be Lonely	PIR 11040	1995
Forever With You	PIR 83090	1998

Album Appearances

You Are My Starship (Norman Connors, feat. Phyllis on "Betcha By Golly Wow" and "We Both Need Each Other")	Buddah 4043	1976

Discography

Premonition (Jon Lucien feat. Phyllis doing backing vocals on "Spring's Arrival")	Columbia 34255	1976
Love Will Find A Way (Pharoah Sanders, feat. Phyllis on "Love Is Here" and "As You Are")	Arista AB4161	1977
Children of Sanchez (Chuck Mangione, feat. Phyllis doing backing vocals on multiple tracks)	A&M 66700	1978
The Fish That Saved Pittsburgh (Original Soundtrack, Phyllis performs "Magic Mona")	Lorimar 36303	1979
Void Where Inhibited (Gotham, feat. Phyllis doing backing vocals on [I'm Your] AC/DC Man")	Aurum AU0002	1979
Sophisticated Ladies (Original Soundtrack, Phyllis performs "It Don't Mean A Thing If It Ain't Got That Swing," "Take The 'A' Train," "In A Sentimental Mood," "I'm Checkin' Out," and "I Got It Bad [And That Ain't Good"])	RCA CB2-4053	1981
Betty Wright (Betty Wright, feat. Phyllis doing backing vocals on "Give A Smile")	Epic 36879	1981
Looking Out (McCoy Tyner, feat. Phyllis on "Love Surrounds Us Everywhere," "I'll Be Around" and "In Search Of My Heart")	Columbia 38053	1982
So Good (The Whispers, feat. Phyllis doing backing vocals on "Suddenly")	Solar 60356-2	1984
Magic (The Four Tops, feat. Phyllis on "Maybe Tomorrow")	Motown 6130	1985
Oasis (Joe Sample, feat. Phyllis on "The Survivor")	MCA 5481	1985
Swing Street (Barry Manilow, feat. Phyllis on "Black and Blue")	Arista 18714	1987

School Daze (Original Soundtrack, Phyllis performs "Be One") — EMI 48680 — 1987

Love Goddess (Lonnie Liston Smith, feat. Phyllis on "Obsession") — Startrak STA-4021 — 1990

Emotionally Yours (The O'Jays, feat. Phyllis as part of the All-Star Gospel Choir on "Emotionally Yours") — Capitol 93390 — 1991

Time Out Of Mind (Grover Washington, Jr., feat. Phyllis on "Sacred Kind of Love") — Columbia 45253 — 1992

Remember Who You Are (Norman Connors, feat. Phyllis on "Remember Who You Are") — MoJazz 7003 — 1993

Acknowledgments

The journey to tell this story has been one of the most challenging, enlightening and growth-producing experiences of my life. I cannot put into words what I have learned or how I have grown, and I'm sure I'll still be unraveling the mysteries of the lessons for years to come. There's no way I could have ever known at this start of this project that it would require me to climb a spiritual Mt. Everest and, to be honest, had I known that I may never have signed up for it in the first place. Many times – *many, many times* – I did not think I was going to make it. Now, on the other side of the mountain … well, like the song says, "my soul looks back in wonder at how I got over."

Friends are truly angels; and often it was the strength of my friends, and not my own, that kept me going. I've made so many wonderful friends along this journey. I really thank Phyllis for that. I think, in a way, her spirit was watching over me and giving me what I needed to keep going and get the job done. Tops on my list, I have to give big ups to my entire project team. Regina Carter, aka Ms. Jazz, you were with me from the beginning. Remember when you got that first email? You had no idea, did you? Bill Schultz, I knew with all we had in common that we were meant to be buds. But you weren't so sure. You made me prove myself to you, and I respect you for that. Nichell Garrett, aka Nissi, whenever my well of enthusiasm threatened to run dry, you were always on hand to fill it back up. David Krause, what I can say? You and Diane and Kristen have become family to me. You saw something in me that I did not see in myself. You pointed it out to me, and now I know it's there. From the bottom of my heart, I thank you for that.

To the rest of my family, both the biological and the spiritual, thank you all for putting up with me. To my mom, for teaching me to be a "simple kind of man" and always encouraging me on my journey even when she didn't understand where this "free bird" was headed; my sister Lynsey Deel for the support, and my grandmother, Opal Lewis, for the roots. (Thanks also to the Irick

Acknowledgements

Family, Dad, Granny and Papa.) To my big bruh, Kavin Coleman, and big sis, Adrene King. You both have taught me so much about how to live and be a better person. I aspire to your wisdom and grace.

Charles Alexander, thank you for all the meals and laughs and the loads of fun we've had in Chicago. Thanks to my aunt, Eula Grooms, for filling in the gap, and to Sylvia Gardocki, for the relaxing lessons in landscaping. Betty Wright, number one soul diva, my old boss and fam forever – thanks for having been in the business long enough to know every-damn-body, and for generously interceding on my behalf when needed.

Glenda Gracia … I don't even know what to say. (And I can't say much for fear you'll proofread it!) With all seriousness, what you've brought to this story is absolutely immeasurable. It was my dream from the start to bring you on board and I'm grateful we were able to align our visions. The prospect of your friendship and what the future holds for us warms my heart and fills it with excitement. I look forward to working with you on the Phyllis Hyman Legacy Campaign and, most importantly, just getting to know you better.

I must also extend my gratitude to Martha David. I said some years ago, before Glenda and I learned to hear each other, that love could build a bridge between us. What I didn't know was that love would take the form of you, Martha. Thank you for being that bridge and for getting us on the same page. I admire and appreciate your dedication to Glenda, as well as to Phyllis's memory.

Additional thanks to editor Stacey Barney for pointing me in the right direction and to Glenda Gracia, herself, for taking my hand and guiding me there; Kyle Jones, my personal assistant; Candace K, my web designer; Kari Helm for the great graphic design; and Arlena Theriot-Triplett, my accountant. To Geraldine, founder of The Light Center in Detroit, Michigan. The Spirit led you to me just when I needed you most. Thank you for getting me back on track. Susan Horowitz and Jan Stevenson, thanks for giving my words a home in your paper for the past nine years. June

Acknowledgements

Washington and Treva Bell Bass, our work is not done. Leslie Warner, thank you for believing. Thanks also to Sean Davis and the Phyllis Hyman Sophisticated Lady MSN Message Board, Michael-Christopher, Ashley Scott, DJ Lisa Sol aka Alisa Berry, Vonne', Robert Tate, Reggie Hamilton, Stacey "Hotwaxx" Hale, Darryl Bonner, Martone Williams, Tim Turner, Kevin Thompson and Kirk Douglas. DLR, as Erykah sings, "I guess I'll see you next lifetime."

Larry Bailey, you get a line all to yourself. Thank you for remembering my promises, even when they momentarily slip my mind. The best is yet to come.

Two people very special to me made their transition while I was in process of writing this story. Billy Herrod (1957-2003) and Kenneth Reese, aka Ken Christopher, (1961-2004) believed in me and in my ability to tell this story. I'm so sorry they aren't here to share this with me, but I'm grateful to have known them both.

Finally, saving the best for last, I thank God for the gift of words, and for gifting the world with the late, great Phyllis Hyman. Phyllis, you had the voice of an angel, though Lord knows you could sure raise some hell. I wish you could have realized how loved you were, but you were never taught to love yourself. I try to apply that lesson to my life each day, in homage to you.

Notes & Sources

A biography is only as good as the research done by the biographer. In the case of *Strength Of A Woman: The Phyllis Hyman Story*, I got lucky. Correction: I was blessed. Since shortly after her passing in 1995, I've had the dream of writing a book about Phyllis. Many wonderful affirmations were sent to me through the intervening years that helped confirm this was meant to me, but none more so than the acquisition of more than 35 boxes of Phyllis's personal papers and memorabilia, for which I offer my sincere thanks to the Hyman family. These papers, which spanned the entire period of Phyllis's career, provided the basis of research for this book. In addition to business records and personal documents, Phyllis kept every single news item that was ever written about her. For compiling these, I thank Phyllis's publicists through the years, Barbara Shelley (during the Buddah and early Arista years) and Sheila Eldridge (from 1982 on). Excellent job, ladies! I scanned hundreds upon hundreds of articles, and those deemed significant to this text are noted here in detail. Phyllis was also in the habit of tape recording her live shows. I listened to and studied over 100 of her concerts, beginning with early shows at Rust Browns in New York in 1976 all the way through to her very last shows in Washington, D.C., just weeks before her death. These tapes provided rare and valuable quotes and allowed me to study the mastery of Phyllis's live technique.

In addition, I found valuable information in the E. Azalia Hackley Collection of the Detroit Public Library and the Lincoln Center Library for the Performing Arts in New York. Also worthy of recognition here is the British Ambassador of Soul, Mr. David Nathan, himself. His work personally and with *Blues & Soul* was extremely helpful. Special thanks to Richard Kenyata and Walid Itayim, who for some years compiled and edited the *Phyllis Hyman Internet Newsletter*. I scoured every issue and extracted many wonderful stories and recollections from fans of Phyllis's from across the world.

Notes & Sources

The Early Years

My sincere thanks, once again, to the Hyman Family for sharing their recollections with me as well as pointing me to other folks who did the same and providing me with many of the rare, personal photographs that are included in this volume. I interviewed Ann Hyman, Jeannie Hyman, Sakinah Shafiq, Mark Hyman, Michael Hyman and Anita Hyman in 2005. My sincere appreciation goes to each of you.

Also interviewed for this section of the text were Phyllis's schoolmate Donna Hubbard (2003), and her first boyfriend, Richard Wall (2005). Music teacher David Tamburri had a profound influence on Phyllis. I thank his widow, Trudy Tamburri (2004), as well as Dick Morgan (2004), who was the first to take Phyllis on the road. In Miami, Joe Donato (2003) allowed Phyllis to front his band, and when she decided to start her own, Hiram Bullock (2006) and Mark Egan (2004) became integral members. Steve Alaimo (2005) auditioned Phyllis for his label, but Sid Maurer (2003) was the first to sign her.

Additionally, I spoke with Betty Wright (2003), Margaret Reynolds (2003) and Phyllis's first producer, George Kerr (2003). My thanks to each of you.

The following print interviews were of great assistance to me in understanding this period of Phyllis's life: *Vibe*, May 2002, "A Life Less Ordinary" by Jonathan Lesser; *Essence*, November 1980, "Phyllis Hyman: A Musical Chameleon" by Kym Cooper; *Eagle & Swan*, September 1979, A Message From Phyllis Hyman's Lifetime" by Nikki Giovanni; *Sepia*, November 1981, "She's Making Her Dreams Come True" by Bever-leigh Banfield; *Oui*, June 1982, "Phyllis Hyman: A Very Sophisticated Lady" by Peter Wolff; *Black Radio Exclusive*, July 1991, "Phyllis Hyman" by Adrien Lores; *Pittsburgh Press*, November 22, 1977, "Singer Phyllis Hyman Home For Heinz Hall Debut" by Pete Bishop; *The Black Collegian*, April/May 1981, "Phyllis Hyman: Sophisticated Lady" by Kalamu ya Salaam; *Greensboro News & Record*,

September 5, 1987, "To Her, Life Is More Than Just A Song" by Susan Ladd; *Los Angeles Times,* September 3, 1981, "Recording Artist Who Had A Plan" by Lydia Lane; *The Washington Post*, January 14, 1981, "Phyllis Hyman: The Barefoot Siren of 'Sophisticated Ladies'" by Jacquelyn Powell; *After Dark*, August/September 1981, "Phyllis Hyman" by Michael Musto; *New Pittsburgh Carrier*, February 3, 1983, "Sultry Phyllis Returns Home" by Timothy Cox; *Philadelphia Tribune*, April 19, 1977, "Phyllis Hyman: Being Very Careful" by Elaine Wells; *N.Y. Amsterdam News*, February 2, 1980, "Phyllis Hyman: Bright Musical Beacon" by Marie Moore; *Associated Press*, August 1981, "Singer Phyllis Hyman Wants To Add Acting To Her Talents" by Mary Campbell; *Right On*, September 1979, "Phyllis Hyman: Too Unique To Be Overlooked" By Shell Slaton; *Black Stars*, September 1979, "The Fury and the Finesse of Phyllis Hyman" by Ashley Samuels; *The Courier-News*, March 31, 1979, "Phyllis Hyman: A Singer By Birth, A Businesswoman By Education" by Marc Hawthorne; St. Louis Sentinel, July 7, 1977, "Phyllis Hyman"; and Rochester, New York *Communicade*, October 22, 1977, "Musically Speaking...Phyllis Hyman Found Success 'Frightening, Puzzling'" by Ken Simmons.

Among the volumes I consulted, *Women Who Don't Sell Out* edited by Lenora Fulani (Castillo International, 1996) and *Jaco* by Bill Milkowski (Backbeat Books, 1996).

Additionally, quotes were culled from Al Beard's May 8, 1988 interview with Phyllis for radio station WYTZ-Chicago, the liner notes from *One On One*, a collection of Phyllis's duets compiled by David Nathan (Hip-O Records, 1998), Phyllis's monologue during her live concert at the Blue Note in New York City on October 22, 1993 and the New York memorial service for Phyllis, which took place at St. Peter's Lutheran Church on July 6, 1995.

The Buddah Years (1976-1977)

For speaking to me about this relatively brief but rather important time in Phyllis's life and career, my thanks go again to the former president of Roadshow Records, Phyllis's first label, Sid Maurer (2003), publicist Barbara Shelley (2003), arranger and Phyllis's musical director for a time Onaje Allan Gumbs (2003), and singer Michael Henderson (2004).

The following print interviews were of great assistance to me in understanding this period of Phyllis's life: *The Philadelphia Inquirer*, April 11, 1989, "Phyllis Hyman Is Back In Town" by Jack Lloyd; *Black Radio Exclusive*, July 1991, "Phyllis Hyman" by Adrien Lores; *The Detroit News*, March 24, 1976, "Phyllis Hyman – Remember That Name" by Dolores Barclay; *The Courier-News*, March 31, 1979, "Phyllis Hyman: A Singer By Birth, A Businesswoman By Education" by Marc Hawthorne; *Players*, September 1976, "Phyllis Hyman: Instrument Of Pleasure" by Clay Goss; Chicago Metro News, June 18, 1977, "Singer Now Standing Tall"; *Michigan Chronicle*, July 12-18, 1995, "In Remembrance Of Phyllis Hyman" by Steve Holsey; *The Sun Reporter*, August 7, 1976, "Phyllis Hyman: Singing Is Not Enough For Me" by Nieda Spigner; *Soul*, July 18, 1977, "Phyllis Hyman: It's All A Fantasy ... But It's Fun" by Connie Johnson; *New York Daily News*, August 6, 1995, "Diva's Final Note" by Phyllis Hyman; *Stereo Review*, November 1977; *Big Apple After Five*, August 6, 1977, "Dialogue With Phyllis Hyman" by Anthony V. Jordan; *Philadelphia Tribune*, April 19, 1977, "Phyllis Hyman: Being Very Careful" by Elaine Welles; *Indianapolis Recorder*, September 24, 1977, "A 'Pushy' Success Story" by Lynn Ford; *N.Y. Amsterdam News*, September 3, 1977, "Phyllis Hyman: Six Feet Of Beauty And Talent" by Ray Jenkins; *Routes*, July 1979, "Phyllis Hyman: A Human Spirit" by Amadeo Richardson; *Pittsburgh Press*, November 22, 1977, Singer Phyllis Hyman Home For Heinz Hall Debut" by Pete Bishop; *Black Stars*, July 1977, "Pittsburgh + New York = Stardom for Phyllis Hyman" by Donald Adderton.

I consulted the volume *The Soulful Divas* by David Nathan (Billboard Books, 1999) and also culled quotes from the online tribute "Norman Connors Remembers Phyllis Hyman" by Stephanie Sheppard as well as Greg Collins's March 4, 1979 interview with Phyllis for radio station KYAC-Seattle.

Notes & Sources

The Arista Years (1978-1983)

You hear about recording stars and the moguls on whose labels they record, but there are a multitude of folks in between the two and they are some of the most valuable when it comes to getting music heard and played. I spoke with Phyllis's product managers at Arista, Andre Perry (2003) and Milton Allen (2003), as well as the label's vice president of A&R, Gerry Griffith (2006). They each provided invaluable insight for which I extend my sincere gratitude.

Tina Stephens (2003) assisted Norman Connors as project coordinator for his work on the *Can't We Fall In Love Again* album and became of dear friend of Phyllis's in the process. Barbara Shelley (2003), once again, still had a hand in Phyllis's publicity at the juncture, and soon Sheila Eldridge (2006) came onboard and began managing those responsibilities quite capably. Michael Henderson (2004) reunited with his old duet partner on that album as well. Sid Maurer (2003) came back into Phyllis's life at this time and took over the reigns of her career in 1982. Thom Bell (2006) produced much of Phyllis's 1983 album *Goddess Of Love*. Before he began his production career, Barry Eastmond (2005) was Phyllis's musical director from 1981-1983. Singer Bobby Caldwell (2006) was Phyllis's special guest star on her Miami television special in 1981. Others also shared their recollections from this time including Patti LaBelle (2006), Dionne Warwick (2004), George Merrill (2003) and David Nathan (2006). My thanks to each of you.

Many books have been written about Whitney Houston. To help understand the climate at Arista upon her arrival, I perused several of them. *Whitney Houston: The Unauthorized Biography* by James Robert Parish (Aurum Press, 2003) was undoubtedly the most comprehensive. But also helpful were *Whitney!* by Mark Bego (PaperJacks, 1986), *Diva: The Totally Unauthorized Biography of Whitney Houston* (Harper, 1995) and *Good Girl Bad Girl: An Insider's Biography of Whitney* Houston (Birch Lane Press, 1996).

I also screened the documentary *The E True Hollywood Story: Whitney & Bobby* (E! Entertainment Network, 2001) for additional information.

Of great assistance to me in understanding the years Phyllis spent on Arista Records were the following articles: *Washington Informer*, April 5, 1979, "Hyman: A Graceful Artist" by Ralph Clarke; *Soul*, March 1980, "Barry Manilow: Soulful At Heart...Where It Counts" by J. Randy Taraborrelli; *Blues & Soul*, April 1979, "Phyllis Hyman: Musical Melting Pot" by David Nathan; *Black Stars*, July 1980, "Phyllis Hyman Dares To Be Different" by Walter Price Burrell; *The New York Times*, April 18, 1979, "Song: Phyllis Hyman, Peabo Bryson" by Ken Emerson; *Los Angeles Times*, February 24, 1979, "Peabo Bryson Packs The House" by Dennis Hunt; *Detroit News*, August 26, 1977, "Phyllis Hyman – From Secretary To Star At 27" by Chuck Bennett; *N.Y. Amsterdam News*, January 12, 1980, "Thom Bell: Rings Success' Musical Bell" by Nelson George; *The Chronicle*, September 20, 1979, "Phyllis Hyman Will Be Entertainer For Ninth Annual Award Dinner"; *Sepia*, August 1979, "Breathing New Life Into The Frazzled Word 'Star'" by Flo Jenkins; *Players*, November 1979, "Phyllis Hyman" by Craig Reid; *Stereo Review*, November 1979; *Philadelphia Tribune*, April 19, 1977, "Phyllis Hyman: Being Very Careful" by Elaine Welles; *Vibe*, May 2002, "A Life Less Ordinary" by Jonathan Lesser; *Essence*, November 1980, "Phyllis Hyman: A Musical Chameleon" by Kym Cooper; *N.Y. Amsterdam News*, February 2, 1980, "Phyllis Hyman: Bright Musical Beacon" by Marie Moore; Eagle & Swan, September 1979, "A Message From Phyllis Hyman's Lifetime" by Nikki Giovanni; *Black Stars*, September 1979, "The Fury and the Finesse of Phyllis Hyman" by Ashley Samuels; *Blues & Soul*, August 25, 1981, "Jingle Belle" by John Abbey; *The Black Collegian*, April/May 1981, "Phyllis Hyman: Sophisticated Lady" by Kalamu ya Salaam; *Blues & Soul*, July 1983, "Phyllis Hyman Puts A Tiger In Her Tank" by John Abbey; *Sepia*, November 1981, "Superstar Phyllis Hyman, She's Making Her Dreams Come True" by Beverleigh Banfield; *Community Leader*, July 23-26, 1981, "Phyllis Hyman A Totally Sophisticated Entertainer"; *Butterick Sewing World*, Spring 1982; *Blactress*, September 1982, "Phyllis Hyman:

Puttin' It All Together" by Dave Frechette; *US*, May 25, 1982, "Clothes For Clergywomen" by Didi Moore; *OUI*, June 1982, "Phyllis Hyman: A Very Sophisticated Lady" by Peter Wolff; *Billboard*, October 23, 1982, concert review by Nelson George; *Philadelphia Daily News*, December 10, 1982, "Phyllis Hyman" by Joseph P. Blake; *Philadelphia Daily News*, December 11, 1982, "Phyllis Hyman Left The Nu-Tec Audience Cold" by Joseph P. Blake; *Philadelphia Tribune*, December 10, 1982, "Phyllis Hyman Has A Soft Spot For Battered Women" by Barbara Faggins; *Los Angeles Times*, February 24, 1983, "Phyllis Hyman Sets Things Right" by Connie Johnson; *Right On/Class*, November 1991, "Phyllis Heads For Philly"; Contrast, June 12, 1981, "Phyllis Hyman Snubs South Africa" by Norman Richmond.

I once again consulted the volume *The Soulful Divas* by David Nathan (Billboard Books, 1999) and also culled quotes from the *Phyllis Hyman Internet Newsletter* #21, "A Day With Phyllis" by Oggi Ogburn, Greg Collins's March 4, 1979 interview with Phyllis for radio station KYAC-Seattle, Morton's Nov. 9, 1994 interview with Phyllis for radio station WBLS-New York and Al Beard's May 8, 1988 interview with Phyllis for radio station WYTZ-Chicago. In addition, quotes were culled from Clayton Riley's liner notes from *The Legacy of Phyllis Hyman* (Arista, 1996), A. Scott Galloway's liner notes from *One On One* (Hip-O Records, 1998), and David Nathan's liner notes from the CD reissue of *You Know How To Love Me* (Arista, 2002). Finally, I culled quotes from various press releases issued by Sheila Eldridge of Orchid on Phyllis's behalf during this period and from Phyllis's monologue during two shows at the Beverly Theatre in Los Angeles, Calif. on December 1, 1983.

Sophisticated Ladies (1981-1982)

To revisit the heady days of *Sophisticated Ladies'* success on Broadway, as well as the turmoil it took to get it there, I spoke with stage manager Ken Hanson (2003) and cast-mates of Phyllis's including Mercedes Ellington (2006), Ty Stephens (2003), Terri Klausner (2003) and Leslie Dockery (2003).

Notes & Sources

A virtual multitude of articles were written about the production. Among those I found extremely helpful were: *Black Stars*, May 1981, "Phyllis Hyman On Broadway"; *Blues & Soul*, August 25, 1981, "Jingle Belle" by John Abbey; *Essence*, September 1981, "Two Sophisticated Ladies Are A Smash On Broadway" by Stephen Gayle; *Eagle & Swan*, June/July 1981, "On Broadway: Sophisticated Ladies"; *Associated Press*, August 1981, "Singer Phyllis Hyman Wants To Add Acting To Her Talents"; *The Washington Post*, January 14, 1981, "Full Speed On The 'A' Train" by James Lardner; *Billboard*, March 28, 1981, "Rhythm Section"; *Players*, July 1981, "Sophisticated Lady Phyllis Hyman On Broadway" by Jared Rutter; *The Washington Post*, February 15, 1981, "'Sophisticated Ladies': Taking The Improved A-Train To Broadway" by James Lardner; *The Washington Post*, January 14, 1981, "Phyllis Hyman: The Barefoot Siren of 'Sophisticated Ladies'" by Jacquelyn Powell; *New York Daily News*, March 2, 1981, "Duke Knew All About 'Sophisticated Ladies'" by Douglas Watt; *Sepia*, June 1981, "The Duke Ain't Dead"; *Dawn Magazine*, April 1981, "Sophisticated Ladies: It's A Hit" by Barbara McGinnis; *Philadelphia Inquirer*, August 23, 1981, "The New Toast Of Broadway Is Phyllis Hyman" by Christine Arnold; *Newsweek*, March 16, 1981, "Snappy Salute To The Duke" by Jack Kroll; *Los Angeles Times*, July 10, 1981, "Aural Revival Of Broadway Hit" by Leonard Feather; *New York Daily News*, July 21, 1981, "Sophisticated Nancy Comes To Town" by Phil Roura and Tom Poster; *Sepia*, November 1981, "Superstar Phyllis Hyman, She's Making Her Dreams Come True" by Bever-leigh Banfield; *Philadelphia Daily News*, December 10, 1982, "Phyllis Hyman" by Joseph P. Blake; *Jet*, January 24, 1983, "'Sophisticated Ladies' Ends Broadway Run; London Show, Touring Company Planned."

Also referenced in this portion of the text is *Transcending Boundaries: My Dancing Life* by Donald McKayle (Routledge Harwood Choreography and Dance Studies, 2002). In addition, I culled quotes from the episode of BET's *Today's Black Woman* that featured Phyllis, as well as Judith Jamison and Hinton Battle, from July 1981, and from an undated *Sophisticated Ladies* rehearsal tape of Phyllis's.

Living All Alone (1984-1987)

My thanks again to Phyllis's siblings for sharing various recollections from this time period, and to Phyllis's niece, Tamani Eldridge (2005), for recalling her summer visits with her aunt. Glenda Gracia (2007) took the reigns of Phyllis's career in 1984 and soon would be assisted by Sydney Francis (2007). Phyllis met and became play mother to Tymm Holloway (2006) during this period. Bill Schultz (2003) and Julie Aponte (2005), longtime friends and assistants, entered the scene here and stayed on board till the end. Miles Jaye (2003) succeeded Barry Eastmond (2005) as Phyllis's musical director, and Terry Burrus (2004) succeeded him. Craig Hentosh (2007) was not just a road manager to Phyllis but a dedicated friend. Kenny Gamble (2007) signed Phyllis to his Philadelphia International record label in 1985. Thom Bell (2006) had a large hand in the production of Phyllis's comeback album, *Living All Alone*, and Nick Martinelli (2003) also produced Phyllis for the first time on that album. Cynthia Biggs (2006) co-wrote the title track, as well as several other tunes on the album, and toured briefly with Phyllis in 1987. In addition, Sheila Eldridge (2006), Tina Stephens (2003) and Gerry Griffith (2006) also had important recollections from this period.

I culled quotes from many published interviews including *New York Daily News*, March 16, 1986, "Phyllis Hyman Starring In New York" by Marion Collins; *Blues & Soul*, March 1987, "Phyllis – A New Chapter Begins" by David Nathan; *Blues & Soul*, June 1992, "Phyllis Hyman Heart To Heart" by Jeff Lorez; *Rhythm & News*, November 1986, "Phyllis Hyman's 'Living All Alone'" by Janice Malone; *Southern Economist*, October 5, 1986, "Phyllis Hyman: Song Stylist Looks To The Future" by Jim Duffy; *The New Times*, November 6, 1995, "Phyllis Hyman's Posthumous Final Album Reflects Hauntingly On Her Life" by Jonathan Takiff; *Scene*, June 18-24, 1987, "Phyllis Hyman: Where She Wants To Be" by Marc Holan; *New York Daily News*, September

5, 1986, "Phyllis Hyman" by Hugh Wyatt; *Stereo Review*, January 1987; *Daily Calumet*, October 17, 1986, "Hyman 'Living All Alone'" by Janis Parker; *N.Y. Amsterdam News*, October 18, 1986, "Phyllis Hyman: Back On Track" by Charles E. Ross; *EM*, February 1987, "Old Friend, New Person" by Raine H. Young; *Chicago Sun Times*, March 20, 1987, "Singer Phyllis Hyman Hopes Her Time Is Now" by Patricia Smith; *The Beacon Journal*, August 28, 1987, "Metaphors Aside, She Can Manage Fine By Herself" by Mark Faris; *The New York Times*, August 12, 1987, "A Jazz Legend At Jezebels: Friends, Food And Memories" by Bryan Miller; *Greensboro News & Record*, September 5, 1987, "To Her, Life Is More Than Just A Song" by Susan Ladd; *The Washington Post*, December 28, 1995, "A Hit Album's Unkindest Cut" by Esther Iverem.

To understand the history of Philadelphia International Records and its position in the industry at the time of Phyllis's arrival, the volumes *A House On Fire: The Rise and Fall of Philadelphia Soul* by John Jackson (Oxford University Press, 2004), *The Death of Rhythm & Blues* by Nelson George (Penguin Books, 1988) and *Hit Men* by Fredric Dannen (Vintage Books, 1990) were extremely helpful.

Other sources referenced in this section include the volume *The Billboard Book Of Number One R&B Hits* by Adam White and Fred Bronson (Billboard Books, 1993), Clayton Riley's liner notes from *The Legacy of Phyllis Hyman* (Arista, 1996), Morton's Nov. 9, 1994 interview with Phyllis for radio station WBLS-New York, Al Beard's May 8, 1988 interview with Phyllis for radio station WYTZ-Chicago, and Donnie Simpson's interview with Phyllis for the television program *Video Soul* (taped November 21, 1992) and from various press releases issued by Sheila Eldridge of Orchid on Phyllis's behalf during this period.

Finally, I culled many quotes from Phyllis's monologues during her shows at Cartoons in Houston, Texas (April 4, 1985), the Whiting Auditorium in Flint, Michigan (May 24, 1987), the Blue Note in New York (December 29, 1987 – January 3, 1988), George's in Chicago, Illinois (May 1988 – exact date unknown), the Wolftrap in Vienna, Virginia (July 22, 1988), Metropol in Pittsburgh, Pennsylvania (May 9, 1990) and Rockefellers in Houston, Texas (January 15, 1994).

Prime Of My Life (1988-1992)

I'm convinced that Phyllis had deep affection for both Martha David (2005) and her one time fiancé Dante James (2005), and I thank them both for sharing their very personal memories with me. Vince Evans (2003) succeeded Terry Burrus (2004) as Phyllis's musical director, and Steven Ford (2004) helped Phyllis assemble a new band in 1992. Jonathan Dubose (2005) was a major part of that band and Ford's eyes and ears on the road. Larry Kendricks (2007) succeeded Tad Fennar as road manager during this period. Nick Martinelli (2003) produced Phyllis's first-ever number one single, "Don't Want To Change The World" and several other songs from the *Prime Of My Life* album. Marti Sharron (2006) produced two tracks for the album, though one, sadly, remains unreleased. Gene McDaniels (2006) produced "Meet Me On The Moon," the song that Phyllis referred to as her "masterpiece." Zoo Entertainment, the company responsible for not only distributing but also promoting the *Prime Of My Life* album, no longer exists. Thankfully I was able to track down its former vice president of urban promotion, Jesus Garber (2006) and promotion man Mark Matlock (2003), both of whom worked diligently on Phyllis's behalf. Fred Williamson (2006) cast Phyllis in his film *Soda Cracker* during this period. Ann Gore (2005) was a good friend and confidant to Phyllis during these years. In addition, the words of Kenny Gamble (2007), Glenda Gracia (2007), Patti LaBelle (2006), Bill Schultz (2003), Barbara Shelley (2003) and Betty Wright (2003) were once again helpful to me as I studied this period of time in Phyllis's life, as were the recollections of Regina Belle (2003), who toured with Phyllis a great deal, and Martha Wash (2005). My thanks to each of you.

I culled quotes from many published interviews to capture the essence of this period of Phyllis's life. They include: *Chicago Sun Times*, May 11, 1988, "Proud, Dramatic Phyllis Hyman Sings With

Strength At George's" by Lynn Voedisch; *Chicago Sun Times*, May 13, 1988, "Chanteuse Hyman Sings With A Passion" by Lynn Voedisch; *Chicago Tribune*, May 19, 1988, "Phyllis Hyman Turns Up Heat On Torch Songs" by John Litweiler; *The Philadelphia Inquirer*, April 11, 1989, "Phyllis Hyman Is Back In Town" by Jack Lloyd; *Philadelphia Daily News*, April 11, 1989, "The Abundant Phyllis Hyman" by Nels Nelson; *USA Today*, April 7, 1989, "Pro-Choice March Signs Up Stars" by Lorrie Lynch; *The Reporter*, April 13, 1989, "You Call That Music? Singer Critical Of Today's Hits" by Kevin C. Johnson; *Chicago Sun Times*, May 21, 1989, "Racism In Music Becomes Crusade For Phyllis Hyman" by Randy Alexander; *Vibe*, May 2002, "A Life Less Ordinary" by Jonathan Lesser; *Blues & Soul*, August 1991, "Prime Time" by David Nathan; *Billboard*, July 20, 1991, "Phyllis Hyman Is Back In 'Prime' Time" by David Nathan; Philadelphia Tribune, August 16, 1991, "Hyman's New Album A Personal Testimony" by Robin Baylor; *Sunday Herald*, March 1, 1992, "Phyllis Hyman In Her Prime" by Paul Freeman; *Chattanooga News-Free Press*, August 15, 1991 "In The Groove Music Reviews"; *Indianapolis Star*, September 2, 1991, "Phyllis Hyman – Prime Of My Life" by Lynn Dean Ford; *Los Angeles Times*, July 29, 1991, "Hyman Tries Her Hand At Milking The Pop Cash Cow" by Dennis Hunt; Michigan Chronicle, July 24, 1991, "In The Prime Of Her Life" by Steve Holsey; *Monday Morning Replay* (Farmington Hills, Michigan), June 24, 1991, "Phyllis Hyman"; *Entertainment Weekly*, November 29, 1991, "Phyllis Hyman: Prime Of My Life" by Amy Linden; Class, November 1991, "From An Emotional Intensity To The Prime Of Her Life" by Donna Henry; *West County Times*, December 6, 1991, "Sad Songs Carried Balladeer To 'Prime'" by Paul Freeman; *Detroit Free Press*, August 1, 1991, "Album Keeps Phyllis Hyman In The Prime Of Life" by Anne Thompson; *Jet*, December 16, 1991, "Phyllis Hyman Says, 'The Man I Wanted, I Made Him Not Want Me And Now I'm All Alone'"; *Blues & Soul*, June 1992, "Phyllis Hyman Heart To Heart" by Jeff Lorez; *The Washington Post*, December 28, 1995, "A Hit Album's Unkindest Cut" by Esther Iverem.

I also culled quotes from the *Phyllis Hyman Internet Newsletter* #18, A. Scott Galloway's liner notes to *One On One* (Hip-O

Records, 1998), and David Nathan's online article "Phyllis Hyman – A Personal Tribute." Also referenced were court documents from the case *G&L Productions v. Phyllis Hyman*, Civil Action No. 92-CA06955 of the Superior Court of the District of Columbia.

Finally, I culled many quotes from Phyllis's monologues during her shows at Richmond's June Jubilee in Richmond, Virginia (June 10, 1988), The Wolftrap in Vienna, Virginia (July 22, 1988), Caravan of Dreams in Ft. Worth, Texas (July 26, 1990) and the Blue Note in Tokyo, Japan (February 1989).

I Refuse To Be Lonely (1993-1995)

As Phyllis began to work on the follow up to *Prime Of My Life*, and in particular following the death of her mother, Phyllis channeled her emotions through songwriting. She collaborated with Nick Martinelli (2003), Barry Eastmond (2005), Gordon Chambers (2005), Lorraine Feather (2005), Denise Rich (2006), Sunny Hilden (2006) and Jerry Barnes (2006) among others. Phyllis hoped that *Blues Bar* would be her grand theatrical comeback, and while the show didn't turn out quite as she had hoped, my thanks still go to director Curtis King (2004) and band member Darryl Craig Harris (2003) for their recollections. Robbie Todd (2005) met Phyllis during these years and became a close friend. Ama Ward's (2006) insight into Phyllis's struggle with her illness was particularly on point. In addition, I once again thank the Hyman family for recalling those difficult days following their mother's death, as well as Phyllis's friends and associates Julie Aponte (2005), Regina Belle (2003), Jonathan Dubose (2005), Kenny Gamble (2007), Ann Gore (2005), Glenda Gracia (2007), Ken Hanson (2003), Tymm Holloway (2006), Larry Kendricks (2007), Bill Schultz (2003), Tina Stephens (2003) and Betty Wright (2003).

I culled quotes from many published interviews that chronicled the last years of Phyllis's life, including: *Fort Worth Star-Telegram*, January 13, 1994, "Phyllis Hyman Gets Going Again As A Songwriter Celebrating Women's Strength" by Dave Ferman; *The*

New Times, November 6, 1995, "Phyllis Hyman's Posthumous Final Album Reflects Hauntingly On Her Life" by Jonathan Takiff; *Blues & Soul*, June 1992, "Phyllis Hyman Heart To Heart" by Jeff Lorez; *New Pittsburgh Courier*, December 23, 1995, "Gone Too Soon: Hyman's Soulful Spirit Lives On In Her Music" by Louis Kendrick; *The Dallas Morning News*, September 23, 1994, "Taking His Show On The Road" by Jerome Weeks; *Jack The Rapper*, September 21, 1994, "Phyllis Hyman & Billy Preston To Star In New Musical, 'Blues Bar'" by Billye Love; The Dallas Morning News, September 24, 1994, "'Blues Bar' Rises On A Tide Of Soul" by Lawson Taitte; *The Washington Post*, December 28, 1995, "A Hit Album's Unkindest Cut" by Esther Iverem; *Vibe*, May 2002, "A Life Less Ordinary" by Jonathan Lesser; *New York Daily News*, August 6, 1995, "Diva's Final Note" by Linda Yglesias; *Philadelphia Inquirer*, July 2, 1995, "Singer Died On Heels Of New Album" by Carolyn Acker; *Washington Afro-American*, July 8, 1995, "Remembering Phyllis Hyman" by Ida Peters; *Essence*, July 1996, "Phyllis Hyman" by Esther Iverem; *New York Beacon*, July 12, 1995, Reflections: The Phyllis Hyman That I Remember" by Don Thomas; *New York Amsterdam News*, July 8, 1995, "There Were 2 Phyllises" by Laura Andrews; *Jet*, July 24, 1995, "Fans And Friends Mourn The Tragic Death Of Singer Phyllis Hyman"; *Jet*, July 24, 1995, "Ex-Boyfriend Of Phyllis Hyman Was Among Last To Talk To Her; Said She Was 'Happy' With Decision To Commit Suicide" by Clarence Waldron and Trudy S. Moore; *Philadelphia Inquirer*, July 12, 1995, "Love For Singer Flows At Memorial" by Suzanne Sataline; *Washington Infor*mer, July 12, 1995, "Silence Is Deadly" by Michael Duane Johnson; *St. Louis Post-Dispatch*, February 8, 1996, "Phyllis Hyman's Last And Best Leaves Pain In Its Wake" by Ray Mark Rinaldi; *The Sun Reporter*, October 19, 1995, "Posthumous Album By Phyllis Hyman Released" by Donna Daniels.

Other sources referenced here include the online tribute "Norman Connors Remembers Phyllis Hyman" by Stephanie Sheppard, Arnetta Scott's remembrance from the *Phyllis Hyman Internet Newsletter #22*, *The Tragedy and Triumph of Lady Day* by Leslie Gourse (Franklin Watts Books, 1995), the liner notes from Tony Scott's *Homage To Billie Holiday* from 1996, *An Unquiet Mind* by

Kay Redfield Jamison (Random House, 1995), *Lady Day Had A Right To Sing The Blues* by Leonard Feather (Creative Concepts Publishing, 1976), *Women Who Don't Sell Out* edited by Lenora Fulani (Castillo International, 1996) and Lorraine Feather's online tribute to Phyllis featured at www.waliditayim.com.

Additionally, quotes were culled from Phyllis's interview with radio station WBLS from November 9, 1994, the transcript from the electronic press kit from the *I Refuse To Be Lonely* album, issued in the fall of 1995, from Phyllis's monologue from her shows at the Circle Star Theatre, San Francisco, California (May 1, 1993); Kimball's East in Oakland, California (December 28, 1993 – January 1, 1994); Caravan of Dreams in Ft. Worth, Texas (January 14, 1994), the Blue Note in New York (May 24, 1994); the Hotel Washington in Washington, D.C. (June 16-18, 1995) and from the New York memorial service for Phyllis (July 6, 1995).

Made in the USA
Middletown, DE
16 February 2024

49932972R00229